# Palm Programming

*The Developer's Guide*

# Palm Programming

*The Developer's Guide*

Neil Rhodes and Julie McKeehan

O'REILLY®

*Beijing · Cambridge · Köln · Paris · Sebastopol · Taipei · Tokyo*

**Palm Programming: The Developer's Guide**
by Neil Rhodes and Julie McKeehan



Published by O'Reilly & Associates, Inc., 101 Morris Street, Sebastopol, CA 95472.

**Editor:** Mark Stone

**Production Editor:** Nancy Wolfe Kotary

**Printing History:**

January 1999: First Edition.

This book is printed on acid-free paper with 85% recycled content, 15% post-consumer waste. O'Reilly & Associates is committed to using paper with the highest recycled content available consistent with high quality.

ISBN: 1-56592-525-4

# Table of Contents

# Foreword

by David Pogue
Author, O'Reilly & Associates' *PalmPilot: The Ultimate Guide*
*http://www.davidpogue.com*

What accounts for the PalmPilot's astonishing success? After all, there are more fully featured handhelds (the dead Apple Newton), smaller ones (Rex), less expensive ones (Avigo), ones with keyboards (Psion), and ones backed by Microsoft (Windows CE devices). Yet all of those palmtops (and many more) put together constitute only 35% of the palmtop market. PalmPilot sales make up the remaining 65%.

Some of the reasons for its success are evident: the PalmPilot is truly shirt-pocketable, inexpensive, fast, and simple, and a pair of AAA batteries drive it for two or three *months* (compare with 15 to 20 hours on a Windows CE gadget). But there's another, bigger reason that overshadows all the others: the PalmPilot is amazingly easy, pleasant, and satisfying to program.

At this writing, there are over 7,000 PalmPilot developers. My guess is that 6,950 of them are teenagers in their bedrooms. But that's just the point—because 3Com/Palm Computing and the Palm OS are so open, so clear, so friendly, almost anyone with a little programming experience can create new software for this addictive piece of circuitry. Maybe that's why 5,000 PalmPilot programs on 500 Web sites are kicking around at this very moment. No other handheld platform offers as many easily accessible development tools—and so much encouragement from Palm Computing, the mother ship.

As a result, it's astonishing that this is the first and only book on PalmPilot programming—and gratifying that it's so meaty, complete, and informative. Authors Neil Rhodes and Julie McKeehan do more than rattle off lists of calls and APIs; in a gentle, book-long arc, the authors lead you through the creation of a sample PalmPilot program. Along the way, you'll learn to create almost every aspect of a Palm OS application, such as databases, beaming, menus, dialogs, data entry, finding, and conduits to the desktop PC.

More than that, you'll learn the Palm OS itself. The authors firmly believe that in creating its OS, Palm Computing got it right the first time; you're encouraged to embrace the same goals of speed, minimization of steps, and elegant design. In other words, this book won't just teach you to become a PalmPilot programmer—it will teach you to be a *good one*.

# *Foreword*

by Daniel Pifko, Phillip B. Shoemaker, and Bill Witte
The Palm Development Tools Team

In 1888, the invention of the ballpoint pen revolutionized the world of writing. In 1995 the invention of the Pilot™ connected organizer revolutionized the world of computing. The concepts behind the Palm Computing® platform have a history longer than the device itself. Before the advent of the Palm Computing platform, Jeff Hawkins and others at a small start-up called Palm Computing were developing software for handheld devices, working with myriad hardware manufacturers to have them adopt the vision of those at Palm Computing. When Jeff and the others finally realized it would never happen, they opted to create the hardware themselves. Years later, out of this primordial ooze of creativity, the Pilot 1000 was born. Then came the Pilot 5000, the PalmPilot™ Personal, the PalmPilot™ Professional, and the Palm III™ connected organizers. Companies started calling upon Palm Computing to partner, and out of those relationships came upgrade cards, pager cards, the IBM WorkPad, the Symbol SPT 1500 with integrated bar code scanner, and the Qualcomm pdQ with integrated cellular phone. And the list continues to grow. Within eighteen months, four products shipped from Palm Computing, and over a million devices were sold. We knew we had a solid and compelling platform that would be popular with developers.

The fundamental idea behind our strategy was first to get a large installed base using the devices as personal organizers, and then to focus on signing up developers to broaden their usefulness. This was a very different approach than those of our predecessors. They believed you needed thousands of partners and a publicly accepted standard to attract a large body of users. A million-plus users later, we have over ten thousand add-on software and hardware developers, and more are signing up daily. They believe, as we do, that the Palm Computing platform represents a new, exciting, and commercially compelling opportunity for companies like themselves. This development community has been and will continue to be an integral part of our success story.

Developers new to the platform will find that the design philosophy that has made Palm's products such a success with users is mirrored in our approach to development. One example is that of minimalistic design. Palm's products have always been designed with only the necessary pieces in mind. Never are arbitrary frills thrown in just to make the device seem more appealing. Instead, we implement features that people will actually use and that are well suited to the constraints present on a small device. True to the philosophy of the devices themselves, the Application Programming Interface (API) has been written with simplicity and applicability to a small device in mind. The functions are tweaked for instant response to user input, easy synchronization and backup, and a simple, consistent user interface in all applications.

We believe that this book will greatly benefit any Palm Computing platform developer who follows the book's advice on how to create the best application with the lowest development cost. To quick-start your own application, you can use the sample programs in the book as building blocks. We hope that they will contribute to the fast development and superior performance of your application—and, in turn, will help it contribute to the growth and power of the Palm Computing platform.

# *Preface*

## *The Palm Phenomenon*

By almost anybody's standard of measure, the PalmPilot and other Palm devices are wildly successful. Everybody loves them: users buy them faster than any other handheld, product reviewers give them awards, and programmers, once they find the platform, never want to leave.

How do we account for this phenomenon? What makes the Palm handheld such a great device? Simple. It's really fast, it's cheap, it does almost anything you ask it to, and it can fit in your shirt pocket. Combine that with loyal users and one of the most ardent developer followings seen since the glory days of the Mac, and you have all the elements of a whirlwind success. If you are a programmer, the question you should really be asking yourself right now is, "What do I need to know to join in the fun?" To find out, keep reading.

## *Who This Book Is For—C Programmers*

If you know C and you want to write applications for Palm devices, then this is the book for you. It doesn't matter if you own a Palm and are an avid user, or if you are only now thinking about getting one. You can be a wretchedly poor student who wants to mess around with a PalmPilot in your spare time using free development tools, or a programmer in a Fortune 500 company who just got told that you have to write an application for the 5,000 units the company is deploying in the field next month.

We have tried hard to make sure that there is useful information for everyone, from beginning Palm programmers to those of you who have already danced around the block with these lovely little devices. If you want to write an application that reads barcodes, we help you; if you want to write an application to deploy a sales force, we show you what to do.

### *Do You Need to Know C++?*

It doesn't hurt if you know C++, but it isn't necessary, either. C is just fine for creating a Palm application. C++ does come in handy if you are going to write a conduit (we will talk more about that in minute).

### *Do You Need to Be a Desktop Expert to Write a Conduit?*

Writing a Palm application can be a two-part adventure. You may want to create an application for the handheld device and a desktop application that will talk to the Palm application. If you want to write a conduit (the code that handles the exchange of data between the Palm and the desktop), then you will need to know about the desktop (Windows or Macintosh). We tell you how to write the conduit, but not a lot about how to create a desktop application. For that you will need some outside resources.

### *Which Flavor Conduit Do You Want—C++ or Java?*

You can use either C++ or Java to write a conduit. We discuss some of the issues and help you figure out which path you want.

## *What This Book Is About and How to Read It*

This book shows you how to create a Palm application and a conduit. It assumes that you have the Palm OS documentation (available at the Palm Computing web site, *http://www.palm.com/devzone*) and know where to find things in it. Before showing you how to create an application, we also spend some time explaining the difference between a good application and a bad one; in other words, we tell you how to design for this platform.

### *The Breakdown of the Chapters*

Part I, *Palm—Why It Works and How to Program It,* gives you the big picture. You learn about the devices, their history, their development environments, and the right way to design a Palm application.

*Chapter 1, The Palm Solution*
: We happily admit that this chapter is unabashedly partisan. Would you want someone who doesn't like the Palm Computing platform telling you about it? We also describe which features can be found on which devices and what you can expect to see in the future.

*Chapter 2, Development Environments and Languages*
: Here we show you the choices in development environments and the range of languages you can use.

*Chapter 3, Designing a Solution*
: We ruminate about the best way to design a Palm application and offer you some advice. We end this chapter by showing you the design of an application and its accompanying conduit that we are going to create in the book.

Part II, *Designing Palm Applications*, takes you inside a Palm application. We describe its structure, user interface elements, and the Application Programming Interface (API) for the various parts of the application.

*Chapter 4, Structure of an Application*
: We take you through the whole cycle of a Palm application, from the time it is launched by the user to the moment it quits.

*Chapter 5, Forms and Form Objects*
: Here you'll learn how to create the various user interface elements of the application—everything from buttons to alerts, from lists to gadgets.

*Chapter 6, Databases*
: We explain the unique way the Palm OS creates data structures and stores data on a Palm device.

*Chapter 7, Menus*
: We show you how to create menus and the items in them. You also learn how to use Palm's Graffiti shortcuts and which menus should be where.

*Chapter 8, Extras*
: We cover a little bit of this and a little bit of that in this chapter. The topics are tables, find, beaming, and barcodes (for use with the Symbol SPT 1500, a Palm Computing platform handheld).

*Chapter 9, Communications*
: This chapter gives you a detailed look at communications on a Palm OS device, everything from serial to TCP/IP.

*Chapter 10, Debugging Palm Applications*
: Last, but most important, we turn to the crucial topic that is the bane of every programmer's existence—debugging. We show you how to figure out what's wrong with your code.

Part III, *Designing Conduits*, covers conduits. Just as we created a Palm application, we do the same for conduits. This section includes everything from a complete description of the parts of a conduit to development platforms for them and code walkthroughs. Unlike the other two sections, these chapters build on each other and should be read in order.

*Chapter 11, Getting Started with Conduits*
: We start once again with the bigger picture. After we describe all the general things you need to know about conduits, we finally turn to a small amount of code that forms the shell of a conduit.

*Chapter 12, Uploading and Downloading Data with a Conduit*
: This chapter takes you a step further, and you see how to upload and download data between the desktop and the conduit.

*Chapter 13, Two-Way Syncing*
: In this chapter, we show you a conduit that uses full-blown data syncing, with the exchange of data depending on where it has last been modified. We also describe the various logic problems you encounter with a device that can synchronize data on various desktops.

*Chapter 14, Debugging Conduits*
: We return to the topic of debugging, this time of conduits.

*Appendix: Where to Go From Here*
: This appendix lists Palm developers' resources.

## How to Read This Book

There are a few standard approaches people use to read a book on programming.

- The skip-through-and-read-what's-interesting approach
- The cover-to-cover approach
- The in-front-of-a-computer-trying-to-create-your-own-application approach

#### The skip-through approach

If you choose this approach, view Part I as background information. This section is more essential for beginners to the Palm Computing platform than for old-timers. If you already know which development environment you are going to use, you can ignore Chapter 2. If you want to understand the design decisions we made in the sample application and what makes the difference between a good and a bad Palm application, then you need to read through Chapter 3.

You can skip around Part II or read its chapters in order. In either case, don't wait too long to read Chapter 10. No matter what, read this chapter before you try to create your own project.

Part III won't make much sense unless you read it in order. Each chapter builds on the previous chapter.

### *The cover-to-cover method*

We didn't write the book in this order, but it seemed like the right progression at the time.

### *The in-front-of-a-computer approach*

Anxious types should read the debugging material before taking too deep a plunge into creating an application. Otherwise, far be it from us to try to slow you down. Get to it!

## *What's in a Name—Is It a Pilot or a Palm?*

We have to take a moment here to talk about both the name of this book, *Palm Programming: The Developer's Guide,* and about Palm devices in general. If you are a loyal Palm user, then you probably call it a Pilot. So does virtually everyone else on the planet, except the company that makes them—3Com. The producers of these dandy devices want you to think of Palm not as a device, but as a platform, the Palm Computing platform. They do this, reasonably enough, so that you realize that all the following devices use the same operating system, even though different companies make and sell them:

- Pilot 1000, Pilot 5000
- PalmPilot Professional
- PalmPilot Personal
- Palm III
- IBM WorkPad
- Symbol SPT 1500

Why 3Com went from the use of Pilot to Palm can be summed up in one word—lawsuit. Lawyers for the French Pilot Pen company contacted lawyers at 3Com and said, "Hey, Pilot is our name; stop using it." So 3Com did. Now, while we could spend hours talking about the questionable wisdom of letting a pen company tell a computer company to throw away a wildly popular, highly recognized trade name, that doesn't change our problem. People call them Pilots; the company calls them Palm devices.

As if the situation weren't interesting enough, add the entrance of the lumbering giant, Microsoft. Noticing the success Palm Computing was having with its popular devices, Microsoft's leaders said, "Hey, we're going to make some, too, and we're going to call them PalmPCs." While Microsoft eventually backed off from the name PalmPC to palm-sized computers, the damage had already been done—the Palm name had been compromised. Now we have to worry that people will not know whether we are talking about a PalmPilot device or a Windows CE–based palm device in this book. It's enough to make a writer cry.

So here's our problem: we want to make the folks at Palm Computing happy, and we want to make sure readers know what we are talking about in the book from just looking at the title. Our compromise solution was *Palm Programming*. We wrote this book to last a long time, and we are betting our title on 3Com's ability to move consumer attachment from the word Pilot to the word Palm.

At the time we went to press, the dust hadn't settled yet; it wasn't clear whether 3Com would be successful in wresting the Palm name away from Microsoft. If they are, the book has the right name, and you picked up *Palm Programming* for the right reasons. If Microsoft wins—not an unbelievable possibility, however unhappy the concept makes us—then you may have picked up this book thinking it would help you with the Microsoft Windows CE programming of palm-sized devices. Sorry for the confusion.

## *Conventions Used in This Book*

We use a couple of conventions worth noting.

*Italic* is used for a variety of things: URLs, filenames, functions, email addresses and other things we wanted to emphasize.

Code comes in either small batches or larger amounts, but it is always represented in `constant width`.

Code elements such as parameters (basically, any code other than function names) also use a `constant-width` font when they are included in a sentence.

Notes with an owl icon consist of tips or hints.

Notes with a turkey icon are warnings.

## How to Contact Us

We have tried very hard to make sure that all the information in this book is accurate. If you find a problem or have a suggestion on how to make the book better, please let us know by writing or emailing us at:

O'Reilly & Associates, Inc.
101 Morris Street
Sebastopol, CA 95472
800-998-9938 (in the U.S. or Canada)
707-829-0515 (international/local)
707-829-0104 (fax)

You can also send us messages electronically. To be put on the mailing list or to request a catalog, send email to:

*nuts@oreilly.com*

To ask technical questions or comment on the book, send email to O'Reilly technical support:

*bookquestions@oreilly.com*

or you can send email to us, the authors:

*neil@pobox.com* (Neil Rhodes)
*julie@pobox.com* (Julie McKeehan)

## Versions of Things

We use a lot of tools in this book. As an easy point of reference, here is each product and the version of it that we used:

- Beta version of CodeWarrior for Palm OS Release 5
- GNU PalmPilot SDK Version 0.5.0
- Palm OS Emulator (POSE) 2.0b3
- 3.0 Conduit Development Kit, beta version
- Gdbplug .02
- Symbol Scanner SDK Beta 1.08

Check O'Reilly's PalmPilot Center at *http://palmpilot.oreilly.com* or see the web page for this book at *http://www.oreilly.com/catalog/palmprog/*.

## What's on the CD?

- Source for all the samples in this book. Updates to the CD can be found at *http://www.oreilly.com/catalog/palmprog/*.
- A demo version of CodeWarrior for Palm OS.
- GNU PalmPilot SDK.
- POSE.
- Palm OS 3.0 SDK—including documentation.
- Symbol Technologies SDK for the SPT 1500.
- Demo version of Satellite Forms.
- Linux versions of gcc, gdb, POSE, and Pilrc in both source and RPM format.

## Whom We Need to Thank

If you haven't already figured out that the people at Palm Computing deserve an enormous amount of gratitude, we will tell you now. Many people deserve our thanks, starting with Maurice Sharp, head of Developer Technical Support (DTS) at Palm Computing. He coordinated the dispersal of proof chapters and had the fortitude to read the whole manuscript while managing all the rest of his duties. Other DTS people who read the entire manuscript were David Fedor, Cheri Leonard, Gary Stratton, Bruce Thompson, and Ryan Robertson. Keith Rollin in Engineering also read the whole manuscript and gave us great comments, especially about debugging tools. If you have ever tried to do a technical review of a proof copy, you know how much work this is. These folks went the extra mile and obviously read on their own time (food spills are a sure-fire indicator of a dedicated individual), and for this we thank them profusely. If this book is useful to you, remember that these people had a great deal to do with that.

Other people at Palm Computing reviewed individual chapters in their own areas of specialty and gave us great advice. These include some folks in Engineering: Dan Chernikoff (for serial port communications), Bob Ebert, Roger Flores, Steve Lemke, Kelly McCraw, Chris Raff, and Tim Wiegman. Three managers also took time out of their schedules to make sure we covered enough of the bigger picture. They are Daniel Pifko (HotSync Product Manager), Phil Shoemaker (Tools Engineering Manager), and Bill Witte (OS/SDK Product Manager). All these people read drafts of chapters and sent back tons of useful technical comments, and we thank them.

The Palm Computing staff also provided a lot of technical assistance. We can't begin to say how nice it is to be able to ask for technical help, ask questions, ask about problems, and get answers, usually within a day or two. The folks at Symbol Technologies also helped us out. Rob Whittle, Product Manager of the SPT 1500, got us a beta unit of the SPT 1500 and gave many useful comments and other help.

We also recruited some readers to see if the book would make sense. These readers included C programmers new to the platform and people who might well know more about programming the Palm than we do. This list of volunteers who deserve recognition includes Stephen Beasley, Edward Keyes, J.B. Parrett, and Stephen Wong. Edward Keyes offered especially insightful and thorough comments.

Now, over to the publishing side of things. Many thanks to our editor, Mark Stone. It was very nice to have an editor who read and actually understood our writing. Mark time and time again caught inconsistencies and sloppy descriptions and gently told us when we were mumbling. For two authors who don't like writing, Mark's competence and professionalism made the task almost palatable.

On the personal side of things, we have a few people to thank as well. As always, we need to thank our children, Nicholas, Alexander, and Nathaniel, who can never figure out why either of us writes books. We also thank our friends and families, who put up with our annoying tendencies to fade out of conversations, be late, and be absolutely boring while we are writing.

# I

# *Palm—Why It Works and How to Program It*

This section is about the big picture. In Chapter 1, *The Palm Solution*, we talk about Palm Computing's success at getting the handheld solution right. In Chapter 2, *Development Environments and Languages*, we discuss how to write programs that run on these devices and your choices in languages and environments. In Chapter 3, *Designing a Solution*, we discuss which applications you can create for this platform—which features the applications support, and what it takes to create a well-designed application.

We tell you what is possible and then show you how to do it. We give you a sample application, the source code, and commentary, so that you can turn around and create Palm applications of your own.

*In this chapter:*
- *Why Palm Succeeded Where So Many Failed*
- *Designing Applications for Palm Devices*
- *Elements in a Palm Application*
- *Summary*

# 1
# *The Palm Solution*

Palm Computing has single-handedly defined the handheld market with the PalmPilot and Palm III pocket organizers—people just go nuts over them. The question is why. Why did this little company succeed when so many giants failed? The answer is that they got the magic formula right—they figured out what customers really wanted and how much they were willing to pay for it.

Understanding how to design an application for this platform requires a bit of backpedaling and a look at the history of these devices. Helping you understand that history and what made Palm such a skyrocketing success will help you know how to design good applications for them. We want you to attack the design of your application with the same magic formula that Palm Computing used. Design does not happen in a vacuum. If you ignore the features and characteristics that made Palm a success, your application will bomb.

## *Why Palm Succeeded Where So Many Failed*

Not everybody knows that the PalmPilot was hardware born out of software, and not even system software, at that. Its origins are in Graffiti, the third-party handwriting recognition software developed for Newton and other Personal Digital Assistants (PDAs).

In 1994, Palm Computing came out with some handwriting-recognition software that promised accuracy and speed in recognition on PDAs at the price of a little bit of shorthand. Many industry experts thought such software was doomed to fail, as it required too much work from the user. They were proved wrong. Speed and accuracy were more important—Graffiti was able to offer enough to compensate for the relatively minor work required to learn the new strokes.

## No One Would Make a Good Enough Device

Buoyed by its success with Graffiti and frustrated by other companies' inability to get the platform right, Palm Computing decided to create its own handhelds. The result was the release of the Pilot 1000 in mid-1996. It and its closely following mate, the Pilot 5000, rapidly made headway. So popular was this product that with the release of its next device 18 months later, the company topped the 1-million-unit mark and clearly dominated the market.

Not only that, but Palm Computing has since been acquired by U.S. Robotics and then again by 3Com. Not to undercut 3Com's new ownership of the Palm OS, but we will continue to refer to the makers of the Palm platform as Palm Computing.

It would be good to stop at this point and ask yourself why this company succeeded when so many other companies failed. How was it alone able to produce a successful handheld? It wasn't experience in hardware design—companies like Apple, Casio, and Hewlett-Packard clearly have more. It wasn't breadth of features—Windows CE and Newton devices have more. It wasn't price—Texas Instruments's Avigo is cheaper. So what does the Palm offer that all these other companies weren't providing? The answer to this question (because Palm Computing figured out what customers wanted) is simple to articulate, but complex to understand. Some insight can be gained by looking at the evolution of Palm devices and their OS relative to other handhelds.

## Palm Device Size and Weight

As you can see in Figure 1-1, Palm Computing (and its licensees) has had a steady progression of products.

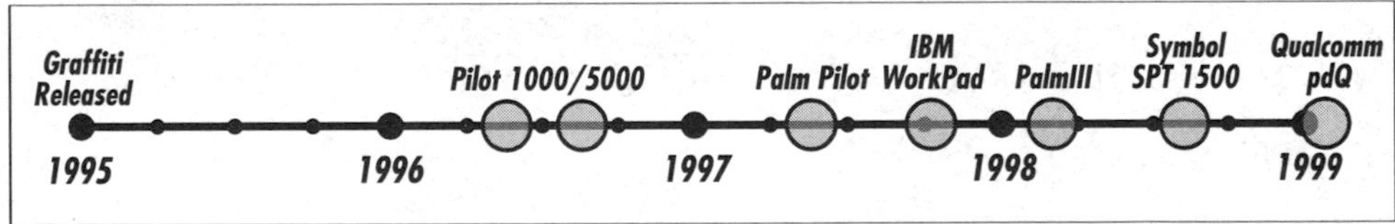


*Figure 1-1. A brief timeline of Palm OS products from Graffiti to the Qualcomm pdQ*

Each of these devices differs in some respects and remains the same in others. One of the most striking similarities is the size or form factor (see Figure 1-2). What differs is the memory, storage space, and the addition of some hardware features like IR support on the Palm III and barcode support on the Symbol SPT 1500, the Palm device from Symbol Technologies. Indeed, there are only a few changes in outward design between the PalmPilot and the Palm III and even less between the Palm III and the SPT 1500. Compared to the PalmPilot, the Palm III has a slightly tapered base, a little bit larger power button, and a sliding serial port cover, and the two scroll buttons have been folded into one seesaw-type button—minor design changes by anybody's measuring stick. The Symbol device differs from the Palm III only in its slightly increased length (to accommodate the barcode reader) and the two green buttons at the top that are used to activate the reader. Figure 1-2 shows most of these differences, plus the Qualcomm pdQ, discussed later.

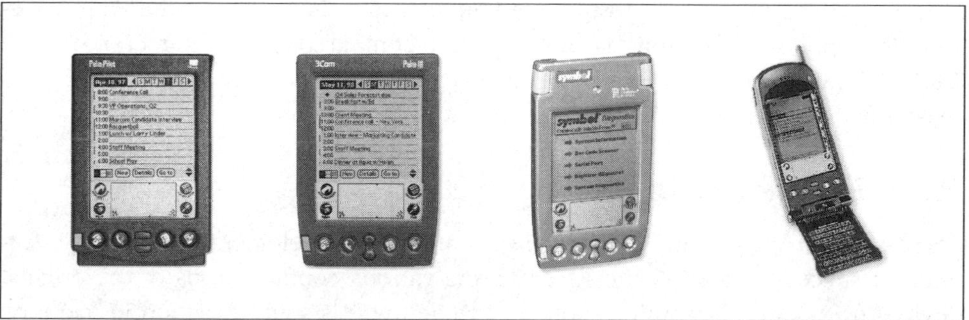

*Figure 1-2. Differences in physical design of Palm OS handhelds (from left to right): PalmPilot, Palm III, Symbol SPT 1500, and Qualcomm pdQ*

The reason Palm Computing didn't change the original design very much was because it was right from the start. The crucial elements that are essentially the same across the entire product line are size and weight (although the Symbol SPT 1500 is ever so slightly taller and heavier due to the addition of a barcode scanner at the top). From these specs, you can see that Palm designers believe that a handheld has to fit easily into a shirt pocket and rest lightly in the hand. This is especially clear when you evaluate the size and weight of Palm devices relative to those of other handhelds (see Table 1-1).

*Table 1-1. Specifications of Various Handhelds*

| Device | Dimensions (in Inches) | Weight (in Ounces) | Price (at Introduction) |
|---|---|---|---|
| PalmPilot | 0.7 × 4.7 × 3.2 | 5.7 | $370 |
| TI Avigo 10 | 0.8 × 5.5 × 3.3 | 7 | $300 |
| Psion Series 5 | 0.9 × 3.5 × 6.7 | 12.5 | $600 |
| Geofox-One | 0.8 × 4.7 × 7.4 | 13.7 | $799 |
| MessagePad 2100 | 1.1 × 8.3 × 4.7 | 22.4 | $1,150 |

Qualcomm's pdQ, a combination wireless cell phone and Palm device, also has the same screen size as other Palm devices. The pdQ has a size of 1.4×6.2×2.6 inches and a weight of 8.2 ounces. This makes it twice as deep, 1.5 inches longer, 0.6 inches narrower, and 2.5 ounces heavier. Given the device's dual functionality, such modifications make sense. Comparing the pdQ in Figure 1-2 to other devices, you can see that it more closely resembles a cell phone than a standard Palm device. What makes this such a nice product, however, is the combination of complementary capabilities. The pdQ is a cell phone with Palm's easy user interface and it has a built-in address book with direct dial functionality.

## *Palm Device Cost*

Moving from form factor to cost, we see another item important in the Palm's success. The price of the units is quite modest compared with other choices (see Table 1-1). It seems that a low entry price is a critical part of the equation in a successful handheld, along with size and weight.

## *Palm Device Features*

The tasks that the handheld accomplishes are the final element in the magic formula of success. Table 1-2 breaks down the various configurations of the original devices from Palm Computing. Note that while there is some variation in memory, there are only a few new feature additions like IR support.

*Table 1-2. Palm Device Specifications*

| | Palm 1000 | Palm 5000 | PalmPilot Personal | PalmPilot Professional and IBM Workpad | Palm III and Symbol SPT 1500 |
|---|---|---|---|---|---|
| **Backlit** | | | ✓ | ✓ | ✓ |
| **High-Contrast LCD** | | | ✓ | ✓ | ✓ |
| **Memory** | 128K | 512K | 512K | 1MB | 2MB |
| **Built-in Apps**[a] | ✓ | ✓ | + Expenses | +Expenses +Mail | +Expenses +Mail |
| **TCP/IP** | | | | ✓ | ✓ |
| **Infared** | | | | | ✓ |
| **Flash Memory** | | | | | ✓ |
| **Barcode Scanner** | | | | | ✓-symbol only |

[a] The built-in applications common to all Palm devices are Address Book, Date Book, To Do List, Memo Pad, Calculator, and Security.

The original Palm Computing built-in applications included Dates, Address Book, To Do List, Memo Pad, Calculator and Password Protection. The PalmPilot added a backlit screen, more memory, and a new built-in application for expenses. The PalmPilot Pro added TCP/IP support, more memory, and a built-in mail application. The Palm III added new IR support and more memory.

From the beginning, Palm devices were extensible by adding applications. Later devices have much more room for third party applications, however.

## *What Palm OS Devices Don't Have and Why*

Almost more important than what Palm OS devices have is what they lack. No Palm OS device has:

- A keyboard
- Full text recognition
- An industry-standard PC card slot
- A powerful processor

Now, reflect for a moment on why this is so. Adding any of these features requires changing the magic combination of speed, size, and price that has made the Palm devices so popular.

### *A keyboard*

Designing a device with a keyboard is a double problem: it radically affects the size, and it changes the types of things a user will attempt to do. If there is a keyboard, a user will expect to be able to enter text easily. But in order to handle a lot of data input, you need a system that can support that type of activity and a processor capable of sorting and displaying it in a responsive way. Once you have both a system and a fast enough processor, the price has crept so high that users go get laptops instead; for just a few dollars more, they get a lot more capability. Windows CE device makers have been learning this lesson the hard way for a long time.

By removing both the keyboard and any real way of handling text input in quantity, Palm Computing kept its focus on what kind of device it was providing. Palm's strategy was to deliberately create a device that was an extension of a desktop computer. Think of the handheld as a "tentacle" (using the metaphor of the creator of the Palm, Jeff Hawkins) reaching back to the desktop. It is a window onto the data that resides on the desktop. Having this sort of window is so useful because it can be taken anywhere. Palm figured out that to be taken anywhere, it has to fit almost anywhere.

There is a really small device called the Franklin Rex, which is no larger than a business card and weighs in at 1.4 oz. It will be interesting to see how successful it is with its input limitation and size advantage relative to the Palm and other handhelds. Watch its progress.

### *Text recognition software*

Besides removing the keyboard, Palm Computing did away with supporting true text recognition. Palm knew from Apple Computer's hard lesson with the Newton (painfully broadcast across the pages of Doonesbury comic strips) that the recognition algorithms were just not good enough. Apple ended up with frustrated people who spent far too much time trying to get their Newtons to recognize what they wrote. Instead, Palm made the nervy choice to ask users to spend a few minutes learning the stroke requirements of Graffiti.

No doubt Apple had many focus group meetings where it asked legions of users the question, "Is it important to you that a handheld device be able to recognize your handwriting?" If faced with this question, users probably universally said yes, it was very important. Palm decided to figure out what users actually wanted instead of what they said they wanted—not always the same thing. Users, it turns out, would rather spend a few minutes learning to write a "T" like "7" than spend three times as much money and have a device take a staggeringly long time to do even the most simple tasks.

### *An industry-standard PC card slot*

Palm devices don't have a card slot, because they couldn't do it and keep the device small and cheap. Palm did install a nonstandard memory card to give users the ability to upgrade the functionality. What the company didn't provide for users was a way to add storage, programs, or updates without being connected to another device (either to the desktop or by modem).

## *Palm-Sized PCs—Are They Palm Killers?*

You can tell that Palm has a successful OS and device strategy because Microsoft has decided to copy it. In this industry you can depend on two things: (1) Microsoft will copy successful products, and (2) prices will drop. What it couldn't accomplish with Windows CE and larger devices, Microsoft is now trying to accomplish with its brand-new Palm-like device. Copying Palm specs almost completely, in January 1998, Microsoft announced a Windows CE–based PalmPC platform. Microsoft later retracted the obvious name ripoff, and the new platform became known as palm-sized PC.

Now these devices are rolling off the assembly line and being compared in the harsh light of reality with Palm devices. Many reviewers of these products ask the question of each new device, "Is it a Palm killer?" The answer seems to be that while each device may have a nifty feature or two, users are better off sticking with their Palm devices. The opinion seems to be pretty widespread that "palm-sized" PCs are no Palm killers.*

# *Designing Applications for Palm Devices*

As you can see from the way its handhelds are designed, Palm Computing was convinced that a handheld device will be successful if it is:

- Small (fits into a shirt pocket)
- Inexpensive (doesn't cost more than a few hundred bucks)
- Able to integrate seamlessly with a desktop computer by placing the handheld in a convenient cradle

These design decisions are only one part of the solution, however. The other part is the software. Palm devices are popular because they contain useful, fast applications and because they are extensible. There were lots of personal organizers before Palm Computing came along. The difference is that those old devices weren't easily extensible—third-party applications couldn't be added. The magic of Palm devices is therefore two-fold. The built-in applications cover a wide range of general activities, giving users access to names, a date book, a to do list, and so on. Crucial, however, is the second part: the platform is also open to other developers. Knowing how important other applications were, Palm provided tools and enough material to gain a wide developer following. These developers, in turn, have added lots of specialized applications. Everybody—Palm, developers, users—benefits.

## *Essential Design Elements*

We spent so much time discussing the history of Palm devices, what makes them popular, and features they don't have because these issues are crucial to your understanding of the design philosophy behind a Palm OS application. These are the essential elements in a Palm application:

- It needs to take into account small screen size.
- It needs to limit text input on the handheld.
- It needs to seamlessly sync to a program on a desktop computer.
- It needs to be small.
- It needs to be fast.

But there is all the difference in the world between listing these elements, and you knowing how to design an application using them. Let's address each point in turn.

---

* For an interesting set of reviews on product comparisons, check out PCWeek's web site, *http://www.zdnet.com/pcweek/*, where electronic versions of their reviews can be found.

### *Designing for a small screen size*

As its history has shown, the form factor of Palm devices is absolutely essential. It's small so people can easily take it anywhere. You should assume that this screen size is here to stay. Unlike some other handhelds that have changed size this way and that, Palm devices will keep this form factor for some time. While you might expect to see some integrated devices with a different screen size, these will be for very specific uses and won't necessarily pertain to the design of most Palm OS applications.

*The size of the Palm Screen is a mere 160×160 pixels in a 6×6 cm area*. The data you present in an application needs to be viewable in this area. Because the area is so small, you will need to break data into parts. While keeping the data in logical groups and relying on different views to show each element will help, you will undoubtedly need to iterate your design several times to get it right.

Look at how the date book handles the presentation of appointments, for example. If the user has a bunch of appointments in a small period of time, that portion of the day is shown. The user doesn't have to scroll through large gaps or look at lots of blank areas. The application shapes the way the data is presented to accommodate a small screen.

Start the design process by mocking up a couple of screens of data. See if the data falls into logical groups that fit nicely in the 160×160 square. If you are requiring your users to continuously scroll back and forth, rethink the organization. Here is the first rule to remember: *the screen size drives the design—not the other way around*.

If you are continually making the user horizontally and vertically scroll through blank areas, redo your design. Trying to display too much data can require the user to do too much scrolling; too little can require flipping between too many views. You have to find the right balance.

### *Limit text input on the handheld*

HotSync technology makes text input far less necessary on the handheld. The small screen size and lack of a keyboard make text entry difficult. All this leads to an ironclad truth for you to remember—a Palm handheld is not a manual text input device. The user has a nice desktop computer that contains lots of good things to facilitate text entry: keyboards, big screens, and fast processors. A Palm handheld has none of these things. These facts lead to another rule in designing for the Palm OS: *data is entered on the desktop, and viewed on the handheld*.

Obviously, we are not excluding all data entry or even trying to limit some types. For example, the application we create in this book is an order entry application. In this case, the handheld user is not required to enter text, but instead picks items from lists. This works nicely because picking things is easy, while entering text is hard. It is also clear that there are some very obvious places where users need to enter data on their handheld, such as in the to-do list. Apart from effortless data entry, you should steer your user toward adding data on the desktop.

A great example of effortless data entry on a large scale is finally available with the arrival of Symbol's SPT 1500. With this device, the user has a way to enter data (via the barcode reader) quickly and easily while not sitting at a desktop. It will be interesting to see how this new device shapes the development of applications with text input options on this platform.

Where your app does allow the user to input something, you will need to support the system keyboard, Graffiti input, and cut, copy, paste, and undo in the standard manner as outlined in the documentation. Likewise, you need to support any shortcuts to text entry that the documentation describes. (These are covered in detail in the Palm OS documentation.)

#### *Seamlessly sync*

The bold stroke of providing a convenient cradle and an easy-to-manage connection with the desktop has been crucial to Palm's success. Palm engineers designed these devices to exist in a symbiotic relationship with another computer. As a result, an enormously important part of your application is the conduit—this is code that runs as part of HotSync on the desktop and transfers information to and from the handheld. In a symbiotic relationship, both organisms rely on each other for something, and both provide something to the other—just as in our Palm OS application and our desktop conduit.

The conduit will handle communication between the handheld and the outside world. The handheld portion of the app will:

- Offer the user data viewing anytime and anywhere
- Allow the user to somewhat modify the data or arrange it differently
- Do tasks with as few taps as possible

Syncing commonly occurs between the handheld and a corresponding application on the desktop. But syncing is not limited to this model. Here are other scenarios for syncing:

- A conduit can transfer data from the handheld to and from a corporate database that exists on a remote server.
- A user might fill out a search form on the handheld that the conduit would read and use to do a Web search. The search result would then be transferred back down to the handheld for the user to view.

- A conduit could sync the Address Book to a web-based Personal Information Manager (PIM). Thus while the data may reside far away, the web-based storage ensures that this information is available to a user who travels anywhere in the world.

### *Make the application small*

The handheld portion of the application needs to take up as little space and memory as possible, because there isn't much heap space and storage to go around. You must be absolutely ruthless about this to end up with a good design. Trim the size, and keep the number of tasks your handheld application performs to a bare minimum.

Later we will talk about ways to optimize your application programmatically. For now we simply want to get your thinking clear about the tasks of the handheld application and the conduit

We pray never to see an Office/Works type of application on the Palm handheld. Rather than make one application do a bunch of tasks, create different apps.

### *Make the application fast*

Handheld users measure time differently than desktop computer users. One is moving; one is sitting still. Handheld users are usually doing more than one thing—whether that is talking on the phone or walking through a store with a list. Contrast this with the desktop user who is sitting at a desk and will most likely be there for a long time.

The desktop user will wait patiently for an application to launch, in contrast to the handheld user who is on the move. If you make the handheld user wait a minute before your program is ready to use, you won't keep that user. Speed is absolutely critical. This is true not only at application launch time but throughout its use. If you make that process too slow or require flipping between too many screens, your user will give up. The Palm is a lively little machine, so don't bog it down with slow apps.

Always remember that there are enormous problems attempting to do things on a handheld that you could do easily on a desktop computer. It has a pip-squeak processor with no more power than a desktop machine in the mid-1980s. As a result, you should precalculate as much as possible on the desktop. The stack space is so abysmally small that you have to be careful of recursive routines, or large amounts of stack-based data. The dynamic memory is so paltry that your global variable space must be limited and large chunks of data can't be allocated in the dynamic heap.

If that were not enough, the amount of storage is tiny. For that reason, your desktop portion of the application needs to pay attention to which data the user really needs in this sync period. In our order entry application, we should download data only on customers that the salesperson is going to use in the near future. Customers that won't be visited in this time period should be left out.

Rather than bemoaning the sparseness of your programming options, however, you should keep in mind two things: (1) it's a great programming challenge to create a clean, quick handheld application under these conditions, and (2) the very existence of these conditions is why Palm devices are outselling everything around. If you design for the device instead of beating your head against the wall for what you can't do, you'll end up with an application that literally millions of people might want.

Palm Computing has done research indicating that nearly all users are aware that they can load third-party applications on their Palm OS device. About two-thirds of the installed base has gone to the trouble of getting third-party software and installing it on their handhelds. This is an enormous user base for your applications.

## *User Interface Guidelines*

The documentation that comes from Palm Computing contains User Interface (UI) Guidelines. These docs cover everything from which type of UI widget to use for each screen control to exactly where they should be placed relative to each other. Follow them.

Palm Computing provides several volumes of documentation on programming for the Palm OS. While not as wonderful as this book, it is nonetheless very useful. It also has a great price—it's free. You can get the entire set of Windows or Macintosh documentation at Palm's developer site: *http://palm.3com.com/devzone.*

Designing your application to behave like the built-in applications is also a good idea. For example, if you have an application that needs to display records similar to Names, then copy the format used in the Names application (including the location of items). Palm Computing has provided the source code to the built-in applications because it wants to facilitate your use of them. Mimic them wherever it makes sense.

The guidelines also discuss the display of different views in your application, navigating between views, and how to convey information to the user. Not surprisingly, the guidelines also emphasize the importance of speed and optimizing in your application. You should also check Palm's web site for system updates and the release of new Palm devices.

# Elements in a Palm Application

Now that you know how to design a Palm application, let's describe its two components. After that we will look at how they communicate with each other.

## The Two-Part Solution

Most Palm solutions are composed of a handheld application and desktop conduit:

*The handheld portion*
: The portion that resides on the handheld and allows the user to view and manipulate data. Part II, *Designing Palm Applications*, deals with the creation of this part.

*The conduit portion*
: Here you have code that handles syncing the data with a desktop application. Part III, *Designing Conduits*, shows you how to create this part.

The handheld portion has an icon that is displayed in the application list. Users will usually use the Palm Install Tool from a Windows or Macintosh machine to install your application (it'll be installed on the next synchronization).

## HotSync Overview

When a user puts a Palm OS device in its cradle and presses the HotSync button, the handheld application begins communicating with the desktop conduit. For example, the Address Book has a built-in conduit that synchronizes the address book information on the handheld with the address book information in the Palm Desktop PIM. If a new entry has been made in either place, it is copied to the other. If an entry has been modified either place, it is copied to the other. If an entry has been deleted in one place, it is usually deleted in the other.

Third parties provide other conduits that replace the Address Book conduit so that the device's address book synchronizes with other PIMs (Microsoft Outlook, for example). You'll usually want to write a conduit for your application's database that will upload/download information in a manner appropriate for your application.

For example, the Expense conduit reads the expense information from the handheld, fills in a spreadsheet based on the information, and then deletes the information from the handheld. From the users' point of view, this is ideal; they get their information in a standard, easy-to-use form: a spreadsheet on the desktop. The Palm OS application doesn't have to worry about creating reports; its only purpose is recording expense information.

If you don't want to write your own conduit, then a backup conduit is provided. It backs up any database that:

- Doesn't already have a conduit responsible for it
- Has been marked as a database that should be backed up

---

There have been four different Windows versions of HotSync shipped to users (1.0, 1.1, 2.0, and 3.0). You'll probably want to target HotSync 1.1 or later. It's also reasonable to target HotSync 3.0, since it is available by download from *http://www.palm.com*.

---

## *Summary*

In this chapter, we have described Palm devices, the circumstances that governed their design, and the history of Palm Computing's success with this combination. Then we discussed application design in light of the devices' history, design, and future directions. Last, we discussed the important elements in a Palm application and gave you some rules to help you in application design.

# 2

# *Development Environments and Languages*

*In this chapter:*
- *Overview*
- *Handheld Development*
- *Alternative Development Environments*
- *High-Level Forms Development*
- *Conduit Development*
- *Conclusion*

This chapter deals with the what and the how of things. First, we show you what you're programming for—the nuts and bolts of the Palm OS. Then we show you how to do it—the available development environments. By the time we are through, you should have a good idea of the range of applications you can create for the Palm OS, the coding requirements, and which development environment you want to use.

## *Overview*

Developing for the Palm OS is in some ways similar to other platforms and in other ways strikingly different. Two important similarities are:

- Applications are event driven.
- You can use anything from standard C code to assembler to scripting.

Differences tend to center around features crucial to the device size and purpose. These include how the Palm OS handles:

- Memory requirements
- Application and data storage
- Connectivity of the device to the desktop

Most important, you should remember that the relationship between the device and the OS is extremely tight. Everything has been built on the premise that the handheld is an extension of the desktop and that it must be responsive to the user.

## *Overview of the OS*

Let's look in more detail at this tight interaction of the OS and the applications on the handheld. The Palm OS runs on top of a preemptive multitasking kernel. One task runs the user interface. Other tasks handle things like monitoring input from the tablet.

The user interface permits only one application to be open at a time. Thus, when your application is open, it (more or less) has control of the entire screen.

---

Applications run within the single-user interface thread and therefore can't themselves be multithreaded.

---

### *Memory*

Memory is handled in an unusual fashion. The RAM on a Palm OS device is used for two purposes:

*For dynamic memory allocation*
: This is memory your application or the system needs while it is running. It also includes the stack your application requires. On a reset, this memory is cleared. This portion of memory is analogous to RAM in a traditional OS.

*For permanent storage*
: This includes downloaded applications as well as data that the user will view, create, and/or edit. To-dos, names and phone numbers, memos, and all the other data for built-in applications also use this memory. On a reset, it is not cleared. This portion of memory is analogous to files on a hard disk in a traditional OS.

For both kinds of memory, allocation is done as chunks. The permanent storage holds databases, with related chunks kept in a single database. For example, all the memos are stored (each as a separate chunk, or database record) in a single database. Another database holds all records from the Address Book application. We cover this in detail in Chapter 6, *Databases.*

Unlike in a traditional desktop operating system, data and code are not copied from permanent storage to dynamic memory but are used in place. For example, when your code executes, it is executing in-place from the permanent storage. Since the permanent store itself is RAM, it can be read by the CPU like any other RAM. Similarly, data can be read (and displayed) directly from storage.

For more information on memory usage in a Palm application see "Memory Is Extremely Limited" in Chapter 4, *Structure of an Application.*

Palm has been careful to ensure that permanent storage is protected against every programmer's ability to accidentally overwrite memory (bugs happen). Palm rightly reasoned that users would be unhappy if one bug in a single application caused all their data to be lost. Thus, while the permanent storage can be read like any other RAM, it is write-protected by the device. It won't allow that portion of RAM to be written. In order to write to specific chunks within permanent memory, you have to use the operating system's mechanism, and that includes a check against attempts to write to places outside the chunk.

### *Resources*

An application on the Palm OS is a resource database that contains many different resources. A resource is simply a database record that has a type and an ID. Stored within these resources are the guts and skin of your application. On the desktop, these resource databases have a *.PRC* extension. You'll find that they are often referred to as PRC files.

Examples of the types of things stored in resources are:

- Your code
- User interface elements
- Text strings
- Forms
- Icons

The user interface elements that appear on the Palm device are initialized based on the contents found in these resources. Because the initialization is not embedded within your code, you can change the appearance of your application (for instance, to localize it for another language) without modifying the code itself. Another advantage is that you can use visual editors to display and edit the user interface portions of your application. Such editors allow you to easily tweak the look or presentation of data without recompiling and redownloading your application. We discuss resources in detail in Chapter 5, *Forms and Form Objects.*

### *Events*

A Palm OS application is event-driven. Events arrive, like pen down or key down, and your application responds to them. Some events are handled by your application; others are handled by the operating system. Once your application begins, it enters an event loop, repeatedly getting, then handling an event. The loop continues until the user launches another application, which causes your application to quit. The event cycle of a Palm application is covered in depth in Chapter 4.

### *Forms and controls*

The Palm OS has built-in support for various controls and for managing forms. Forms are similar to windows on a desktop operating system. Because of the simpler user interface on the Palm OS, only one form is active even though several forms may be displayed.

The Palm OS provides a rich API for forms that includes many user-interface elements. Some of these elements are:

- Checkboxes
- Radio buttons
- Push buttons
- Lists (one-column)
- Pickers (pop-up lists)
- Tables (multicolumn)
- Scrollbars
- Static text labels
- Editable text fields
- Menus

Because these elements are stored as resources rather than in your code, you can create a prototype of your application very quickly. The simplicity of adding the User Interface (UI) elements and the variety of them makes it easy to try out various application designs. Chapter 5 contains a description of these.

### *Communications*

The Palm OS supports a variety of communication methods. As communicating is an essential aspect of the Palm's success, you should expect this area of the OS to be critical both in current and future applications. Current communication protocols are:

- Serial communication.
- TCP/IP with a socket interface.
- Infrared. Low-level infrared support is via IrDA (Infrared Data Assocation).
- A higher-level object exchange is provided that allows exchanging information between Palm devices and other devices using an industry-standard object exchange. This object exchange currently runs only over IRDA, although other ways of exchanging information may be provided in the future.

Chapter 9, *Communications*, is devoted to a full discussion of communication features of the Palm OS.

### Palm 3.0 OS features

The 3.0 system added new features to the OS. The most important of these are:

*Grayscale*
: The Palm 3.0 OS supports limited grayscale in 2-bit mode. Your applications can switch between 1- and 2-bit mode with specific system routines. Later devices and OS versions will undoubtedly increase grayscale support.

*Fonts*
: An additional larger bold font has been added to the ROM. Applications also have system support for the use of custom fonts.

*Heaps*
: The dynamic heap is larger, and the storage area has been folded into a single large heap. We discuss heap size and manipulating memory chunks in "Memory Is Extremely Limited" in Chapter 4.

*Objects larger than 64K*
: The system now allows you to manage objects that are larger than 64K with a new set of APIs.

*Sound*
: There is support for volume control, asynchronous tones, custom alert sounds, and Standard MIDI (Musical Instrument Digital Interface) Files (SMFs).

*Dynamic UI*
: New APIs are available that make it possible for you to create controls at runtime.

*Serial number*
: Many devices (including the Palm III) have a unique programmer-accessible serial number. This allows greater flexibility with security measures. (Note: future devices are not guaranteed have this type of identification.)

Applications that use these new features should check the version of the OS on which they are running and either fail gracefully or not use 3.0-specific features.

### Miscellaneous

The Palm OS has various other APIs for things like:

- Strings—searching within strings, copying, converting to/from numbers.
- Date and time.
- Alarms—setting an alarm for a particular date and time. Your application is then notified when that date and time are reached (even though it may not be running at the moment).

- Find—the Palm OS provides a device-wide find that allows the user to search for a string anywhere within the device. Each application does its part by searching for the specified string within its own databases.

With all these features, you can see that the Palm OS provides for rich and varied applications. Text and the presentation of content are supported by a wide variety of tools that aid in the visual display of information.

The subsystems of the Palm OS are called managers, and the naming convention for functions designate the manager that they are in. For example, all memory manager routines begin with `Mem`. All database manager routines begin with `Dm`. All form manager routines begin with `Frm`.

## *Overview of Conduits*

The second part of the Palm application is the desktop connection. Because Palm devices act as an extension of the desktop, it is crucial that information be easily exchanged. Conduits are the mechanism for doing this.

A conduit is code on the desktop that is called during a HotSync synchronization to manage the flow of information to and from databases on the handheld. Conduits register the database or databases for which they are responsible. Note that each database should have only one conduit responsible for it.

Conduits (Figure 2-1) are created using Conduit Development Kits for Windows (C/C++), Mac OS (C/C++), or Java.

Applications that do not have a conduit portion use a system-provided one instead. This Palm-created conduit is used for backups and is part of HotSync. This backup conduit copies the application data or database from the device and stores it as a file. You specify the backup conduit when you create a database. Think of this as the "If you can't afford an attorney, one will be appointed for you at no charge" conduit—the conduit of last resort.

During a HotSync session, the backup conduit is called for databases that don't have another conduit and which have been marked as needing a backup. At this point, it copies each record from the database and copies database header information into a file. This file can then be used to restore the state of the device if necessary.

More sophisticated conduits do more than this basic copying of information. They can read/write specific information to or from the device. For example, a conduit for a sales application might handle the downloads of new price lists, overwriting any existing price list that has expired. It might also be responsible for uploading a database of sales orders.

*Figure 2-1. Conduits control the exchange of information*

The most sophisticated conduits are those that synchronize records on the handheld with information on the desktop. Good examples of these include conduits that synchronize the Date Book records with various desktop PIMs like Outlook or Lotus Organizer. These synchronization conduits usually work by assigning each record a unique ID and tracking when a particular record has been changed.

# Handheld Development

Many different development tools are available for Palm programming. There is everything from a collection of tools that let you write C code to polished forms based packages that require only modest amounts of scripting. From this gamut of choices, you should be able to pick the right tool for the type of application you want to create. Before we discuss the advantages and disadvantages of each choice, however, it's worth looking at a description of each option.

For the development of the handheld portion of your Palm application, you can write code on Windows 95/98/NT, Unix, or Macintosh platforms. Palm's official development environment, CodeWarrior, is available for both Windows and Macintosh. Unix and Windows programmers have access to the free set of tools—GNU C compiler, or GCC—and there are two packages for Windows-based forms development. Last, but not least, Windows programmers can also program in 68K assembler or use a proprietary language called CASL.

## *CodeWarrior for Palm OS*

The official development environment for the Palm OS is Metrowerks's CodeWarrior for Palm OS. This commercial development environment allows you to create ANSI C and C++ programs on either Windows 95/98/NT or Macintosh systems. It currently includes Palm's Conduit Software Development Kit, and Palm's own documentation assumes that you are using it. CodeWarrior for Palm OS is available on a subscription basis with one year of free updates. It costs approximately $369. Here is a description of the tools that CodeWarrior gives you for Palm OS development:

*Metrowerks's Constructor*
: Constructor is a graphical resource editor (see Figure 2-2) that you use to create the user interface elements of your application.

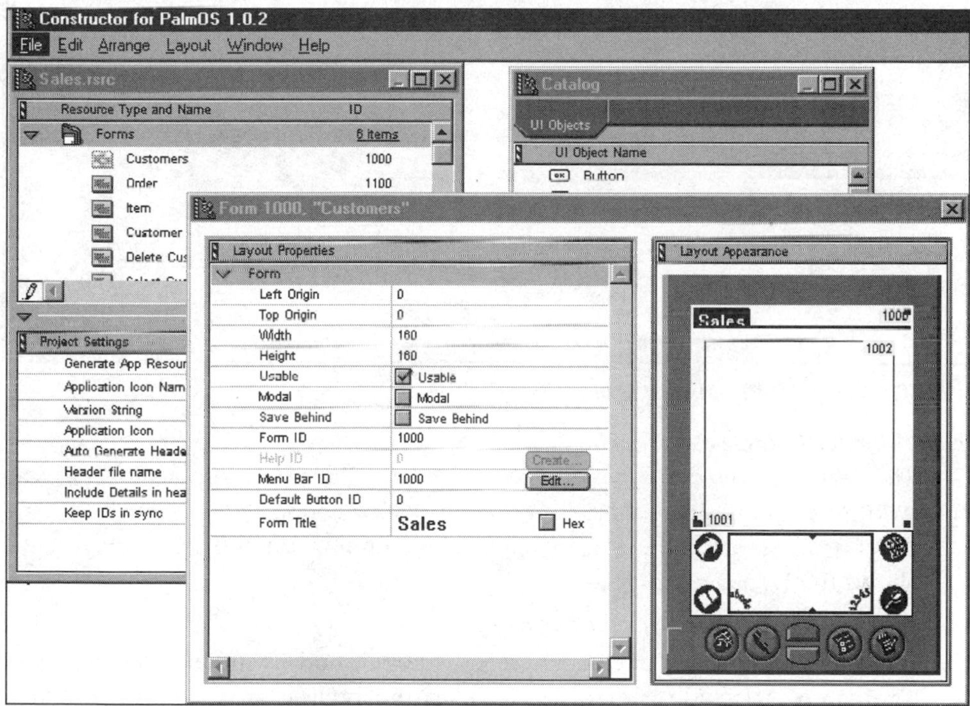


*Figure 2-2. Creating an application's resources using Metrowerks Constructor*

*CodeWarrior Integrated Development Environment (IDE)*
: This is a project-based IDE (see Figure 2-3) that includes:

- A Motorola 68000 C/C++ compiler
- A linker
- PalmRez (formerly called PilotRez), which creates PRC files from the compiled 68000 code and converts resources from Constructor format to PRC format

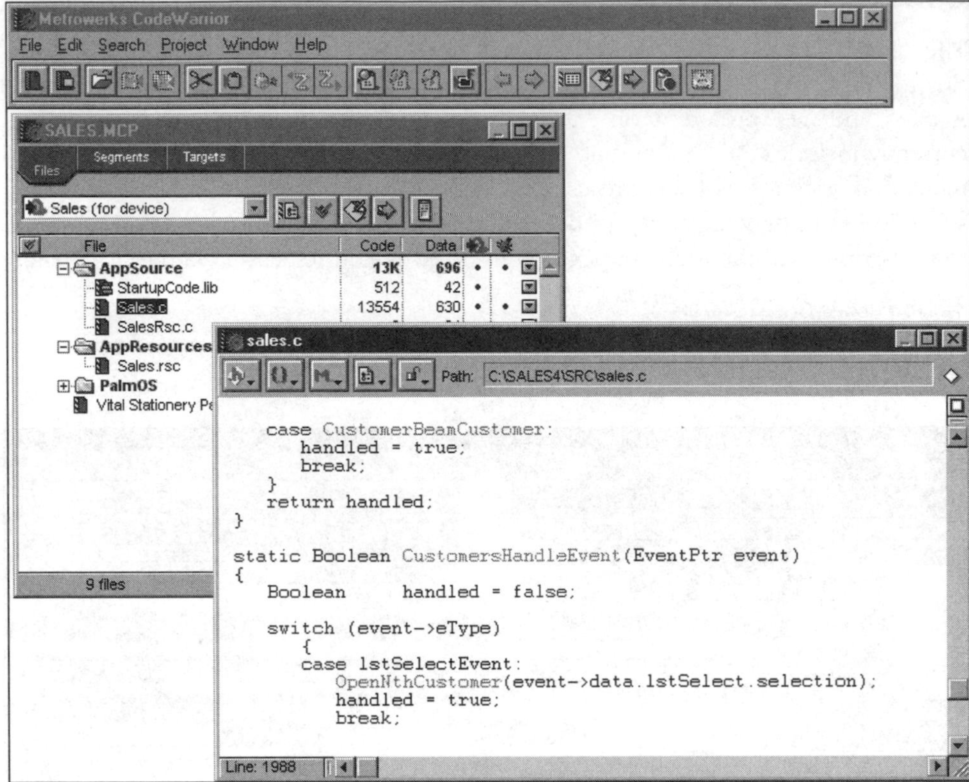


*Figure 2-3. CodeWarrior IDE editing a project*

*CodeWarrior Debugger*
: This source-level debugger is used to debug Palm OS applications. It can debug an application running on a Palm device connected to your host computer via a serial cable, or an application running on the POSE. Figure 2-4 shows the Debugger in action.

*Palm Software Development Kit (SDK)*
: Includes header files, documentation, a tutorial, and invaluable sample code. The samples include the source code to the built-in applications: Expense, Memo, Address Book, and To Do.

*Conduit SDK*
: This SDK is used to create conduits. The SDK is available separately, but is bundled as a courtesy. Note that the SDK requires Microsoft Visual C++ for Windows in order to create Windows conduits. Metrowerks's CodeWarrior for Mac OS can be used to create Macintosh conduits.

### *Developing on the Macintosh*

If you're already developing software on the Macintosh, you're probably using CodeWarrior and therefore have a good idea of what to expect from this product.

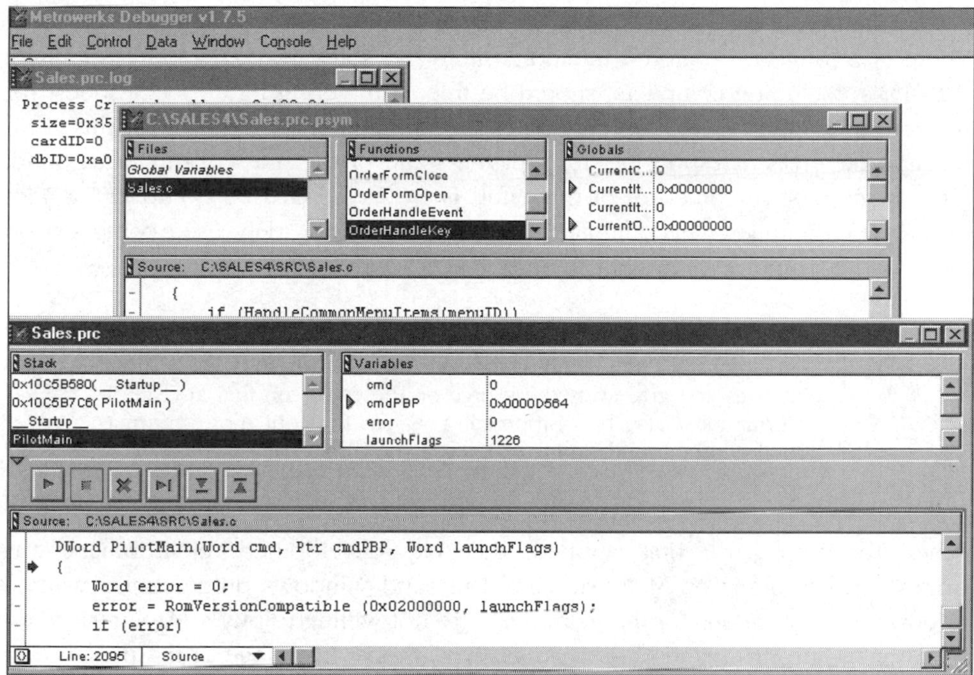


*Figure 2-4. Metrowerks Debugger being used on a Palm OS application*

For those Macintosh users who don't have CodeWarrior, you can assume that Metrowerks's reputation for creating quality development environments is deserved. Most users are very happy with its products.

### *Developing on Windows*

CodeWarrior was originally a Macintosh-only development environment that has been ported to Windows. While it works quite reliably, many Windows users find that the CodeWarrior IDE does not have a Windows look and feel. Because it looks more like a Macintosh product and some keystrokes don't work as expected, some Windows users find it annoying.

You should assume that Metrowerks will fix the problems with the look of the Windows product. It is certainly worth your time to check out the most current version. CodeWarrior can be purchased directly from Metrowerks (*http://www.metrowerks.com*) or from mail-order houses such as PC Zone (*http://www.pczone.com*). A demo version of CodeWarrior for Palm OS (on Windows) is available from *http://www.metrowerks.com/lite/*.

## GCC

There is a long and honored tradition within the software developer community that tools, including compilers, should be free. A towering figure in the quest for free programming tools is the Free Software Foundation. Volunteers for this organization have been responsible for creating some of the finest compilers around. One of the best to come out of this effort is GCC (the GNU C Compiler), a general C/C++ compiler. This compiler is one of the most widely used compilers on Unix, and it even enjoys broad use on Win32 platforms.

Free Software Foundation volunteers create compilers for various platforms and give away the source on the condition that any modifications must also be distributed. You can find out more information about the foundation from its web site (*http://www.gnu.org/fsf*).

When the Pilot 1000 first shipped, the only development environment was CodeWarrior running on Mac OS. Many Unix and Windows programmers wanted to develop applications for the Palm but were not willing to buy a Macintosh to do so. Some enterprising and helpful programmers took advantage of the presence of GCC and added a PalmPilot port of the compiler that creates Palm OS binaries. A collection of tools was put together in what is officially known as GNU PalmPilot SDK—however, most folks just call the entire thing GCC.

#### *What is in GNU PalmPilot SDK*

This SDK is a collection of tools that allow you to create C/C++ Palm OS applications on Unix or Windows. The tools include:

*GCC*
: The most important of these tools is the GNU C Compiler (GCC), which compiles C/C++ code to Motorola 68K.

*GDB*
: A source-level debugger.

*PilRC*
: This resource compiler creates Palm resources from textual descriptions of the resources. These text files contain resource descriptions and end in the extension *.RCP*.

*PilrcUI*
: This application displays RCP files graphically, previewing what they'll look like on the handheld. Figure 2-5 shows an example of PilrcUI.

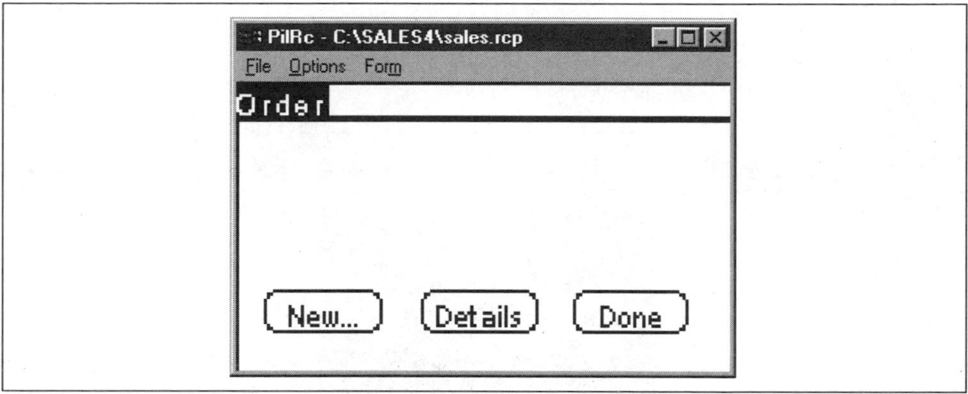


*Figure 2-5. PilrcUI displaying the resources of an application*

*Copilot*

This application emulates the Palm device at the hardware level. It requires a ROM image from an actual Palm device and acts almost exactly like a Palm device. Further development of this has been taken over by Palm—see Chapter 10, *Debugging Palm Applications*, for more details.

#### *Where to get GCC*

There are several sources on the Net for GCC, depending on whether you want GCC for Unix or for Windows. As new places become available all the time, it is worth checking Palm's web site for more recent information. If you get all the parts at once, it is a big download (15MB), so make sure that you leave ample time for it. Our favorite place to acquire all of GCC at once is Ray's Software Archive (*http://www.palmcentral.com*).

If you use GCC, you still need to figure out what to do for the conduit portion of your application. You have two choices. You can purchase the Conduit SDK Tool Kit from Palm for $99, or you can rely on the backup conduit that Palm supplies.

## *Tools Directly from Palm Computing*

Palm offers a lot of useful stuff as well. All of the following resources can be found at Palm's developer web site (*http://www.palm.com/devzone*):

*POSE*

This application is a further development of Copilot. It serves as a replacement for an actual Palm OS device while you do development. Because it can load a ROM image from disk, it usefully emulates different versions of the Palm OS. Figure 2-6 shows how POSE appears on your monitor.

Of course, final testing of your application should take place with actual Palm OS devices. Do not ship an application having tested it only on the emulator.

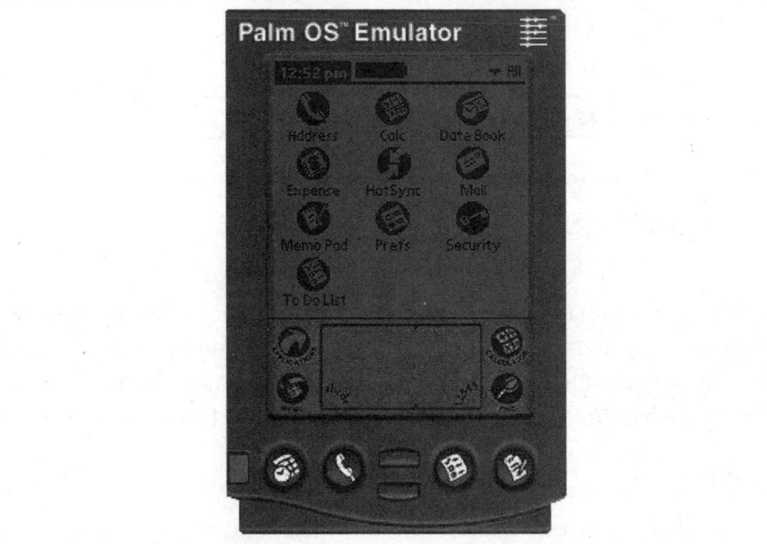


*Figure 2-6. POSE in a desktop window emulating a Palm III device*

*Debug ROMs*
: There are 2.0 and 3.0 OS ROM images that you can use with POSE. They are not the version of the ROM used in production devices, as they have added, among other things, extra debugging code that does sanity checking of parameters.

*Palm OS documentation*
: All the documentation for the Palm OS can be found on Palm's web site. There are numerous FAQs, tech notes, and white papers. This documentation is updated frequently.

*Palm tutorial*
: This is a walkthrough that shows the building of an application from start to finish. The tutorial assumes you'll be using CodeWarrior for Palm OS. This very thorough tutorial is quite good in its description of the intricate details of application development (what buttons go where, how you add a button to a form, and so on). There are Windows and Macintosh versions of the tutorial that can be downloaded for free (*http://www.palm.com/devzone*).

*Conduit Development Kit (CDK)*

This is the SDK for creating conduits for Mac OS and/or Windows using C or C++. This SDK costs $99, but is included as part of CodeWarrior for Palm OS. The Windows version requires Visual C++. The Macintosh version requires CodeWarrior for Mac OS.

*Conduit SDK, Java Edition*

This is the SDK for creating conduits for Mac OS and/or Windows using Java. This SDK costs $99.

# Alternative Development Environments

The following sections describe several useful alternative development environments for the Palm OS.

## Assembler SDK (ASDK)

This SDK allows development of applications written in Motorola 68K assembler. It includes Pila (Pilot Assembler). To us this would be sheer agony, but apparently some developers enjoy writing applications in assembly language. To each their own poison. You certainly can't beat the price—it's free.

For more information, see Darren Massena's web site (*http://www.massena.com*), which is an indispensable Palm developer resource in its own right.

## Jump

This novel environment allows you to write your application in Java using a Palm class library and your favorite Java development environment. Jump then compiles the resulting Java *.class* files into Motorola 68K code. Jump includes a very small runtime library that provides crucial Java support like garbage collection.

The only disappointing aspect of Jump is that the Palm OS is not completely supported. For example, any calls that require a callback function as a parameter (such as *LstSetDrawFunction* and *FrmSetEventHandler*) won't work.

This development environment is free, and source code is provided. Jump is the brainchild of Greg Hewgill; you can get it from *http://www.hewgill.com.*

## CASL

This commercial package provides cross-platform support. You write an application once in the CASL language (a BASIC-like proprietary language) and then deploy it on Palm OS or on other operating systems. This approach offers you ease of cross-platform dispersion as you write your applications in one language for multiple platforms. The code is compiled into a p-code for a virtual machine. There is a virtual machine for Palm OS, and one will be available for Windows CE in 1998. You can test your applications under Windows, as well. Figure 2-7 shows an example of application development using CASL. As you can see, development is simpler than directly using C or C++.

CASL runs only on Windows and is currently priced at $64.95 (a free demo version is available). See *http://www.caslsoft.com* for more details.

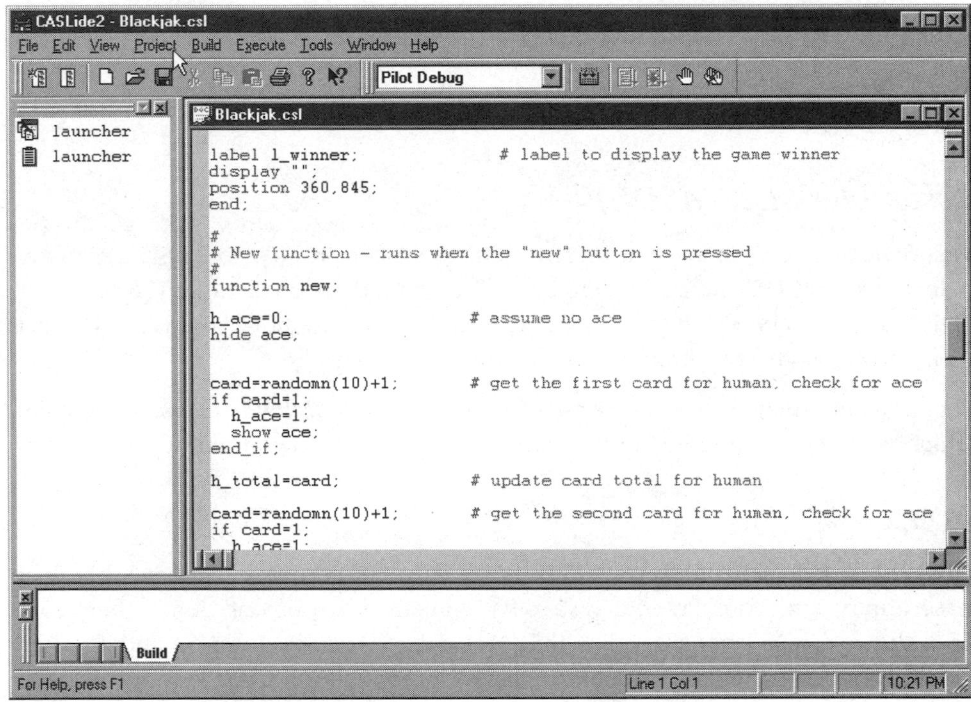


*Figure 2-7. Using the CASL IDE*

# *High-Level Forms Development*

Palm devices are so numerous and applications so popular that there are even a couple of third-party development environments specifically for creating specialized forms–based Palm applications.

## *Pendragon Forms*

This Windows application provides a very easy way to create simple multipage forms that contain text fields, checkboxes, radio buttons, etc.

Pendragon Forms also provides a conduit that automatically uploads information into comma-separated values (CSV) files. These files can then be easily imported into spreadsheet or database programs. Looking at Figure 2-8, you can see how simple it is to make the form being displayed on the Palm device in Figure 2-9.

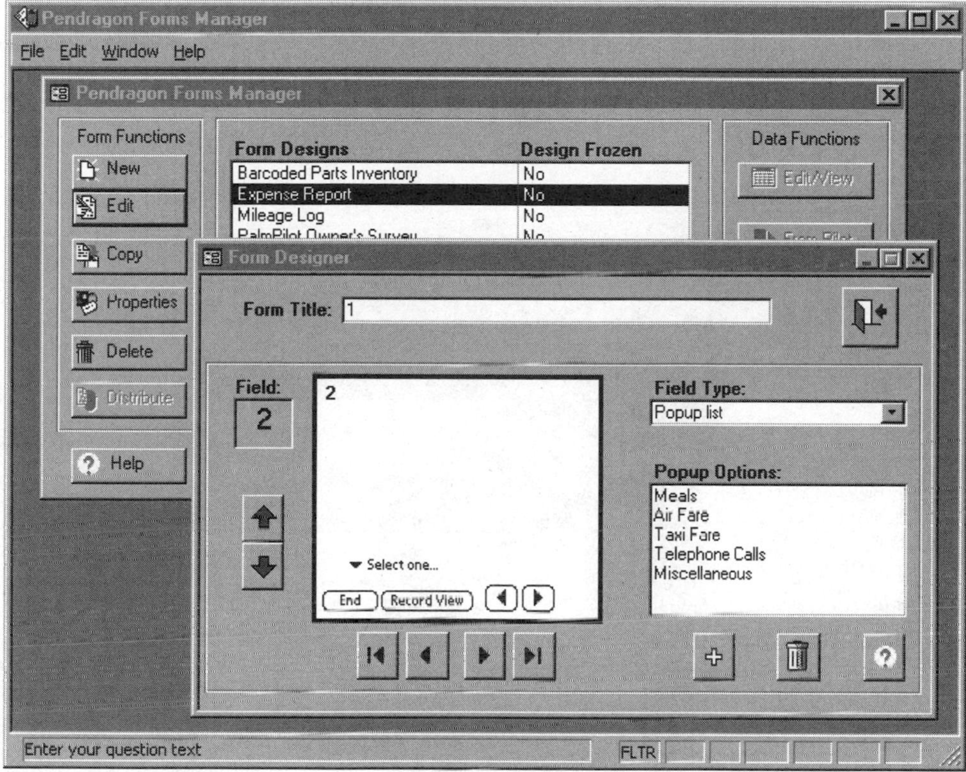


*Figure 2-8. Developing a form using Pendragon Forms*

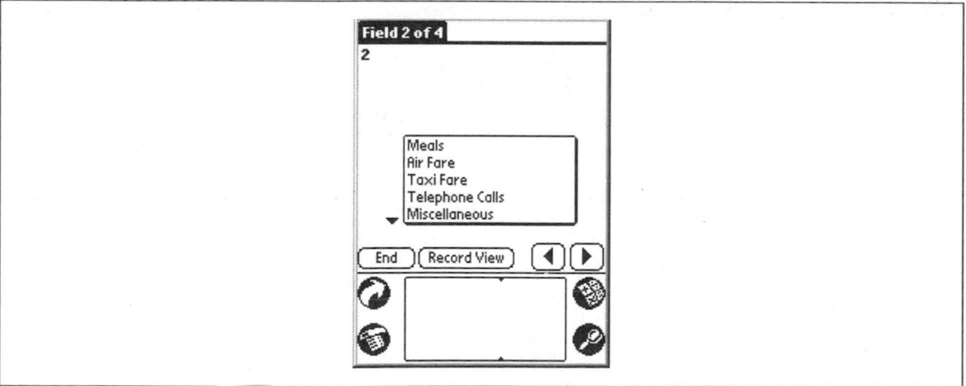


*Figure 2-9. Running an application created with Pendragon Forms*

Pendragon Forms is $50, and, nicely enough, there is no runtime fee necessary for deploying forms. See *http://www.pendragon-software.com* for further details.

## Satellite Forms

Satellite Forms, by SoftMagic, is an environment for creating very sophisticated Palm OS applications. In Satellite Forms, your application consists of a number of database tables and forms. Each form is tied to a specific table and can display elements of that table. Figure 2-10 shows an example table in Satellite Forms. Figure 2-11 shows an example form. Figure 2-12 shows the resulting form on a Palm device.

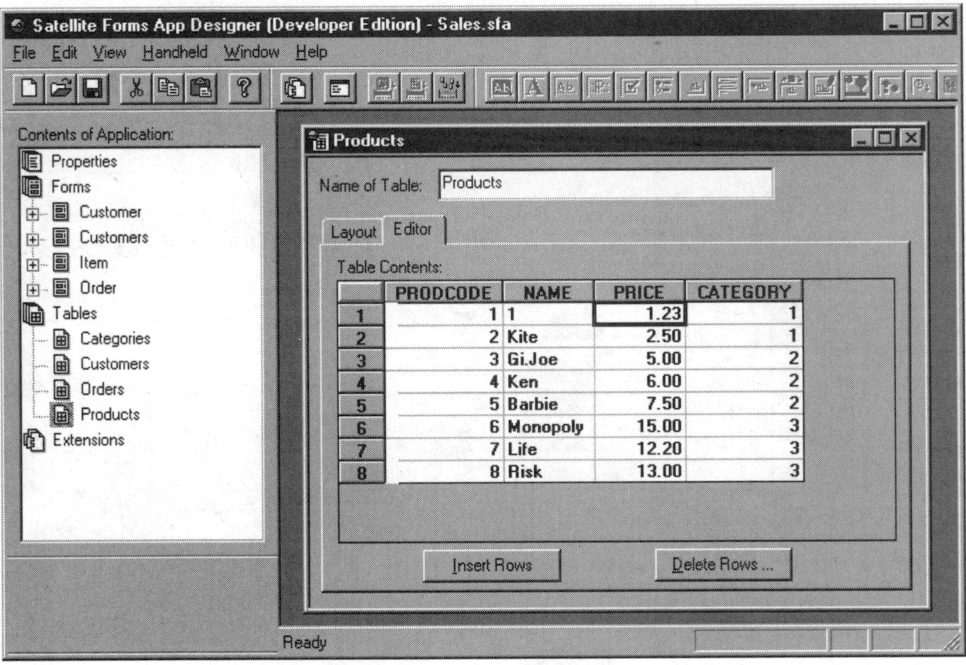


*Figure 2-10. Creating a table in Satellite Forms*

Instead of using C/C++ code, you control the actions of the application in one of two ways:

- You specify a set of built-in actions that occur when the user taps a control. For instance, when a button is pressed, you could request (among many choices) that a new form be opened or that you return to the previous form.
- You specify custom code that you want executed. The code is created using a scripting language that is very similar to Visual Basic.

The application comes with a number of built-in controls as well as a library of routines. Satellite Forms also has an extension mechanism that allows you to write

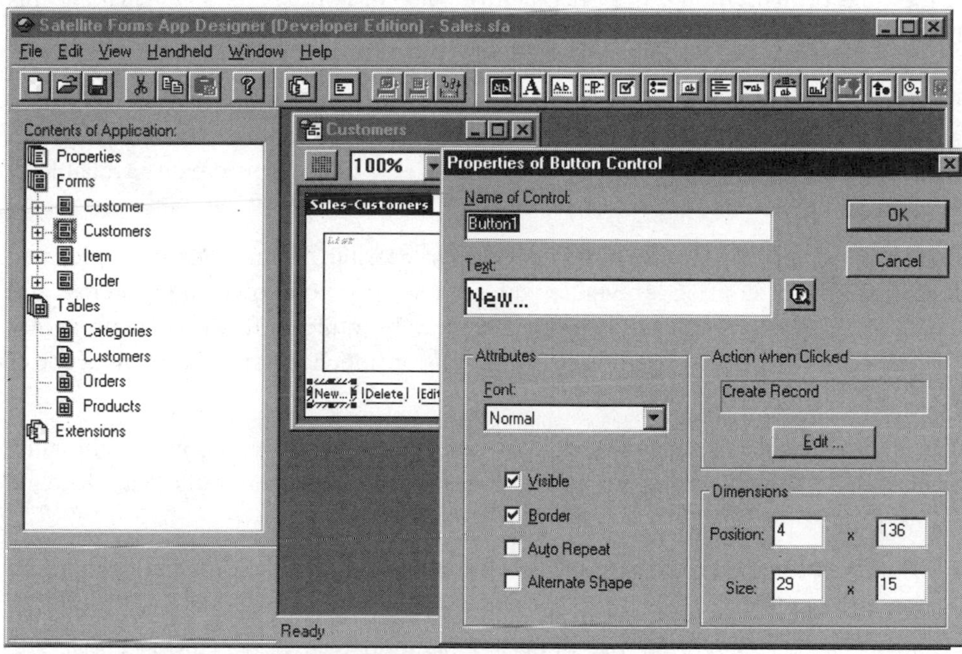


*Figure 2-11. Creating a form in Satellite Forms*

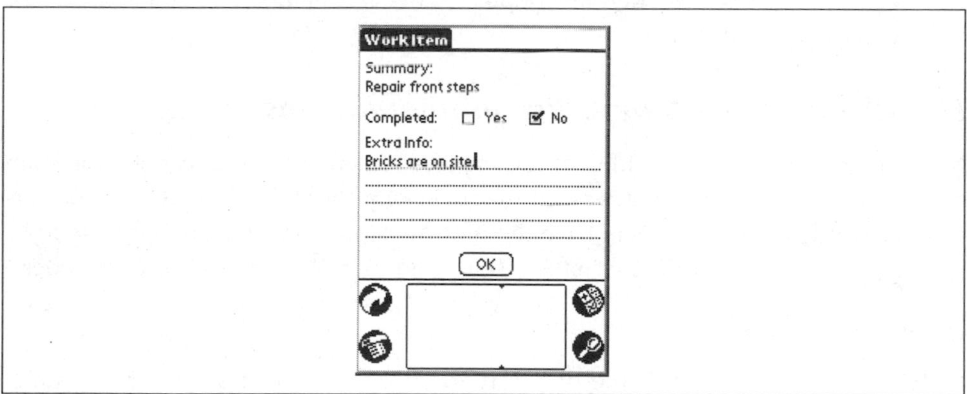


*Figure 2-12. A running Satellite Forms application*

C code for your own new controls and new libraries (imagine, for instance, a library of financial routines or a new user interface control).

Satellite Forms has an ActiveX control that is connected to a HotSync conduit. You can use the ActiveX control during HotSync to copy any table to, or from, the Palm device. The tables are stored on the desktop as DBX files, which can be easily integrated with any database.

At the time of this writing, the price tag for Satellite Forms was $595 (making this the most expensive environment). You have a couple of requirements, as well. It only runs on Windows, and applications you create require a runtime library on the Palm device (the runtime is free). After you hand over the initial money, there is no additional cost to deploying applications built with Satellite Forms. There is a demo version (which limits the number and size of tables you create) available at the company's web site (*http://www.softmagic.com*).

There are certain things that can't be done in Satellite Forms. For example, you don't have direct control of events, you can't specify your own menu items, and text fields have a maximum length. It also may be quite difficult to create a very specialized user interface (although the extension mechanism does allow a lot of flexibility).

This is a very sophisticated package that can be used to create commercial-quality applications. The following commercial products have been built with Satellite Forms:

- *Punch List* by Strata Systems. This is project management software for the construction industry.
- *Real Estate Companion* by Mobile Generation Software. This is client and property information for real estate professionals.
- *Helpdesk on the Go* by Kerem Krikpinar. This is a field service companion for technical support desks.

## Handheld Development Recommendations

Now that you have a good idea of the choices for creating applications for Palm devices, it's time to figure out which is the right one for you. As should not be surprising, Windows programmers have the most flexibility; Macintosh and Unix folks have none. Let's look at the Macintosh, Unix, and then Windows choices in order.

### Developing using Mac OS

CodeWarrior for Palm OS is the only way to do development at the current time. The good news is that CodeWarrior for Palm OS started life on Macintosh, so you can be assured that it's a robust, elegant product.

### Developing using Unix

You'll be using GCC tools for your development environment. This isn't really a disadvantage, however. If you are accustomed to twiddling around with Unix in the first place, then the slightly more complex setup of GCC (the need to use makefiles) won't even get a twitch out of you. Plus, it's free.

### *Developing using Windows*

You've got quite a bit of choice, as every environment we have discussed is available on Windows. Let's try to eliminate some of the options by focusing on what might be a factor in your decisions:

*Assembly programming*
: If programming in assembly is your cup of tea, then ASDK is for you.

*C/C++ programming*
: If you are an ardent C programmer, you will be using CodeWarrior or GCC. If you are an occasional or hobbyist programmer, then GCC is probably your best choice, given its attractive sticker price. While it is more flexible, it is also more difficult to use (it requires familiarity with makefiles and command lines).*

  For greater usability, we suggest that you go with CodeWarrior. The inclusion of Palm's Conduit SDK as part of the package, the documentation and source code provided by both Metrowerks and Palm, and Palm's support make this development environment the obvious winner.

*Forms-based script development*
: If price is an important factor, then we think Pendragon Forms is a good low-cost way to create simple forms for inputting data. If we were writing a simple survey-type application on a tight budget, this would be the tool of choice.

### *The choice for rapid prototyping, fast development, and great usability*

We are very excited about Satellite Forms and view it as comparable to Visual Basic on Windows. If you can afford it, you should use it. Even if your final shipping application is based in C, this environment is great for rapid prototyping. It allows quick development of applications without forcing you to get involved in the low-level nuts and bolts of creating an application from scratch.

Let's put it this way—if we (veteran C/C++ programmers) were writing *any* application for the Palm OS, we'd first look to see whether we could use Satellite Forms. We give this strong a recommendation because of the experience we had with porting the sample application in this book to Satellite Forms. Don't be fooled by the simplicity of the environment. You can create quite sophisticated applications very quickly with little or no custom code. For example, consider the Sales application that we are developing in this book. Using C, this application has more than 2,000 lines of code and took weeks to write. *Using Satellite forms, we created an application with similar functionality in about three hours—this includes the time it took to learn how to use Satellite Forms.*

---

* While we have never used any, we have heard that there are visual frontends to GCC that make it somewhat easier to use.

On the CD-ROM are versions of the Sales application. Compare the CodeWarrior/GCC version of it with the one we created using Satellite forms. We think you'll be amazed at the similarity. Figure 2-13 shows the final Satellite Forms version running on the Palm handheld.

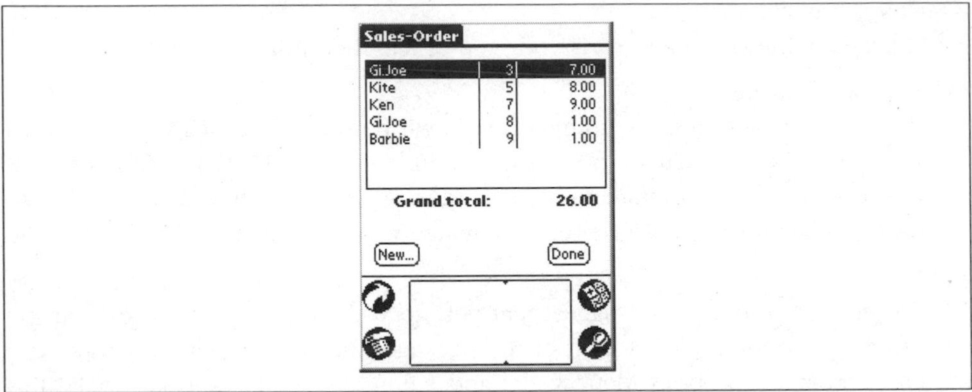


*Figure 2-13. Sales application written using Satellite Forms*

### *Switching platforms*

If you are changing development platforms, there are a few issues for you to consider. CodeWarrior is compatible across platforms, as projects and files can be moved from Macintosh to Windows and vice versa.

You also have cross-platform compatibility between Windows and Unix if you are using GCC. The only thing to watch for is line break conventions—they are different on the two operating systems.

Metrowerks Constructor uses Mac OS resource forks. (If you're not familiar with Mac OS resource forks, now is not the time to learn.) While this creates no problem for the Mac OS, Windows is another matter. A Windows project requires two separate files for your Constructor resource files, one for the data fork and one for the resource fork. This can cause some confusion on Windows, since both these files are visible. Additionally, in order to get these two separate files created, you have to copy Constructor files on a floppy—copying over the network won't work.

This problem will go away in the future when Constructor is rewritten to use normal data files that provide true cross-platform compatibility.

### *Switching development environments*

Switching from CodeWarrior to GCC or vice versa is possible but not easy. The source code is not much of a problem, even though there are some differences between the two C/C++ compilers. The resources are a different matter. If you are moving from GCC to CodeWarrior, you have to do the following:

1. On a Mac OS machine, use *prc2rsrc* to convert your PRC file to a Macintosh resource file. (That's right—you need a Macintosh to convert from Unix to Windows!)
2. Next, use ResEdit to modify the `MBAR` resource into an `MBAR` resource and separate `MENU` resources as required by Constructor.

Going from CodeWarrior to GCC is much easier:

1. Use PTools (which is written in Java and therefore available on any platform) to open your *.PRC* file.
2. Next, display each resource in PilRC format. Copy each of the resources into one big *.RCP* file, and use this as input to PilRC.

The sample application in this book, Sales, compiles with both CodeWarrior and GCC and has both PilRC resource files and Metrowerks Constructor files. Thus, it can be built in either environment. Most of these tools (demo or complete versions), along with the sample code, are available on the CD.

## *Conduit Development*

If you are creating a conduit for your Palm application, you need to do so on Macintosh or Windows using Palm's Conduit SDK. The Conduit SDK comes with:

- Header files
- Debug and nondebug libraries
- Source code for sample conduits

### *What Is a Conduit?*

Under Windows, a conduit is a Dynamic Link Library (DLL) that is called as HotSync occurs. An install DLL is provided with which you register your conduit with HotSync. On Mac OS, a conduit is a shared library.

Conduits have access to databases on the Palm OS. The Conduit Manager handles the complexities of communication; it is not your concern. You simply call routines to read and write records in the database. The Conduit Manager handles the communication protocol.

### *Using C/C++*

In order to develop conduits for Windows, you must use Visual C++ 5.0 (or later). For Mac OS, you can use any development environment that has the ability to create shared libraries (CodeWarrior for Mac OS is a likely candidate).

C++ classes that simplify creating a synchronization conduit are provided by Palm (frequently referred to by the names *basemon* and *basetbl*). These C++ classes are the basis of the conduits for the built-in applications. If your application's synchronization needs are similar to those of the built-in applications, then these C++ classes work well. As your application's sync needs differ, the C++ classes become less useful, and you might wish to consider reverting to the underlying C/C++ Conduit Manager API to make things work properly. You do, however, have another alternative.

There are other C++ classes recently provided by Palm to aid in the creation of conduits. These classes (called Generic Conduit) are not officially supported by Palm (at the time of this book's writing), but they do offer an alternative—in many ways easier—method of conduit creation.

### *Using Java*

Presently, Java conduits work only on Windows. Conduits written in Java can take advantage of Java Database Classes (JDBC) for easy interaction with database engines. The sample code that is part of the Conduit SDK, Java Edition, uses JDBC to interact with an Oracle database.

## *Conclusion*

You should now have a good idea of which development environment you want to use to write your Palm OS applications. You should also know enough about the features in the Palm OS and of the devices to make intelligent decisions about the types of applications that you can create for Palm devices. Next, we discuss the sample application that we are developing throughout this book.

# 3

# *Designing a Solution*

Now that you know about the features of the Palm OS and you have figured out what development environment you are going to use, it is time to create a new application. To do this, you first need to know what the Palm OS provides in the way of user interface elements. Second, you need a description of the elements common to every application.

From this general overview, we move to a concrete example. For this purpose, we discuss a sample application that we are going to create and then dissect in this book. We show you its design, what actions the user performs, how we prototyped it, and the design complications we encountered. Once we've covered the handheld portion of the application, we turn to a description of the conduit.

## *User Interface Elements in an Application*

The Palm OS provides you with an abundance of user interface elements. The following is a description of these elements. We also show you some common examples of each type.

## Alerts

Figure 3-1 contains an example of a typical alert. It is simply a modal dialog that displays a title, a message, an icon, and one or more buttons. You are responsible for setting the text of the title, the message, and the button(s). You also specify the type of alert. It can be any of the following types (ordered from mildest in consequence to most severe):

*Information*
: This has an "i" icon. The alert provides to the user some information (for example, that an action can't be completed). No data loss has occurred.

*Confirmation*
: This has a "?" icon. The alert asks the user a question, asking the user to confirm an action or to choose from possibilities.

*Warning*
: This has a "!" icon. You are asking the user if the action is really intentional. Data loss could occur if the action is completed. The Memo Pad uses a confirmation alert for deleting memos, since the user can choose to save an archive on the PC (thus the data is not lost). However, the system uses a warning dialog when the user chooses to delete an application, since after the delete, the application is completely gone. Figure 3-1 is a warning alert.

*Error*
: This has a stop sign. This alert tells the user that an error occurred as a result of the last action.

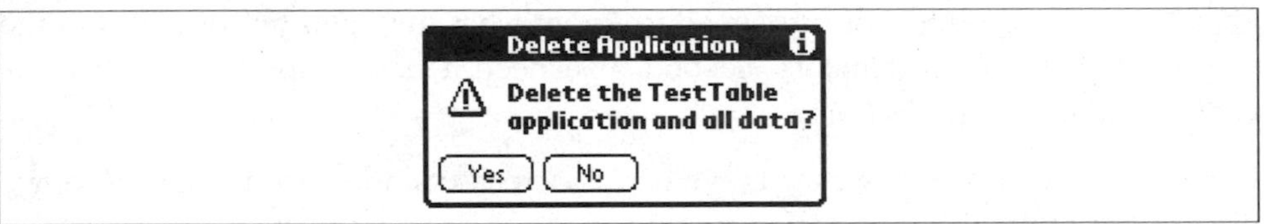


*Figure 3-1. A warning alert*

## Forms

A form is a general purpose container for one or more other user interface elements. A form can contain buttons, lists, tables, controls, and icons. It can also have a menubar associated with it. Forms can be anything from modal dialogs to containers for lists or tables of data. Forms can be small or fill the entire screen of the handheld.

The look of a form, including the proper placement of buttons, is covered in the Palm OS documentation. You need to scrupulously follow placement guidelines for all elements in a form. Figure 3-2 contains three different forms from the built-in applications to give you an idea of the variability they can have.

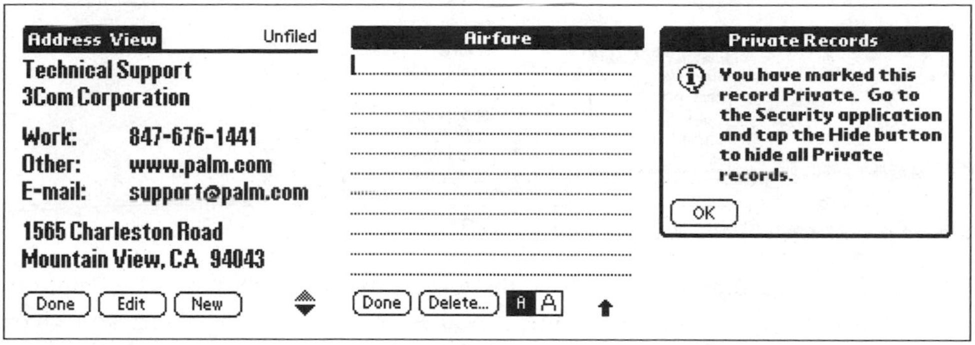

*Figure 3-2. Three forms containing various controls*

## *Menus, Menu Items, and Menubars*

Menus, menu items, and menubars are related to one another. A menubar contains one or more menus. A menu contains one or more menu items. Menu items often have Graffiti shortcuts associated with them. Figure 3-3 contains an example of a menubar with two menus in it. One of the menus is open, and it contains six menu items (plus an additional separator bar item). We discuss these features in detail in Chapter 7, *Menus*.

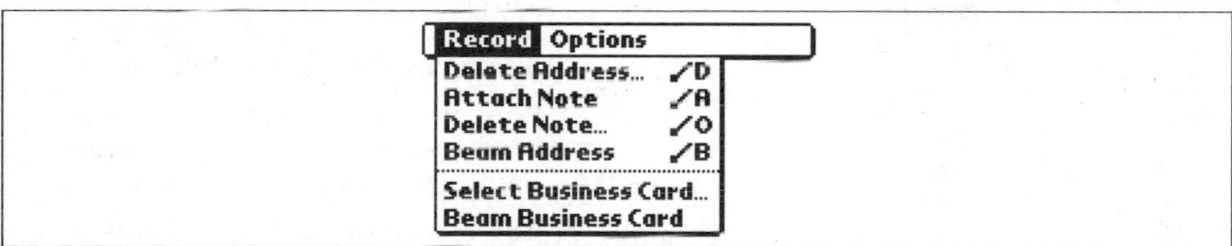


*Figure 3-3. A menubar with two menus; the first menu has six items (plus a separator bar)*

## *Tables and Lists*

Tables and lists are used for similar purposes. Use a table when you want to displays multiple columns of data and use lists when you need to display a single column. We discuss this further in the section "Tables" in Chapter 8, *Extras*. Figure 3-4 contains an example of a list on the left and a table on the right. As you can see in Figure 3-4, tables can support different types of data.

## *Miscellaneous User Interface Elements*

There are a number of other user interface elements. These include buttons, checkboxes, bitmaps, fields, gadgets, labels, Graffiti shift indicators, pop-up triggers, push buttons, repeating buttons, scrollbars, and selectors. Table 3-1 contains

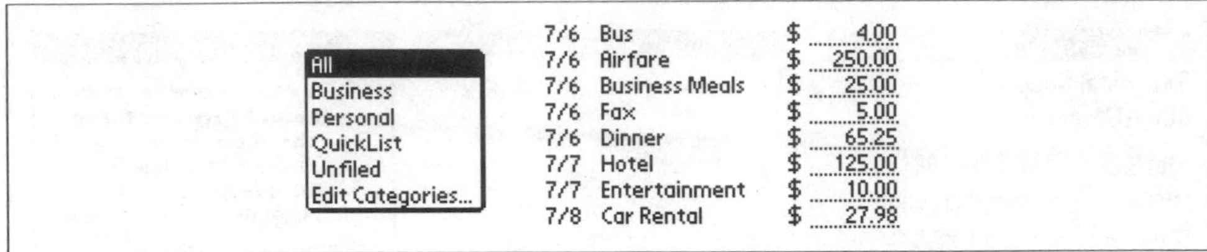


*Figure 3-4. A list (left) and a table (right)*

an example and a brief description of the typical use for each item. The Palm OS documentation describes in detail the attributes of each type of object and gives you information on where each item should be placed in a form.

*Table 3-1. Miscellaneous User Interface Elements*

| User Interface Element | Typical Example | Brief Description of Use |
|---|---|---|
| Button | New | A button is a tappable object with a label. An action occurs when it is tapped. |
| Checkbox | ☐ 1 Here is a checkbox and a string<br>☑ 1 Here is a checked check box | A checkbox represents an on/off state. |
| Field | New Name | This is for user data entry. It has one or more lines of editable text. It can also be used for text that isn't editable. |
| Form Bitmap | | This is a bitmap object that is usually black and white. Look for grayscale and color support in the future. |
| Gadget | S M T W T F S<br>5 6 7 8 9 10 11<br>8:00<br>10:00<br>12:00<br>2:00<br>4:00<br>6:00 | This is a custom UI object that is limited only by your imagination. You can create gadgets for simple or complicated uses.<br>This example gadget comes from the Calendar application and was created to handle the display of custom appointment times. |
| Graffiti Shift Indicator | ⬆ | This shows the current Graffiti shift state (punctuation, symbol, uppercase shift, or uppercase lock). This indicator should be in any form that allows text entry and should be at the lower right of the form. |
| Label | First name: | This is a noneditable text object. |

*Table 3-1. Miscellaneous User Interface Elements (continued)*

| User Interface Element | Typical Example | Brief Description of Use |
|---|---|---|
| Pop-up Trigger | ▾ All | Tap on this to display a pop-up list. The pop-up trigger displays the currently selected text from the list. |
| Push Button | Priority: 1 2 3 4 5 | Push buttons represent an on/off state and, as a rule, are grouped so that only one of a group is selected at a time. |
| Repeating Button | | This works like a button but causes a repeating action while the button is held down. |
| Scrollbar | | This object is often used for scrolling text or tables. It allows one-line scrolling, page scrolling, and direct navigation to a particular location. Scrollbars are not available prior to Palm OS 2.0. If you plan to support the 1.0 OS, your code will need to handle scrolling using the hardware scroll buttons. |
| Selector Trigger | 1:00 pm - 2:00 pm | When a user taps this object, a dialog box pops up to allow the user to edit the value. A gray rectangle surrounds the trigger. |

# *General Design of a Palm Application*

Most applications will contain a certain core number of user interface elements. Even the simplest application will, at the very least, need a form and some controls. Most applications go well beyond the minimal number of features and have multiple menus, forms, and dialogs as well.

When you sit down to design your application, you'll need to ask yourself the following questions and come up with some reasonable answers to them:

*What tasks does the application accomplish?*

Obviously, this is a question one would ask about any application on any platform. That doesn't make it any less relevant here. You need to lay out as clearly as possible what the user can do with your application, what tasks the user can perform. Just as importantly, you should have a clear idea of possible tasks that the user can't do.

The essence of the Palm OS and the handhelds is speed and accessibility. Putting a possible feature on the chopping block because it ruins either of these is something to be proud of and is terribly difficult to do in this era of "kitchen sink" applications.

*What forms does the application have?*
: There is minimally a startup form that the user sees when tapping the application icon. Every dialog (other than an alert) or other data view is also a new form. A good rule of thumb is that you will have one form for every view of data. Forms add up fast when you count this way.

*What menus does the application have?*
: Commonly, you will support the Record, Edit, and Option menus. They will be similar to those found in the built-in applications with the same menu items. Often custom menus are also a part of the application.

*What dialog boxes does the application have?*
: Alert dialog boxes give information, ask questions, issue warnings, and report errors.

*What is the structure of the application's database or databases?*
: The database is where you store information that is displayed on the handheld. You need to decide how many databases you will need, how the records are ordered, and what is stored in each record.

*What versions of the OS will you support?*
: You need to decide what versions of the Palm OS you are targeting. As we write this, there are three versions: 1.0, 2.0, and 3.0.

  A Palm study found that less than five percent of the Palm OS devices in use were running the 1.0 version of the OS. This number will only shrink as more post–1.0 OS devices are sold and users upgrade their 1.0 devices to the 3.0 OS.

  Our recommendation is not to worry about compatibility with the Palm 1.0 OS. Users can upgrade to the 3.0 OS (including IR support and 2MB of memory) for around $100 at the time of this writing. A user unwilling to spend that kind of money is probably unwilling to buy your software. Of course, your particular situation may dictate that you support the 1.0 version of the OS.

  Here are the major changes in the 2.0 and 3.0 operating systems:

  *Palm OS 2.0*
  : Many new APIs, some changed APIs. Support for TCP/IP (on ≥ 1MB devices), support for scrollbars, and support for IEEE Floating Point (32-bit floats, 64-bit doubles)

  *Palm OS 3.0*
  : Added support for infrared (devices include an IR port), additional sound support, additional font support, progress manager, possible unique device ID

It's very easy to write an application that is intended to support the 1.0 OS and accidentally uses a post-1.0 call (like *EvtSysEventAvail*). To catch this type of error, include a header file that flags any calls to a 2.0-or-later routine. You can find this header on the CD-ROM. You can also test your applications with POSE using older ROMs.

*What does the conduit do?*

If all you want to do is save the handheld data to the desktop as a backup, use the backup conduit. If the user needs to look at or edit the data on the desktop, or if the user needs to transfer data from the desktop to the handheld, then you need to design a conduit and determine what it can and can't do with data. You need to figure out what data is transferred, whether data will be uploaded, downloaded, or synchronized, and what application on the desktop the user will use to view the data.

### General Optimization

There are also some important ways to optimize when designing an application:

- Minimize the number of taps to complete frequent actions
- Minimize screen clutter by hiding infrequent actions
- Provide command buttons for common multistep activities
- Minimize switching screens

## How the Sample Applications Are Useful

Some of you may be wondering how useful the Sales application will be to you. Does it show you how to implement all the APIs? Does it contain the essential components of most Palm applications? Here are some answers. The Sales application uses most of the Palm API (except for Category UI) and to that extent offers a broad treatment. Because it isn't an exact clone of the built-in apps, you also see some new design issues and code. It also covers databases, beaming, menus, dialog boxes, and Find. Another crucial component is the detailed description of its conduit. We hope that much of what is mystifying about conduits is clarified in our descriptions and the code we create.

We also cover some Palm OS features in smaller sample applications. We handle tables, barcoding, serial, and TCP/IP in this manner. The bad news is that the Palm OS is so feature-rich that there are indeed some other areas we don't cover in this detail. We hope there are no glaring omissions. Our goal was not to cover every topic but only the most difficult or important ones. Our examples are created with this goal in mind. (If we goofed, let us know and we will try to correct it in the future.)

# *User Interface of the Sales Application*

The sample application we are creating is a forms-based application that will be used to record orders. This application is for a person who sells toys to stores.

This sample application will be used as a basis for our code discussions throughout the book. It and the source code are available on the CD-ROM.

These are the activities we want the salesperson to be able to accomplish in the application:

- Modify, delete, or create a new customer
- Create a new order for a customer
- Delete an order
- Delete or modify items in an order
- Beam a company to another device

## *The Sales Application Customer List*

The user starts the application and picks a customer from a list.

### *The customer list*

This is the startup form of the application. It is a list of all the customers that our salesperson normally sells toys to during that selling period. The user can tell which customers already have orders because those without orders are in bold.

We admit that bolding an item to indicate status is a subtle, if not obscure, design element. Its presence is reasonable when you remember the audience of this application. The same user will use it day in and day out for taking orders. The bolding of an item in a constantly used application may be warranted, while it may not be in a more general purpose application. In any case, a user who doesn't know what the bold is for is not hurt—it's just a shortcut for the experienced user.

When a name is selected from the customer list (see Figure 3-5), the individual Customer form is opened.

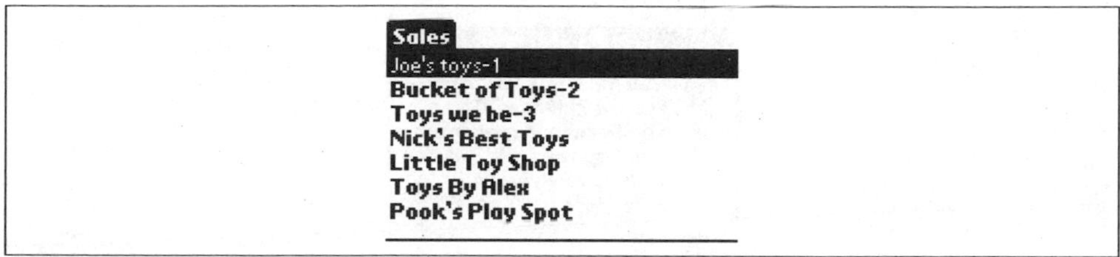


*Figure 3-5. Picking a customer from a list*

Occasionally the salesperson may want to create a new customer while out in the field, so we provide this capability on the handheld. On Palm devices with IR capability, the salesperson might also want to beam customer information. Both these actions are handled in this form as part of the Customer List Record menu (see Figure 3-6).

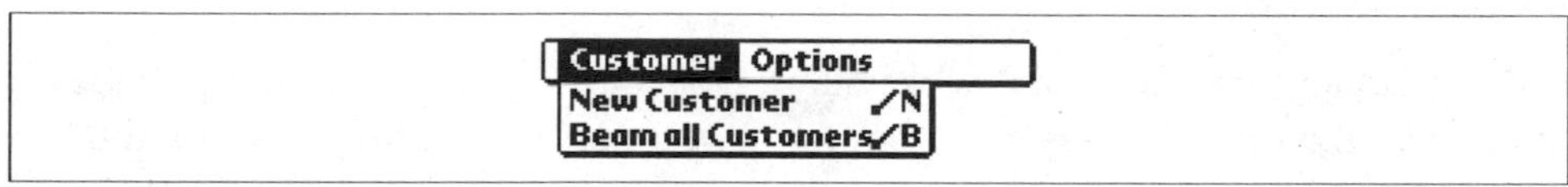


*Figure 3-6. Customer Menu in the Customer List form*

### *New Customer*

When the user selects New Customer or performs the Graffiti shortcut, the New Customer dialog you see in Figure 3-7 is shown.

*Figure 3-7. New Customer dialog*

Note that customer records can be labeled private. When a user selects this option and the preferences are set to view all records, we put up a dialog explaining why that customer is still visible (see Figure 3-8).

The user clearly expects something to happen when selecting the private checkbox. If preferences have been set to hide private records, the record disappears

*Figure 3-8. Explanation on private record checkbox*

from view when the user taps OK. We put up the dialog to prevent confusion on the user's part when all records are viewable. This is a good example of explaining logical, but unexpected, results.

## Beam All Customers

If the handheld has IR (infrared beaming) capabilities, this menu item provides a quick way for the salesperson to transfer all the customer information to another device. When Beam All Customers is selected, the user get the message shown in Figure 3-9. The person receiving the customers also gets status information (see Figure 3-9).

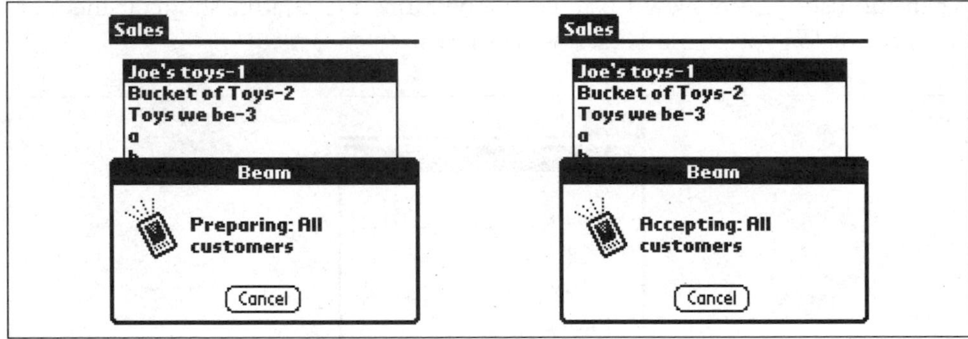


*Figure 3-9. The status when beaming customers*

If the Palm device is not IR capable, the user never sees the item in the Customer List menu. The built-in sample applications always show the Beam menu, but then tell users they can't beam on a non-IR-capable device—we like our way better.

## The Customer Order Form

Once a customer is tapped on, the user is shown the individual Customer form. Most of the activity in the application happens here.

### Creating an order

The most important activity is the creation of an order. This is done by selecting toys and adding them to the customer's order. Figure 3-10 shows an empty Order sheet and one that has several items in it.

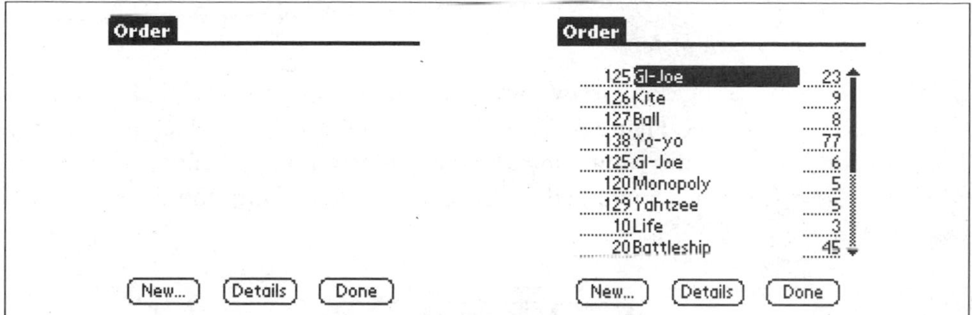


*Figure 3-10. A new order and one containing several items*

Figure 3-11 shows the toys listed by category. First the user selects a category (if the current category is wrong) and then selects one of the toys in it.

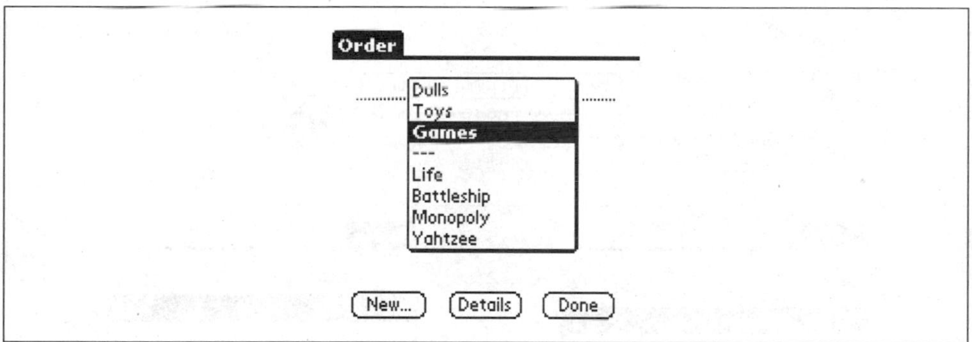


*Figure 3-11. Selecting a category and toy*

Once an order is complete, the salesperson closes it and moves on to another customer. Orders can be revisited, if necessary. As there is only one order per customer, selecting that customer from the list automatically takes the user back to the order.

Ideally, a customer should be able to have more than one order associated with the customer form. In a shipping application, we would certainly add that functionality. For the purposes of this book, however, the extra programming doesn't add much new to our explanation of the Palm OS. We leave it as an additional exercise for eager readers.

### *Modifying an item in an order*

The user can modify an item by tapping on the part of it that needs changing. If the toy is wrong, a new toy can be selected. When the item is changed, the item stock number automatically updates to reflect the new toy. If the number is wrong, that can be changed separately.

### *Deleting an item in an order*

Deleting the item can be done in two ways. The quick way is to select Delete Item in the Record menu (see Figure 3-12). If the user failed to first select an item, we give a dialog box reminder prompting an item's selection (see Figure 3-13). Otherwise, we show the user a confirmation dialog just to make sure the delete request was valid (see Figure 3-13).

Record Edit Options
Delete Item ⁄D
Delete Customer...
Customer Details... ⁄E
New... Details Done

*Figure 3-12. Deleting from the Record Menu*

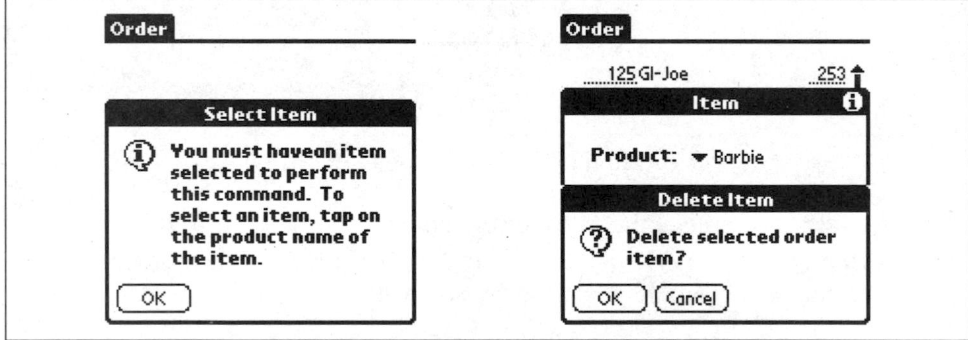


*Figure 3-13. Deleting an item from an order*

It is difficult to say whether it is better to require a user to constantly confirm deletion requests or to allow the accidental deletion of items instead. Two points that drove our decision here were the smallness of the Palm screen and the real likelihood that the user would be moving when selecting items. Remember, there are only a couple of pixels of space between Delete Customer and Delete Item in the Record menu. If you give the user no warning before deleting an item, you can easily turn a mistap into a terrible mistake.

Another way to delete an item is by selecting the Details button, which brings up the Details dialog (see the right side of Figure 3-13). A deletion confirmation dialog is also shown. A third way is to set the quantity to 0, and then tap on a different row.

## Changing Customer Information

To change information about a customer, the user selects Customer Details in the Record menu (see Figure 3-17). Delete Customer is used to get rid of the customer entirely. (We talk more about why this information is handled here in "Design Tradeoffs in the Sample Application," later in this chapter.)

There are two different details forms: one for the customer and one for the item. They have different user interfaces. When you follow the logic of the Palm UI, and look at the number of times a user is likely to do either of these tasks, you will understand our positioning of each of these choices.

### The Customer Details

The Customer Details is the form in which you change information about the customer or, secondarily, delete the customer entirely (see Figure 3-14). This is not something we commonly expect the user to want to do. Indeed, this is information that is primarily entered and maintained on the desktop. We allow editing to give the user flexibility, not because we think this form will be edited very often. The user is more likely to look at this form to get the customer's telephone number than to change it. As access is through the Record menu, this form is difficult to get to, and it may be hard for the user to remember its location. This is okay if it allows better access for a more frequent activity. It does—to the Item Details form.

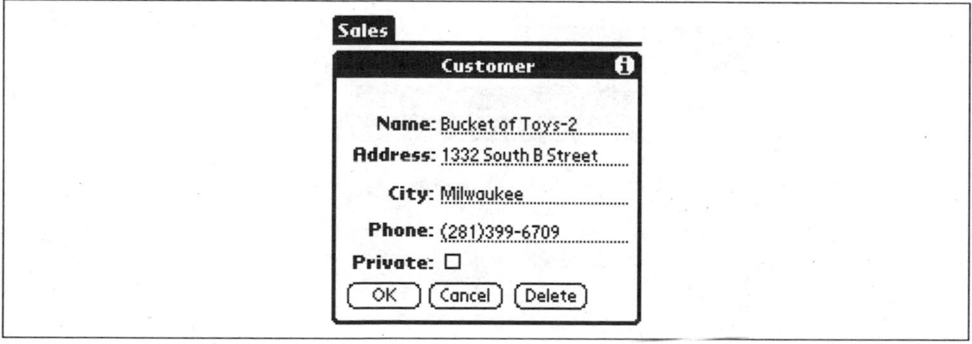


*Figure 3-14. Customer information*

### The Item Details

Every customer has an detail screen associated with the order, as well. In this form, the user can do three things (from most frequent to least):

- Delete the item from the order
- Change the quantity of the item being ordered
- Change the type of item being ordered

The activity most likely to occur is the deletion of an item, because the item amount or type can also be changed in the order itself (see Figure 3-15). But the salesperson can only delete an item from an order in this form. As this is a more common activity than viewing information about the customer, this form is easier to get to for the user.

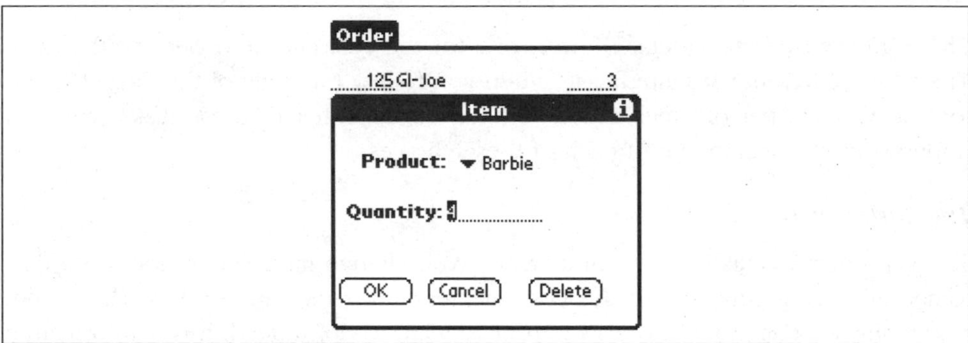


*Figure 3-15. The Item Details screen*

## Deleting the Customer

If the user selects the Delete Customer menu item, a confirmation dialog is shown (see Figure 3-16). A much slower way to delete an item is to select the Customer Details menu item and tap the Delete button in that form.

*Figure 3-16. Deleting a customer*

We provide the user with an option to archive the customer information on the PC, as opposed to deleting it completely from both the handheld and the PC.

### *Beaming the Customer*

The user of an IR-capable device can also beam information about a single user. Selecting the menu item Beam Customer takes care of this. We make sure that non-IR-capable devices don't show the item in the menu (see Figure 3-17 for a comparison).

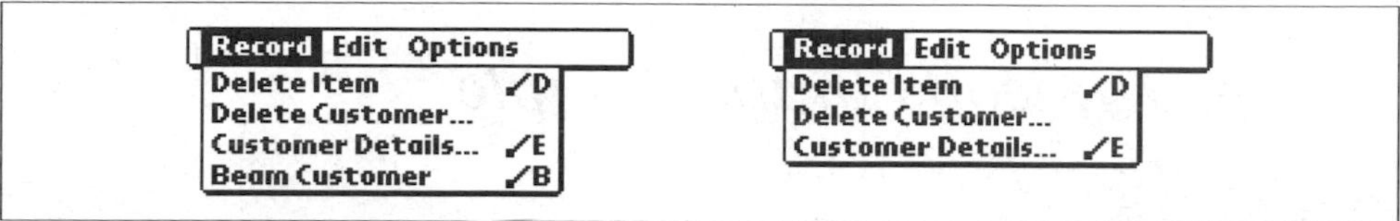


*Figure 3-17. The Record menu with beam present and not present*

### *Edit and Options Menus*

Last, but not least, we offer Edit and Options menus in our application with the standard Graffiti shortcuts (see Figure 3-18).

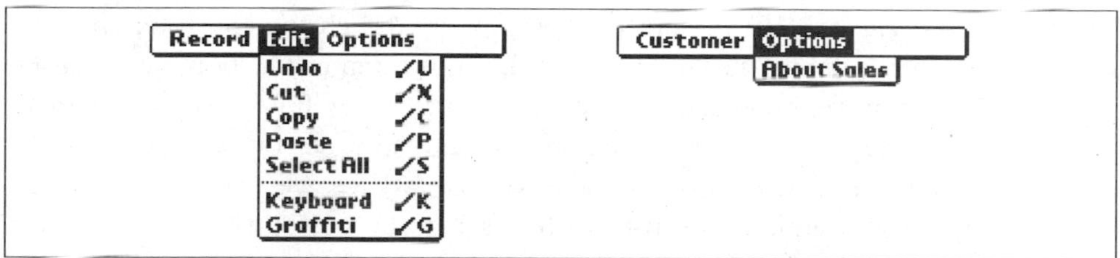


*Figure 3-18. Sales application Edit and Options menus*

## Developing a Prototype

Now that we've shown you the application in its final form, let's back up and show you the process and decisions we made to get there. First, let's look at how we prototyped it.

### *Clarify the Flow of Events*

Our prototype design was a mock-up of the basic views that we wanted to have in the application. We came up with those views by listing the actions we wanted the user to be able to do and the order in which we thought they would occur; we discussed the flow of events. Our strategy was to optimize the application so that the more frequent the action the fewer steps it took to complete. We also wanted to emulate the design of the built-in applications wherever possible.

### The Start Screen

The first and most important view to create well is the start screen—what your user sees when the application is launched. In the Sales application, the place to start seemed straightforward—with a list of the salesperson's customers. This is a list that can be modified on the handheld, but ordinarily would be created on the desktop. The desktop application should be clever about culling customers from the list if the salesperson isn't visiting them on this trip. It might also want to order the customers either alphabetically or by visit (as the salesperson prefers).

## Design Tradeoffs in the Sample Application

As with any design, we made some modifications that changed the look and functionality of this application. We think it will be useful to you to explain how we meandered about with these decisions.

### Adding Items to an Order

There are a couple of things to notice about the design that we ended up with for this action (see Figure 3-19). When the user taps on the customer name, an order form immediately presents itself. As this is the most common action, we focused on minimizing the steps necessary to complete it. In our final design, we managed to reduce the number of steps required to take an order by one. Look at two possible designs in Figure 3-19, and you will see where we saved a step. The example on the left requires the user to first select the customer name and then tap the New Order button below the list (two actions). The example on the right brings the order forward with one less action.

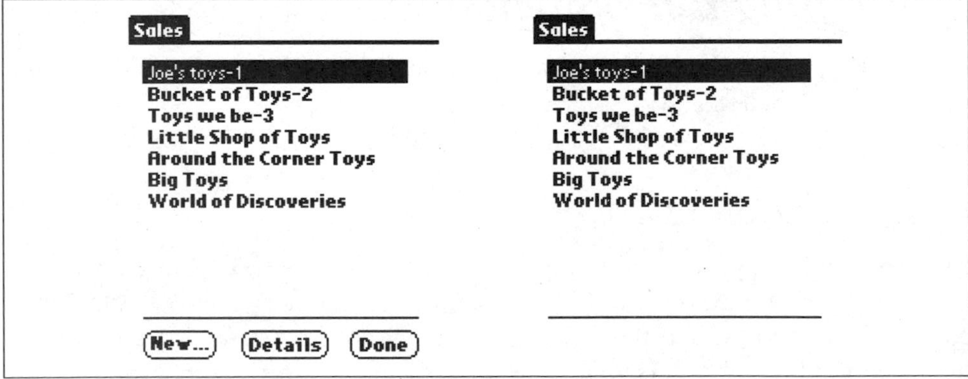


*Figure 3-19. Two ways to design the selection of a new order*

The tradeoff here affects two things. We can make an order easier to create (our solution) or make customers easier to create and edit. For us the choice is obvious; we assume that the salesperson rarely adds new customers or modifies old ones. This is the standard list of customers that our user always deals with when selling toys. In a world where customers came and went more often, we might have chosen differently.

## *Where to Put Customer Information*

The next design issue we tackled was how the user accesses, modifies, and deletes customer information. Menu items or buttons could go either in the startup screen or in the order form. Both choices carry their own set of advantages and disadvantages. Before showing you the logic of our choices, back up and look again at what we want the user of the Palm device to be able to do:

- Create a new customer
- Beam a customer list
- Beam a single customer
- Modify a customer
- Delete a customer

In a desktop application, we are certain that all of these activities would be put in the same menu. On the handheld, we weren't so sure they should be kept together. After some consideration, we chose to put creating a new customer and beaming a customer list in the startup view, because these are the only two general customer items. Every other action has to do with a particular customer, whether that is creating an order, changing the customer's information, or deleting the information from the unit.

### *Creating a new customer*

Clearly, the time when a user is going to create a new customer is in the startup screen while looking at the list of customers. The right user interface for this is a menu item, not a button. This is an infrequent action, so we don't want to waste valuable screen real estate with a button for it. In our solution, getting to the New Customer form takes two actions: pressing the built-in Menu button and selecting New Customer from the Customer menu.

### *Beaming a list of customers*

Our users might share customers with each other; we wanted to give them an easy way of sending customer information to each other (we chose not to support beaming orders, though). The menu item was our way of doing this. It takes two steps to accomplish this task. The user first pushes the built-in Menu button and then selects the item from the Customer menu.

### *Deleting a customer*

You could place this item in the startup Customer List form or in the Customer form. If you put it in the menu of the startup Customer List form, as we did in an earlier version of this application, you need a way for the user to select which customer to delete. The user selects Delete Customer from the Customer menu and a picklist is brought forth from which customers can be deleted one at a time or in group (see Figure 3-20).

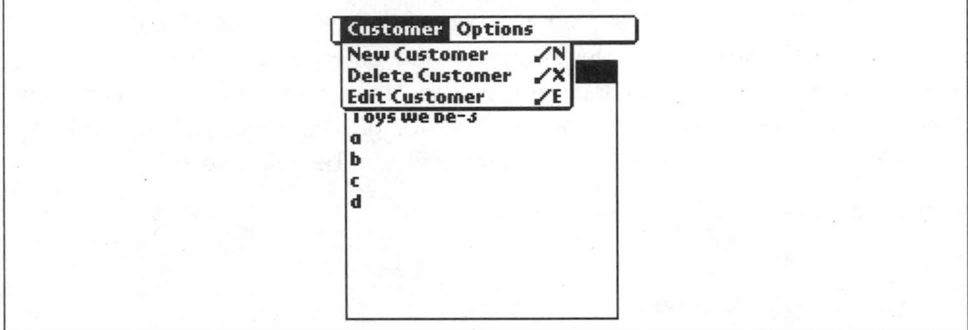


*Figure 3-20. One way to delete customers*

However, there's a faster way that requires fewer taps (and no new picklists). Within the Palm user interface model, you delete an item while you are viewing it. Look at the built-in Names and Memos applications (see Figure 3-21). Notice that you start with a list of items and select one. Only at this point can you use a Record menu item to delete the name or memo you are viewing.

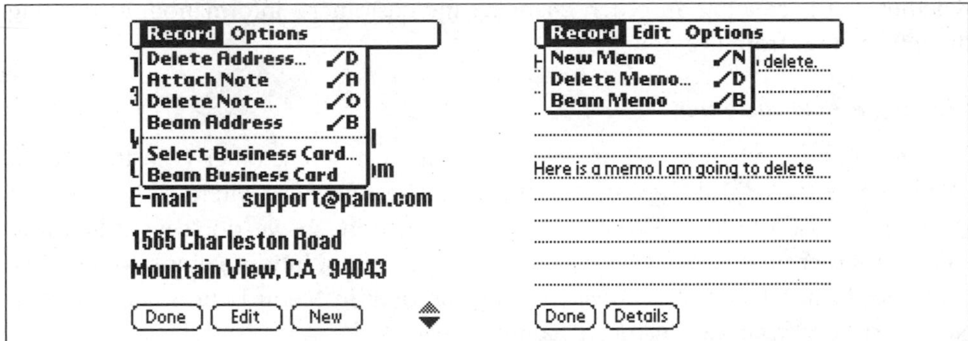


*Figure 3-21. How the built-in Names and Memos applications handle actions*

Likewise, in our application the customer is selected from a list and then, while viewing the customer form, the user can delete that client.

A desktop application would not be designed this way. Single-clicking on a customer from the list would select it. At that point, the Delete menu item would delete it, while the Open menu item (or, as a shortcut, a double-click) would open the Order form for the customer. However, the Palm OS is not a desktop OS. Double-taps aren't part of the idiom. Users of a Palm OS device expect a single tap to make an action occur.

You might ask why this model has been adopted. The design makes sense when you realize that the initial items in the startup list are "hot." If you touch them, something happens immediately to switch you to another form. The Palm OS does not have a tap, double-tap model. The Palm model is attractive because it cuts down on the number of steps required to complete the most common actions. Each of these very common actions takes a smaller number of steps because picklist items are hot:

- Viewing a name in the Names application requires pushing the built-in Names button and tapping the name in the list.
- Opening a memo requires pushing the built-in Memo button and tapping the appropriate memo.
- Creating a new order for a customer requires opening the application and tapping a customer.

## Designing for a Small Screen

One of the biggest challenges you face as a handheld application designer is how to fit data in the screen space on a Palm device. In the Sales application, this challenge happens when we are trying to figure out the right way to select a toy. We assume that there are more toys than would fit on one list on the screen. One approach might have been to have one long scrolling list—the least favorable solution. Toys, like many other types of items, naturally fall into obvious groups. We chose to take advantage of this by first putting the toys into categories.

Table 3-2 contains three ways that we could have organized the items. Our solution was to go with a category organization. This makes things like special sales promotional items easy to handle. A fast-food restaurant might use a similar approach for taking orders. In both cases, the customer is going to go through categories in certain obvious groupings.

Organizing things alphabetically is another possibility, but one that doesn't make as much sense for our application. Neither the customer nor the salesperson is likely to think about the toys in this way.

Organizing the items by number might have been a good choice from the salesperson's point of view. It is not uncommon to memorize part numbers of items you work with all the time; however, where this organization strategy breaks down is from the customer's point of view. The customer is not necessarily going to request items by number. We imagine the customer thinks in terms of the store's shelves which are themselves organized by category. Our strategy is to match the customer's organizational model. Doing so minimizes the number of steps required to add an item to the order (less category switching).

*Table 3-2. Ways of Categorizing Toys*

| By Category | Alphabetically | By Item Number |
|---|---|---|
| **Games** | **A-C** | **001-99** |
| • Acquire<br>• Mousetrap<br>• Monsterwalk<br>• Siege Towers | Absolute Terror Tim<br>Acquire<br>Aardvark Arnie<br>Chubby Bunny | 1–Aardvark Arnie<br>2–Jane Sit and Spit<br>3–Pretty Patty<br>4–Zebra with baby |
| **Dolls** | **D-H** | **100-199** |
| • Aardvark Arnie<br>• Jane, Sit and Spit<br>• Zebra with baby | Glow in the Dark Pumpkin<br>Halloween-Princess<br>Happy Bunny PlayAlong | 101–Marbles by the 100s<br>102–Ball and Jacks<br>104–Glowing Glop |
| **Action Figures** | **I-P** | **200-299** |
| • Absolute Terror Tim<br>• Chubby Bunny<br>• Daredevil Dan<br>• Sissy Sunny | Jane, Sit and Spit<br>Monsterwalk<br>Mousetrap<br>Pretty Patty | 200–Siege Towers<br>201–Acquire<br>202–Moustrap<br>203–Monsterwalk |
| **Promotional** | **Q-Z** | **900-999** |
| • Glow in the Dark Pumpkin<br>• Halloween-Princess<br>• Halloween-Pirate | Siege Towers<br>Sissy Sunny<br>Zooming Eyes | 900–Glow in the Dark Pumpkin<br>901–Halloween-Princess<br>903–Happy Bunny PlayAlong |

## *Designing the Databases*

Once you have figured out how to organize the data, your next big decision is to determine the number of databases you should use. We settled on four databases in the Sales application; they are customers, products, orders, and categories.

*Customers*

The customer database contains the information about the customers. Each customer record contains five items:

*Customer ID*

A unique customer code assigned at corporate headquarters. If a new customer is created on the handheld, it is assigned a temporary negative customer ID. Corporate headquarters is responsible for assigning a permanent ID after a HotSync.

*Name*

A string.

*Address*

A string.

*City*

A string.

*Phone*

A string.

The order in the database is the order in which they are displayed in the list. New customers are added at the beginning. There are at least two possible ways to reasonably organize the customer database—alphabetically or by visit order (the first name is the first customer the salesperson visits, the second name is the second visit, and so on).

*Products*

The product database contains information about each of the toys that can be ordered by the customer. Each product record contains:

*Product ID*

An integer. This is assigned by corporate headquarters.

*Price*

A number. This is a cent amount that we can store as an integer rather than as a floating point number.

*Name*

A string.

*Category number*

A number. The value is from 0 to 15 and is stored as an index into the category database.

Instead of storing the category number as a separate piece of data directly in the record, we use the category feature of the database manager to store it (see Chapter 6, *Databases*). Doing so saves a small amount of space and gives us a pedagogical excuse to discuss this feature of databases.

*Orders*

The order database contains records for each of the salesperson's orders. The order database does not contain records for customers with no orders. Each order record contains:

*Customer ID*

In order to match a customer to an order, each order contains the customer ID.

*Number items ordered*

An integer. This is the quantity of each item that was ordered.

*Items*

An array of items where each item contains a product ID and a quantity.

We considered having the customer's order be part of the customer database, but decided to separate them as a precursor to providing multiple orders for each customer in the future.

*Categories*

There's a Category UI that we don't implement in the Sales application. It is inappropriate to our application because it is a mechanism for allowing the storing of editable category names. The Category UI has folders at the top-right and items are stored within these categories. The Category UI also provides a mechanism for editing the category names. This is the feature we wish to restrict in our application—products come from the desktop and are unchangeable.

We didn't want to hardcode the category names into the application, either, as product lists have been known to change on occasion. We chose instead to store the information in the application info block of the products database (see "Creating the Application Info Block in a Database" on page 145). This way we can modify it during a HotSync.

The categories are stored sequentially as null-terminated strings. The order of the categories matches the category numbers used in the products database—record 0 of this database contains the name of category 0. For example, if we want to know the name of category 4, we go to the fourth null-terminated string in the app info block.

# Designing the Conduit

A conduit is a desktop application made in a desktop development environment. It uses HotSync synchronization to connect the desktop to the handheld; conduits are responsible for the transfer of data to and from the handheld and the desktop. The user views the data using some application (a spreadsheet, for example, for viewing expense report items). The conduit needs to make sure that this desktop application has the data it needs to handle processor-intensive tasks. Before looking at the design of the Sales application conduit, let's examine this issue of off-loading processor-intensive tasks.

## Processor-Intensive Tasks

Using the conduit to transfer the data, move processor-intensive tasks onto the PC and off of the handheld. If you can't move tasks, you should almost always get rid of them.

Palm devices are noted for being both fast and cheap—two of the key features that have made them so popular. One of the reasons they are cheap is they have little bitty processors that don't have much horsepower. Your job as a good application designer is to avoid taxing the handheld's processing abilities. Don't turn it into a slow device—there are already plenty of those around. This means that you may end up making design decisions about your database that don't make sense from a desktop database designer's point of view, but do make sense when you take into account the desktop's superior processing abilities. Here is an example.

Recently, we were involved in porting an application from another handheld platform (with a fast processor) to the Palm platform. This is an application that keeps track of a bunch of vending machines: when they need filling, what products go in what slots, how much money is collected, and so on. The account screen provides a summary of the machines that belong in that account (an account could have many machines or just a few). The machine screen provides a summary of items for that particular machine. In the original platform, as we entered an account screen at runtime, we'd run through the database, summarizing and totalling (for instance, we'd total how many machines needed to be serviced for an account, along with how many total machines an account had).

When we began our port of the application to the Palm platform, this way of handling the task no longer made sense. The hit the user would endure when opening a machine or account screen was too long. So we bit the bullet and moved the summarizing and totalling to the desktop application. This information is now stored in the account database. The price we had to pay is duplicate data in every account (upping by a small amount the size of our databases). It was worth it, however, to have a zippy account screen that instantly displays information about machines.

The built-in Expense application provides another useful example. Let's approach the issue from the point of view of a question.

*Q: What feature is missing from the Expense application?*

*A:* There is no expense total.

Why? you might ask. We think it is to avoid an unnecessary processing task that doesn't really provide the user with necessary information. Totals are things a user will care about back at the office when sitting calmly at a desktop computer, not when she or he is rushing from a cab through an airport to catch a flight.

The moral of the story is not to make users pay for processor-intensive tasks if there is any way to avoid it. Sometimes that means keeping functionality but moving the processing elsewhere (as in our ported vending machine application); sometimes that means not offering a feature in the first place (as in the Expense application with no total).

Tasks that may be fast on the handheld but can't be implemented well for other reasons should also be moved to the desktop. For example, think of subtotalling a list of figures in an expense report. This task is easy to do on a big screen using a mouse and a combination of keys to select and total the figures. It is much harder to do on a tiny screen (you can't see many of the items at one time), where data is close together (it's easy to hit the wrong figure), and selecting is complex (items are hot and tapping does something). Desktop applications and handheld ones should complement each other and extend functionality in ways that neither could handle alone—they should not duplicate features.

## *Design of the Sales Application Conduit*

Our Sales application conduit handles the following tasks during a HotSync synchronization:

- Opening and closing the sales, customer, and product databases on the Palm device.
- Iterating through the records in the databases on the handheld.
- Uploading customer orders from the handheld to the desktop.
- Downloading the product database from the desktop to the handheld.
- Comparing customer records so that only modified records are synced.
- Appropriately adding, deleting, and modifying customer records on the handheld and on the desktop.
- Reordering records in a database after new records have been added.
- Public portions of data, such as product information, are kept in the application desktop folder; private portions of data, such as customer lists, are kept in user folders.
- Converting the data in the application's database records to a text-delimited file that can be read into a database on the desktop computer.

The conduit also needs to be installed and uninstalled. With a commercial application, this process should be handled automatically, invisible from the user.

Use an installer program to automate the installation and uninstallation of the conduit; it is fairly straightforward (we tell you about this in "Automatically Installing and Uninstalling a Conduit" on page 311). For information on manual installation, see "Registering and Unregistering Manually Using CondCfg" on page 311.

# *Design Summary*

By now, you should have a good feel for how to design a Palm application and conduit. You also know about the range and types of tools available to help you with this project. You should also have a good feeling for what types of applications will work well on a Palm device and the types of user interface elements you can easily add to them. Now it is time to turn away from design issues and to the code you need to write to create your application.

# II

# *Designing Palm Applications*

Now it is time to see what is inside a Palm application. We cover everything you need to know, from the application's structure and user interface elements to the API for the various parts of the application. Chapter 4, *Structure of an Application*, takes you through the whole cycle of a Palm application, from the time it is launched by the user to the moment that it receives the command to quit. Chapter 5, *Forms and Form Objects*, shows you how to create the various user interface elements of the application, everything from buttons to lists to dialogs. Chapter 6, *Databases*, shows you how to work with and store data in a Palm application. Chapter 7, *Menus*, is an examination of menus and the items they contain. Chapter 8, *Extras*, covers a little bit of this and a little bit of that—topics that are important, but too small to require their own chapter. Chapter 9, *Communications*, gives you a detailed look at serial and TCP/IP. Last, but most importantly, in Chapter 10, *Debugging Palm Applications*, we turn to that crucial topic that is every programmer's necessary evil in life—debugging.

In this chapter:
- Terminology
- A Simple Application
- Scenarios
- Memory Is Extremely Limited
- Other Times Your Application Is Called
- Summary

# 4

# Structure of an Application

The overall flow and content of a Palm OS application is the subject of this chapter. You will learn:

- The standard code routines found in every Palm application
- All about the application's lifecycle—its starting, running, and closing
- How the application processes each event and hands it off to the appropriate manager
- How memory is organized on a Palm device; how the application can use it
- All the times that an application needs to be available to the system and how these instances are handled in the code

## Terminology

Like every operating system and coding interaction, the Palm OS has it own set of necessary terminology for you to learn. Much of it may already be familiar to you from other applications you have written. We suggest that you skim through this list and concentrate on the items that are new to you. New and unique terminology is listed first.

*Form*

An application window (what many people would think of as a view) that usually covers the entire screen. A form optionally contains controls, text areas, and menus. *In a Palm OS application, there is only one active form allowed at a time*. Chapter 5, *Forms and Form Objects*, covers forms in detail.

*Window*

A rectangular area in which things like dialogs, forms, and menus are drawn by the application. The Window Manager makes sure that windows properly display relative to each other (for example, it has the ability to restore the old contents when a window is closed). Note in a rather Shakespearian twist of logic that all forms are windows, even though all windows are not forms.

*Database*

A collection of persistent memory chunks. There are two kinds: resource and record databases.

*Resource*

A piece of data stored in a resource database. Each resource is identified by a resource type and number. A Palm application is a collection of resources. Chapter 5 covers resources in more detail.

*Record*

A data structure identified by a unique record ID. Applications typically store data in record databases.

*Event*

A data structure that describes things that happen in an application. Events can be low-level hardware events like a pen down, pen up, or hardware key press. They can also be higher-level events like a character entered, a menu item selected, or a software button pressed.

*The Palm OS is an event-driven system*. Only one application is open at a time. When that application is running, it runs an event loop that retrieves events and continues to handle them until the user starts another application.

*Main event loop*

The main loop of execution in an application, which repeatedly retrieves events and then acts on them.

*Launch code*

A parameter passed to an application that specifies what the application should do when that particular launch code is executed. An application typically handles more than one launch code. This is the communication method used between the OS and an application and between applications.

*Menu*

Menus are stored in resources grouped together into menubars and are displayed when the user taps the menu area. See Chapter 7, *Menus*, for more details.

*Menubar*

A collection of menus stored in a resource. Each form can have a menubar associated with it.

*Dialog*

A window containing controls that require the user to make a decision. In other words, the dialog must be dismissed (usually by tapping on one of its buttons) before the application can continue.

*Alert*

A warning or information dialog that needs to be dismissed by the user.

These brief descriptions cover the most important terminology. In the following section, we look at the basic elements of a very small Palm OS application.

# A Simple Application

Creating a small application before tackling a more complex one is a good way to gain familiarity with a new coding challenge. First, we tell you what our little application does and show you the code for it. After that we do a code walk-through and point out important elements.

## What the Application Does

Our Hello World application displays the words "Hello World" and provides a button to press. Pressing the button displays an alert, as shown in Figure 4-1, which is dismissed by tapping OK. There are two menus, each with one menu item (see Figure 4-2). As this is a very simple application, you just get a beep when you choose either menu item.

*Figure 4-1. Dialog shown after tapping the button*

*Figure 4-2. The menus of Hello World*

## The Hello World Source Code

Now that you have an idea of what the application can do, look at Example 4-1 to see the code that produces it. Once you have looked through it for yourself, we will discuss it.

*Example 4-1. The Hello World Source Code*

```
#include <Pilot.h>
#ifdef __GNUC__
#include "Callback.h"
#endif
#include "HelloWorldRsc.h"

static Err StartApplication(void)
{
  FrmGotoForm(HelloWorldForm);
  return 0;
}

static void StopApplication(void)
{
}

static Boolean MyFormHandleEvent(EventPtr event)
{
  Boolean     handled = false;

#ifdef __GNUC__
   CALLBACK_PROLOGUE
#endif
   switch (event->eType) {
   case ctlSelectEvent:  // A control button was pressed and released.
      FrmAlert(GoodnightMoonAlert);
      handled = true;
      break;

   case frmOpenEvent:
      FrmDrawForm(FrmGetActiveForm());
      handled = true;
      break;

   case menuEvent:
      if (event->data.menu.itemID == FirstBeep)
         SndPlaySystemSound(sndInfo);
      else
         SndPlaySystemSound(sndStartUp);
      handled = true;
      break;
   }
#ifdef __GNUC__
   CALLBACK_EPILOGUE
#endif
   return handled;
}
```

*Example 4-1. The Hello World Source Code (continued)*

```
static Boolean ApplicationHandleEvent(EventPtr event)
{
   FormPtr  frm;
   Int    formId;
   Boolean  handled = false;

   if (event->eType == frmLoadEvent) {
      //Load the form resource specified in the event then activate it
      formId = event->data.frmLoad.formID;
      frm = FrmInitForm(formId);
      FrmSetActiveForm(frm);

      // Set the event handler for the form.  The handler of the currently
      // active form is called by FrmDispatchEvent each time it is called
      switch (formId) {
      case HelloWorldForm:
         FrmSetEventHandler(frm, MyFormHandleEvent);
         break;
      }
      handled = true;
   }

   return handled;
}

static void EventLoop(void)
{
   EventType   event;
   Word        error;

   do {
    EvtGetEvent(&event, evtWaitForever);
    if (! SysHandleEvent(&event))
       if (! MenuHandleEvent(0, &event, &error))
          if (! ApplicationHandleEvent(&event))
             FrmDispatchEvent(&event);
   } while (event.eType != appStopEvent);
}

DWord PilotMain(Word launchCode, Ptr cmdPBP, Word launchFlags)
{
  Err err;

  if (launchCode == sysAppLaunchCmdNormalLaunch) {
     if ((err = StartApplication()) == 0) {
        EventLoop();
        StopApplication();
     }
   }

   return err;
}
```

## A Code Walkthrough of Hello World

Let's start at the beginning with the `#include` files.

### The #include files

*Pilot.h* is an include file that itself includes most of the standard Palm OS include files (using CodeWarrior, *Pilot.h* actually includes a prebuilt header file to speed compilation). To keep things simple, our application doesn't use anything beyond the standard Palm OS include files. Indeed, any calls outside the standard ones would have necessitated the use of other specific Palm OS include files.

The second include file, *Callback.h*, defines some macros needed if you are using GCC. They are needed to handle callbacks from the Palm OS to your code. We discuss this in "Callbacks in GCC" on page 78.

The third include file, *HelloWorldRsc.h*, defines constants for all the application's resources (for example, `HelloWorldForm`). As we'll see in Chapter 5, if you use Constructor, this file is generated automatically (see Example 4-2). If you use the GNU PalmPilot SDK, you usually create this file yourself (see Example 4-3).

*Example 4-2. HelloWorldRsc.h Generated by Constructor (Used with CodeWarrior)*

```
// Header generated by Constructor for Pilot 1.0.2
//
// Generated at 9:55:01 PM on Thursday, August 20, 1998
//
// Generated for file: Macintosh HD:Palm:HelloWorld:Rsc:Hello.rsrc
//
// THIS IS AN AUTOMATICALLY GENERATED HEADER FILE FROM CONSTRUCTOR FOR PALMPILOT;
// - DO NOT EDIT - CHANGES MADE TO THIS FILE WILL BE LOST
//
// Pilot App Name:       "Hello World"
//
// Pilot App Version:       "1.0"

// Resource: tFRM 1000
#define HelloWorldForm                                    1000
#define HelloWorldButtonButton                            1003

// Resource: Talt 1101
#define GoodnightMoonAlert                                1101
#define GoodnightMoonOK                                   0

// Resource: MBAR 1000
#define HelloWorldMenuBar                                 1000

// Resource: MENU 1010
#define FirstMenu                                         1010
#define FirstBeep                                         1010

// Resource: MENU 1000
#define SecondMenu                                        1000
#define SecondBeepmore                                    1000
```

*Example 4-3. HelloWorldRsrc.h Created by Hand (Used with GNU PalmPilot SDK)*

```
#define HelloWorldForm                                  1000
#define HelloWorldButtonButton                          1003
#define HelloWorldMenuBar                               1000

#define GoodnightMoonAlert                              1101

#define FirstBeep                                       1010

#define SecondBeepmore                                  1000
```

### *The main routine: PilotMain*

Example 4-4 shows the main entry point into your application. The first parameter is the launch code. If your application is being opened normally, this parameter is the constant `sysAppLaunchCmdNormalLaunch`. The second and third parameters are used when the application is opened at other times.

*Example 4-4. PilotMain*

```
DWord PilotMain(Word launchCode, Ptr cmdPBP, Word launchFlags)
{
   Err err;

   if (launchCode == sysAppLaunchCmdNormalLaunch) {
      if ((err = StartApplication()) == 0) {
         EventLoop();
         StopApplication();
      }
   }

   return err;
}
```

If the launch code is `sysAppLaunchCmdNormalLaunch`, we do an initialization in *StartApplication* and run our event loop until the user does something to close the application. At that point, we handle termination in *StopApplication*.

### *The startup routine: StartApplication*

In the routine shown in Example 4-5, we handle all the standard opening and initialization of our application. In more complicated applications, this would include opening our databases and reading user preference information. In our rudimentary Hello World application, all we need to do is tell the Form Manager that we want to send our (one and only) form. This queues up a `frmLoadEvent` in the event queue.

*Example 4-5. StartApplication*

```
static Err StartApplication(void)
{
   FrmGotoForm(HelloWorldForm);
   return 0;
}
```

### The closing routine: StopApplication

Because we are creating such a simple application, we don't actually have anything to do when it's closing time. We provided the routine in Example 4-6 so that our Hello World source code would have the same standard structure as other Palm applications.

*Example 4-6. An Empty StopApplication*

```
static void StopApplication(void)
{
}
```

Normally in *StopApplication* we handle all the standard closing operations, such as closing our database, saving the current state in preferences, and so on.

### The main event loop

In *PilotMain*, you will notice that after the initialization there is a call to the one main event loop (see Example 4-7). In this loop, we continually process events—handing them off wherever possible to the system. We go through the loop, getting an event with *EvtGetEvent*, and then dispatch that event to one of four nested event handlers, each of which gets a chance to handle the event. If an event handler returns true, it has handled the event and we don't process it any further. *EvtGetEvent* then gets the next event in the queue, and our loop repeats the process.

The loop doggedly continues in this fashion until we get the `appStopEvent`, at which time we exit the function and clean things up in *StopApplication*.

*Example 4-7. EventLoop*

```
static void EventLoop(void)
{
   EventType  event;
   Word       error;

   do {
    EvtGetEvent(&event, evtWaitForever);                system routine
    if (! SysHandleEvent(&event))                       system routine
       if (! MenuHandleEvent(0, &event, &error))        system routine
          if (! ApplicationHandleEvent(&event))         routine we write
             FrmDispatchEvent(&event);                  system routine
   } while (event.eType != appStopEvent);
}
```

### Handling events with EvtGetEvent

This Event Manager routine's sole purpose in life is to get the next event from the queue. It takes as a second parameter a time-out value (in ticks—hundredths of a second). *EvtGetEvent* returns either when an event has occurred (in which case it returns true) or when the time-out value has elapsed (in which case it returns false and fills in an event code of `nilEvent`).

We don't have anything to do until an event occurs (this application has no background processing to do), so we pass the `evtWaitForever` constant, specifying that we don't want a time-out.

#### *The event queue and application event loop*

Let's step back for a moment and look at the events that are received from *EvtGetEvent*. Events can be of all different types, anything from low-level to high-level ones. In fact, one useful way to look at a Palm application is simply as an event handler—it takes all sorts of events, handing them off to various managers, which in turn may post a new event back to the queue, where it is handled by another event handler. We will discuss more sophisticated examples of this later (see "Scenarios" later in this chapter), but for now look at a very simple set of events to get an idea of how this all works together. Imagine the user has our application open and taps the stylus on the screen in the area of the silk-screened Menu button. The first time through the event queue the *SysHandleEvent* routine handles the event, interprets it, and creates a new event that gets put back in the queue (see Figure 4-3).

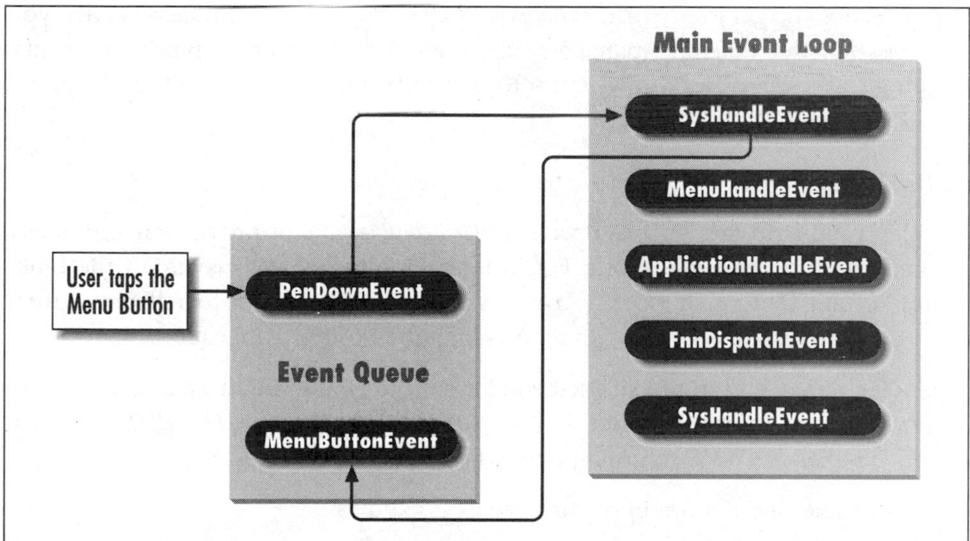


*Figure 4-3. An event in the event loop*

This new event, when it comes through the loop, gets passed through *SysHandleEvent* and on to the *MenuHandleEvent*, as it is now recognizable as a menu request (see Figure 4-4). *MenuHandleEvent* displays the menubar and drops down one of the menus. If the user now taps outside the menu, the menus disappear.

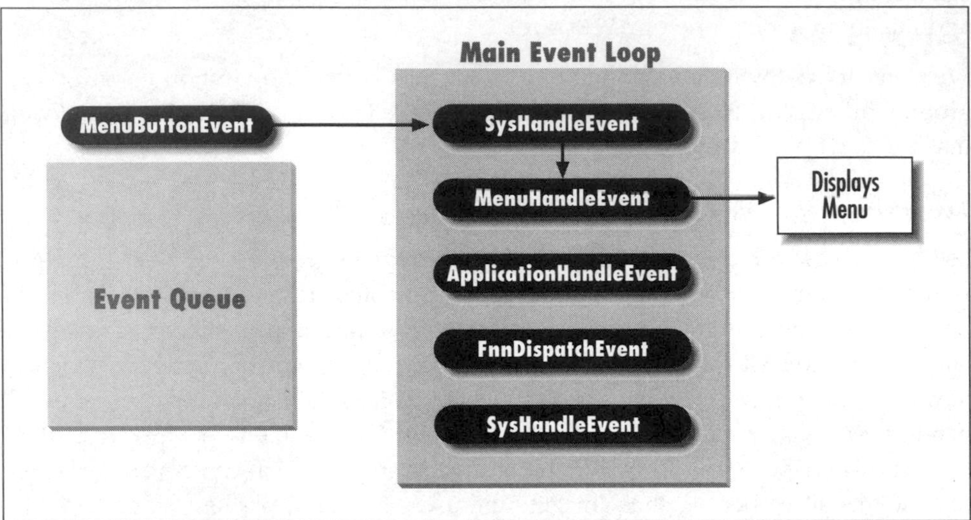


*Figure 4-4. A regurgitated event in the event loop*

If a menu item is selected, however, a new event is generated and sent to the queue. This event is retrieved by the event loop, where it is passed through *SysHandleEvent* and on to *MenuHandleEvent*. Given the way this process works, you can see that the different managers are interested in different types of events. Keeping this in mind, let's now return to our code and look at the event loop and the four routines in it.

### *SysHandleEvent*

The first routine in the loop is always *SysHandleEvent*, as it provides functionality common to all Palm applications. For instance, it handles key events for the built-in application buttons. It does so by posting an *appStopEvent* to tell the current application to quit; the system can then launch the desired application.

It handles pen events in the silk-screened area (the Graffiti input area and the silk-screened buttons). For example, if the user taps on Find, *SysHandleEvent* completely handles the Find, returning only when the Find is done.

Here are some of the more important events it handles:

`keyEvent`
: Occurs, among other times, when one of the built-in buttons is pressed. The keycode specifies which particular button is pressed. *SysHandleEvent* handles pen events in the Graffiti input area. When a character is written, *SysHandleEvent* posts a `keyEvent` with the recognized character.

`penDownEvent`
: Occurs when the user presses the stylus to the screen.

`penMoveEvent`
: Occurs when the user moves the stylus on the screen.

`penMoveEvents` aren't actually stored in the event queue, because there are so many of them. Instead, when *EvtGetEvent* is called, if no other events are pending, *EvtGetEvent* will return a `penMoveEvent` if the pen is down and has moved since the last call.

### *MenuHandleEvent*

The second routine in our event loop is *MenuHandleEvent*. As you might have imagined, the *MenuHandleEvent* handles events involving menus. These events occur when a user:

- Taps on the Menu silk-screened button. The function finds the menubar for the current form and displays it by creating a window.
- Taps somewhere else while a menu is being displayed. The function closes the menu when the user taps outside it.

*MenuHandleEvent* also switches menus if the user taps on the menubar. As would be expected, it closes the menu and menubar if the user taps on a menu item. At this point, it posts a menu event that will be retrieved in a later call to *EvtGetEvent*.

### *ApplicationHandleEvent*

The third routine, *ApplicationHandleEvent*, is also a standard part of the event loop and is responsible for loading forms and associating an event handler with the form. Note that this is also the first time our application is doing something with an event. Here is the code in our Hello World application for that routine:

```
static Boolean ApplicationHandleEvent(EventPtr event)
{
   FormPtr  frm;
   Int    formId;
   Boolean  handled = false;

   if (event->eType == frmLoadEvent) {
   // Load the form resource specified in the event and activate the form.
      formId = event->data.frmLoad.formID;
      frm = FrmInitForm(formId);
      FrmSetActiveForm(frm);

  // Set the event handler for the form.  The handler of the currently
  // active form is called by FrmDispatchEvent each time it gets an event.
```

```
        switch (formId) {
        case HelloWorldForm:
           FrmSetEventHandler(frm, MyFormHandleEvent);
           break;
        }
        handled = true;
     }
     return handled;
  }
```

While we'll see a more complex example of *ApplicationHandleEvent* in Chapter 5, you can at least see that our routine handles the request to load our sole form.

### *Callbacks in GCC*

We need to swerve down a tangent for a moment to discuss GCC. There is one way that your code will differ depending on whether you use GCC or CodeWarrior. Even if you're not using GCC, it's still worth reading this section to learn why we sprinkled a bunch of "`#ifdef __GNUC__` " in our functions.

The GCC compiler's calling conventions differ from those in the Palm OS. In particular, the GCC compiler expects at startup that it can set up the A4 register (which it uses to access global variables) and that it will remain set throughout the life of the application. Unfortunately, this is not true when a GCC application calls a Palm OS routine that either directly or indirectly calls back to a GCC function (a callback).

The most common example of this occurrence is when we've installed an event handler for a form with *FrmSetEventHandler*. Once we've done that, a call to *FrmDispatchEvent* (a Palm OS routine) can call our form's event handler (a GCC function, if we've compiled our application with GCC). At this point, if our event handler tries to access global variables, it'll cause a spectacular application crash.

The solution is to use a set of macros that set the A4 register on entry to the callback function and restore it on exit. You need to provide a *Callback.h* header file as part of your project (see Example 4-8) and `#include` it in your file. Then, every callback needs to add the `CALLBACK_PROLOGUE` macro at the beginning of the callback function (just after variables are declared) and a `CALLBACK_EPILOGUE` macro at the end of the callback function. Here's a very simple example:

```
static int MyCallback()
{
   int myReturnResult;
   int anotherVariable;
#ifdef __GNUC__
   CALLBACK_PROLOGUE
#endif
   // do stuff in my function
#ifdef __GNUC__
   CALLBACK_EPILOGUE
   return myReturnResult;
}
```

It's crucial that you don't try to access global variables before the CALLBACK_PROLOGUE macro. For example, here's code that will blow up because you're accessing globals before the macro has had a chance to set the A4 register:

```
static int MyCallback()
{
   int myVariable = gSomeGlobalVar;
#ifdef __GNUC__
   CALLBACK_PROLOGUE
#endif
   ...
}
```

It's also important that you return from your function at the bottom. If you must ignore our advice and return from your function in the middle, make sure to add yet another instance of the CALLBACK_EPILOGUE right before the return.

*Example 4-8. The Callback.h File, Needed for GCC*

```
#ifndef __CALLBACK_H__
#define __CALLBACK_H__

/* This is a workaround for a bug in the current version of gcc: gcc assumes
   that no one will touch %a4 after it is set up in crt0.o. This isn't true
   if a function is called as a callback by something that wasn't compiled by
   gcc (like FrmCloseAllForms()). It may also not be true if it is used as a
   callback by something in a different shared library. We really want a function
   attribute "callback" that inserts this prologue and epilogue automatically.
- Ian */

register void *reg_a4 asm("%a4");

#define CALLBACK_PROLOGUE \
   void *save_a4 = reg_a4; asm("move.l %%a5,%%a4; sub.l #edata,%%a4" : :);
#define CALLBACK_EPILOGUE reg_a4 = save_a4;

#endif
```

There's been some discussion among those who use the GCC compiler about a more convenient solution to the Example 4-8 workaround. Some folks want to get rid of the macros by modifying the GCC compiler with a callback attribute to the function declaration. This would cause the compiler to add code that manages A4 correctly. Here's an example:

```
callback int MyCallback()
{
   // code which can safely access globals
}
```

Others want a more radical solution. They want to be able to use all functions as callbacks without any special declaration.

### *FrmDispatchEvent*

This fourth and last routine in the event loop is the one that indirectly provides form-specific handling. This routine handles standard form functionality (for example, a pen-down event on a button highlights the button, a pen-up on a button posts a `ctlSelectEvent` to the event queue). Cut/copy/paste in text fields are other examples of functionality handled by *FrmDispatchEvent*. In order to provide form-specific handling, *FrmDispatchEvent* also calls the form's installed event handler. Therefore, when *FrmDispatchEvent* gets an event, it calls our own *MyFormHandleEvent* routine:

```
static Boolean MyFormHandleEvent(EventPtr event)
{
   Boolean     handled = false;

   switch (event->eType) {
    case ctlSelectEvent:  // A control button was pressed and released.
       FrmAlert(GoodnightMoonAlert);
       handled = true;
       break;

    case frmOpenEvent:
       FrmDrawForm(FrmGetActiveForm());
       handled = true;
       break;

    case menuEvent:
       if (event->data.menu.itemID == FirstBeep)
          SndPlaySystemSound(sndInfo);
       else
          SndPlaySystemSound(sndStartUp);
      handled = true;
      break;
   }
   return handled;
}
```

As the code indicates, we take an action if the user taps on our button or chooses either of the two menu items. We beep in either case.

## *Hello World Summary*

In this simple application, we have all the major elements of any Palm application. In review, these are:

- A set of necessary include files
- A startup routine called *StartApplication*, which handles all our initial setup
- A *PilotMain* routine, which starts an event loop to handle events passed to it by the system

- An event loop, which continually hands events to a series of four managing routines—*SysHandleEvent*, *MenuHandleEvent*, *ApplicationHandleEvent*, and *FrmDispatchEvent*
- A set of routines to handle our form-specific functionality
- A closing routine called *StopApplication*, which handles the proper closing of our application

# *Scenarios*

Now that you have a better understanding of the code in the Hello World application, let's take a close look at what happens as events are passed from the event queue into the event loop. Unlike our earlier example, where we hand-waved through the technical parts of what happens when a menu was chosen, we will now look with great detail at three different user actions and the flow through the code as these scenarios occur.

This first code excerpt shows what happens when a user opens the application by tapping on the application's icon. Example 4-9 shows the flow of events. Pay particular attention to the `frmLoadEvent`, which is handled by *ApplicationHandleEvent*, and the `frmOpenEvent`, which is handled by *MyFormHandleEvent*.

*Example 4-9. Flow of Control as Hello World Application Is Opened*

```
PilotMain (enter)
  StartApplication (enter)
    FrmGotoForm(HelloWorldForm)                  open the HelloWorldForm
  StartApplication (exit)                        returns 0 (proceed)
  EventLoop (enter)
   EvtGetEvent                                   returns frmLoadEvent (formID
                                                    HelloWorldForm)
    SysHandleEvent                               returns false
    MenuHandleEvent                              returns false
    ApplicationHandleEvent (enter)
      FrmInitForm(HelloWorldForm)                load the form
      FrmSetActiveForm(frm)                      activate the form
      FrmSetEventHandler(frm, MyFormHandleEvent) set the event handler
    ApplicationHandleEvent (exit)                returns true
  EvtGetEvent                                    returns frmOpenEvent
  SysHandleEvent                                 returns false
  MenuHandleEvent                                returns false
  ApplicationHandleEvent                         returns false
  FrmDispatchEvent (enter)                       calls form's event handler
    MyFormHandleEvent (enter)
      FrmDrawForm(FrmGetActiveForm())            draws the form and its contents
    MyFormHandlEvent (exit)                      returns true
```

In Example 4-10 our user taps on the button labeled "Button," which in turn puts up an alert. Notice that eventually, the `penDownEvent` is transformed into a `ctlSelectEvent`, which is handled by our routine, *MyFormHandleEvent*.

*Example 4-10. Flow of Control in Event Loop When "Button" Button Is Pressed*

```
EvtGetEvent                        returns penDownEvent
SysHandleEvent                     returns false
MenuHandleEvent                    returns false
ApplicationHandleEvent             returns false
FrmDispatchEvent (enter)
  MyFormHandleEvent                returns false
  CtlHandleEvent                   standard control-manager routine that posts
                                     ctlEnterEvent to the event queue and returns true.
                                     a tap hits a usable control; a ctlEnterEvent is sent
FrmDispatchEvent (exit)            returns true

EvtGetEvent                        returns ctlEnterEvent
SysHandleEvent                     returns false
MenuHandleEvent                    returns false
ApplicationHandleEvent             returns false
FrmDispatchEvent (enter)
  MyFormHandleEvent                returns false
  CtlHandleEvent                   inverts the button and waits for the pen to be lifted
                                     (EvtGetPen); when the pen is lifted, inverts
                                     the button; posts ctlSelectEvent to the event queue
                                     as the pen is lifted from the control; returns true
FrmDispatchEvent (exit)            returns true

EvtGetEvent                        returns ctlSelectEvent
SysHandleEvent                     returns false
MenuHandleEvent                    returns false
ApplicationHandleEvent             returns false
FrmDispatchEvent (enter)
  MyFormHandleEvent (enter)
    FrmAlert                       returns after the OK button has been pressed
                                     (FrmDoAlert has its own event loop)
  MyFormHandleEvent (exit)         returns true

EvtGetEvent                        returns penUpEvent
SysHandleEvent                     returns false
MenuHandleEvent                    returns false
ApplicationHandleEvent             returns false
FrmDispatchEvent (enter)
  MyFormHandleEvent                returns false
FrmDispatchEvent (exit)            returns false
```

Last, but not least, examine Example 4-11 to see what happens when the user finally chooses a menu item. The `penDownEvent` is transformed into a `keyEvent` (tapping on the hardware keys or on the soft buttons causes a `keyEvent` to be posted). When the user finally taps on a particular menu item, a `menuEvent` is posted to the event queue, which is once again handled by *MyFormHandleEvent*.

*Example 4-11. Event Loop Handling a Menu Item*

| | |
|---|---|
| | *Tap on Menu button* |
| `EvtGetEvent` | *returns penDownEvent* |
| `SysHandleEvent` | *tracks pen; doesn't return until pen up; returns true* |
| `EvtGetEvent` | *returns penUpEvent* |
| `SysHandleEvent` | *posts keyDownEvent on the event queue and returns true* |
| `EvtGetEvent` | *returns keyDownEvent with key: menuChr (0x105). This is a special system key event that triggers menu code in MenuHandleEvent* |
| `SysHandleEvent` | *returns false* |
| `MenuHandleEvent` | *puts up menu bar and "First" menu and returns true* |
| | *Tap on Second menu* |
| `EvtGetEvent` | *returns penDownEvent* |
| `SysHandleEvent` | *returns false* |
| `MenuHandleEvent` | *puts up "Second" menu and returns true* |
| `EvtGetEvent` | *returns penUpEvent* |
| `SysHandleEvent` | *returns false* |
| `MenuHandleEvent` | *returns false* |
| `ApplicationHandleEvent` | *returns false* |
| `FrmDispatchEvent (enter)` | *calls MyFormHandleEvent* |
| `  MyFormHandleEvent` | *returns false* |
| `FrmDispatchEvent (exit)` | *returns false* |
| | *Tap on Beep Another Item* |
| `EvtGetEvent` | *returns penDownEvent* |
| `SysHandleEvent` | *returns false* |
| `MenuHandleEvent` | *removes menubar and menu and posts menuEvent to the event queue and returns true* |
| `EvtGetEvent` | *returns menuEvent with itemID: 1000* |
| `SysHandleEvent` | *returns false* |
| `MenuHandleEvent` | *returns false* |
| `ApplicationHandleEvent` | *returns false* |
| `FrmDispatchEvent (enter)` | *calls MyFormHandleEvent* |
| `  MyFormHandleEvent` | *beeps and returns true* |
| `FrmDispatchEvent (exit)` | *returns true* |
| `EvtGetEvent` | *returns penUpEvent* |
| `SysHandleEvent` | *returns false* |
| `MenuHandleEvent` | *returns false* |
| `ApplicationHandleEvent` | *returns false* |
| `FrmDispatchEvent (enter)` | *calls MyFormHandleEvent* |
| `  MyFormHandleEvent` | *returns false* |
| `FrmDispatchEvent (exit)` | *returns false* |

## Memory Is Extremely Limited

Now that you have an idea of how the system hands events off to the application, it's time to look at how memory is handled. To start off, it will help if you remember one crucial point: *memory is an extremely limited resource on Palm OS devices.* Because of this, Palm OS applications need to be written with careful attention to memory management.

To that end, let's examine the memory architecture on Palm devices. RAM is divided into two areas: storage and dynamic (see Figure 4-5). The storage area of memory is managed by the Database Manager, which we discuss in Chapter 6, *Databases.* It is dynamic memory, which is handled by the Memory Manager, that we discuss here.

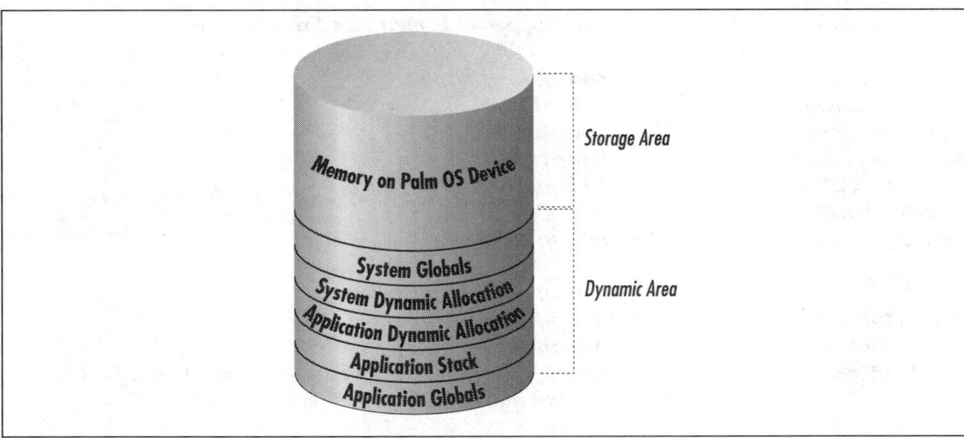


*Figure 4-5. Memory map*

The dynamic memory is used for Palm OS globals, Palm OS dynamic allocations, your application's global variables (note that C statics are a form of globals), your application's stack space, and any dynamic memory allocations you make. As you can see in Table 4-1, the size available depends on the operating system and on the amount of total memory on the device.

*Table 4-1. Dynamic Memory Usage for Various Palm OS Configurations*

| System Resources | OS 3.0 (>1 MB) | OS 2.0 (1 MB; has TCP/IP) | OS 2.0 (512 KB; no TCP/IP) |
|---|---|---|---|
| System Globals | 6KB | 2.5KB | 2.5KB |
| System dynamic allocation (TCP/IP, IRDA, etc.) | 50KB | 47KB | 15KB |
| Application stack (call stack and local variables) | 4KB (by default) | 2.5KB | 2.5KB |

*Table 4-1. Dynamic Memory Usage for Various Palm OS Configurations (continued)*

| System Resources | OS 3.0 (>1 MB) | OS 2.0 (1 MB; has TCP/IP) | OS 2.0 (512 KB; no TCP/IP) |
|---|---|---|---|
| Remainder (application globals dynamic allocation) | 36KB | 12KB | 12KB |
| Total dynamic memory | 96KB | 64KB | 32KB |

## *The Dynamic Heap*

The dynamic memory area is called the *dynamic heap*. You can allocate from the heap as either nonrelocatable chunks (called pointers) or relocatable chunks (called handles). It is always preferable to use handles wherever possible (if you're going to keep something locked for its entire existence, you might as well use a pointer). This gives the memory manager the ability to move chunks around as necessary and to keep free space contiguous.

In order to read or modify the contents of a relocatable block, you temporarily lock it. When a memory allocation occurs, any unlocked relocatable block can be relocated (see Figure 4-6 for a diagram of unlocked relocatable blocks moving due to a memory allocation).

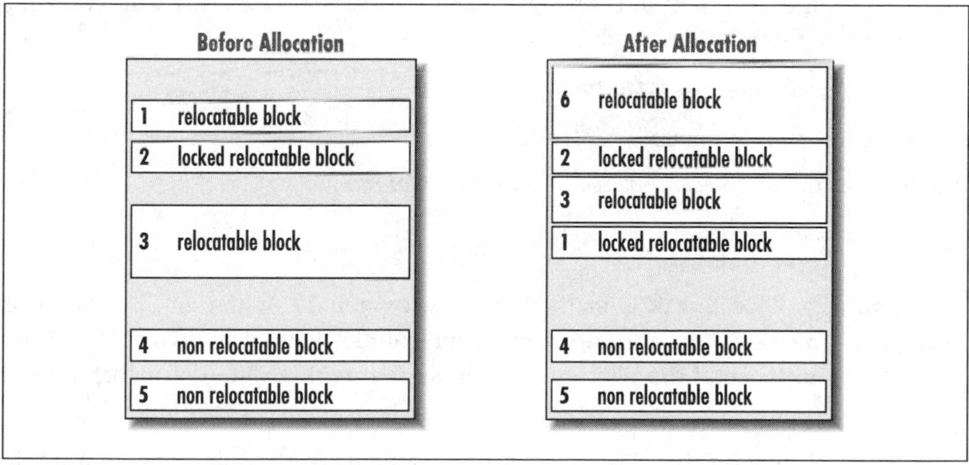


*Figure 4-6. The dynamic heap before and after doing an allocation*

## *Memory API*

Here is the API for using handles in your code. *MemHandleNew* lets you allocate a handle like this:

```
VoidHand myHandle = MemHandleNew(chunkSize)
```

`MemHandleNew` will return NULL if the allocation was unsuccessful.

Before you read from or write to a handle in your program, you need to lock it. You do so by calling *MemHandleLock*, which returns a pointer to the locked data. While the handle is locked, the relocatable block can't be moved and you can do things like reading and writing of the data. In general, you should keep a handle locked for as short a time as possible (keeping in mind, however, that there is a performance cost to repetitive locking and unlocking); locked handles tend to fragment free memory when compaction takes place. Here is the code to lock and unlock a memory handle:

```
void *myPointer = MemHandleLock(myHandle);
// do something with myPointer
MemHandleUnlock(myHandle);
```

*MemHandleLock* and *MemHandleUnlock* calls can be nested, because *MemHandleLock* increments a lock count (you can have a maximum of 15 outstanding locks per handle). *MemHandleUnlock* decrements the lock count. Note that it doesn't actually allow the chunk to move unless the lock count hits 0. If you get overeager and try to lock a handle that's already been locked 15 times, you get a runtime "chunk overlocked" error message. Similarly, unlocking a handle that is already unlocked (whose lock count is 0) generates a "chunk underlocked" error message.

Alternatively, you can call *MemPtrUnlock*. This may be more convenient, especially when the unlock is in a separate routine from the lock. This way you only have to pass around the locked pointer.

To allocate a pointer, use *MemPtrNew*:

```
struct s *myS = MemPtrNew(sizeof(struct s));
```

To free a chunk, use *MemPtrFree* or *MemHandleFree*:

```
MemPtrFree(myPointer);
MemHandleFree(myHandle);
```

As a chunk is allocated, it is marked with an owner ID. When an application is closed, the Memory Manager deallocates all chunks with that owner ID. Other chunks (for instance, those allocated by the system with a different mark) are not deallocated.

You shouldn't rely on this cleanup, however. Instead, you should code your application to free all its allocated memory explicitly. Just consider the system cleanup to be a crutch for those application writers who aren't as fastidious as you. However, in the rare case that you might forget a deallocation, the system will do it for you.

This cleanup makes the lives of Palm device users much happier. They are no longer prey to every poorly written application with a memory leak. Without this behavior, there would be no cleanup of memory allocated by an application but never deallocated. Imagine an application that allocates 50 bytes every time it is

## *Lock Counts*

A lock count allows nested locking to work. For example, imagine the following code:

```
void A(VoidHand h)
{
VoidPtr p = MemHandleLock(h);

// do stuff with P
B(h);
// code after B
MemHandleUnlock(h);
}

void B(VoidHand h)
{
VoidPtr s = MemHandleLock(h);
// do stuff with s
MemHandleUnlock(h);
}
```

When A locks h, its lock count goes to 1. When A calls B, it passes this locked handle. When B locks it again, the lock count goes to 2. When B unlocks it, it goes down to 1. After B returns, the handle is still locked, with a lock count of 1. After A unlocks it, it is really unlocked.

If *MemHandleLock* and *MemHandleUnlock* didn't use lock counts (some operating systems do provide handle locking but don't use lock counts), there would be a problem with the previous code. When B unlocked the handle, it would in fact be unlocked. Then, in A's code after the call to B, but before the call to unlock the handle, the handle would be unlocked. If A's code used the pointer p during that time, havoc could ensue, as p is no longer valid once its handle is unlocked (actually, it's still valid until the chunk moves, but that could happen any time after the handle is unlocked).

Lock counts add a small amount of complexity to the Memory Manager, but make applications easier to code.

run but never deallocates it. Running the application twice a day for two weeks uses 1,400 bytes of dynamic memory that could be reclaimed only by a reset. A Palm device isn't like a desktop computer that is rebooted fairly often (at least we know *our* desktop computers are rebooted fairly often!). Instead, a Palm device *should* run months or years without a reset. The fact that handhelds need a reset button is a flaw. (Don't get us wrong, though; given the current state of affairs, handhelds do need reset buttons.)

The Memory Manager provides other facilities, including finding the size of a chunk, resizing a chunk, and finding a handle given a locked pointer. For more information about these routines, you should see the Memory Manager documentation (or the include file *MemoryMgr.h*).

Last, there are two useful memory utility routines you should know about. They are *MemSet* and *MemMove*:

```
MemSet(void *p, ULong numBytes, Byte value)
MemMove(void *from, void *to, ULong numBytes)
```

*MemSet* sets a range of memory to the specified byte value. *MemMove* copies the specified number of bytes from a particular range to another range (it correctly handles the case where the two ranges overlap).

# Other Times Your Application Is Called

The Palm OS makes a distinction between communicating with the active application and communicating with a possibly inactive application. In this first case, the active application is busy executing an event loop and can be communicated with by posting events to the event queue. As shown in Hello World, this was how our application got closed; the `appStopEvent` was posted to the event queue. When the active application gets that event, it quits.

Because there are other times that your application gets called by the Palm OS, there needs to be a way to communicate with it in those instances. First, let's look at a list of the circumstances under which the system might want to talk to your application:

- When the user does a Find, the system must ask each installed application to look for any records that match the Find request.
- When beamed data is received, the system must ask the appropriate application (the one that is registered to receive the data) to handle the incoming item.
- When a synchronization occurs, each application is notified after its data has been synced.
- After a reset, each application is notified that a reset has occurred.
- If the system time or date changes, each application is notified.
- If the country changes, each application is notified.

In all these cases, a communication must take place to an inactive or closed application. The question is how the system does this. The answer is launch codes; all these communications are handled by your application's launch codes.

## *Launch Codes*

Within the Palm OS, the *launch code* specifies to the application which of the circumstances just listed exist and what the application needs to do. These codes arrive at the application's *PilotMain* routine by way of its `launchCode` parameter. Here are some common launch codes:

*sysAppLaunchFind*
: This code tells the application to look up a particular text string and return information about any matching data.

*sysAppLaunchGoTo*
: This code tells the application to open, if it isn't already open, and then to go to the specified piece of data.

*sysAppLaunchNormal*
: As we have already seen, this code opens the application normally.

## *Launch Flags*

Associated with these launch codes are various launch flags. The launch flags specify important information about how the application is being executed. Here are some examples:

- Whether the application's global variables are available. Globals are not available on many launch codes.
- Whether the application is now the active application.
- Whether it had already been open as the active application.
- Whether some other application is active.

## *A Few Scenarios*

To help make this whole relationship between the application and when it gets called by the system clear, let's look at some examples of when this happens and what the flow of the code is like.

Example 4-12 shows what happens when a user does a Find when the built-in application Memo Pad is open. The *PilotMain* of Hello World is called with the `sysAppLaunchCmdFind` launch code and with no launch flags.

*Example 4-12. Flow of Control When User Chooses Find When MemoPad Is Open*

```
MemoPad's                                          sysAppLaunchFlagNewStack AND
PilotMain(sysAppLaunchCmdNormalLaunch,params,      sysAppLaunchFlagNewGlobals AND
flags)                                             sysAppLaunchFlagUIApp
  MemoPad's EventLoop
  SysHandleEvent (enter)
```

*Example 4-12. Flow of Control When User Chooses Find When MemoPad Is Open (continued)*

```
                                          after user taps Find
  Loop through all applications:
    MemoPad's PilotMain(sysAppLaunchCmdFind,
      parameters, sysAppLaunchFlagSubCall)
    PilotMain(sysAppLaunchCmdFind,        calls HelloWorld's PilotMain
      parameters, 0)
SysHandleEvent (exit)
```

Now take a look in Example 4-13. This is what happens when we do a Find with our application already open. In this case, HelloWorld's *PilotMain* is called with the same launch code, **sysAppLaunchCmdFind**, but with the launch flag **sysAppLaunchFlagSubCall**, specifying that the HelloWorld application is already open and running. This signifies that global variables are available and that the *StartApplication* routine has been called.

*Example 4-13. Flow of Control When User Chooses Find When Hello World Is Open*

```
HelloWorld's PilotMain(                   sysAppLaunchFlagNewStack AND
sysAppLaunchCmdNormalLaunch, params,      sysAppLaunchFlagNewGlobals AND
flags)                                    sysAppLaunchFlagUIApp
  HelloWorld's EventLoop
  SysHandleEvent (enter)
                                          after user taps Find
    Loop through all applications:
      HelloWorld's PilotMain(sysAppLaunchCmdFind,
       parameters, sysAppLaunchFlagSubCall)
      PilotMain(sysAppLaunchCmdFind,parameters,
       0)
  SysHandleEvent (exit)
```

# Summary

In this chapter, we have given you a description of how an application interacts with the system on a Palm device. We have also done a code walkthrough of a sample program that contains all the code components that are standard to all Palm applications. You have learned that the Palm application is an event driven system. The system's event queue feeds a constant flow of events to your application, and it is up to you to handle them. You have also seen the wide variety of instances under which your application may get called by the system and the resources available to you to deal with these instances. Last, but not least, we have discussed some of the more important elements in handling memory in a Palm application.

From all this information, you should now be well on your way to understanding this application architecture. In the following chapters, you will use this information to create a full-featured application.

*In this chapter:*
- *Resources*
- *Forms*
- *Form Objects*
- *Resources, Forms, and Form Objects in the Sales Application*

# 5

# *Forms and Form Objects*

This chapter describes forms and form objects. Before we cover these subjects, however, we explain how the resources associated with the forms are created and used. Your application is stored in the form of resources. Once we discuss resources and forms in general, we give you some programming tips for creating specific types of forms (like alerts). Last, we turn to a discussion of resources and forms in the sample application.

## *Resources*

A resource is a relocatable block marked with a four-byte type (usually represented as four characters, like CODE or tSTR) and a two-byte ID. Resources are stored in a resource database (on the desktop, these files end in the extension *.PRC*).

An application is a resource database. One of the resources in this database contains code, another resource contains the application's name, another the application's icon, and the rest contain the forms, alerts, menus, strings, and other elements of the application. The Palm OS uses these resources directly from the storage heap (after locking them) via the Resource Manager.

The two most common tools to create Palm OS application resources are CodeWarrior's Constructor tool or PilRC as part of the GCC collection of tools. Our discussion turns to Constructor first and PilRC second.

### *Creating Resources in Constructor*

CodeWarrior's Constructor is a visual resource editor: you lay out the user interface object resources using a graphical layout tool.

In the following example, we take a peek at the Forms section of the resource file. You will see how to use the New Form Resource menu item and select the name and change it to be called "Main" (see Figure 5-1).

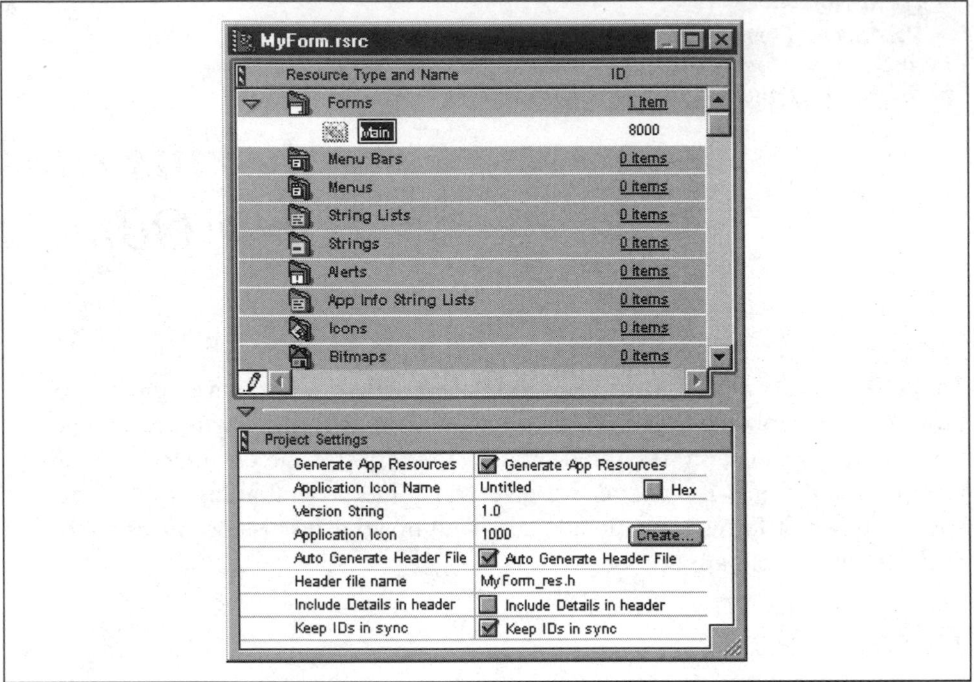


*Figure 5-1. Creating a form resource in Constructor*

The following discussion is not a tutorial on how to use Constructor. The Code Warrior documentation does a fine job at that. Rather, it is intended to be just enough information to give you a clear idea of what it's like to create a resource using Constructor.

To add a particular type of object resource to a form—a button, for instance—you drag it from the catalog window and drop it into the form (see Figure 5-2). Clicking on any item that has been dropped into the form allows you to edit its attributes. Double-clicking brings up a separate window.

If you look at Figure 5-3, you will see several windows: one shows you all the items in your form; another shows you the hierarchy of your form and its objects (as shown in the Object Hierarchy window); and last, but not least, another shows editing a form. In Figure 5-3, the top left window is the form window used to edit the form shown at the top right. The bottom left window is an editor for the Done button. The bottom right window shows the hierarchy of items on this particular form.

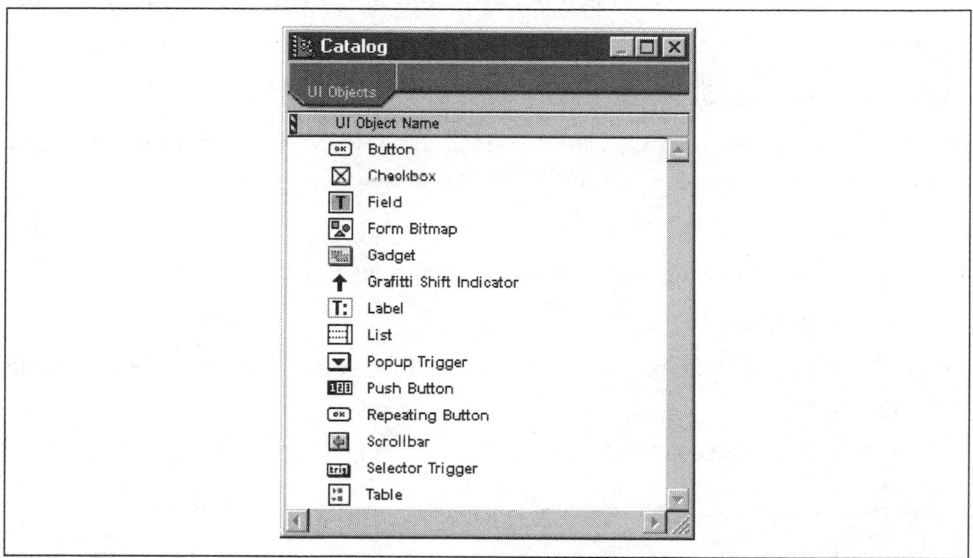


*Figure 5-2. The catalog window from which you can drag-and-drop an item to a form*

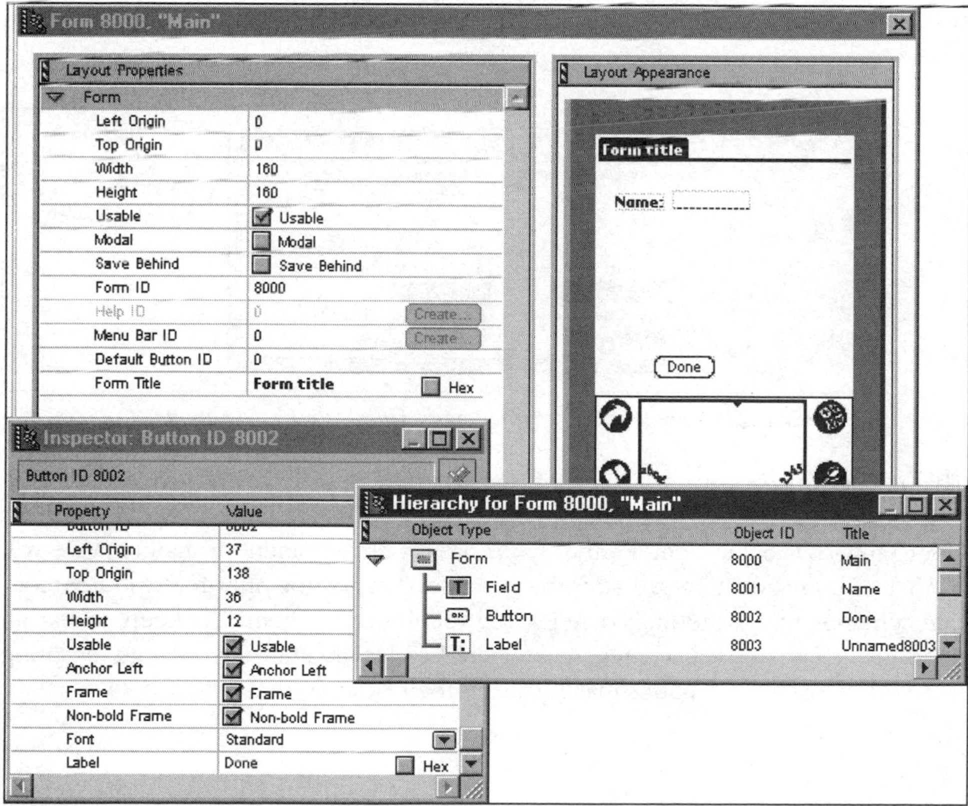


*Figure 5-3. Editing a form*

There are a couple of worthwhile things to know about creating resources in Constructor.

### *Use constants rather than raw resource IDs*

When using Constructor to create resources, you won't be embedding resource IDs directly in your code as raw numbers like this:

```
FrmAlert(1056);
```

Instead, you should create symbolic constants for each of the resource IDs:

```
#define  TellUserSomethingAlert 1056
```

Thus, when you use the resource with a function, you will have code that looks like this:

```
FrmAlert(TellUserSomethingAlert);
```

### *Using constants for your resources*

Constructor rewards you for creating symbolic constants for your resources. When it saves the resource file, it also saves a corresponding header file with all symbolic constant definitions nicely and neatly laid out for you (Figure 5-4 shows you how to choose the header filename). The names it creates are based on the type of the resource and the resource name you've provided.

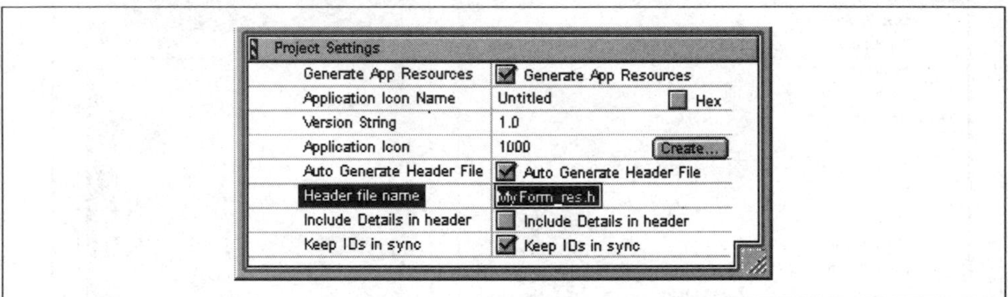


*Figure 5-4. Specifying the header file Constructor generates with ID definitions*

This is Constructor's way of keeping you from editing the resource file directly—that's Constructor's job and strictly hands off to you. For one thing, Constructor can change IDs on an item. Further, your project development or maintenance will not work correctly. You are supposed to use Constructor only for resource editing, whether that is adding, deleting, or renumbering them. To keep things all lined up nicely, Constructor regenerates the header file after any change, ensuring that your constant definitions match exactly the resources that exist.

Constructor creates constants not only for resource IDs, but for form object IDs (see "Form Objects," later in this chapter) as well.

Here's the header file generated by Constructor for the resource file we created in Figure 5-3. As you can see in the comments, you are not supposed to fiddle with this file:

```
// Header generated by Constructor for Pilot 1.0.2
//
// Generated at 10:55:44 AM on Friday, July 10, 1998
//
// Generated for file: Macintosh HD::MyForm.rsc
//
// THIS IS AN AUTOMATICALLY GENERATED HEADER FILE FROM
// CONSTRUCTOR FOR PALMPILOT;
// - DO NOT EDIT - CHANGES MADE TO THIS FILE WILL BE LOST
//
// Pilot App Name:     "Untitled"
//
// Pilot App Version: "1.0"

// Resource: tFRM 8000
#define MainForm                                            8000
#define MainDoneButton                                      8002
#define MainNameField                                       8001
#define MainUnnamed8003Label                                8003
```

Constructor has generated constants for every resource in the file; one for the form and three for the form objects.

## Creating Resources in PilRC

PilRC is a resource compiler that takes textual descriptions (stored in an *.RCP* file) of your resources and compiles them into the binary format required by a *.PRC* file. Unlike Constructor, PilRC doesn't allow you to visually create your resources; instead, you type in text to designate their characteristics. There is a way to see what that PilRC text-based description will look like visually, however. You can use PilRCUI, a tool that reads an *.RCP* file and displays a graphic preview of that file. This allows you to see what your resource objects are going to look like on the Palm device (see Figure 5-5).

### *The pretty points of PilRC*

PilRC does do some of the grunt work of creating resources for you. For example, you don't need to specify a number for every item's top and left coordinates, and

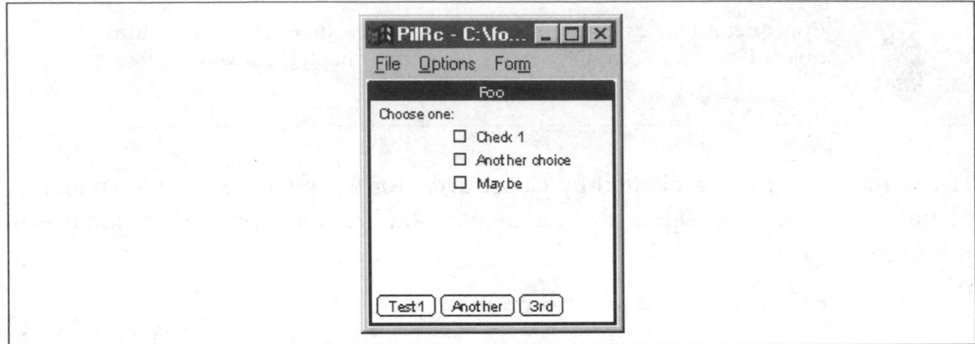


*Figure 5-5. PilRCUI displaying a preview of a form from an .RCP file*

every item's width and height. PilRC has a mechanism for automatically calculating the width or height of an item based on the text width or height. This works especially well for things like buttons, push buttons, and checkboxes.

It also allows you to specify the center justification of items. Beyond this, you can even justify the coordinates of one item based on those of another; you use the width/height of the previous item. These mechanisms also make it possible to specify the relationships between items on a form, so that changes affect not just one, but related groups of items. Thus, you can move an item or resize it and have that change affect succeeding items on the form as well.

### *PilRC example*

Here's a PilRC example. It is a simple form that contains:

- A label
- Three checkboxes whose left edges line up under the right edge of the label
- Three buttons at the bottom of the form, each with three pixels of space between the borders of the buttons

Figure 5-5 shows you what this text description looks like graphically:

```
FORM ID 1 AT (2 2 156 156)
USABLE
MODAL
BEGIN
   TITLE "Foo"
   LABEL "Choose one:" 2001  AT (8 16)

   CHECKBOX "Check 1" ID 2002 AT (PrevRight PrevBottom+3 AUTO AUTO) GROUP 1
   CHECKBOX "Another choice" ID 2003 AT (PrevLeft PrevBottom+3 AUTO AUTO)
      GROUP 1
   CHECKBOX "Maybe" ID 2004 AT (PrevLeft PrevBottom+3 AUTO AUTO) GROUP 1
```

```
    BUTTON "Test1" ID 2006 AT (7 140 AUTO AUTO)
    BUTTON "Another" ID 2007 AT (PrevRight+5 PrevTop AUTO AUTO)
    BUTTON "3rd" ID 2008 AT (PrevRight+5 PrevTop AUTO AUTO)
END
```

Just as Constructor discourages you from embedding resource IDs directly into your code as raw numbers (see Figure 5-3), similarly, you shouldn't embed resource IDs directly into your *.RCP* files. The right way to do this with PilRC is to use constants.

### *Using constants for your resources*

PilRC doesn't automatically generate symbolic constants, as Constructor does. PilRC does, however, have a mechanism for unification. If you create a header file that defines symbolic constants, you can include that header file both in your C code and in your PilRC *.RCP* definition file. PilRC allows you to include a file using **#include** and understands C-style **#define** statements. You'll simply be sharing your **#defines** between your C code and your resource definitions.

PilRC does have an **-H** flag that automatically creates resource IDs for symbolic constants you provide.

Here's a header file we've created, *ResDefs.h*, with constant definitions (similar to the kind that Constructor generates automatically):

```
#define MainForm          8000
#define MainDoneButton    8002
#define MainNameField     8001
```

We include that in our *.c* file and then include it in our *resources.rcp* file:

```
#include "ResDefs.h"

FORM ID MainForm AT (0 0 160 160)
BEGIN
   TITLE "Form title"
   LABEL "Name:" AUTOID AT (11 35) FONT 1
   FIELD ID MainNameField AT (PrevRight PrevTop 50 AUTO) UNDERLINED
      MULTIPLELINES MAXCHARS 80
   BUTTON "Done" ID MainDoneButton AT (CENTER 143 AUTO AUTO)
END
```

Note that the label doesn't have an explicit ID but uses **AUTOID**. An ID of **AUTOID** causes PilRC to create a unique ID for you automatically. This is handy for items on a form that you don't need to refer to programmatically from your code as is often the case with labels, for example.

### Reading Resources

Occasionally, you may need to use the Resource Manager to directly obtain a resource from your application's resource database. Here's what you do:

1. Get a handle to the resource.
2. Lock it.
3. Mess with it, doing whatever you need to do.
4. Unlock it.
5. Release it.

You modify a resource with a call to *DmGetResource*. This function gives you a handle to that resource as an unlocked relocatable block. To find the particular resource you want, you specify the resource type and ID when you make the call. *DmGetResource* searches through the application's resources and the system's resources. When it finds the matching resource, it marks it busy and returns its handle. You lock the handle with a call to *MemHandleLock*. When you are finished with the resource, you call *DmReleaseResource* to release it.

Here's some sample code that retrieves a string resource, uses it, and then releases it:

```
Handle  h;
CharPtr s;

h = DmGetResource('tSTR', 1099);
s = MemHandleLock(h);
// use the string s
MemHandleUnlock(h);
DmReleaseResource(h);
```

Actually, *DmGetResource* searches through the entire list of open resource databases, including the system resource database stored in ROM. Use *DmGet1Resource* to search through only the topmost open resource database; this is normally your application.

### Writing Resources

Although it is possible to write to resources (see "Modifying a Record" on page 150), it is uncommon; most resources are used only for reading.

## Forms

As we discussed earlier, a form is a container for the application's visual elements. A form is created based on information from a resource (of type "tFRM") that describes the elements. There are both modal and modeless forms in an application. The classic example of a modal form is an alert. Other forms can be made modal but require extra work on your part.

A modal dialog is different from a modeless form in:

- Appearance: a modal dialog has a full-width titlebar with the title centered and with buttons from left to right along the bottom. Most modal dialogs should have an info button that provides additional help.
- Behavior: the Find button doesn't work while a modal dialog is being displayed.

In the following material, we first discuss alerts and then modal forms. We also offer several tips in each section.

## Alerts

An alert is a very constrained form (based on a "Talt" resource); it is a modal dialog with an icon, a message, and one or more buttons at the bottom that dismiss the dialog (see Figure 5-6). As we discussed in Chapter 3, *Designing a Solution*, there are four different types of alerts (information, warning, confirmation, and error). The user can distinguish the alert type by the icon shown.

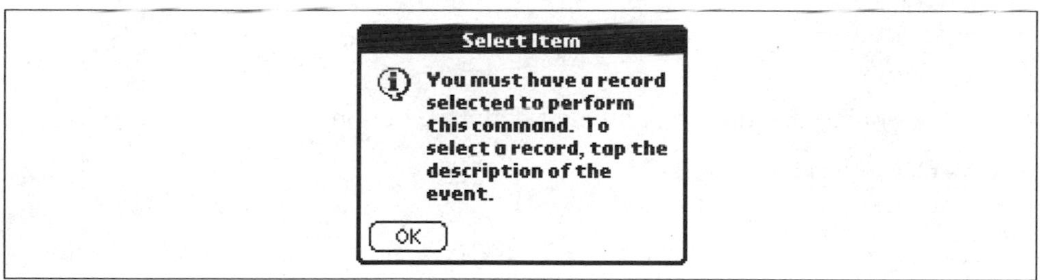


*Figure 5-6. An alert showing an icon, a message, and a button*

The return result of *FrmAlert* is the number of the button that was pressed (where the first button is number 0).

### Customizing an alert

It is worth noting that you can customize the message in an alert. You do so with runtime parameters that allow you to make up to three textual substitutions in the message. In the resource, you specify a placeholder for the runtime text with ^1, ^2, or ^3. Instead of calling *FrmAlert*, you call *FrmCustomAlert*. The first string replaces any occurrence of ^1, the second replaces any occurrence of ^2, and the third replaces occurrences of ^3.

When you call *FrmCustomAlert*, you can pass `NULL` as the text pointer only if there is no corresponding placeholder in the alert resource. If there is a corresponding placeholder, then passing `NULL` will cause a crash; pass a string with one space in it (`" "`) instead.

That is, if your alert message is `"My Message ^1 (^2)"`, you can call:

```
FrmCustomAlert(MyAlertID, "string", " ", NULL)
```

but not this:

```
FrmCustomAlert(MyAlertID, "string", NULL, NULL)
```

User interface guidelines recommend that modal dialogs have an info button at the top right that provides help for the dialog. To do so, create a string resource with your help text and specify the string resource ID as the help ID in the alert resource.

Make sure that any alerts you display with *FrmAlert* don't have ^1, ^2, or ^3 in them. `FrmAlert(alertID)` is equivalent to `FrmCustomAlert(alertID, NULL, NULL, NULL)`. The Form Manager will try to replace any occurrences of ^1, ^2, or ^3 with `NULL`, and this will certainly cause a crash.

### *Alert example*

Here's a resource description of an alert with two buttons:

```
#define MyAlert 1000

ALERT ID MyAlert
CONFIRMATION
BEGIN
    TITLE "My Alert Title (^1)"
    MESSAGE "My Message (^1) (^2)  (^1)"
    BUTTONS "OK" "Cancel"
END
```

If you display the alert with *FrmCustomAlert*, it appears as shown in Figure 5-7:

```
if (FrmCustomAlert(MyAlert, "foo", "bar", NULL) == 0) {
   // user pressed OK
} else {
   // user pressed Cancel
}
```

*Figure 5-7. An alert displayed with FrmCustomAlert; note that FrmCustomAlert doesn't replace strings in the title*

### *Tips on creating alerts*

Here are a few tips that will help you avoid common mistakes:

*Button capitalization*
: Buttons in an alert should be capitalized. Thus, a button should be titled "Cancel" and not "cancel".

*OK buttons*
: An "OK" button should be exactly that. Don't use "Ok", "Okay", "ok", or "Okey-dokey". OK?

*Using ^1, ^2, ^3*
: The ^1, ^2, ^3 placeholders aren't replaced in the alert title or in buttons but are replaced only in the alert message.

## *Modal Dialogs*

The easiest way to display a modal dialog is to use *FrmAlert* or *FrmCustomAlert*. The fixed structure of alerts (icon, text, and buttons) may not always match what you need, however. For example, you may need a checkbox or other control in your dialog.

### *Modal form template*

If you need this type of flexible modal dialog, use a form resource (setting the `modal` attribute of the form) and then display the dialog using the following code:

```
// returns object ID of hit button
static Word DisplayMyFormModally(void)
{
    FormPtr previousForm = FrmGetActiveForm();
    FormPtr frm = FrmInitForm(MyForm);
    Word    hitButton;

    FrmSetActiveForm(frm);

// Set an event handler, if you wish, with FrmSetEventHandler
// Initialize any form objects in the form
```

```
    hitButton = FrmDoDialog(frm);

    // read any values from the form objects here
    // before the form is deleted

    if (previousForm)
        FrmSetActiveForm(previousForm);
    FrmDeleteForm(frm);
    return hitButton;
}
```

*FrmDoDialog* is documented to return the number of the tapped button, where the first button is 0. Actually, it returns the button ID of the tapped button.

For example, if you've got a form with an icon, a label, and two buttons, where the first button has a button ID of 1002 and the second button has a button ID of 1001, *FrmDoDialog* will return either 1002 or 1001, depending on whether the first or second button is pressed.

### *Modal form example*

Here we have an example that displays a modal dialog with a checkbox in it (see Figure 5-8). The initial value of the checkbox is determined by the parameter to *TrueOrFalse*. The final value of *TrueOrFalse* is the value of the checkbox (if the user taps OK) or the initial value (if the user taps Cancel). This demonstrates setting form object values in a modal form before displaying it and reading values from a modal form's objects after it is done:

```
// takes a true/false value and allows the user to edit it
static Boolean TrueOrFalse(Boolean initialValue)
{
   FormPtr previousForm = FrmGetActiveForm();
   FormPtr frm = FrmInitForm(TrueOrFalseForm);
   Word    hitButton;
   ControlPtr  checkbox = FrmGetObjectPtr(frm,
            FrmGetObjectIndex(frm, TrueOrFalseCheckbox));
   Boolean  newValue;

   FrmSetActiveForm(frm);

// Set an event handler, if you wish, with FrmSetEventHandler

   CtlSetValue(checkbox, initialValue);

   hitButton = FrmDoDialog(frm);

   newValue = CtlGetValue(checkbox);

   if (previousForm)
      FrmSetActiveForm(previousForm);
```

```
        FrmDeleteForm(frm);
        if (hitButton == TrueOrFalseOKButton)
           return newValue;
        else
           return initialValue;
    }
```

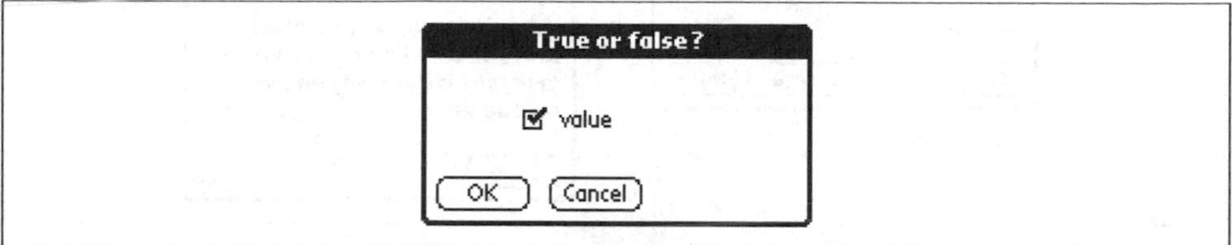


*Figure 5-8. The modal form that allows you to edit a true/false value with a checkbox*

### *A tip for modal forms*

When you call *FrmDoDialog* with a modal form, your event handler won't get a `frmOpenEvent`, and it doesn't have to call *FrmDrawForm*. Since your event handler won't be notified that the form is opening, any form initialization must be done before you call *FrmDoDialog*.

### *Modal form sizes*

You don't want your modal form to take up the entire screen real estate. Center it horizontally at the bottom of the screen, and make sure that the borders of the form can be seen. You'll need to inset the bounds of your form by at least two pixels in each direction.

### *Help for modal forms*

The Palm user interface guidelines specify that modal dialogs should provide online help through the "i" button at the top right of the form (see Figure 5-9). You provide this help text as a string resource (`tSTR`) that contains the appropriate help message. In your form (or alert) resource, you then set the help ID to the string resource ID. The Palm OS takes care of displaying the "i" button (only if the help ID is nonzero) and displaying the help text if the button is tapped.

## *Form Objects*

The elements that populate a form are called form objects. Before we get into the details of specific form objects, however, there are some very important things to know about how forms deal with all form objects.

Many of the form objects post specific kinds of events when they are tapped on, or used. To use a particular type of form object, you need to consult the Palm OS documentation to see what kinds of events that form object produces.

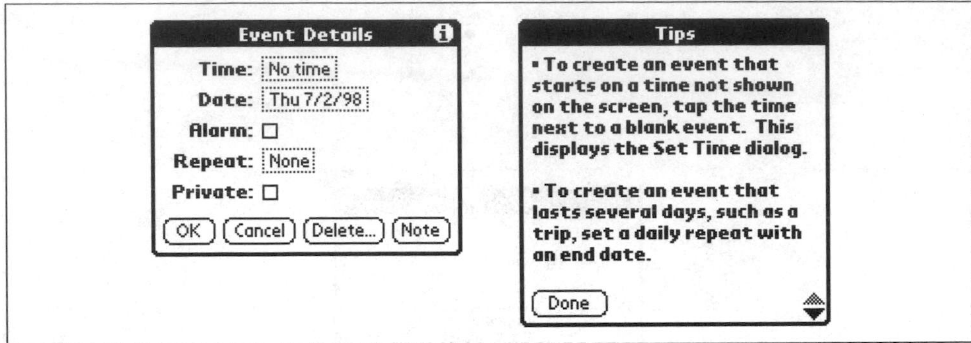


*Figure 5-9. Modal dialog (left) with "i" button bringing up help (right)*

## Dealing with Form Objects in Your Form Event

Form objects communicate their actions by posting events. Most of the form objects have a similar structure:

1. When the stylus is pressed on the object, it sends an enter event.
2. In response to the enter event, the object responds appropriately while the stylus is pressed down. For example: a button highlights while the pen is within the button and unhighlights while it is outside the button; a scrollbar sends `sclRepeatEvents` while the user has a scroll arrow tapped; a list highlights the row the stylus is on and scrolls, if necessary, when the pen reaches the top or bottom of the list.
3. When the stylus is released:
   a. If it is on the object, it sends a select event.
   b. If it is outside the object, it sends an exit event.

In all these events, the ID of the tapped form object and a pointer to the form object itself are provided as part of the event. The ID allows you to distinguish between different instances that generate the same types of events. For example, two buttons would both generate a `ctlSelectEvent` when tapped; you need the IDs to know which is which.

#### *Events generated by a successful tap*

Most often, you want to know only when an object has been successfully tapped; that is, the user lifts the stylus while still within the boundaries of the object. You'll be interested in these events:

- `ctlSelectEvent`
- `frmTitleSelectEvent`

- `lstSelectEvent`
- `popSelectEvent`
- `tblSelectEvent`

### *Events generated by repeated taps*

Sometimes, you'll need to be notified of a repetitive action while a form object is being pressed. The events are `ctlRepeatEvent` (used for repeating buttons) and `sclRepeatEvent`.

### *Events generated by the start of a tap*

Occasionally, you'll want to know when the user starts to tap on a form object. For example, when the user starts to tap on a pop-up trigger you may want to dynamically fill in the contents of the pop-up list before it is displayed. You'd do that in the `ctlEnterEvent`, looking for the appropriate control ID. The events sent when the user starts to tap on a form object are:

- `ctlEnterEvent`
- `fldEnterEvent`
- `frmTitleEnterEvent`
- `lstEnterEvent`
- `sclEnterEvent`
- `tblEnterEvent`

### *Events generated by the end of an unsuccessful tap*

Rarely, you'll want to know when a form object has been unsuccessfully tapped (the user tapped the object, but scuttled the stylus outside the boundaries before lifting it). For example, if you allocate some memory in the enter event, you'd deallocate the memory in both the select event and in the corresponding exit event (covering all your bases, so to speak). The events are `ctlExitEvent`, `lstExitEvent`, `sclExitEvent`, and `tblExitEvent`.

Note that although there is a `frmTitleSelectEvent`, there is no corresponding `frmTitleExitEvent`. We know of no reason why this is so.

## Getting an Object from a Form

Whenever you need to do something with an object, you will need to get it from the form. You do this with a pointer and the function *FrmGetObjectPtr*. Note that *FrmGetObjectPtr* takes an object index and not an object ID. The return result of *FrmGetObjectPtr* depends on the type of the form object.

### Types of form object pointers

*FrmGetObjectPtr* returns one of the following, depending on the type of the form object kept at that index:

- `FieldPtr`
- `ControlPtr`
- `ListPtr`
- `TablePtr`
- `FormBitmapPtr`
- `FormLabelPtr`
- `FormTitlePtr`
- `FormPopupPtr`
- `FormGraffitiStatePtr`
- `FormGadgetPtr`
- `ScrollBarPtr`

### Code example

If you pass the correct index into *FrmGetObjectPtr*, you can safely typecast the return result. For example, here we get a field from the form and cast it to a `FieldPtr`:

```
FormPtr frm = FrmGetActiveForm();
FieldPtr fld = FrmGetObjectPtr(frm, FrmGetObjectIndex(frm, MainMyField));
```

C doesn't require an explicit typecast when casting from a `void *` such as the return result of *FrmGetObjectPtr*. It automatically typecasts for you. C++, on the other hand, requires an explicit typecast in that situation.

### *Error checking*

You can use *FrmGetObjectType* with *FrmGetObjectPtr* to ensure that the type of the form object you retrieve is the type you expect. Here's an example that retrieves a `FieldPtr`, using additional error checking to verify the type:

```
FieldPtr GetFieldPtr(FormPtr frm, Word objectIndex)
{
    ErrNonFatalDisplayIf(FrmGetObjectType(frm, objectIndex <> frmFieldObj,
      "Form object isn't a field"
   return (FieldPtr) FrmGetObjectPtr(frm, objectIndex);
}
```

In a finished application, of course, your code shouldn't be accessing form objects of the wrong type. During the development process, however, it is frightfully easy to accidentally pass the wrong index to *FrmGetObjectPtr*. Thus, using a safety checking routine like *GetFieldPtr* can be helpful in catching programming errors that are common in early development.

## *Form Object "Gotchas"*

Here are a couple of problems to watch out for when dealing with form functions and handling form objects:

*Remember which form functions require object IDs versus object indexes*

You must keep track of which form functions require form object IDs and which require form object indexes. If you pass an object ID to a routine that expects an object index, you'll probably cause the device to crash. Remember that you can translate back and forth between these two using *FrmGetObjectID* and *FrmGetObjectIndex* whenever it's necessary.

*Bitmaps don't have object IDs*

Bitmaps on a form don't have an associated object ID. This can be a problem if you want to do hit-testing on a bitmap, for instance. In such cases, you can create a gadget that has the same bounds as the bitmap and do hit-testing on it. This has an associated object ID.

## *Specific Form Objects*

Now that you have an idea how forms interact with form objects, it is time to look at the quirks associated with programming particular form objects. Concerning these form objects there is both good news and bad. Let's start with the good.

We don't discuss any of the following objects, because their creation and coding requirements are well documented and straightforward:

- Buttons
- Checkboxes
- Form bitmaps
- Graffiti shift indicators
- Push buttons
- Repeating buttons
- Selector triggers

The bad news is that the rest of the form objects require further discussion. Indeed, some objects, like editable text field objects, require extensive help before you can successfully add them to an application. Here is the list of objects that we are going to discuss further:

- Labels
- Gadgets
- Lists
- Pop-up triggers
- Text
- Scrollbars
- Tables (we actually describe these later in Chapter 8, *Extras*, on page 206)

## Label Objects

Label objects can be a little bit tricky if you are going to change the label at runtime. They are a snap if the label values don't switch.

### *Changing the text of a label*

To change the text of a label form object, use *FrmCopyLabel*. Unfortunately, *FrmCopyLabel* only redraws the new label, while not erasing the old one. You can have problems with this in the case where the new text is shorter than the old text; remnants of the old text are left behind. One way to avoid this problem is to hide the label before doing the copy and then show it afterward. Here is an example of that:

```
FormPtr frm = FrmGetActiveForm();
Word    myLabelObjectIndex = FrmGetObjectIndex(frm, MainMyLabel);

FrmHideObject(frm, myLabelObjectIndex);
```

```
FrmCopyLabel(FrmGetActiveForm(), MainMyLabel, "newText");
FrmShowObject(frm, myLabelObjectIndex);
```

To change the label of a control (like a checkbox, for instance), use *CtlSetLabel*, not *FrmCopyLabel*.

#### *Problems with labels longer than the resource specification*

You will also have trouble if the length of the new label is longer than the length specified in the resource. Longer strings definitely cause errors, since *FrmCopyLabel* blindly writes beyond the space allocated for the label.

In general, you should realize that labels aren't well suited for text that needs to change at runtime. In most cases, if you've got some text on the screen that needs to change, you are better off not using a label. A preferable choice, in such instances, is a field that has the editable and underline attributes turned off.

## *Gadget Objects*

Once you have rifled through the other objects and haven't found anything suitable for the task you have in mind, you are left with using a gadget. A gadget is the form object you use when nothing else will do.

A gadget is a custom form object with an on-screen bounds that can have data programmatically associated with it. (You can't set data for a gadget from a resource.) It also has an object ID. That's all the Form Manager knows about a gadget: bounds, object ID, and a data pointer. Everything else you need to handle yourself.

#### *What the gadget is responsible for*

The two biggest tasks the gadget needs to handle are:

- All the drawing of the gadget on the screen
- All the taps on the gadget

There are two times when the gadget needs to be drawn—when the form first gets opened and whenever your event handler receives a `frmUpdateEvent` (these are the same times you need to call *FrmUpdateForm*).

If you'll be saving data associated with the gadget, use the function *FrmSetGadgetData*. You also need to initialize the data when your form is opened.

Although you could draw and respond to taps without a gadget, it has three advantages over a totally custom-coded structure:

- The gadget maintains a pointer that allows you to store gadget-specific data.
- The gadget maintains a rectangular bounds specified in the resource.
- Gremlins, the automatic random tester (see page 297), recognizes gadgets and taps on them. This is an enormous advantage, because Gremlins relentlessly tap on them during testing cycles. While it is true that it will tap on areas that lie outside the bounds of any form object, it is a rare event. Gremlins are especially attracted to buttons and objects and like to spend time tapping in them. If you didn't use gadgets, your code would rarely receive taps during this type of testing.

### *A sample gadget*

Let's look at an example gadget that stores the integer 0 or 1 and displays either a vertical or horizontal line. Tapping on the gadget flips the integer and the line. Here's the form's initialization routine that initializes the data in the gadget and then draws it:

```
FormPtr  frm = FrmGetActiveForm();
VoidHand h = MemHandleNew(sizeof(Word));

if (h) {
   * (Word *) MemHandleLock(h) = 1;
   MemHandleUnlock(h);
   FrmSetGadgetData(frm, FrmGetObjectIndex(frm, MainG1Gadget), h);
}

// Draw the form.
FrmDrawForm(frm);
GadgetDraw(frm, MainG1Gadget);
```

When the form is closed, the gadget's data handle must be deallocated:

```
VoidHand h;
FormPtr  frm = FrmGetActiveForm();

h = FrmGetGadgetData(frm, FrmGetObjectIndex(frm, MainG1Gadget));
if (h)
   MemHandleFree(h);
```

Here's the routine that draws the horizontal or vertical line:

```
// draws  | or - depending on the data in the gadget
static void GadgetDraw(FormPtr frm, Word gadgetID)
```

```
{
   RectangleType  bounds;
   UInt           fromx, fromy, tox, toy;
   Word           gadgetIndex = FrmGetObjectIndex(frm, gadgetID);
   VoidHand       data = FrmGetGadgetData(frm, gadgetIndex);

   if (data) {
      WordPtr        wordP = MemHandleLock(data);

      FrmGetObjectBounds(frm, gadgetIndex, &bounds);
      switch (*wordP) {
      case 0:
         fromx = bounds.topLeft.x + bounds.extent.x / 2;
         fromy = bounds.topLeft.y;
         tox = fromx;
         toy = fromy + bounds.extent.y - 1;
         break;
      case 1:
         fromx = bounds.topLeft.x;
         fromy = bounds.topLeft.y + bounds.extent.y / 2;
         tox = fromx + bounds.extent.x - 1;
         toy = fromy;
         break;
      default:
         fromx = tox = bounds.topLeft.x;
         fromy = toy = bounds.topLeft.y;
         break;
      }
      MemHandleUnlock(data);
      WinEraseRectangle(&bounds, 0);
      WinDrawLine(fromx, fromy, tox, toy);
   }
}
```

Every time the user taps down on the form, the form's event handler needs to check to see whether the tap is on the gadget. It does so by comparing the tap point with the gadget's bounds. Here is an example:

```
case penDownEvent:
   {
      FormPtr        frm = FrmGetActiveForm();
      Word           gadgetIndex = FrmGetObjectIndex(frm, MainG1Gadget);
      RectangleType  bounds;

      FrmGetObjectBounds(frm, gadgetIndex, &bounds);
      if (RctPtInRectangle (event->screenX, event->screenY, &bounds)) {
         GadgetTap(frm, MainG1Gadget, event);
         handled = true;
      }
   }
   break;
```

The *GadgetTap* function handles a tap and acts like a button (highlighting and unhighlighting as the stylus moves in and out of the gadget):

```
// it'll work like a button: Invert when you tap in it.
// Stay inverted while you stay in the button. Leave the button, uninvert,
// let go outside, nothing happens; let go inside, data changes/redraws
static void GadgetTap(FormPtr frm, Word gadgetID, EventPtr event)
{
   Word           gadgetIndex = FrmGetObjectIndex(frm, gadgetID);
   VoidHand       data = FrmGetGadgetData(frm, gadgetIndex);
   SWord          x, y;
   Boolean        penDown;
   RectangleType  bounds;
   Boolean        wasInBounds = true;

   if (data) {
      FrmGetObjectBounds(frm, gadgetIndex, &bounds);
      WinInvertRectangle(&bounds, 0);
      do {
         Boolean  nowInBounds;

         PenGetPoint (&x, &y, &penDown);
         nowInBounds = RctPtInRectangle(x, y, &bounds);
         if (nowInBounds != wasInBounds) {
            WinInvertRectangle(&bounds, 0);
            wasInBounds = nowInBounds;
         }
      } while (penDown);
      if (wasInBounds) {
         WordPtr  wPtr = MemHandleLock(data);
         *wPtr = !(*wPtr)
         MemHandleUnlock(data);

         // GadgetDraw will erase--we don't need to invert
         GadgetDraw(frm, gadgetID);
      } // else gadget is already uninverted
   }
}
```

If we wanted to have multiple gadgets on a single form, we'd need to modify the form open and close routines to allocate and deallocate handles for each gadget in the form. In addition, we'd have to modify the event handler to check for taps in the bounds of each gadget, rather than just the one.

## List Objects

A list can be used as is without any programmatic customization. In the resource, you can specify the text of each list row and the number of rows that can be displayed at one time (the number of visible items). The list will automatically provide scroll arrows if the number of items in the list is greater than the number that can be shown.

Lists are used both alone and with pop-up triggers (see "Pop-up Trigger Objects" later in this chapter). If you are using a standalone list, you'll receive a `lstSelectEvent` when the user taps on (and releases) a list item. The list manager automatically highlights the selected item.

You can manipulate the display of a list in two ways:

- You can programmatically set the default selection using *LstSetSelection*.
- You can make a specific item visible with *LstMakeItemVisible*; the list will scroll, if necessary, to display that item.

You can get information from it using three different routines:

- You can retrieve information from the list by using *LstGetNumberOfItems*, *LstGetVisibleItems*, or *LstGetSelectionText*.

### *Sample that displays a specific list item*

Here's some sample code that selects the 11th item in a list (the first item is at 0) and scrolls the list, if necessary, so that it is visible:

```
FormPtr  frm = FrmGetActiveForm();
ListPtr  list = FrmGetObjectPtr(frm, FrmGetObjectIndex(frm, MainMyList));

LstSetSelection(list, 10);
LstMakeItemVisible(list, 10);
```

### *Custom versus noncustom lists*

If you want to specify the contents of the list at runtime, there are two ways to do it:

- Use *LstSetArrayChoices* to pass an array of strings that will become the new items. The List Manager retains the strings and draws each string as necessary.
- Use *LstSetDrawFunction* to provide a callback function that is responsible for drawing the contents of each row.

You'll find that the second way is almost always easier than the first. Let's look at a sample written twice, using the first approach and again using the second.

The sample draws a list composed of items in a string list resource. A string list resource contains:

- Two bytes at the beginning used for an undisclosed, highly secret piece of industry gossip
- A byte with the number of strings
- The null-terminated strings concatenated together

There's no particular significance to retrieving the items from a string list resource; we just needed some example that required the runtime retrieval of the strings.

Here's a C structure defining a string resource:

```
typedef struct StrListType {
      Word      unused;
      char      numStrings;
      char      firstString[1]; // more than 1-all concated together.
} *StrListPtr;
```

Using the first approach, we need to create an array with each element pointing to a string. The easiest way to create such an array is with *SysFormPointerArray-ToStrings*. This routine takes a concatenation of null-terminated strings and returns a newly allocated array that points to the beginning of each string in the concatenation. We lock the return result and pass it to *LstSetListChoices*:

```
static void MainViewInit(void)
{
   FormPtr          frm = FrmGetActiveForm();

   gStringsHandle = DmGetResource('tSTL', MyStringList);
   if (gStringsHandle) {
      ListPtr  list = FrmGetObjectPtr(frm,
         FrmGetObjectIndex(frm, MainMyList));
      StrLstPtr   stringsPtr = = MemHandleLock(gStringsHandle);

      gStringArrayH = SysFormPointerArrayToStrings(
         stringsPtr->firstString, stringsPtr->numStrings);
      LstSetListChoices(list, MemHandleLock(gStringArrayH),
         stringsPtr->numStrings);
   }
   // Draw the form.
   FrmDrawForm(frm);
}
```

The resource handle and the newly allocated array are stored in global variables so that they can be deallocated when the form closes:

```
static VoidHand  gStringArrayH = 0;
static VoidHand  gStringsHandle = 0;
```

Here's the deallocation routine where we deallocate the allocated array, and unlock and release the resource:

```
static void MainViewDeInit(void)
{
   if (gStringArrayH) {
      MemHandleFree(gStringArrayH);
      gStringArrayH = NULL;
   }

   if (gStringsHandle) {
      MemHandleUnlock(gStringsHandle);
```

```
        DmReleaseResource(gStringsHandle);
        gStringsHandle = NULL;
    }
}
```

Here's the alternative way of customizing the list at runtime. Our drawing function to draw each row is similar. Our initialization routine must initialize the number of rows in the list and must install a callback routine:

```
static void MainViewInit(void)
{
    FormPtr         frm = FrmGetActiveForm();

    VoidHand stringsHandle = DmGetResource('tSTL', MyStringList);
    if (stringsHandle) {
        StrListPtr  stringsPtr;
        ListPtr  list = FrmGetObjectPtr(frm,
            FrmGetObjectIndex(frm, MainMyList));

        stringsPtr = MemHandleLock(stringsHandle);
        LstSetListChoices(list, NULL, stringsPtr->numStrings);
        MemHandleUnlock(stringsHandle);
        DmReleaseResource(stringsHandle);

        LstSetDrawFunction(list, ListDrawFunc);
    }

    // Draw the form.
    FrmDrawForm(frm);
}
```

*ListDrawFunc* gets the appropriate string from the list and draws it. If the callback routine had wanted to do additional drawing (lines, bitmaps, etc.), it could have:

```
static void ListDrawFunc(UInt itemNum, RectanglePtr bounds, CharPtr *data)
{
    VoidHand stringsHandle = DmGetResource('tSTL', MyStringList);
    if (stringsHandle) {
        StrListPtr  stringsPtr;
        FormPtr     frm = FrmGetActiveForm();
        ListPtr     list = FrmGetObjectPtr(frm,
            FrmGetObjectIndex(frm, MainMyList));
        CharPtr     s;

        stringsPtr = MemHandleLock(stringsHandle);
        s = stringsPtr->firstString;
        while (itemNum-- > 0)
            s += StrLen(s) + 1;  // skip this string, including null byte
        WinDrawChars(s, StrLen(s), bounds->topLeft.x, bounds->topLeft.y);
        MemHandleUnlock(stringsHandle);
        DmReleaseResource(stringsHandle);
    }
}
```

There is no cleanup necessary when the form is completed.

Note that the two different approaches had roughly the same amount of code. The first used more memory (because of the allocated array). It also kept the resource locked the entire time the form was open, resulting in possible heap fragmentation.

The second approach was somewhat slower, since, for each row, the resource was obtained, locked, iterated through to find the correct string, and unlocked. Note that if we'd been willing to keep the resource locked as we did in the first case, the times would have been very similar. The second approach had more flexibility in that the drawing routine could have drawn text in different fonts or styles, or could have done additional drawing on a row-by-row basis.

## Pop-up Trigger Objects

Pop-up triggers need an associated list. The list's bounds should be set so that when it pops up, it will be equal to or bigger than the trigger. Otherwise, you get the ugly effect of a telltale fragment of the original trigger under the list. In addition, the `usable` attribute must be set to false so that it won't appear until the pop-up trigger is pressed.

When the pop-up trigger is pressed, the list is displayed. When a list item is chosen, the pop-up label is set to the chosen item. These actions occur automatically; no code needs to be written. When a new item is chosen from the pop-up, a `popSelectEvent` is sent. Some associated data goes with it that includes the list ID, the list pointer, a pointer to the trigger control, and the indexes of the previously selected item and newly selected items.

Here's an example resource:

```
#define MainForm          1100
#define MainTriggerID     1102
#define MainListID        1103

FORM ID 1100 AT (0 0 160 160)
BEGIN
    POPUPTRIGGER "States" ID MainTriggerID AT (55 30 44 12)
        LEFTANCHOR NOFRAME FONT 0
        POPUPLIST ID MainTriggerID MainListID
    LIST "California" "Kansas" "New Mexico" "Pennsylvania" "Rhode Island"
        "Wyoming" ID MainListID AT (64 29 63 33) NONUSABLE DISABLED FONT 0
END
```

Here's an example of handling a `popSelectEvent` in an event handler:

```
case popSelectEvent:
      // do something with following fields of event->data.popSelect
      //   controlID
      //   controlPtr
      //   listID
```

```
    //   listP
    //   selection
    //   priorSelection
  break;
```

## *Text Objects*

Editable text objects require attention to many details.

### *Setting text in a field*

Accessing an editable field needs to be done in a particular way. In the first place, you must use a handle instead of a pointer. The ability to resize the text requires the use of a handle. You must also make sure to get the field's current handle and expressly free it in your code. Here is some sample code that shows you how to do this:

```
static FieldPtr SetFieldTextFromHandle(Word fieldID, Handle txtH)
{
   Handle       oldTxtH;
   FormPtr      frm = FrmGetActiveForm();
   FieldPtr     fldP;


   // get the field and the field's current text handle.
   fldP      = FrmGetObjectPtr(frm, FrmGetObjectIndex(frm, fieldID));
   ErrNonFatalDisplayIf(!fldP, "missing field");
   oldTxtH   = FldGetTextHandle(fldP);

   // set the field's text to the new text.
   FldSetTextHandle(fldP, txtH);
   FldDrawField(fldP);

   // free the handle AFTER we call FldSetTextHandle().
   if (oldTxtH)
      MemHandleFree(oldTxtH);

   return fldP;
}
```

The previous bit of code is actually quite tricky. The Palm OS documentation doesn't tell you that it's your responsibility to dispose of the field's old handle. (We get the field handle with *FldGetTextHandle* and dispose of it with *MemHandleFree* at the end of the routine.)

Were we not to dispose of the old handles of editable text fields in the application, we would get slowly growing memory leaks all over the running application. Imagine if every time an editable field were modified programmatically, its old handle were kept in memory, along with its new handle. It wouldn't take long for our running application to choke the application heap with its vampire-like hunger for memory. Further, debugging such a problem would require diligent sleuthing as the cause of the problem would not be readily obvious.

Last, we redraw the field with *FldDrawField*. If we had not done so, the changed text wouldn't be displayed.

Note that when a form closes, each field within it frees its handle. If you don't want that behavior for a particular field, call `FldSetTextHandle(fld, NULL)` before the field is closed. If a field has no handle associated with it, when the user starts writing in the field, the Field Manager automatically allocates a handle for it.

Here are some utility routines that are wrappers around the previous routine. The first one sets a field's text to that of a string, allocates a handle, and copies the string for you:

```
// Allocates new handle and copies incoming string
static FieldPtr SetFieldTextFromStr(Word fieldID, CharPtr strP)
{
   Handle      txtH;

   // get some space in which to stash the string.
   txtH  = MemHandleNew(StrLen(strP) + 1);
   if (!txtH)
      return NULL;

   // copy the string to the locked handle.
   StrCopy(MemHandleLock(txtH), strP);

   // unlock the string handle.
   MemHandleUnlock(txtH);

   // set the field to the handle
   return SetFieldTextFromHandle(fieldID, txtH);
}
```

The second utility routine clears the text from a field:

```
static void ClearFieldText(Word fieldID)
{
   SetFieldTextFromHandle(fieldID, NULL);
}
```

### *Modifying text in a field*

One way to make changes to text is to use *FldDelete*, *FldSetSelection*, and *FldInsert*. *FldDelete* deletes a specified range of text. *FldInsert* inserts text at the current selection (*FldSetSelection* sets the selection). By making judicious calls to these routines, you can change the existing text into whatever new text you desire. The routines are easy to use. They have a flaw, however, that may make them inappropriate to use in some cases: *FldDelete* and *FldInsert* redraw the field. If you're making multiple calls to these routines for a single field (let's say, for example, you were replacing every other character with an "X"), you'd see the field redraw after every call. Users might find this distracting. Be careful with **FldChanged** events, as well, as they can overflow the event queue if they are too numerous.

An alternative approach exists that involves directly modifying the text in the handle. However, you must not change the text in a handle while it is being used by a field. Changing the text while the field is using it confuses the field and its internal information is not updated correctly. Among other things, line breaks won't work correctly.

To properly change the text, first remove it from the field, modify it, and then put it back. Here's an example of how to do that:

```
FormPtr     frm = FrmGetActiveForm();
FieldPtr    fld;
Handle      h;

// get the field and the field's current text handle.
fld       = FrmGetObjectPtr(frm, FrmGetObjectIndex(frm, Main1Field));
h = FldGetTextHandle(fld);
if (h) {
   CharPtr  s;

   FldSetTextHandle(fld, NULL);
   s = MemHandleLock(h);
  // change contents of s
   while (*s != '\0') {
      if (*s >= 'A' && *s <= 'Z')
         StrCopy(s, s+1);
      else
         s++;
   }

   MemHandleUnlock(h);
   FldSetTextHandle(fld, h);
   FldDrawField(fld);
}
```

This no-brainer example simply removes any uppercase characters in the field.

### *Getting text from a field*

To read the text from a field, you can use *FldGetTextHandle.* It is often more convenient, however, to obtain a pointer instead by using *FldGetTextPtr.* It returns a locked pointer to the text. Note that this text pointer can become invalid if the user subsequently edits the text (if there isn't enough room left for new text, the field manager unlocks the handle, resizes it, and then relocks it).

If the field is empty, it won't have any text associated with it. In such cases, *FldGetTextPtr* returns NULL. Make sure you check for this case.

### *Other aspects of a field that require attention*

When a form containing editable text fields is displayed, one of the text fields should contain the focus; this means it displays an insertion point and receives any Graffiti input. You must choose the field that has the initial focus by setting it in your code. The user can change the focus by tapping on a field. The Form Manager handles changing the focus in this case.

You must also handle the `prevFieldChr` and `nextFieldChr` characters; these allow the user to move from field to field using Graffiti (the Graffiti strokes for these characters are ∨ and ∧).

To move the focus, use *FrmSetFocus*. Here's an example that sets the focus to the `MyFormMyTextField` field:

```
FormPtr frm = FrmGetActiveForm();

FrmSetFocus(frm, FrmGetObjectIndex(frm, MyFormMyTextField));
```

Do not use *FldGrabFocus*. It changes the insertion point, but doesn't notify the form that the focus has changed. *FrmSetFocus* ends up calling *FldGrabFocus* anyway.

### *Field "gotchas"*

As might be expected with such a complicated type of field, there are a number of things to watch out for in your code:

*Preventing deallocation of a handle*

When a form containing a field is closed, the field frees its handle (with *FldFreeMemory*). In some cases, this is fine (for instance, if the field automatically allocated the handle because the user started writing into an empty field). In other cases, it is not. For example, when you've used *FldSetTextHandle* so that a field will edit your handle, you may not want the handle deallocated—you may want to deallocate it yourself or retain it.

To prevent the field from deallocating your handle, call *FldSetTextHandle(fld, NULL)* to set the field's text handle to `NULL`. Do this when your form receives a `frmCloseEvent`.

*Preventing memory leaks*

When you call *FldSetTextHandle*, any existing handle in the field is not automatically deallocated. To prevent memory leaks, you'll normally want to:

1. Get the old handle with *FldGetTextHandle*
2. Set the new handle with *FldSetTextHandle*
3. Deallocate the old handle

*Don't use FldSetTextPtr and FldSetTextHandle together*
: *FldSetTextPtr* should be used only for noneditable fields for which you'll never call *FldSetTextHandle.* The two routines do not work well together.

*Remove the handle when editing a field*
: If you're going to modify the text within a field's handle, first remove the handle from the field with *FldSetTextHandle(fld, NULL)*, modify the text, and then set the handle back again.

*Compacting string handles*
: The length of the handle in a field may be longer than the length of the string itself, since a field expands a handle in chunks. When a handle has been edited with a field, call *FldCompactText* to shrink the handle to the length of the string (actually, one longer than the length of the string for the trailing null byte).

## Scrollbar Objects

A scrollbar doesn't know anything about scrolling or about any other form objects. It is just a form object that stores a current number, along with a minimum and maximum. The user interface effect is a result of the scrollbar's allowing the user to modify that number graphically within the constraints of the minimum and maximum.

Scrollbars were introduced in Palm OS 2.0 and therefore aren't available in the 1.0 OS. If you intend to run on 1.0 systems, your code will need to do something about objects that rely on scrollbars.

### Scrollbar coding requirements

There are a few things that you need to handle in your code:

- You must respond to a change in the scrollbar's current value by scrolling the objects the scrollbar is supposed to be moving over.

  Here is how you do that. Your event handler receives a `sclRepeatEvent` while the user holds the stylus down and a `sclExitEvent` when the user releases the stylus. Your code is on the lookout for one or the other event, depending on whether your application wants to scroll immediately (as the user is scrolling with the scrollbar) or postpone the scrolling until the user has gotten to the final scroll position with the scrollbar.

- You must change the scrollbar if the current scroll position changes through other appropriate user actions; for example, if the user pushes the built-in Scroll buttons or does drag-scrolling through text.

- You must change the scrollbar if the scroll maximum value changes. It would do so, for example, when typing changes the total number of lines. A field sends a `fldChangedEvent` at this point if its resource attribute `hasScrollbar` is set.

### *Updating the scrollbar based on the insertion point*

Let's look at the code for a sample application that has a field connected to a scrollbar. We need a routine that will update the scrollbar based on the current insertion point, field height, and number of text lines (*FldGetScrollValues* is designed to return these values):

```
static void UpdateScrollbar(void)
{
   FormPtr        frm = FrmGetActiveForm();
   ScrollBarPtr   scroll;
   FieldPtr       field;
   Word           currentPosition;
   Word           textHeight;
   Word           fieldHeight;
   Word           maxValue;

   field = FrmGetObjectPtr(frm, FrmGetObjectIndex(frm, Main1Field));
   FldGetScrollValues(field, &currentPosition, &textHeight, &fieldHeight);

   // if the field is 3 lines, and the text height is 4 lines
   // then we can scroll so that the first line is at the top
   // (scroll position 0) or so the second line is at the top
   // (scroll postion 1). These two values are enough to see
   // the entire text.
   if (textHeight > fieldHeight)
      maxValue = textHeight - fieldHeight;
   else if (currentPosition)
      maxValue = currentPosition;
   else
      maxValue = 0;

   scroll = FrmGetObjectPtr(frm, FrmGetObjectIndex(frm, MainMyScrollBar));

   // on a page scroll, want to overlap by one line (to provide context)
   SclSetScrollBar(scroll, currentPosition, 0, maxValue, fieldHeight - 1);
}
```

We update the scrollbar when the form is initially opened:

```
static void MainViewInit(void)
{
   UpdateScrollbar();
   // Draw the form.
   FrmDrawForm(FrmGetActiveForm());
}
```

### *Updating the scrollbar when the number of lines changes*

We've also got to update the scrollbar whenever the number of lines in the field changes. Since we set the **hasScrollbar** attribute of the field in the resource, when the lines change, the **fldChangedEvent** passes to our event handler (in fact, this is the only reason for the existence of the **hasScrollbar** attribute). Here's the code we put in the event handler:

```
case fldChangedEvent:
   UpdateScrollbar();
   handled = true;
   break;
```

At this point, the scrollbar updates automatically as the text changes.

### *Updating the display when the scrollbar moves*

Next, we've got to handle changes made via the scrollbar. Of the two choices open to us, we want to scroll immediately, so we handle the **sclRepeatEvent**:

```
case sclRepeatEvent:
   ScrollLines(event->data.sclRepeat.newValue -
      event->data.sclRepeat.value, false);
   break;
```

*ScrollLines* is responsible for scrolling the text field (using *FldScrollField*). Things can get tricky, however, if there are empty lines at the end of the field. When the user scrolls up, the number of lines is reduced. Thus, we have to make sure the scrollbar gets updated to reflect this change (note that up and down are constant enumerations defined in the Palm OS include files):

```
static void ScrollLines(int numLinesToScroll, Boolean redraw)
{
   FormPtr        frm = FrmGetActiveForm();
   FieldPtr       field;

   field = FrmGetObjectPtr(frm, FrmGetObjectIndex(frm, Main1Field));
   if (numLinesToScroll < 0)
      FldScrollField(field, -numLinesToScroll, up);
   else
      FldScrollField(field, numLinesToScroll, down);

   // if there are blank lines at the end and we scroll up, FldScrollField
   // makes the blank lines disappear. Therefore, we've got to update
   // the scrollbar
   if ((FldGetNumberOfBlankLines(field) && numLinesToScroll < 0) ||
      redraw)
      UpdateScrollbar();
}
```

#### *Updating the display when the scroll buttons are used*

Next on the list of things to do is handling the Scroll buttons. When the user taps either of the Scroll buttons, we receive a `keyDownEvent`. Here's the code in our event handler that takes care of these buttons:

```
case keyDownEvent:
  if (event->data.keyDown.chr == pageUpChr) {
      PageScroll(up);
      handled = true;
    } else if (event->data.keyDown.chr == pageDownChr) {
      PageScroll(down);
      handled = true;
   }
   break;
```

#### *Scrolling a full page*

Finally, here's our page scrolling function. Of course, we don't want to scroll if we've already scrolled as far as we can. *FldScrollable* tells us if we can scroll in a particular direction. We use *ScrollLines* to do the actual scrolling and rely on it to update the scrollbar:

```
static void PageScroll(DirectionType direction)
{
   FormPtr        frm = FrmGetActiveForm();
   FieldPtr       field;

   field = FrmGetObjectPtr(frm, FrmGetObjectIndex(frm, Main1Field));
   if (FldScrollable(field, direction)) {
      int linesToScroll = FldGetVisibleLines(field) - 1;

      if (direction == up)
         linesToScroll = -linesToScroll;
      ScrollLines(linesToScroll, true);
   }
}
```

# *Resources, Forms, and Form Objects in the Sales Application*

Now that we have given you general information about resources, forms, and form objects, we will add them to the Sales application. We'll show you the resource definitions of all the forms, alerts, and help text. We won't show you all the code, however, as it would get exceedingly repetitious and not teach you anything new. In particular, we won't show the code to bring up every alert. We also postpone adding the table to the order form until "Tables in the Sample Application" on page 218.

We cover the forms and the code for them in order of increasing complexity. This yields the following sequence:

- Alerts
- The Delete Customer dialog
- The Edit Customer form
- The Item Details form
- The Customers form
- Switching forms

All the resources are shown in text as PilRC format. (This format is easier to explain than a bunch of screen dumps from Constructor.)

## Alerts

Here are the defines for the alert IDs and for the buttons in the Delete Item alert (this is the alert that has more than one button):

```
#define RomIncompatibleAlert                          1001
#define DeleteItemAlert                               1201
#define DeleteItemOK                                  0
#define DeleteItemCancel                              1
#define NoItemSelectedAlert                           1000
#define AboutBoxAlert                                 1100
```

Here are the alerts themselves:

```
ALERT ID NoItemSelectedAlert
INFORMATION
BEGIN
    TITLE "Select Item"
    MESSAGE "You must have an item selected to perform this command. " \
            "To select an item, tap on the product name of the item."
    BUTTONS "OK"
END
ALERT ID RomIncompatibleAlert
ERROR
BEGIN
    TITLE "System Incompatible"
    MESSAGE "System Version 2.0 or greater is required to run this " \
            "application."
    BUTTONS "OK"
END

ALERT ID DeleteItemAlert
CONFIRMATION
BEGIN
    TITLE "Delete Item"
    MESSAGE "Delete selected order item?"
    BUTTONS "OK" "Cancel"
END
```

```
ALERT ID AboutBoxAlert
INFORMATION
BEGIN
   TITLE "Sales v. 1.0"
   MESSAGE "This application is from the book \"Palm Programming: The " \
      Developer's Guide\" by Neil Rhodes and Julie McKeehan."
   BUTTONS "OK"
END
```

We won't show every call to *FrmAlert* (the call that displays each of these alerts). Here, however, is a piece of code from *OrderHandleMenuEvent*, which shows two calls to *FrmAlert*. The code is called when the user chooses to delete an item. If nothing is selected, we put up an alert to notify the user of that. If an item is selected, we put up an alert asking if they really want to delete it:

```
if (!gCellSelected)
   FrmAlert(NoItemSelectedAlert);
else if (FrmAlert(DeleteItemAlert) == DeleteItemOK) {
     // code to delete an item
}
```

## Delete Customer

Our Delete Customer dialog has a checkbox in it, so we can't use an alert. We use a modal form, instead. Here are the resources for the form:

```
#define DeleteCustomerForm                      1400
#define DeleteCustomerOKButton                  1404
#define DeleteCustomerCancelButton              1405
#define DeleteCustomerSaveBackupCheckbox        1403
```

We have only one define to add:

```
#define DeleteCustomerHelpString                          1400
```

Here is the Delete Customer dialog:

```
STRING ID DeleteCustomerHelpString "The Save Backup Copy option will " \
   "store deleted records in an archive file on your desktop computer " \
   "at the next HotSync. Some records will be hidden but not deleted " \
   "until then."

FORM ID DeleteCustomerForm AT (2 40 156 118)
MODAL
SAVEBEHIND
HELPID DeleteCustomerHelpString
BEGIN
   TITLE "Delete Customer"
   FORMBITMAP AT (13 29) BITMAP 10005
   LABEL "Delete selected customer?" ID 1402 AT (42 30) FONT 1
   CHECKBOX "Save backup copy on PC?" ID DeleteCustomerSaveBackupCheckbox
      AT (12 68 140 12) LEFTANCHOR  FONT 1 GROUP 0 CHECKED
   BUTTON "OK" ID DeleteCustomerOKButton AT (12 96 36 12) LEFTANCHOR FRAME
      FONT 0
```

```
    BUTTON "Cancel" ID DeleteCustomerCancelButton AT (56 96 36 12)
        LEFTANCHOR FRAME FONT 0
END
```

The bitmap is a resource in the system ROM; the Palm OS header files define `ConfirmationAlertBitmap` as its resource ID.

Here's the code that displays the dialog. Note that we set the value of the checkbox before calling *FrmDoDialog*. We take a look at it again to see if the user has changed the value after *FrmDoDialog* returns but before we delete the form:

```
static Boolean AskDeleteCustomer(void)
{
    FormPtr  previousForm = FrmGetActiveForm();
    FormPtr frm = FrmInitForm(DeleteCustomerForm);
    Word  hitButton;
    Word  ctlIndex;

    FrmSetActiveForm(frm);
    // Set the "save backup" checkbox to its previous setting.
    ctlIndex = FrmGetObjectIndex(frm, DeleteCustomerSaveBackupCheckbox);
    FrmSetControlValue(frm, ctlIndex, gSaveBackup);

    hitButton = FrmDoDialog(frm);
    if (hitButton == DeleteCustomerOKButton)
    {
        gSaveBackup = FrmGetControlValue(frm, ctlIndex);
    }
    if (previousForm)
        FrmSetActiveForm(previousForm);
    FrmDeleteForm(frm);
    return hitButton == DeleteCustomerOKButton;
}
```

## Edit Customer

We have a bunch of resources for the Edit Customer form. Here are the `#defines`:

```
#define CustomerForm                                    1300
#define CustomerOKButton                                1303
#define CustomerCancelButton                            1304
#define CustomerDeleteButton                            1305
#define CustomerPrivateCheckbox                         1310
#define CustomerNameField                               1302
#define CustomerAddressField                            1307
#define CustomerCityField                               1309
#define CustomerPhoneField                              1313
```

Now we get down to business and create the form:

```
FORM ID CustomerForm AT (2 20 156 138)
MODAL
SAVEBEHIND
HELPID CustomerhelpString
```

```
MENUID DialogWithInputFieldMenuBar
BEGIN
   TITLE "Customer Information"
   LABEL "Name:" AUTOID AT (15 29) FONT 1
   FIELD ID CustomerNameField AT (54 29 97 13) LEFTALIGN FONT 0 UNDERLINED
      MULTIPLELINES MAXCHARS 80
   BUTTON "OK" ID CustomerOKButton AT (7 119 36 12) LEFTANCHOR FRAME
      FONT 0
   BUTTON "Cancel" ID CustomerCancelButton AT (49 119 36 12) LEFTANCHOR
      FRAME FONT 0
   BUTTON "Delete" ID CustomerDeleteButton AT (93 119 36 12) LEFTANCHOR
      FRAME FONT 0
   LABEL "Address:" AUTOID AT (10 46) FONT 1
   FIELD ID CustomerAddressField AT (49 46 97 13) LEFTALIGN FONT 0
      UNDERLINED MULTIPLELINES MAXCHARS 80
   LABEL "City:" AUTOID AT (11 67) FONT 1
   FIELD ID CustomerCityField AT (53 66 97 13) LEFTALIGN FONT 0 UNDERLINED
      MULTIPLELINES MAXCHARS 80
   CHECKBOX "" ID CustomerPrivateCheckbox AT (54 101 19 12) LEFTANCHOR
      FONT  0 GROUP 0
   LABEL "Private:" AUTOID AT (9 102) FONT 1
   LABEL "Phone:" AUTOID AT (12 86) FONT 1
   FIELD ID CustomerPhoneField AT (51 86 97 13) LEFTALIGN FONT 0
      UNDERLINED  MULTIPLELINES MAXCHARS 80
END
```

Here's the event handler for the form. It's responsible for bringing up the Delete Customer dialog if the user taps on the Delete button:

```
static Boolean CustomerHandleEvent(EventPtr event)
{
#ifdef __GNUC__
   CALLBACK_PROLOGUE
#endif
   if (event->eType == ctlSelectEvent &&
      event->data.ctlSelect.controlID == CustomerDeleteButton) {
      if (!AskDeleteCustomer())
         return true;   // don't bail out if they cancel the delete dialog
   } else if (event->eType == menuEvent) {
      if (HandleCommonMenuItems(event->data.menu.itemID))
         return true;
   }
#ifdef __GNUC__
   CALLBACK_EPILOGUE
#endif
   return false;
}
```

Last, but not least, here is the code that makes sure the customer was handled correctly:

```
static void EditCustomerWithSelection(UInt recordNumber, Boolean isNew,
   Boolean *deleted, Boolean *hidden, struct frmGoto *gotoData)
{
   FormPtr  previousForm = FrmGetActiveForm();
   FormPtr  frm;
```

```
UInt      hitButton;
Boolean   dirty = false;
ControlPtr  privateCheckbox;
UInt      attributes;
Boolean     isSecret;
FieldPtr nameField;
FieldPtr addressField;
FieldPtr cityField;
FieldPtr phoneField;
Customer theCustomer;
UInt      offset = offsetof(PackedCustomer, name);
VoidHand    customerHandle = DmGetRecord(gCustomerDB, recordNumber);

*hidden = *deleted = false;
// code deleted that initializes isSecret based on the record

frm = FrmInitForm(CustomerForm);
FrmSetEventHandler(frm, CustomerHandleEvent);
FrmSetActiveForm(frm);

UnpackCustomer(&theCustomer, MemHandleLock(customerHandle));

nameField = GetObjectFromActiveForm(CustomerNameField);
addressField = GetObjectFromActiveForm(CustomerAddressField);
cityField = GetObjectFromActiveForm(CustomerCityField);
phoneField = GetObjectFromActiveForm(CustomerPhoneField);

SetFieldTextFromStr(CustomerNameField,     (CharPtr) theCustomer.name);
SetFieldTextFromStr(CustomerAddressField,
   (CharPtr) theCustomer.address);
SetFieldTextFromStr(CustomerCityField,     (CharPtr) theCustomer.city);
SetFieldTextFromStr(CustomerPhoneField,    (CharPtr) theCustomer.phone);

// select one of the fields
if (gotoData && gotoData->matchFieldNum) {
   FieldPtr selectedField =
      GetObjectFromActiveForm(gotoData->matchFieldNum);
   FldSetScrollPosition(selectedField, gotoData->matchPos);
   FrmSetFocus(frm, FrmGetObjectIndex(frm, gotoData->matchFieldNum));
   FldSetSelection(selectedField, gotoData->matchPos,
      gotoData->matchPos + gotoData->matchLen);
} else {
   FrmSetFocus(frm, FrmGetObjectIndex(frm, CustomerNameField));
   FldSetSelection(nameField, 0, FldGetTextLength(nameField));
}
// unlock the customer
MemHandleUnlock(customerHandle);

privateCheckbox = GetObjectFromActiveForm(CustomerPrivateCheckbox);
CtlSetValue(privateCheckbox, isSecret);

hitButton = FrmDoDialog(frm);

if (hitButton == CustomerOKButton) {
   dirty = FldDirty(nameField) || FldDirty(addressField) ||
      FldDirty(cityField) || FldDirty(phoneField);
```

```
        if (dirty) {
            theCustomer.name = FldGetTextPtr(nameField);
            if (!theCustomer.name)
                theCustomer.name = "";
            theCustomer.address = FldGetTextPtr(addressField);
            if (!theCustomer.address)
                theCustomer.address = "";
            theCustomer.city = FldGetTextPtr(cityField);
            if (!theCustomer.city)
                theCustomer.city = "";
            theCustomer.phone = FldGetTextPtr(phoneField);
            if (!theCustomer.phone)
                theCustomer.phone = "";
        }
        PackCustomer(&theCustomer, customerHandle);
        if (CtlGetValue(privateCheckbox) != isSecret) {
            // code deleted that sets information about secret records
        }
    }

    if (hitButton == CustomerDeleteButton) {
        // code deleted that deletes the record
    }
    else if (hitButton == CustomerOKButton && isNew &&
        !(StrLen(theCustomer.name) || StrLen(theCustomer.address) ||
        StrLen(theCustomer.city) || StrLen(theCustomer.phone))) {
        // code deleted that deletes the record
    }
    else if (hitButton == CustomerCancelButton && isNew) {
        // code deleted that deletes the record
    }

    if (previousForm)
        FrmSetActiveForm(previousForm);
    FrmDeleteForm(frm);
}
```

Note that in the code we set *CustomerHandleEvent* as the event handler, and we initialize each of the text fields before calling *FrmDoDialog*. After the call to *FrmDoDialog*, the text from the text fields is copied if the OK button was pressed and any of the fields have been changed.

## Item Details

This modal dialog allows editing the quantity and product for an item. The interesting part of this dialog is the pop-up trigger that contains both product categories and products.

The code uses the following globals:

```
static UInt         gCurrentCategory = 0;
static Long         gCurrentSelectedItemIndex = -1;
static UInt         gNumCategories;
```

`gCurrentCategory` contains the current category number. `ProductsOffset-InList` shows where in the list the products start.

When the Item Details form opens, here is the code that gets called:

```
static void ItemFormOpen(void)
{
   ListPtr  list;

   FormPtr  frm = FrmGetActiveForm();
   FieldPtr fld = GetObjectFromActiveForm(ItemQuantityField);
   char  quantityString[kMaxNumericStringLength];

   // initialize quantity
   StrIToA(quantityString, gCurrentItem->quantity);
   SetFieldTextFromStr(ItemQuantityField, quantityString);

   // select entire quantity (so it doesn't have to be selected before
   // writing a new quantity)
   FrmSetFocus(frm, FrmGetObjectIndex(frm, ItemQuantityField));
   FldSetSelection(fld, 0, StrLen(quantityString));

   list = GetObjectFromActiveForm(ItemProductsList);
   LstSetDrawFunction(list, DrawOneProductInList);

   if (gCurrentItem->productID) {
      Product  p;
      VoidHand h;
      UInt     index;
      UInt     attr;

      h = GetProductFromProductID(gCurrentItem->productID, &p, &index);
      ErrNonFatalDisplayIf(!h, "can't get product for existing item");
      // deleted code that sets finds attr--the category;
      SelectACategory(list, attr & dmRecAttrCategoryMask);
      LstSetSelection(list,
         DmPositionInCategory(gProductDB, index, gCurrentCategory) +
         (gNumCategories + 1));

      CtlSetLabel(GetObjectFromActiveForm(ItemProductPopTrigger),
         (CharPtr) p.name);
      MemHandleUnlock(h);
   } else
      SelectACategory(list, gCurrentCategory);
}
```

First, we set the quantity field. Next, we set a custom draw function. Finally, if the current item already has a product selected, we initialize the list using *SelectACategory*. We use *LstSetSelection* to set the current list selection and *CtlSetLabel* to set the label of the trigger. If no product is selected, we initialize the list using whatever category has been previously used.

Here's *SelectACategory*, which sets the current category, initializes the list with the correct number of items, and sets the list height (the number of items shown concurrently):

```
static void SelectACategory(ListPtr list, UInt newCategory)
{
   Word     numItems;

   gCurrentCategory = newCategory;
   // code deleted that sets numItems based on the
   // product category
   LstSetHeight(list, numItems);
   LstSetListChoices(list, NULL, numItems);
}
```

When the user taps on the trigger, the list is shown. We've used *DrawOneProductInList* to draw the list. It draws the categories at the top (with the current category in bold), a separator line, and then the products for that category:

```
static void DrawOneProductInList(UInt itemNumber, RectanglePtr bounds,
   CharPtr *text)
{
   FontID   curFont;
   Boolean  setFont = false;
   const char  *toDraw = "";

#ifdef __GNUC__
   CALLBACK_PROLOGUE
#endif
   if (itemNumber == gCurrentCategory) {
      curFont = FntSetFont(boldFont);
      setFont = true;
   }
   if (itemNumber == gNumCategories)
      toDraw = "---";
   else if (itemNumber < gNumCategories) {
      // code deleted that sets toDraw based on category name
   } else {
      // code deleted that sets toDraw based on product name
   }
   DrawCharsToFitWidth(toDraw, bounds);
   if (setFont)
      FntSetFont(curFont);
#ifdef __GNUC__
   CALLBACK_EPILOGUE
#endif
}
```

When the user selects an item from the pop-up, a `popSelectEvent` is generated. Here's the event handler for that event:

```
static Boolean ItemHandleEvent(EventPtr event)
{
   Boolean     handled = false;
```

```
#ifdef __GNUC__
   CALLBACK_PROLOGUE
#endif
   switch (event->eType) {
      // code deleted that handles other kinds of events

      case popSelectEvent:
         if (event->data.popSelect.listID == ItemProductsList){
            HandleClickInProductPopup(event);
            handled = true;
         }
         break;

      }
#ifdef __GNUC__
   CALLBACK_EPILOGUE
#endif
   return handled;
}
```

*HandleClickInProductPopup* actually handles the selection. If a product is selected, the trigger's label is updated (as is the item). If a new category is selected, the list is updated with a new category, and *CtlHitControl* is called to simulate tapping again on the trigger. This makes the list reappear without work on the user's part:

```
static void HandleClickInProductPopup(EventPtr event)
{
   ListPtr     list = event->data.popSelect.listP;
   ControlPtr  control = event->data.popSelect.controlP;

   if (event->data.popSelect.selection < (gNumCategories + 1)) {
      if (event->data.popSelect.selection < gNumCategories)
         SelectACategory(list, event->data.popSelect.selection);
      LstSetSelection(list, gCurrentCategory);
      CtlHitControl(control);
   } else {
      // code deleted that sets s.name to product name
      CtlSetLabel(control, (CharPtr) s.name);
   }
}
```

## Customers Form

Here's the form containing only one form object, the list. Here are the resource definitions of the form, the list, and a menu:

```
#define CustomersForm                             1000
#define CustomersCustomersList                    1002
#define CustomersMenuBar                          1000
```

Here is the Customers form:

```
FORM ID CustomersForm AT (0 0 160 160)
MENUID CustomersCustomerMenu
```

```
BEGIN
    TITLE "Sales"
    LIST "" ID CustomersCustomersList AT (0 15 160 132) DISABLED FONT 0
END
```

Our initialization routine (which we call on a `frmOpenEvent`) sets the draw function callback for the list and sets the number (by calling *InitNumberCustomers*):

```
static void CustomersFormOpen(void)
{
   ListPtr  list = GetObjectFromActiveForm(CustomersCustomersList);
   InitNumberCustomers();
   LstSetDrawFunction(list, DrawOneCustomerInListWithFont);

   // code deleted that sets different menus on a pre-3.0 device
}
```

*InitNumberCustomers* calls *LstSetListChoices* to set the number of elements in the list. It is called when the form is opened and when the number of customers changes (this happens if a customer is added):

```
static void InitNumberCustomers(void)
{
   ListPtr  list = GetObjectFromActiveForm(CustomersCustomersList);
   // code deleted that sets numCustomers from the databas
   LstSetListChoices(list, NULL, numCustomers);
}
```

Our event handler handles an open event by calling *CustomersFormOpen*, then draws the form:

```
case frmOpenEvent:
   CustomersFormOpen();
   FrmDrawForm(FrmGetActiveForm());
   handled = true;
   break;
```

A `lstSelectEvent` is sent when the user taps (and releases) on a list entry. Our event handler calls *OpenNthCustomer* to open the Order form for that customer:

```
case lstSelectEvent:
   OpenNthCustomer(event->data.lstSelect.selection);
   handled = true;
   break;
```

*OpenNthCustomer* calls *SwitchForm* to switch to a different form:

```
static void OpenNthCustomer(UInt customerIndex)
{
   Long  customerID = GetCustomerIDForNthCustomer(customerIndex);

   if ((gCurrentOrder =  GetOrCreateOrderForCustomer(
      customerID, &gCurrentOrderIndex)) != NULL)
      SwitchForm(OrderForm);
}
```

*SwitchForm* calls *FrmGotoForm* to open a new form (and to save the ID of the new form):

```
static void SwitchForm(Word formID)
{
   FrmGotoForm(formID);
   gCurrentView = formID;
}
```

The event handler has to handle the up and down scroll keys. It calls the list to do the actual scrolling (note that we scroll by one row at a time, instead of by an entire page):

```
case keyDownEvent:
   if (event->data.keyDown.chr == pageUpChr ||
      event->data.keyDown.chr == pageDownChr) {
      ListPtr  list = GetObjectFromActiveForm(CustomersCustomersList);
      enum directions   d;
      if (event->data.keyDown.chr == pageUpChr)
         d = up;
      else
         d = down;
      LstScrollList(list, d, 1);
   }
   handled = true;
   break;
```

When a new customer is created, code in *CustomerHandleMenuEvent* calls *EditCustomer* to put up a modal dialog for the user to enter the new customer data. When the modal dialog is dismissed, the Form Manager automatically restores the contents of the Customers form. The Customers form also needs to be redrawn, as a new customer has been added to the list. *CustomerHandleMenuEvent* calls *FrmUpdateForm*, which sends our event handler a `frmUpdateEvent`:

```
EditCustomer(recordNumber, true);
FrmUpdateForm(CustomersForm, frmRedrawUpdateCode);
```

By default, the Form Manager redraws the form when a `frmUpdateEvent` occurs. However, it doesn't erase the form first. We need to have the list erased before it is redrawn, since we've changed the contents of the list. So, we erase the list with *LstEraseList* and then update the list with the new number of customers. We set `handled` to `false` so the default behavior (redrawing the form) will occur.

```
case frmUpdateEvent:
   LstEraseList(GetObjectFromActiveForm(CustomersCustomersList));
   InitNumberCustomers();
   handled = false;
   break;
```

## Switching Forms

The *ApplicationHandleEvent* needs to load forms when a **frmLoadEvent** occurs (not necessary for forms shown with *FrmDoDialog*):

```
static Boolean ApplicationHandleEvent(EventPtr event)
{
   FormPtr  frm;
   Int      formId;
   Boolean  handled = false;

   if (event->eType == frmLoadEvent)
   {
      // Load the form resource specified in event then activate the form.
      formId = event->data.frmLoad.formID;
      frm = FrmInitForm(formId);
      FrmSetActiveForm(frm);

      // Set the event handler for the form.  The handler of the currently
      // active form is called by FrmDispatchEvent each time it receives
      // an event.
      switch (formId)
      {
      case OrderForm:
         FrmSetEventHandler(frm, OrderHandleEvent);
         break;

      case CustomersForm:
         FrmSetEventHandler(frm, CustomersHandleEvent);
         break;

      }
      handled = true;
   }
   return handled;
}
```

We keep a variable that tells us which is the current form, the **CustomersForm** or the **OrderForm**. This variable can be saved in the application's preferences entry so that when the application is reopened, it can return to the form the user was last viewing:

```
static Word gCurrentView = CustomersForm;
```

In our *PilotMain*, we open the form specified by **gCurrentView**. We also check to make sure that we're running on a 2.0 OS or greater (since we want our application to take advantage of some calls not present in the 1.0 OS):

```
error = RomVersionCompatible(0x02000000, launchFlags);
if (error)
   return error;
```

```
if (cmd == sysAppLaunchCmdNormalLaunch)
{
   error = StartApplication();
   if (!error)
   {
      FrmGotoForm(gCurrentView);
      EventLoop();

      StopApplication();
   }
}
```

The *RomVersionCompatible* checks whether the OS version of the handheld device is at least that required to run. It puts up an alert telling the user that a newer OS is required (only if the application's launch flags specify that it should interact with the user):

```
static Err RomVersionCompatible(DWord requiredVersion, Word launchFlags)
{
   DWord         romVersion;
   // See if we're on a minimum required version of the ROM or later.
   // The system records the version number in a feature.  A feature is a
   // piece of information that can be looked up by a creator and feature
   // number.
   FtrGet(sysFtrCreator, sysFtrNumROMVersion, &romVersion);
   if (romVersion < requiredVersion)
      {
      // If the user launched the app from the launcher, explain
      // why the app shouldn't run.  If the app was contacted for
      // something else, like it was asked to find a string by the
      // system find, then don't bother the user with a warning dialog.
      // These flags tell how the app was launched to decided if a
      // warning should be displayed.
      if ((launchFlags &
         (sysAppLaunchFlagNewGlobals | sysAppLaunchFlagUIApp))
         == (sysAppLaunchFlagNewGlobals | sysAppLaunchFlagUIApp)) {
         FrmAlert(RomIncompatibleAlert);

         // Pilot 1.0 will continuously relaunch this app unless we switch
         // to another safe one.  The sysFileCDefaultApp is
         // considered "safe".
         if (romVersion < 0x02000000) {
            Err err;

            AppLaunchWithCommand(sysFileCDefaultApp,
               sysAppLaunchCmdNormalLaunch, NULL);
         }
      }
      return sysErrRomIncompatible;
   }
   return 0;
}
```

That is all there is of interest to the resources, forms, and form objects in the Sales application. This material took so much space simply because of the large number of objects we needed to show you, rather than because of the complexity of the subject material. This is all good news, however, as a rich set of forms and form objects means greater flexibility in the types of applications you can create for Palm OS devices.

*In this chapter:*
- *Overview of Databases and Records*
- *Creating, Opening, and Closing Databases*
- *Working with Records*
- *Examining Databases in the Sales Sample*

# 6

# Databases

As we described earlier, permanent data resides in memory. This memory is divided into two sections: the dynamic and storage heaps. Permanent data resides in the storage heap and is controlled by the Data Manager (the dynamic heap is managed strictly by the Memory Manager).

Data is organized into two components: databases and records. The relationship between the two is straightforward. A database is a related collection of records. Records are relocatable blocks of memory (handles). An individual record can't exceed 64KB in size.

## Overview of Databases and Records

A database, as a collection of records, maintains certain key information about each record (see Figure 6-1):

- The location of the record.
- A three-byte unique ID. This ID is unique only within a given database. It is assigned automatically by the Data Manager when the record is created.
- A one-byte attribute. This attribute contains a 4-bit category: a deleted bit, an archived bit, a busy bit, and a secret (or private) bit.

In the Palm 3.0 OS, there is one large storage heap; in previous versions, there were many small ones. A database resides in a storage heap, but its records need not be in the same heap (see Figure 6-1).

Databases also contain the following other types of information:

*An application info block*
: This usually contains category names as well as any other database-wide information.

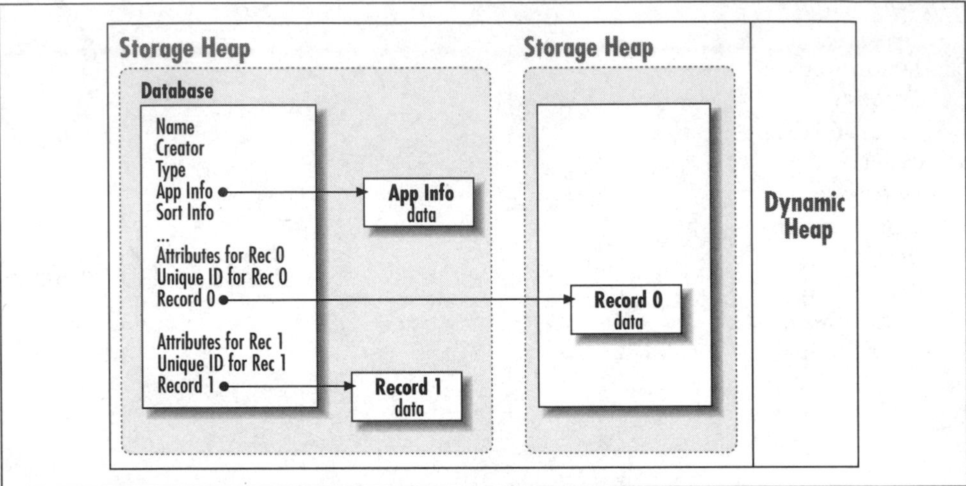


*Figure 6-1. Database with two records in a database in persistent memory*

*A sort info block*

This is where you store a list of record numbers in a variant order. For example, address book entries might be sorted by company rather than by a person's name. Most applications don't use a sort info block.

*Name, type, and creator*

Databases are created with a name (which must be unique), a type, and a creator. When a user deletes an application, the Palm OS automatically deletes all databases that share the same creator. The preferences record is removed at the same time. So that this cleanup can happen correctly, it's important that your databases use the creator of their application.

## Write-Protected Memory

In order to maintain the integrity of the storage heap, it is hardware write-protected. This ensures that a rogue application referencing a stray pointer can't accidentally destroy important data or applications. Therefore, changes to the databases can only be made through the Data Manager API. These APIs check that writes are made only within an allocated chunk of memory—writes to random areas or past the end of an allocated chunk are not allowed.

## Palm 3.0 OS Heap Changes

In pre-3.0 versions of the OS, a database heap is limited to at most 64KB. The persistent area of memory is therefore divided into many different database heaps. In this pre-3.0 world, it is much harder to manage memory, since each allocated record must fit within one heap. The 3.0 OS does not have that 64KB limit on database heaps. Instead, the persistent memory area contains just one large database heap.

The multiple database heaps lead to a problem: although there is free memory available, there might not be enough available for a record. The situation occurs when you have, for example, 10 databases heaps, each of size 64KB, and each half full. Although there is 320KB memory available, a record of size 40KB can't be allocated (because no single heap can hold it). The original 1.0 OS exacerbated this problem with an ill-chosen strategy for database allocations: records were allocated by attempting to keep heaps equally full. This made large record allocations more and more difficult as previous allocations were made.

The 2.0 OS switched to a first-fit strategy (a record is allocated in the first heap in which it will fit). A change to the 2.0 OS (found in the System Update 2.0.4) modified the strategy (if there isn't room in an existing heap for a chunk, chunks from the most empty heap are moved out of that heap until there is enough space). It isn't until 3.0, however, that a full fix (one large heap) is in place.

## Where Databases Are Stored

Although all current Palm OS devices have only one memory card, the Palm OS supports multiple cards. Cards are numbered, starting with the internal card, which is 0. When you create a database, you specify the card on which it is created. If and when multiple cards are supported, there will need to be some user interface to decide default locations. Until that time, you create your databases on card 0.

While creating databases on card 0 is fine, other code in the application shouldn't rely on the value of the card being 0. By not hardcoding this value, the application will work with multiple card devices.

## How Records Are Stored Versus How They Are Referenced

While your application is running, reference database records using handles. Database records are not stored this way, however. Within the database heap they are stored as local IDs. A local ID is an offset from the beginning of the card on which it is located. Because items are stored this way, the base address of the card can change without requiring any changes in the database heap.

A future Palm device OS with multiple card slots would have separate base addresses for each slot. Thus, the memory address for a chunk on a memory card would depend on what slot it was in (and thus what its base address was).

This is relevant to your job as an application writer when you get to the application info block in the Database. Application info (and sort info) blocks are stored as local IDs. Also, if you need to store a reference to a memory chunk within a record, you can't store a handle (because they are valid only while your application is running). Instead, you'd need to convert the handle to a local ID (using a Memory Manager function) and store the local ID.

# Creating, Opening, and Closing Databases

You handle these standard operations in a straightforward manner in Palm applications.

## Creating a Database

To create a database, you normally use *DmCreateDatabase*:

```
Err DmCreateDatabase(UInt cardNo, CharPtr nameP, ULong creator,
     ULong type, Boolean resDB)
```

The `creator` is the unique creator you've registered at the Palm developer web site (*http://www.palm.com/devzone*). You use the `type` to distinguish between multiple databases with different types of information in them. The `nameP` is the name of the database, and it *must be unique*.

Until Palm Developer Support issues guidelines on how to use multiple card numbers, just use 0 as your card number when creating databases.

In order to guarantee that your database name is unique, you need to include your creator as part of your database name. Developer Support recommends that you name your database with two parts, the database name followed by a hyphen (-) and your creator code. An application with a creator of "Neil" that created two databases might name them:

```
Database1-Neil
Database2-Neil
```

### *Create your database in your StartApplication routine*

You normally create your database from within your *StartApplication* routine. This is in cases where the database does not yet exist. Here is a typical code sequence to do that:

```
// Find the Customer database.  If it doesn't exist, create it.
gDB = DmOpenDatabaseByTypeCreator(kCustType, kSalesCreator, mode);
if (! gDB) {
   err = DmCreateDatabase(0, kCustName, kSalesCreator,
      kCustType, false);
   if (err)
      return err;

   gDB = DmOpenDatabaseByTypeCreator(kCustType, kSalesCreator, mode);
   if (!gDB)
      return DmGetLastErr();

   // code to initialize records and application info
}
```

### *Creating a database from an image*

If your application has a database that should be initialized with a predefined set of records, it may make sense to "freeze-dry" a database as a resource in your application. Thus, when you build your application, add an existing database image to it. Then, when your application's *StartApplication* routine is called, if the database doesn't exist, you can create it and initialize it from this freeze dried image.

Of course, you could just provide your user with a Palm database (PDB) file to download. The advantage is that your application is smaller; the disadvantage is that the user might not download the file. In this case, you'd still need to check for the existence of your databases.

Here's an example:

```
gDB = DmOpenDatabaseByTypeCreator(kCustType, kSalesCreator, mode);
if (!gDB) {
   VoidHand imageHandle = DmGetResource('DBIM', 1000);

   err = DmCreateDatabaseFromImage(MemHandleLock(imageHandle));
   MemHandleUnlock(imageHandle);
   DmReleaseResource(imageHandle);

   if (err)
      return err;
   gDB = DmOpenDatabaseByTypeCreator(kCustType, kSalesCreator, mode);
   if (!gDB)
      return DmGetLastErr();
}
```

This code assumes that there's a resource of type `DBIM` with ID 1000 in your application's resource database that contains an appropriate image.

You can create the database on a Palm OS device, and then do a HotSync to back up the database. The file that Palm Desktop creates is a database image (a PDB file).

The exercise of getting a data file into a resource in your application is not covered here. Your development environment determines how you do this.

## Opening a Database

You usually open your database by type and creator with a call like this:

```
gDB = DmOpenDatabaseByTypeCreator(kCustType, kSalesCreator, mode);
```

In your application, use a `mode` of `dmModeReadWrite`, since you may be modifying records in the database. If you know that you aren't making any modifications, then use a `dmModeReadOnly` mode.

If your application supports private records, then you should honor the user's preference of whether to show private records by setting `dmModeShowSecret` to the mode, as necessary. Here's code that adds the `dmModeShowSecret` appropriately:

```
SystemPreferencesType sysPrefs;

// Determine if secret records should be shown.
PrefGetPreferences(&sysPrefs);

if (!sysPrefs.hideSecretRecords)
   mode |= dmModeShowSecret;

gDB = DmOpenDatabaseByTypeCreator(kCustType, kSalesCreator, mode);
```

## Closing a Database

When you are finished with a database, call *DmCloseDatabase*:

```
err = DmCloseDatabase(gDB);
```

Don't leave databases open unnecessarily, because each open database takes approximately 100 bytes of room in the dynamic heap. A good rule of thumb might be that if the user isn't in a view that has access to the data in that database, it shouldn't be open.

Note that when you close a database, records in that database that are locked or busy remain that way. If for some reason your code must close a database while you have locked or busy records, call *DmResetRecordStates* before calling *DmCloseDatabase*:

```
err = DmResetRecordStates(gDB);
err = DmCloseDatabase(gDB);
```

The Data Manager doesn't do this resetting automatically from *DmCloseDatabase* because of the performance penalty. The philosophy is that you shouldn't penalize the vast majority of applications that have released and unlocked all their records. Instead, force the minority of applications to make the extra call and incur the speed penalty in these rare cases.

## *Creating the Application Info Block in a Database*

The application info block is a block of memory that is associated with your database as a whole. You can use it for database-wide information. For example, you might have a database of checks and want to keep the total value of all the checks. Or you might allow the user to choose from among more than one sort order and need to keep track of the current sort order. Or you might need to keep track of category names. In each of these cases, the application info block is an appropriate place to keep this information. Here's a snippet of code (normally used when you create your database) to allocate and initialize the application info block:

```
UInt            cardNo;
LocalID         dbID;
LocalID         appInfoID;
MyAppInfoType   *appInfoP;

if (DmOpenDatabaseInfo(gDB, &dbID, NULL, NULL, &cardNo, NULL))
   return dmErrInvalidParam;

h = DmNewHandle(gDB, sizeof(MyAppInfoType));
if (!h)
   return dmErrMemError;

appInfoID = MemHandleToLocalID(h);
DmSetDatabaseInfo(cardNo, dbID, NULL, NULL, NULL,
   NULL, NULL, NULL, NULL, &appInfoID, NULL, NULL, NULL);

appInfoP = (MyAppInfoType *) MemHandleLock(h);
DmSet(appInfoP, 0, sizeof(MyAppInfoType), 0);

// Code deleted to initialize fields in appInfoP

// Unlock
MemPtrUnlock(appInfoP);
```

Note that you can't use *MemHandleNew* to allocate the block, because you want the block to be in the same heap as the database and not in the dynamic heap.

Therefore, use *DmNewHandle*. Also, you can't directly store the handle in the database. Instead, you must convert it to a local ID.

---

Remember that a local ID is an offset from the beginning of the card. This is necessary for the future in case multiple cards are supported. In such a case, the memory addresses would be dependent on the slot in which the card was placed.

---

If you use the Category Manager to manage your database, you need to make sure the first field in your application info block is of type `AppInfoType` (this stores the mapping from category number to category name). To initialize this field, call *CategoryInitialize*:

```
CategoryInitialize(&appInfoP->appInfo, LocalizedAppInfoStr);
```

The second parameter is the resource ID of an application string list (resource type `tAIS`) that contains the initial category names. You need to add one of these to your resource file (it's common to initialize it with "Unfiled", "Business", and "Personal").

# Working with Records

Now that you know how to set up databases, you need to populate them with records. How you sort and therefore find a record is usually determined when you create it. Let's first look at the mechanics of finding a record. After that, we'll create a new record.

## Finding a Record

If your records are sorted based on the value of a field (or fields) within the record, you can do a binary search to find a particular record. If your records aren't sorted (or you are looking for a record based on the value of an unsorted field), you need to iterate through all the records, testing each record to see whether it is the one you want. "Iterating Through the Records in a Database or Category" later in this chapter shows how to iterate through all records. If you are looking for a unique ID, there's a call to find a record.

### *Finding a record given a unique ID*

If you've got the unique ID, you get the record number using *DmFindRecordByID*:

```
UInt     recordNumber;
err = DmFindRecordByID(gDB, uniqueID, &recordNumber);
```

Note that this search starts at the first record and keeps looking until it finds the one with a matching unique ID.

### *Finding a record given a key*

If you have records sorted by some criterion (see "Sorting the Records in a Database" later in this chapter), you can do a binary search to find a specific record. First, you need to define a comparison routine that compares two records and determines the ordering between the two. Here are the possible orderings:

- The first is greater than the second
- The second is greater than the first
- They are equal

The comparison routine takes six parameters:

- Record 1
- Record 2
- An "other" integer for your own use
- The attributes and unique ID for record 1
- The attributes and unique ID for record 2
- The application info block

The extra parameters (beyond just the records) are there to allow sorting based on further information. This is information found outside the record and includes such things as attributes (its category, for instance), a unique ID, and a specified sort order. The "other" integer parameter is necessary whenever you call a routine that requires a comparison routine; it is then passed on to your comparison routine. This parameter is commonly used to pass a sort order to your sorting routine. Note that the application info block is rarely used as part of a comparison routine—perhaps to sort by alphabetized categories (Business first, then Personal, then Unfiled). Since the category names are stored in the application info block, it's needed by a comparison routine that wants to take into account category names.

Here's an example comparison function that compares first by `lastName` field and then by `firstName` field. The attributes, unique ID, application info block, and extra integer parameter are not used:

```
static Int CompareRecordFunc(MyRecordStruct *rec1, MyRecordStruct *rec2,
   Int unusedInt, SortRecordInfoPtr unused1, SortRecordInfoPtr unused2,
   VoidHand appInfoH)
{
   Int   result;

   result = StrCompare(rec1->lastName, rec2->lastName);
```

```
    if (result == 0)
        result = StrCompare(rec1->firstName, rec2->firstName);
    return result;
}
```

The *DmFindSortPosition* is used to find a record (or to find where a record would be placed if it were in the database). It takes five parameters:

- The database
- The record to search for (filled in with the fields the comparison routine will look for)
- The attributes and the unique ID for the record (necessary because the record you're passing in isn't necessarily part of the database and doesn't really have attributes or a unique ID)
- The comparison function
- The additional integer parameter to be passed to the comparison routine

Here's a search for a specific record. Note that *DmFindSortPosition* returns a number in the range `0..numberOfRecords`. A return result of `0` signifies that the passed-in record is less than any existing records. A return result equal to the number of records signifies that the passed-in record is the last record. A return result, `i`, in the range `1..numberOfRecords-1` signifies that *record* $i-1 \leq$ *passed-in record* < *record i*. Here's a use of *DmFindSortPosition* that finds the record, if present:

```
Boolean           foundIt = false;
MyRecordStruct    findRecord;
UInt              recordNumber;

findRecord.lastName = "Rhodes";
findRecord.firstName = "Neil";
recordNumber = DmFindSortPosition(gDB, &findRecord, 0,
   (DmComparF *) CompareRecordFunc, 0);

if (recordNumber > 0) {
   MyRecordStruct    *record;
   Handle          theRecordHandle;

   theRecordHandle = DmQueryRecord(gDB, recordNumber - 1);

   record = MemHandleLock(theRecordHandle);
   foundIt = StrCompare(findRecord.lastName, record->lastName) == 0 &&
      StrCompare(findRecord.firstName, record->firstName);
   MemHandleUnlock(theOrderHandle);
}
if (foundIt) {
   // recordNumber - 1 is the matching record
} else {
   // record at recordNumber < findRecord < record at recordNumber+1
}
```

## *Creating a New Record*

You create a new record with *DmNewRecord*:

```
myRecordHandle = DmNewRecord(gDB, &recordIndex, recordSize)
```

The `recordSize` is the initial record size; you can change it later with *MemHandleSetSize*, just as you would with any handle. Make sure you specify a positive record size; zero-size records are not valid.

You'll notice that you need to specify the index number of the record as the second parameter. You initialize it with the desired record index; when *DmNewRecord* returns, it contains the actual record index.

Record indexes are zero-based; they range from 0 to one less than the number of records. If your desired record index is in this range, the new record will be created with your desired record index. All the records with that index and above are shifted up (their record indexes are increased by one). If your desired record index is ≥ the number of records, your new record will be created after the last record, and the actual record index will be returned.

### *Adding at the beginning of the database*

To add to the beginning of the database, use 0 as a desired record index:

```
UInt recordIndex = 0;
myRecordHandle = DmNewRecord(gDB, &recordIndex, recordSize)
```

### *Adding at the end of the database*

To add to the end of the database, use `dmMaxRecordIndex` as your desired record index:

```
UInt recordIndex = dmMaxRecordIndex;
myRecordHandle = DmNewRecord(gDB, &recordIndex, recordSize)
// now recordIndex contains the actual index
```

You should rarely add to the end of the database, because archived and deleted records are kept at the end.

### *Adding in sort order*

Use *DmFindSortPosition* to determine where to insert the record:

```
UInt             recordIndex;
MyRecordStruct   newRecord;
VoidHand         myRecordHandle;
MyRecordStruct  *newRecordPtr;

// initialize fields of newRecord
recordIndex = DmFindSortPosition(gDB, &newRecord, 0,
   (DmComparF *) CompareRecordFunc, 0);
```

```
myRecordHandle = DmNewRecord(gDB, &recordIndex, sizeof(MyRecordStruct));
newRecordPtr = MemHandleLock(myRecordHandle);
DmWrite(newRecordPtr, 0, &newRecord, sizeof(newRecord));
MemHandleUnlock(myRecordHandle);
```

The `recordNumber` returned by *DmFindSortPosition* is the record number you use with *DmNewRecord*.

## Reading from a Record

Reading from a record is very simple. Although records are write-protected, they are still in RAM; thus you can just get a record from a database, lock it, and then read from it. Here's an example:

```
VoidHand myRecord = DmQueryRecord(gDB, recordNumber);
StructType *s = MemHandleLock(myRecord);
DoSomethingReadOnlyi(s->field);
MemHandleUnlock(myRecord);
```

The *DmQueryRecord* call returns a record that is read-only; it can't be written to, as it doesn't mark the record as busy.

## Modifying a Record

In order to modify a record, you must use *DmGetRecord*, which marks the record busy. Call *DmReleaseRecord* when you're finished with it. Because you can't just write to the pointer (the storage area is write-protected), you must use either *DmSet* (to set a range to a particular character value) or *DmWrite*.

Often, a record has a structure associated with it. You usually read and write the entire structure:

```
VoidHand myRecord = DmGetRecord(gDB, recordNumber);
StructType *s = MemHandleLock(myRecord);
StructType theStructure;

theStructure = *s;
theStructure.field = newValue;
DmWrite(gDB, s, 0, &theStructure, sizeof(theStructure));
MemHandleUnlock(myRecord);
DmReleaseRecord(gDB, recordNumber, true);
```

Another alternative is to write specific fields in the structure. A very handy thing to use in this case is the standard C `offsetof` macro (`offsetof` returns the offset of a field within a structure):

```
VoidHand myRecord = DmGetRecord(gDB, recordNumber);
StructType *s = MemHandleLock(myRecord);

DmWrite(s, offsetof(StructType, field), &newValue, sizeof(newValue));
MemHandleUnlock(myRecord);
DmReleaseRecord(gDB, recordNumber, true);
```

The second approach has the advantage of writing less data; it writes only the data that needs to change.

The third parameter to *DmReleaseRecord* tells whether the record was actually modified or not. Passing the value true causes the record to be marked as modified. If you modify a record but don't tell *DmReleaseRecord* that you changed it, during a HotSync the database's conduit may not realize the record has been changed.

## Handling Secret Records

In order for a Palm OS user to feel comfortable maintaining sensitive information on his device, the Palm OS supports secret (also called private) records. In the Security application, the user can specify whether to show or hide private records. The user can specify a password that is required before private records are shown.

Each record has a bit associated with it (in the record attributes) that indicates whether it is secret. As part of the mode you use when opening a database, you can request that secret records be skipped. "Opening a Database" on page 144 shows the code you need. Once you make that request, some of the database operations on that open database completely ignore secret records. The routines that take index numbers (like *DmGetRecord* or *DmQueryRecord*) don't ignore secret records, nor does *DmNumRecords*. *DmNumRecordsInCategory* and *DmSeekRecordInCategory* do ignore secret records, though. You can use these to find a correct index number.

The user sets the secret bit of a record in a Details dialog for that record. Here is some code that handles that request:

```
ControlPtr        privateCheckbox;
UInt        attributes;
Boolean        isSecret;

DmRecordInfo(CustomerDB, recordNumber, &attributes, NULL, NULL);
isSecret = (attributes & dmRecAttrSecret) == dmRecAttrSecret;

privateCheckbox = GetObjectFromActiveForm(DetailsPrivateCheckbox);
   CtlSetValue(privateCheckbox, isSecret);

hitButton = FrmDoDialog(frm);

if (hitButton == DetailsOKButton) {
   if (CtlGetValue(privateCheckbox) != isSecret) {
      if (CtlGetValue(privateCheckbox)) {
         attributes |= dmRecAttrSecret;
         // tell user how to hide private records
         if (!gHideSecretRecords)
            FrmAlert(privateRecordInfoAlert);
      } else
         attributes &= ~dmRecAttrSecret;
```

```
        DmSetRecordInfo(CustomerDB, recordNumber, &attributes, NULL);
    }
}
```

Note that we must put up an alert (see Figure 6-2) if the user marks a record as private while show all records is enabled. As we are still showing private records, this might be confusing for a new user, who sees this private checkbox, marks something as private, and expects something to happen as a result.

*Figure 6-2. Alert shown when user marks a record as private while showing private records*

## Iterating Through the Records in a Database or Category

Whether you want only the items in a particular category or all the records, you still need to use category calls. These calls skip over deleted or archived (but still present) and private records (if the database is not opened with `dmModeShowSecret`).

Here's some code to visit every record:

```
UInt theCategory = dmAllCategories;      // could be a specific category
UInt totalItems = DmNumRecordsInCategory(gDB, theCategory);
UInt i;
UInt recordNum = 0;

for (i = 0; i < totalItems; i++) {
   VoidHand recordH = DmQueryNextInCategory (gDB, &recordNum,
      theCategory);
   // at this point, recordNum contains the desired record number.
   // You could use DmGetRecord to get write-access, and then
   // DmReleaseRecord when finished

   // do something with recordH
}
```

## Sorting the Records in a Database

Just as finding an item in a sorted database requires a comparison routine, sorting a database requires a similar routine. There are two different sort routines you can use. The first, *DmInsertionSort*, uses an insertion sort (similar to the way most people sort a hand of cards, placing each card in its proper location one by one). The insertion sort works very quickly on an almost-sorted database. For example, if you change one record in a sorted database it may now be out of place while all the other records are still in sorted order. Use the insertion sort to put it back in order.

The second routine, *DmQuickSort*, uses a *quicksort* (it successively partitions the records). If you don't know anything about the sort state of the database, use the quicksort. Changing the sort order (for instance, by name instead of by creation date) causes all records to be out of order. This is an excellent time to use the quicksort.

*Insertion sort*

```
err = DmInsertionSort(gDB,  (DmComparF *) CompareRecordFunc, 0);
```

*Quicksort*

```
err = DmQuickSort(gDB,  (DmComparF *) CompareRecordFunc, 0);
```

Both sorting routines put deleted and archived records at the end of the database (deleted records aren't passed to the comparison routine, since there's no record data). Keeping deleted and archived records at the end of the database isn't required, but it is a widely followed convention used by the sorting routines and by *DmFindSortPosition*.

One other difference between the two sorting routines is that *DmInsertionSort* is a stable sort, while *DmQuickSort* is not. That is, two records that compare the same will remain in the same relative order after *DmInsertionSort* but might switch positions after *DmQuickSort*.

## Deleting a Record

Deleting a record is slightly complicated because of the interaction with conduits and the data on the desktop. The simplest record deletion is to completely remove the record from the database (using *DmRemoveRecord*). This is used when the user creates a record but then immediately decides to delete it. Since there's no corresponding record on the desktop, there's no information that needs to be maintained in the database so that synchronization can occur.

When a preexisting record is deleted, it also needs to be deleted on the desktop during the next Hotsync. To handle this deletion from the desktop, the unique ID and attributes are still maintained in the database (but the record's memory chunk is freed). The deleted attribute of the record is set. The conduit looks for this bit setting and then deletes such records from the desktop and from the handheld on the next HotSync. *DmDeleteRecord* does this kind of deletion, leaving the record's unique ID and attributes in the database.

The final possibility is that the user requests that a deleted record be archived on the desktop (see Figure 6-3). In this case, the memory chunk can't be freed (because the data must be copied to the desktop to be archived). Instead, the archived bit of the record is set, and it is treated on the handheld as if it were deleted. Once a HotSync occurs, the conduit copies the record to the desktop and then deletes it from the handheld database. *DmArchiveRecord* does this archiving.

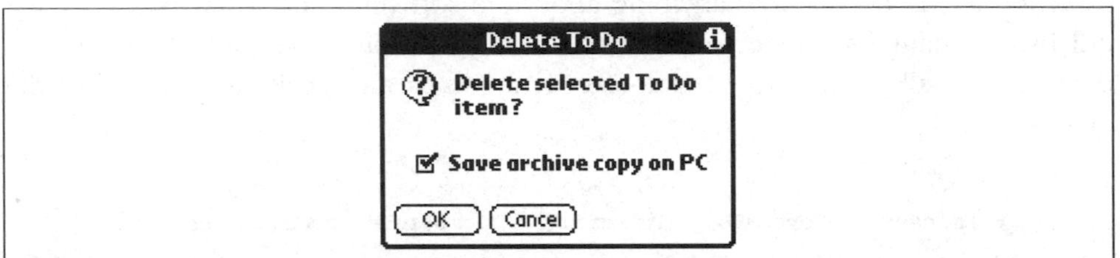


*Figure 6-3. Dialog allowing the user to archive a record on the desktop (it shows up after the user asks to delete a record)*

Newly archived and deleted records should be moved to the end of the database (the sorting routines and *DmFindSortPosition* rely on archived and deleted records being only at the end of the database). Here's the logic you'll probably want to use when the user deletes a record:

```
if (isNew && !gSaveBackup)
   DmRemoveRecord(gDB, recordNumber); // remove all traces
else {
   if (gSaveBackup) //need to archive it on PC
      DmArchiveRecord(gDB, recordNumber);
   else
     DmDeleteRecord(gDB, recordNumber); // leave the unique ID and attrs
   // Deleted records are stored at the end of the database
   DmMoveRecord (gDB, recordNumber, DmNumRecords(gDB));
}
```

If the user doesn't explicitly request that a record be deleted, but implicitly requests it by deleting necessary data (for instance, ending up with an empty memo in the Memo Pad), you don't need to archive the record. Here's the code you use:

```
if (recordIsEmpty) {
   if (isNew)
      DmRemoveRecord(gDB, recordNumber); // remove all traces
   else {
      DmDeleteRecord(gDB, recordNumber); // leave the unique ID and attrs
      // Deleted records are stored at the end of the database
      DmMoveRecord (gDB, recordNumber, DmNumRecords(gDB));
   }
}
```

## *Dealing with Large Records*

The maximum amount of data a record can hold is slightly less than 64KB of data. If you've got larger amounts of data to deal with, there are a couple of ways to tackle the problem.

### *File streaming*

If you're using Palm OS 3.0, you can use the File Streaming Manager. The File Streaming Manager provides a file-based API (currently implemented as separate chunks within a database heap). You create a uniquely named file and a small record that stores only that filename. We suggest you use as a filename the database creator followed by the database type, followed by the record's unique ID. Use *FileOpen* to create a file:

```
FileHand fileHandle;
UInt     cardNo = 0;

fileHandle = FileOpen(cardNo, uniqueFileName, kCustType, kSalesCreator,
   fileModeReadWrite, &err);
```

Store the filename as the contents of the record. Read and write with *FileRead* and *FileWrite*. When you are done reading and writing, close the file with *FileClose*. When you delete the record, you can delete the file with *FileDelete*.

One disadvantage of file streams is that your conduit has no access to these files.

### *Multiple chunks in a separate database*

If you are running Palm OS 2.0 or earlier, the File Stream Manager isn't available. Therefore, you need to allocate multiple chunks in a separate database yourself. The record stores the unique IDs of each of the chunks in the separate chunk database. Here's a rough idea of how you might support a record of up to 180KB (we'll have 18 records of 10KB each—we don't want each record to be too big, since it's easier to pack smaller objects into the many 64KB heaps than it is to pack fewer larger ones). We assume we've got two open databases: `gDB`, where our "large" records are, and `gChunkDB`, which contains our chunks:

```
#define kNumChunks 18
#define kChunkSize (10 * 1024)
typedef struct {
   ULong uniqueIDs[kNumChunks];
} MyRecordType;
MyRecordType newRecord;
```

```
MyRecordType *newRecordPtr = 0;
Handle    h;
int       i;
UInt      numRecordsInChunkDatabase;

// keep track of original number of records
// so in case a problem occurs we can delete
// any we've added
numRecordsInChunkDatabase = DmNumRecords(gChunkDB);

for (i = 0; i < kNumChunks; i++) {
   UInt  chunkRecordNumber = dmMaxRecordIndex;
   h = DmNewRecord(gChunkDB, &chunkRecordNumber, kChunkSize);
    if (!h)
      break;
   if (DmRecordInfo(gChunkDB, chunkRecordNumber, NULL,
      &newRecord.uniqueIDs[i], NULL) != 0)
      break;
   DmReleaseRecord(gChunkDB, chunkRecordNumber, true);
}
if (i >= kNumChunks) {
   // we were able to allocate all the chunks
   UInt recordNumber = 0;
   h = DmNewRecord(gDB, &recordNumber, sizeof(MyRecordType));
   if (h) {
      newRecordPtr = MemHandleLock(h);
      DmWrite(newRecordPtr, 0, &newRecord, sizeof(newRecord));
      DmReleaseRecord(gDB, recordNumber, true);
   }
}
if (!newRecordPtr) {
   // unable to allocate all chunks and record
   // delete all the chunks we allocated
   UInt  recordNumToDelete;
   recordNumToDelete = DmNumRecords(gChunkDB) - 1;
   while (recordNumToDelete >= numRecordsInChunkDatabase)
      DmRemoveRecord(gChunkDB, recordNumToDelete--);
}
```

Now that you've allocated the record (and the chunks it points to), it's fairly straightforward to edit any of the 180KB bytes of data. You use the unique ID to go into the appropriate chunk (reading it from the chunk database after finding the index with *DmFindRecordByID*).

## Editing a Record in Place

The Field Manager can be set to edit a string field in place. The string need not take up the entire record; you specify the starting offset of the string and the current string length. The Field Manager resizes the handle as necessary while the string is edited.

This mechanism is a great way to handle editing a single string in a record. However, you can't have multiple fields simultaneously editing multiple strings in a record. For example, if you have a record containing both last name and first name, you can't create two fields in a single form to edit both the last name and first name in place. (This makes sense, because each of the fields may want to resize the handle.)

The following sections explain this mechanism.

### *Initialize the field with the handle*

This code shows how to initialize the field with the handle:

```
typedef struct {
   int   field;
   // other fields
   char textField[1];      // may actually be longer, null-terminated
} MyRecType;

Handle      theRecordHandle;
Handle      oldTextHandle = FldGetTextHandle(fld);

if (fld) {
   // must dispose of the old handle, or we'll leak memory
   MemHandleFree(oldTextHandle);
}
theRecordHandle = DmGetRecord(gDB, recordNumber);
recPtr = MemHandleLock(theRecordHandle);
FldSetText(fld, theRecordHandle, offsetof(MyRecType, textField),
   StrLen(theRecordHandle.textField) + 1);
```

### *Cleanup once the editing is finished*

When the editing is done (this usually occurs when the form is closing), three things need to be done:

- Compact the text. When a field is edited, the text handle is resized in chunks rather than one byte at a time. Compacting the text resizes the text block to remove the extra space at the end of the block.
- Reset the text handle. When a field is freed, it frees its text handle. We don't want the record in the database to be freed, so we set the field's handle to 0.
- Release the record back to the database.

Here's the code:

```
Boolean dirty = FldDirty(fld);
if (dirty)
   FldCompactText(fld);
FldSetTextHandle(fld, NULL);
DmReleaseRecord(gDB, recordNumber, dirty);
```

# Examining Databases in the Sales Sample

Now that you understand how databases and records function within the storage heap space, let's look at how we use them in our Sales application.

## Defining the Sales Databases

The Sales application has three different databases. The first holds customers, the second orders (one record for each order), and the third items. Here are the constant definitions for the names and types:

```
#define kCustomerDBType         'Cust'
#define kCustomerDBName         "Customers-Sles"
#define kOrderDBType            'Ordr'
#define kOrderDBName            "Orders-Sles"
#define kProductDBType          'Prod'
#define kProductDBName          "Products-Sles"
```

## Reading and Writing the Customer

The customer is stored as the customer ID followed by four null-terminated strings back to back (it's "packed," so to speak). Here's a structure we use for the customer record (there's no way to represent the four strings, so we just specify the first one):

```
typedef struct {
   SDWord customerID;
   char  name[1]; // actually may be longer than 1
} PackedCustomer;
```

When we're working with a customer and need to access each of the fields, we use a different structure:

```
typedef struct {
   SDWord       customerID;
   const char *name;
   const char *address;
   const char *city;
   const char *phone;
} Customer;
```

Here's a routine that takes a locked *PackedCustomer* and fills out a customer—it unpacks the customer. Note that each field points into the *PackedCustomer* (to avoid allocating additional memory). The customer is valid only while the *PackedCustomer* remains locked (otherwise, the pointers are not valid):

```
// packedCustomer must remain locked while customer is in use
static void UnpackCustomer(Customer *customer,
   const PackedCustomer *packedCustomer)
```

```
{
   const char *s = packedCustomer->name;
   customer->customerID = packedCustomer->customerID;
   customer->name = s;
   s += StrLen(s) + 1;
   customer->address = s;
   s += StrLen(s) + 1;
   customer->city = s;
   s += StrLen(s) + 1;
   customer->phone = s;
   s += StrLen(s) + 1;
}
```

We have an inverse routine that packs a customer:

```
static void PackCustomer(Customer *customer, VoidHand customerDBEntry)
{
   // figure out necessary size
   UInt     length = 0;
   CharPtr     s;
   UInt     offset = 0;

   length = sizeof(customer->customerID) + StrLen(customer->name) +
      StrLen(customer->address) + StrLen(customer->city) +
      StrLen(customer->phone) + 4;  // 4 for string terminators

   // resize the VoidHand
   if (MemHandleResize(customerDBEntry, length) == 0) {
      // copy the fields
      s = MemHandleLock(customerDBEntry);
      offset = 0;
      DmWrite(s, offset, (CharPtr) &customer->customerID,
         sizeof(customer->customerID));
      offset += sizeof(customer->customerID);
      DmStrCopy(s, offset, (CharPtr) customer->name);
      offset += StrLen(customer->name) + 1;
      DmStrCopy(s, offset, (CharPtr) customer->address);
      offset += StrLen(customer->address) + 1;
      DmStrCopy(s, offset, (CharPtr) customer->city);
      offset += StrLen(customer->city) + 1;
      DmStrCopy(s, offset, (CharPtr) customer->phone);
      MemHandleUnlock(customerDBEntry);
   }
}
```

## *Reading and Writing Products*

Similarly, we have structures for packed and unpacked products:

```
typedef struct {
   ULong productID;
   ULong price;   // in cents
   const char  *name;
} Product;
```

```
typedef struct {
   DWord productID;
   DWord price;    // in cents
   char  name[1]; // actually may be longer than 1
} PackedProduct;
```

Since the structure for packed and unpacked products is so similar, we could write our code to not distinguish between the two. However, in the future, we may want to represent the data in records differently from the data in memory. By separating the two now, we prepare for possible changes in the future.

The `productID` is unique within the database. We keep the price in cents so we don't have to deal with floating-point numbers.

We have routines that pack and unpack:

```
static void PackProduct(Product *product, VoidHand productDBEntry)
{
   // figure out necessary size
   UInt     length = 0;
   CharPtr  s;
   UInt     offset = 0;

   length = sizeof(product->productID) + sizeof(product->price) +
      StrLen(product->name) + 1;

   // resize the VoidHand
   if (MemHandleResize(productDBEntry, length) == 0) {
      // copy the fields
      s = MemHandleLock(productDBEntry);
      DmWrite(s, offsetof(PackedProduct, productID), &product->productID,
         sizeof(product->productID));
      DmWrite(s, offsetof(PackedProduct, price), &product->price,
         sizeof(product->price));
      DmStrCopy(s, offsetof(PackedProduct, name), (CharPtr) product->name);
      MemHandleUnlock(productDBEntry);
   }
}

// packedProduct must remain locked while product is in use
static void UnpackProduct(Product *product,
   const PackedProduct *packedProduct)
{
   product->productID = packedProduct->productID;
   product->price = packedProduct->price;
   product->name = packedProduct->name;
}
```

## Working with Orders

Orders have a variable number of items:

```
typedef struct {
   DWord productID;
   DWord quantity;
```

```
} Item;

typedef struct {
   SDWord   customerID;
   Word  numItems;
   Item  items[1];   // this array will actually be numItems long.
} Order;
```

There is zero or one order per customer. An order is matched to its customer via the `customerUniqueID`.

We have variables for the open databases:

```
static DmOpenRef      gCustomerDB;
static DmOpenRef      gOrderDB;
static DmOpenRef      gProductDB;
```

## *Opening, Creating, and Closing the Sales Databases*

Here's our *StartApplication* that opens the databases (after creating each one, if necessary):

```
static Err StartApplication(void)
{
   UInt                     prefsSize;
   UInt                     mode = dmModeReadWrite;
   Err                      err = 0;
   CategoriesStruct         *c;
   Boolean                  created;

   // code that reads preferences deleted

   // Determime if secret records should be shown.
   gHideSecretRecords = PrefGetPreference(prefHidePrivateRecords);
   if (!gHideSecretRecords)
      mode |= dmModeShowSecret;

   // Find the Customer database.  If it doesn't exist, create it.
   OpenOrCreateDB(&gCustomerDB, kCustomerDBType, kSalesCreator, mode,
      0, kCustomerDBName, &created);
   if (created)
      InitializeCustomers();

   // Find the Order database.  If it doesn't exist, create it.
   OpenOrCreateDB(&gOrderDB, kOrderDBType, kSalesCreator, mode,
      0, kOrderDBName, &created);
   if (created)
      InitializeOrders();

   // Find the Product database.  If it doesn't exist, create it.
   OpenOrCreateDB(&gProductDB, kProductDBType, kSalesCreator, mode,
      0, kProductDBName, &created);
   if (created)
      InitializeProducts();
```

```
    c = GetLockedAppInfo();
    gNumCategories = c->numCategories;
    MemPtrUnlock(c);

    return err;
}
```

It uses a utility routine to open (and create, if necessary) each database:

```
// open a database. If it doesn't exist, create it.
static Err OpenOrCreateDB(DmOpenRef *dbP, ULong type, ULong creator,
    ULong mode, UInt cardNo, char *name, Boolean *created)
{
    Err   err;

    *created = false;
    *dbP = DmOpenDatabaseByTypeCreator(type, creator, mode);
    err = DmGetLastErr();
    if (! *dbP)
    {
        err = DmCreateDatabase(0, name, creator, type, false);
        if (err)
            return err;
        *created = true;

        *dbP = DmOpenDatabaseByTypeCreator(type, creator, mode);
        if (! *dbP)
            return DmGetLastErr();
    }
    return err;
}
```

It uses another utility routine to read the categories from the application info block for the product database:

```
static CategoriesStruct *GetLockedAppInfo()
{
    UInt  cardNo;
    LocalID  dbID;
    LocalID  appInfoID;
    Err      err;

     if ((err = DmOpenDatabaseInfo(gProductDB, &dbID, NULL, NULL,
        &cardNo, NULL)) != 0)
        return NULL;
    if ((err = DmDatabaseInfo(cardNo, dbID, NULL, NULL, NULL, NULL, NULL,
        NULL, NULL, &appInfoID, NULL, NULL, NULL)) != 0)
        return NULL;
    return MemLocalIDToLockedPtr(appInfoID, cardNo);
}
```

When the application closes, it has to close the databases:

```
static void StopApplication(void)
{
    // code that saves preferences deleted
```

```
    // Close all open forms,  this will force any unsaved data to
    // be written to the database.
    FrmCloseAllForms();

    // Close the databases.
    DmCloseDatabase(gCustomerDB);
    DmCloseDatabase(gOrderDB);
    DmCloseDatabase(gProductDB);
}
```

## Initializing the Sales Databases

We have routines to initialize each of the databases. At some point, these routines could be removed (instead, our conduit would initialize the database during a HotSync).

### Initializing the customer database

Here's the initialization routine for customers:

```
static void InitializeCustomers(void)
{
   Customer c1 = {1, "Joe's toys-1", "123 Main St." ,"Anytown",
      "(123) 456-7890"};
   Customer c2 = {2, "Bucket of Toys-2", "" ,"", ""};
   Customer c3 = {3, "Toys we be-3", "" ,"", ""};
   Customer c4 = {4, "a", "" ,"", ""};
   Customer c5 = {5, "b", "" ,"", ""};
   Customer c6 = {6, "c", "" ,"", ""};
   Customer c7 = {7, "d", "" ,"", ""};
   Customer *customers[7];
   UInt  numCustomers = sizeof(customers) / sizeof(customers[0]);
   UInt  i;

   customers[0] = &c1;
   customers[1] = &c2;
   customers[2] = &c3;
   customers[3] = &c4;
   customers[4] = &c5;
   customers[5] = &c6;
   customers[6] = &c7;
   for (i = 0; i < numCustomers; i++) {
      UInt  index = dmMaxRecordIndex;
      VoidHand h = DmNewRecord(gCustomerDB, &index, 1);
      if (h) {
         PackCustomer(customers[i], h);
         DmReleaseRecord(gCustomerDB, index, true);
      }
   }
}
```

### *Initializing the product database*

Here's the routine to initialize products:

```
static void InitializeProducts(void)
{
#define  kMaxPerCategory 4
#define  kNumCategories 3
   Product prod1 = {125, 253 ,"GI-Joe"};
   Product prod2 = {135, 1122 ,"Barbie"};
   Product prod3 = {145, 752 ,"Ken"};
   Product prod4 = {9,   852 ,"Skipper"};
   Product prod5 = {126, 253 ,"Kite"};
   Product prod6 = {127, 350 , "Silly-Putty"};
   Product prod7 = {138, 650 ,"Yo-yo"};
   Product prod8 = {199, 950 ,"Legos"};
   Product prod9 = {120, 999 ,"Monopoly"};
   Product prod10= {129, 888 , "Yahtzee"};
   Product prod11= {10, 899 ,  "Life"};
   Product prod12= {20, 1199 ,"Battleship"};
   Product *products[kNumCategories][kMaxPerCategory];
   UInt  i;
   UInt  j;
   VoidHand h;

   products[0][0] = &prod1;
   products[0][1] = &prod2;
   products[0][2] = &prod3;
   products[0][3] = &prod4;
   products[1][0] = &prod5;
   products[1][1] = &prod6;
   products[1][2] = &prod7;
   products[1][3] = &prod8;
   products[2][0] = &prod9;
   products[2][1] = &prod10;
   products[2][2] = &prod11;
   products[2][3] = &prod12;
   for (i = 0; i < kNumCategories; i++) {
      for (j = 0; j < kMaxPerCategory && products[i][j]->name; j++) {
         UInt          index;
         PackedProduct  findRecord;
         VoidHand       h;

         findRecord.productID = products[i][j]->productID;
         index = DmFindSortPosition(gProductDB, &findRecord, 0,
            (DmComparF* ) CompareIDFunc, 0);
         h = DmNewRecord(gProductDB, &index, 1);
         if (h) {
            UInt  attr;
            // Set the category of the new record to the category it
            // belongs in.
            DmRecordInfo(gProductDB, index, &attr, NULL, NULL);
            attr &= ~dmRecAttrCategoryMask;
            attr |= i;        // category is kept in low bits of attr
```

```
                DmSetRecordInfo(gProductDB, index, &attr, NULL);
                PackProduct(products[i][j], h);
                DmReleaseRecord(gProductDB, index, true);
            }
        }
    }

    h = DmNewHandle(gProductDB,
        offsetof(CategoriesStruct, names[kNumCategories]));
    if (h) {
        char  *categories[] = {"Dolls", "Toys", "Games"};
        CategoriesStruct  *c = MemHandleLock(h);
        LocalID            dbID;
        LocalID            appInfoID;
        UInt             cardNo;
        UInt             num = kNumCategories;
        Err                err;

        DmWrite(c, offsetof(CategoriesStruct, numCategories), &num,
            sizeof(num));
        for (i = 0; i < kNumCategories; i++)
            DmStrCopy(c,
                offsetof(CategoriesStruct, names[i]), categories[i]);
        MemHandleUnlock(h);
            appInfoID = MemHandleToLocalID( h);
            err = DmOpenDatabaseInfo(gProductDB, &dbID, NULL, NULL,
                &cardNo, NULL);
            if (err == 0) {
            err = DmSetDatabaseInfo(cardNo, dbID, NULL, NULL, NULL, NULL,
                NULL, NULL, NULL, &appInfoID, NULL, NULL, NULL);
            ErrNonFatalDisplayIf(err, "DmSetDatabaseInfo failed");
        }
    }
}
```

The code inserts the products sorted by product ID (an alternative would be to create the products in unsorted order and then sort them afterward). Note also that the attributes of each record are modified to set the category of the product.

### *The comparison routine for sorting*

Here's the comparison routine used for sorting products, companies, and orders:

```
static Int CompareIDFunc(SDWord *p1, SDWord *p2, Int i,
    SortRecordInfoPtr s1, SortRecordInfoPtr s2, VoidHand appInfoH)
{
    // can't just return *p1 - *p2 because that's a long that may overflow
    // our return type of Int.  Therefore, we do the subtraction ourself
    // and check
    long difference = *p1 - *p2;
    if (difference < 0)
        return -1;
    else if (difference > 0)
        return 1;
```

```
    else
        return 0;
    return (*p1 - *p2);
}
```

### *Initializing the orders database*

Finally, the orders must be initialized:

```
static void InitializeOrders(void)
{
    Item item1 =  {125, 253};
    Item item2 =  {126, 999};
    Item item3 =  {127, 888};
    Item item4 =  {138, 777};
    Item item5 =  {125, 6};
    Item item6 =  {120, 5};
    Item item7 =  {129, 5};
    Item item8 =  {10,  3};
    Item item9 =  {20,  45};
    Item item10 = {125, 66};
    Item item11 = {125, 75};
    Item item12 = {125, 23};
    Item item13 = {125, 55};
    Item item14 = {125, 888};
    Item item15 = {125, 456};
    Item items[15];
    VoidHand h;
    Order    *order;
    UInt  recordNum;
    UInt  numItems = sizeof(items) / sizeof(items[0]);

    items[0] =  item1;
    items[1] =  item2;
    items[2] =  item3;
    items[3] =  item4;
    items[4] =  item5;
    items[5] =  item6;
    items[6] =  item7;
    items[7] =  item8;
    items[8] =  item9;
    items[9] =  item10;
    items[10] = item11;
    items[11] = item12;
    items[12] = item13;
    items[13] = item14;
    items[14] = item15;

    order= GetOrCreateOrderForCustomer(1, &recordNum);

    // write numItems
    DmWrite(order, offsetof(Order, numItems), &numItems, sizeof(numItems));

    // resize to hold more items
    h = MemPtrRecoverHandle(order);
```

```
        MemHandleUnlock(h);
        MemHandleResize(h, offsetof(Order, items) + sizeof(Item) * numItems);
        order = MemHandleLock(h);

        // write new items
        DmWrite(order, offsetof(Order, items), items, sizeof(items));

        // done with it
        MemHandleUnlock(h);
        DmReleaseRecord(gOrderDB, recordNum, true);
    }
```

## Adding Records

All we do is add some items to the first customer. The remaining customers we treat as still needing an order. (We do this primarily to test later code that shows which customers do and do not have orders.) We use a routine that takes a customer ID and returns the corresponding order (or creates it as necessary). This routine is used not only for initializing the database, but also at other points in the program:

```
static Order *GetOrCreateOrderForCustomer(Long customerID,
    UInt *recordNumPtr)
{
    VoidHand theOrderHandle;
    Order    *order;
    Boolean  exists;

    *recordNumPtr = OrderRecordNumber(customerID, &exists);
    if (exists) {
        theOrderHandle = DmGetRecord(gOrderDB, *recordNumPtr);
        ErrNonFatalDisplayIf(!theOrderHandle, "DMGetRecord failed!");
        order = MemHandleLock(theOrderHandle);
    } else {
        Order o;
        theOrderHandle = DmNewRecord(gOrderDB, recordNumPtr, sizeof(Order));
        if (!theOrderHandle) {
            FrmAlert(DeviceFullAlert);
            return NULL;
        }
        o.numItems = 0;
        o.customerID = customerID;
        order = MemHandleLock(theOrderHandle);
        DmWrite(order, 0, &o, sizeof(o));
    }
    return order;
}
```

*OrderRecordNumber* returns the record number of a customer's order or the location at which the order should be inserted, if no such order exists:

```
// returns record number for order, if it exists, or where it
// should be inserted
static UInt OrderRecordNumber(Long customerID, Boolean *orderExists)
```

```
{
   Order     findRecord;
   UInt      recordNumber;

   *orderExists = false;
   findRecord.customerID = customerID;
   recordNumber = DmFindSortPosition(gOrderDB, &findRecord, 0,
      (DmComparF *) CompareIDFunc, 0);

   if (recordNumber > 0) {
      Order *order;
      VoidHand theOrderHandle;
      Boolean  foundIt;

      theOrderHandle = DmQueryRecord(gOrderDB, recordNumber - 1);
      ErrNonFatalDisplayIf(!theOrderHandle, "DMGetRecord failed!");

      order = MemHandleLock(theOrderHandle);
      foundIt = order->customerID == customerID;
      MemHandleUnlock(theOrderHandle);
      if (foundIt) {
         *orderExists = true;
         return recordNumber - 1;
      }
   }
   return recordNumber;
}
```

## The Customers Form

Let's now look at how the customers are displayed in the Customers form. Customers are displayed in a list that has a drawing callback function that displays the customer for a particular row (since it's called by the system, it must have the CALLBACK macros for GCC). The customers that already have an order are shown in bold, to distinguish them from the others. The text pointer is unused, since we don't store our customer names in the list but obtain them from the database. Here's the routine:

```
static void DrawOneCustomerInListWithFont(UInt itemNumber, RectanglePtr
bounds, CharPtr *text)
{
   VoidHand h;
   Int      seekAmount = itemNumber;
   UInt  index = 0;

#ifdef __GNUC__
   CALLBACK_PROLOGUE
#endif
   // must do seek to skip over secret records
   DmSeekRecordInCategory(gCustomerDB, &index, seekAmount, dmSeekForward,
      dmAllCategories);
   h = DmQueryRecord(gCustomerDB, index);
   if (h) {
```

```
        FontID   curFont;
        Boolean  setFont = false;
        PackedCustomer *packedCustomer = MemHandleLock(h);

        if (!OrderExistsForCustomer(packedCustomer->customerID)) {
           setFont = true;
           curFont = FntSetFont(boldFont);
        }
        DrawCharsToFitWidth(packedCustomer->name, bounds);
        MemHandleUnlock(h);

        if (setFont)
           FntSetFont(curFont);
     }
#ifdef __GNUC__
   CALLBACK_EPILOGUE
#endif
}
```

The routine uses two other routines: one that finds the unique ID for a specific row number and one that tells whether an order exists. Here's the routine that returns a unique ID:

```
static ULong GetCustomerIDForNthCustomer(UInt itemNumber)
{
   Long           customerID;
   UInt           index = 0;
   Int               seekAmount = itemNumber;
   VoidHand          h;
   PackedCustomer *packedCustomer;

   // must do seek to skip over secret records
   DmSeekRecordInCategory(gCustomerDB, &index, seekAmount, dmSeekForward,
      dmAllCategories);
   h = DmQueryRecord(gCustomerDB, index);
   ErrNonFatalDisplayIf(!h,
      "can't get customer in GetCustomerIDForNthCustomer");
   packedCustomer = MemHandleLock(h);
   customerID = packedCustomer->customerID;
   MemHandleUnlock(h);

   return customerID;
}
```

Note the use of *DmSeekRecordInCategory*, which skips over any secret records. Here's the code that calls *OrderRecordNumber* to figure out whether an order exists (so that the customer name can be bolded or not):

```
static Boolean OrderExistsForCustomer(Long customerID)
{
   Boolean  orderExists;

   OrderRecordNumber(customerID, &orderExists);
   return  orderExists;
}
```

## Editing Customers

Here's the *EditCustomerWithSelection* routine that handles editing customers, deleting customers, and setting/clearing the private record attribute. The `gotoData` parameter is used to preselect some text in a field (used for displaying the results of a Find):

```
static void EditCustomerWithSelection(UInt recordNumber, Boolean isNew,
   Boolean *deleted, Boolean *hidden, struct frmGoto *gotoData)
{
   FormPtr  previousForm = FrmGetActiveForm();
   FormPtr  frm;
   UInt     hitButton;
   Boolean  dirty = false;
   ControlPtr  privateCheckbox;
   UInt     attributes;
   Boolean     isSecret;
   FieldPtr nameField;
   FieldPtr addressField;
   FieldPtr cityField;
   FieldPtr phoneField;
   Customer theCustomer;
   UInt     offset = offsetof(PackedCustomer, name);
   VoidHand     customerHandle = DmGetRecord(gCustomerDB, recordNumber);

   *hidden = *deleted = false;
   DmRecordInfo(gCustomerDB, recordNumber, &attributes, NULL, NULL);
   isSecret = (attributes & dmRecAttrSecret) == dmRecAttrSecret;

   frm = FrmInitForm(CustomerForm);
   FrmSetEventHandler(frm, CustomerHandleEvent);
   FrmSetActiveForm(frm);

   UnpackCustomer(&theCustomer, MemHandleLock(customerHandle));

   // code deleted that initializes the fields

   // unlock the customer
   MemHandleUnlock(customerHandle);

   privateCheckbox = GetObjectFromActiveForm(CustomerPrivateCheckbox);
   CtlSetValue(privateCheckbox, isSecret);

   hitButton = FrmDoDialog(frm);

   if (hitButton == CustomerOKButton) {
      dirty = FldDirty(nameField) || FldDirty(addressField) ||
         FldDirty(cityField) || FldDirty(phoneField);
      if (dirty) {
         // code deleted that reads the fields into theCustomer
      }
      PackCustomer(&theCustomer, customerHandle);
      if (CtlGetValue(privateCheckbox) != isSecret) {
```

```
            dirty = true;
            if (CtlGetValue(privateCheckbox)) {
               attributes |= dmRecAttrSecret;
               // tell user how to hide private records
               if (gHideSecretRecords)
                  *hidden = true;
               else
                  FrmAlert(privateRecordInfoAlert);
            } else
               attributes &= ~dmRecAttrSecret;
            DmSetRecordInfo(gCustomerDB, recordNumber, &attributes, NULL);
         }
      }

      DmReleaseRecord(gCustomerDB, recordNumber, dirty);
      if (hitButton == CustomerDeleteButton) {
         *deleted = true;
         if (isNew && !gSaveBackup)
            DmRemoveRecord(gCustomerDB, recordNumber);
         else {
            if (gSaveBackup)  // Need to archive it on PC
               DmArchiveRecord(gCustomerDB, recordNumber);
            else
               DmDeleteRecord(gCustomerDB, recordNumber);
            // Deleted records are stored at the end of the database
            DmMoveRecord(gCustomerDB, recordNumber,
               DmNumRecords(gCustomerDB));
         }
      }
      else if (hitButton == CustomerOKButton && isNew &&
         !(StrLen(theCustomer.name) || StrLen(theCustomer.address) ||
         StrLen(theCustomer.city) || StrLen(theCustomer.phone))) {
         *deleted = true;
         // delete Customer if it is new & empty
         DmRemoveRecord(gCustomerDB, recordNumber);
      }
      else if (hitButton == CustomerCancelButton && isNew) {
         *deleted = true;
         DmRemoveRecord(gCustomerDB, recordNumber);
      }

      if (previousForm)
         FrmSetActiveForm(previousForm);
      FrmDeleteForm(frm);
   }
```

We have a utility routine we use that doesn't require a `gotoData` parameter:

```
static void EditCustomer(UInt recordNumber, Boolean isNew, Boolean *deleted,
Boolean *hidden)
{
   EditCustomerWithSelection(recordNumber, isNew, deleted, hidden, NULL);
}
```

## The Order Form

Most of the functionality in this form is provided in a table (see "Tables" on page 206). We won't look at the table parts specifically, but it's worth knowing that each visible row of the table has an item index number associated with it (this is retrieved with *TblGetRowID*). Here's the code that draws a product name for a particular row:

```
static void OrderDrawProductName(VoidPtr table, Word row, Word column,
   RectanglePtr bounds)
{
   VoidHand h = NULL;
   Product  p;
   UInt  itemNumber;
   ULong productID;
   CharPtr  toDraw;

#ifdef __GNUC__
   CALLBACK_PROLOGUE
#endif
   toDraw = "-Product-";
   itemNumber = TblGetRowID(table, row);
   productID = gCurrentOrder->items[itemNumber].productID;
   if (productID) {
      h = GetProductFromProductID(productID, &p, NULL);
      if (h)
         toDraw = (CharPtr) p.name;
   }
   DrawCharsToFitWidth(toDraw, bounds);
   if (h)
      MemHandleUnlock(h);
#ifdef __GNUC__
   CALLBACK_EPILOGUE
#endif
}
```

### Looking up a product

*GetProductFromProductId* looks up a product given a product ID. Here's the code for that:

```
// if successful, returns the product, and the locked VoidHand
static VoidHand GetProductFromProductID(ULong productID, Product *theProduct,
UInt *indexPtr)
{
   UInt          index;
   PackedProduct findRecord;
   VoidHand      foundHandle = 0;

   findRecord.productID = productID;
   index = DmFindSortPosition(gProductDB, &findRecord, 0,
      (DmComparF *) CompareIDFunc, 0);
```

```
        if (index > 0) {
            PackedProduct  *p;
            VoidHand       h;

            index--;
            h = DmQueryRecord(gProductDB, index);
            p = MemHandleLock(h);
            if (p->productID == productID) {
                if (theProduct)
                    UnpackProduct(theProduct, p);
                else
                    MemHandleUnlock(h);
                if (indexPtr)
                    *indexPtr = index;
                return h;
            }
            MemHandleUnlock(h);
        }
        return NULL;
    }
```

### *Editing an item*

The code to display the product ID and quantity doesn't use the Database Manager (so we don't show that code).

Here's a snippet of code from *OrderSaveAmount* that modifies the quantity, if it has been edited:

```
CharPtr textP = FldGetTextPtr(fld);
Item  oldItem = gCurrentOrder->items[gCurrentSelectedItemIndex];

if (table->currentColumn == kQuantityColumn) {
   if (textP)
      oldItem.quantity = StrAToI(textP);
   else
      oldItem.quantity = 0;
}
DmWrite(gCurrentOrder,
   offsetof(Order, items[gCurrentSelectedItemIndex]),
   &oldItem, sizeof(oldItem));
```

Note that *DmWrite* is used to modify `gCurrentOrder`, since `gCurrentOrder` is a record in the order database and can't be written to directly.

### *Deleting an item*

We need to delete an item in certain circumstances (if the user explicitly chooses to delete an item, or sets the quantity to 0, and then stops editing that item). Here's the code that does that (note that it uses *DmWrite* to move succeeding items forward and uses *MemPtrResize* to make the record smaller):

```
// gCurrentOrder changes after this routine.
// gCurrentItem is no longer valid
```

```
static void DeleteNthItem(UInt itemNumber)
{
   UInt     newNumItems;
   ErrNonFatalDisplayIf(itemNumber >= gCurrentOrder->numItems,
      "bad itemNumber");

   // move items from itemNumber+1..numItems down 1 to
   // itemNumber .. numItems - 1
   if (itemNumber < gCurrentOrder->numItems - 1)
      DmWrite(gCurrentOrder,
         offsetof(Order, items[itemNumber]),
         &gCurrentOrder->items[itemNumber+1],
         (gCurrentOrder->numItems - itemNumber - 1) * sizeof(Item));

   // decrement numItems;
   newNumItems = gCurrentOrder->numItems - 1;
   DmWrite(gCurrentOrder,
      offsetof(Order, numItems), &newNumItems, sizeof(newNumItems));

   // resize the pointer smaller. We could use MemPtrRecoverHandle,
   // MemHandleUnlock, MemHandleResize, MemHandleLock.
   // However, MemPtrResize will always work
   // as long as your are making a chunk smaller.  Thanks, Bob!
   MemPtrResize(gCurrentOrder,
      offsetof(Order, items[gCurrentOrder->numItems]));
}
```

### *Adding a new item*

Similarly, we must have a routine to add a new item:

```
// returns true if successfull. itemNumber is location at which it was
// added
static Boolean AddNewItem(UInt *itemNumber)
{
   VoidHand theOrderHandle;
   Err      err;
   UInt  numItems;
   Item  newItem = {0, 0};

   ErrNonFatalDisplayIf(!gCurrentOrder, "no current order");
   theOrderHandle = MemPtrRecoverHandle(gCurrentOrder);
   MemHandleUnlock(theOrderHandle);
   err = MemHandleResize(theOrderHandle,
      MemHandleSize(theOrderHandle) + sizeof(Item));
   gCurrentOrder = MemHandleLock(theOrderHandle);
   if (err != 0) {
      FrmAlert(DeviceFullAlert);
      return false;
   }
   numItems = gCurrentOrder->numItems + 1;
   DmWrite(gCurrentOrder, offsetof(Order, numItems), &numItems,
      sizeof(numItems));
   *itemNumber = gCurrentOrder->numItems - 1;
```

```
        DmWrite(gCurrentOrder, offsetof(Order, items[*itemNumber]), &newItem,
            sizeof(newItem));
        gCurrentOrderChanged = true;
        return true;
    }
```

Note that if we can't resize the handle, we display the system alert telling the user that the device is full.

### *Finishing an order record*

When the Order form is closed, the records in the order database must be updated. If there are no items, the entire order is deleted:

```
static void OrderFormClose(void)
{
    VoidHand theOrderHandle;
    UInt  numItems;

    OrderDeselectRowAndDeleteIfEmpty();
    numItems = gCurrentOrder->numItems;
    // unlock the order
    theOrderHandle = MemPtrRecoverHandle(gCurrentOrder);
    MemHandleUnlock(theOrderHandle);

    // delete Order if it is empty; release it back to the database otherwise
    if (numItems == 0)
        DmRemoveRecord(gOrderDB, gCurrentOrderIndex);
    else
        DmReleaseRecord(gOrderDB, gCurrentOrderIndex, gCurrentOrderChanged);
}
```

## *The Item Form*

Once the form is initialized, the user interacts with it until a button is tapped. The event handler for the form handles the button tap:

```
static Boolean ItemHandleEvent(EventPtr event)
{
    Boolean     handled = false;
    FieldPtr    fld;

#ifdef __GNUC__
    CALLBACK_PROLOGUE
#endif
    switch (event->eType) {
        case ctlSelectEvent:
            switch (event->data.ctlSelect.controlID) {
            case ItemOKButton:
                {
                    char  *textPtr;
                    ULong quantity;
```

```
            fld = GetObjectFromActiveForm(ItemQuantityField);
            textPtr = FldGetTextPtr(fld);
            ErrNonFatalDisplayIf(!textPtr, "No quantity text");
            quantity = StrAToI(textPtr);
            DmWrite(gCurrentOrder,
               offsetof(Order, items[gCurrentItemNumber].quantity),
               &quantity, sizeof(quantity));

            if (gHaveProductIndex) {
               VoidHand      h;
               PackedProduct  *p;

               h = DmQueryRecord(gProductDB, gCurrentProductIndex);
               ErrNonFatalDisplayIf(!h, "Can't find the record");
               p = MemHandleLock(h);
               DmWrite(gCurrentOrder,
                  offsetof(Order, items[gCurrentItemNumber].productID),
                  &p->productID, sizeof(p->productID));
               MemHandleUnlock(h);
            }
         }
         break;

         case ItemCancelButton:
            break;

         case ItemDeleteButton:
            if (FrmAlert(DeleteItemAlert) == DeleteItemOK)
               DeleteNthItem(gCurrentItemNumber);
            else
               handled = true;
            break;
         }
      break;

      // code for other events deleted

      }
#ifdef __GNUC__
   CALLBACK_EPILOGUE
#endif
   return handled;
}
```

If the user taps OK, the code updates the quantity and product ID of the current item (if the user has edited it). If the user taps Delete, the code calls *DeleteNthItem* (which we've already seen). On a Cancel, the code doesn't modify the current order.

*In this chapter:*
- *Menu User Interface*
- *Menu Resources*
- *Application Code for Menus*
- *Adding Menus to the Sample Application*

# 7

# *Menus*

In this chapter, we explain how to create menus. Along with a discussion of the menu source code, we highlight potential problems and show workarounds for them. First, however, we need to clarify some terminology and describe the user interface for menus.

## *Menu User Interface*

Every Palm application that contains menus uses the same framework for them. If you look at Figure 7-1, you see a sample menubar containing two menus: Customer and Options. The open Customer menu contains three menu items: New Customer, Delete Customer, Edit Customer.

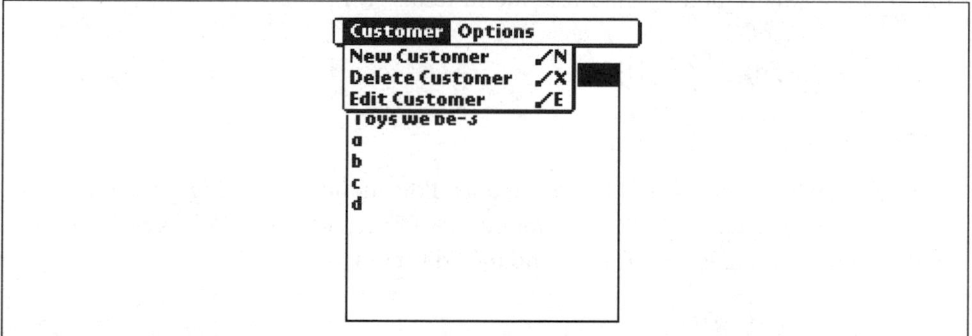


*Figure 7-1. Application menubar, menus, and menu items*

Note that menu items commonly have shortcuts associated with them. These are Graffiti letters that are unique to each menu item. By doing the stroke-and-letter shortcut, the user can perform the operation without first selecting the menu item.

For example, the "/ N" brings up a New Customer form. As a rule, you should add these shortcuts to menu items wherever necessary and always with standard menu items. Make sure that the most frequent operations have shortcuts, and don't put a shortcut on an infrequent action (such as the About Box).

## Common Menu Shortcuts

Table 7-1 contains common menus and the standard shortcut letters used with them. Keep the same letters so that users can expect the same behavior from different applications. Items with an asterisk are less common.

*Table 7-1. Standard Shortcut Letters*

| Record | | Edit | | Options | |
|---|---|---|---|---|---|
| New <*Item*> | N | Undo | U | *Font | F |
| Delete <*Item*> | D | Cut | X | Preferences | R |
| *Attach <*Item*> | A | Copy | C | *Display Options | Y |
| Beam <*Item*> | B | Paste | P | *HotSync Options | H |
| *Purge | E | Select All | S | | |
| | | Keyboard | K | | |
| | | Graffiti Help | G | | |

## Arranging Menus

Menus can also be arranged with separator bars in them to group similar items together (see Figure 7-2). Note that menus and menu items are never dimmed (grayed out). We discuss how to handle menu items that aren't applicable in certain situations in "Handling Unusable Menu Items" on page 191.

## Standard Menu Items

### Edit menu

Most forms with a text field should have an Edit menu containing, at a minimum, Undo, Cut, Copy, Paste. Most Edit menus also include Select All, Keyboard, and Graffiti Help. See Figure 7-2 for a standard Edit menu.

Password dialogs shouldn't support Cut, Copy, or Paste.

### *About application*

You should have an About *myApplication* menu item; it is usually found in an Options menu. This menu should bring up an alert/dialog containing information about your application (who wrote it, version number, name, email address, web site, and technical support information). This dialog is often called an About Box.

## *Applications Can Have Multiple Sets of Menus*

A set of menus is always associated with a particular form or window in the application. Thus, if you look at the Order form of our Sales application in Figure 7-2, you see that it has its own new set of menus.

*Figure 7-2. The Order form of the Sales application*

You should also note that different forms in an application may share a similar set of menus and menu items. For example, the Order form and the Customer Details form both have an Edit menu with the same items (see Figure 7-3).

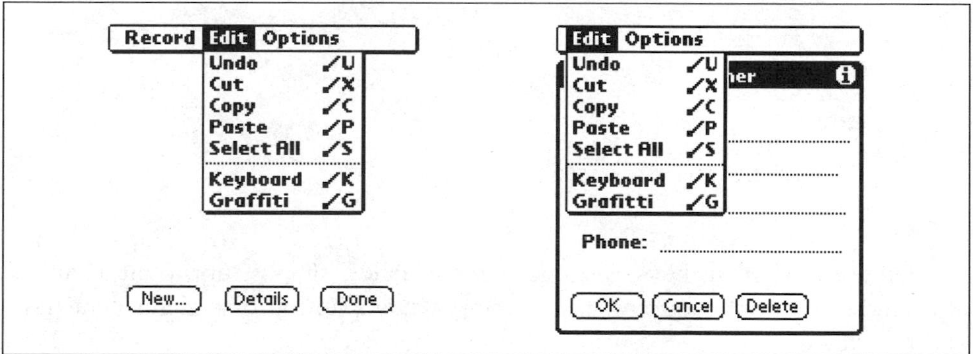


*Figure 7-3. The Edit menu in two different forms*

# Menu Resources

Menus are created and stored as resources in your application. Depending on the development environment you use, you make the menus in different ways. First, we show you how to create menus with PilRC (the GNU PalmPilot SDK resource creator) and then using CodeWarrior's Constructor. In either case, the menus end up in a *.PRC* resource file.

## The .PRC file

The *.PRC* file contains an MBAR resource for each menubar in your application. These MBAR resources are in turn composed of a number of menus, each of which contains menu items. Each menu item has associated with it a menu ID and, optionally, a shortcut key. When you design your menubars, you need to make sure that no two menu items in menus displayed at the same time have the same key shortcut—each shortcut must be unique.

## Using PilRC

To create your *.PRC* file using GCC, use the PilRC Resource Compiler. PilRC allows you to directly create menubar resources; later you will learn that this is a tremendous advantage. PilRC is a textual, rather than a graphical, resource editor.

Here's a simple MBAR (ID 1000) Resource with two menus, each with two items (the item IDs are 1001, 1002, 1011, and 1012):

```
MENU 1000
BEGIN
    PULLDOWN "Menu1"
    BEGIN
        MENUITEM "Item1"   1001      "I"
        MENUITEM "Item2"   1002
    END
    PULLDOWN "Menu2"
    BEGIN
        MENUITEM "Item3"   1011
        MENUITEM "Item4"   1012
    END
END
```

To define the shortcut keys of menu items in PilRC, simply supply the character surrounded by double quotes. In our simple example, the first menu item has a shortcut key of "I".

Of course, you'll commonly use named constants instead of raw numbers in your *.RCP* file. Here is a good technique for numbering your resources: make your MBAR resource IDs multiples of 1000 and your menu resource IDs multiples of 10 starting 1 unit higher (this assumes that no menu will have more than 10 items in it). For example:

| MBAR | MENU |
|---|---|
| 1000 | 1001 |
| | 1011 |
| 2000 | 2001 |
| | 2011 |
| | 2021 |

## *Using Constructor*

While simple to use, Constructor does give you some problems with menu construction. First, look at how Constructor creates menus, and then we will describe the problems.

### *How Constructor creates menus*

You create menus in a Constructor project by graphically laying out menu elements. Figure 7-4 shows you how simple this is to do. The left side of Figure 7-4 contains a simple Constructor project with a couple of menubars and menus. The record menu on the right side contains some menu items (two of which have shortcuts) that were selected from the Constructor Edit menu.

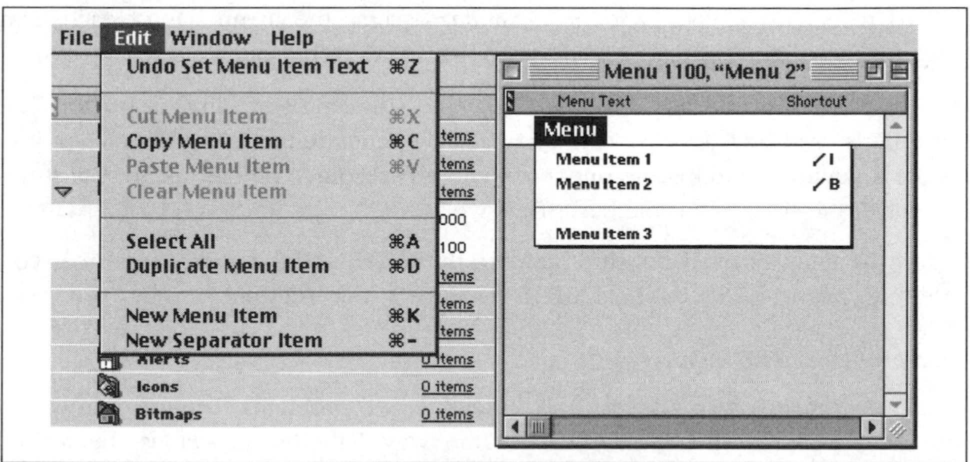


*Figure 7-4. A small project showing the graphical interface for menu creation in Constructor*

### *How Constructor creates MENU resources*

Constructor doesn't directly create MBAR resources in the format needed by a *.PRC* file. Instead, it creates MENU resources (one for each menu). First, you graphically lay out the menus, then Constructor takes over and generates unique resource IDs for all these menus (see Figure 7-5). It does so by keeping track of the MENU resources in an MBAR resource via a list of MENU resource IDs.

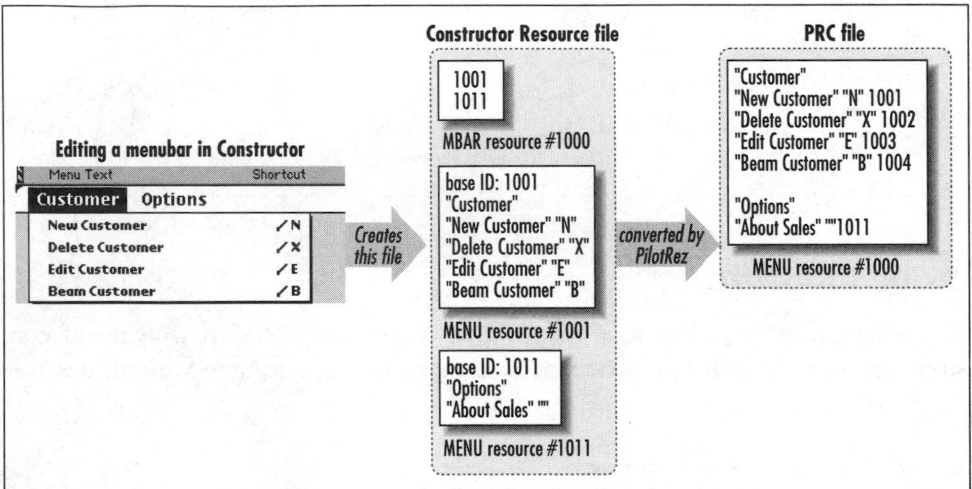


*Figure 7-5. Editing a MENU resource in Constructor*

When you edit a MENU resource, you can edit the resource ID, the text of each menu item, and the shortcut key. You can do all of this in Constructor. What you can't do is edit a menu ID. Here is why: CodeWarrior uses PalmRez, a post-linking tool, to create the MBAR resource in the *.PRC* file. It uses the MBAR and MENU resources in your *.RSC* file. PalmRez assigns the menu IDs of each item sequentially, starting with a base ID stored in the MENU resource itself.

This base ID is not the MENU resource ID, and you can't see it in Constructor. The base ID is used by Constructor to automatically generate the menu IDs. When you create a new menu, duplicate one, or modify the resource ID of a menu, Constructor automatically changes the base ID as well.

Figure 7-6 shows the relationship between the MBAR and the MENU resources you edit in Constructor and the final MBAR resource in the *.PRC* file.

### *Two problems with menus*

Generating menus with Constructor can lead to two problems. The first one has to do with duplicate menus. Because of the way PalmRez processes the MENU resources (deleting each MENU resource as it processes it), you can't share one

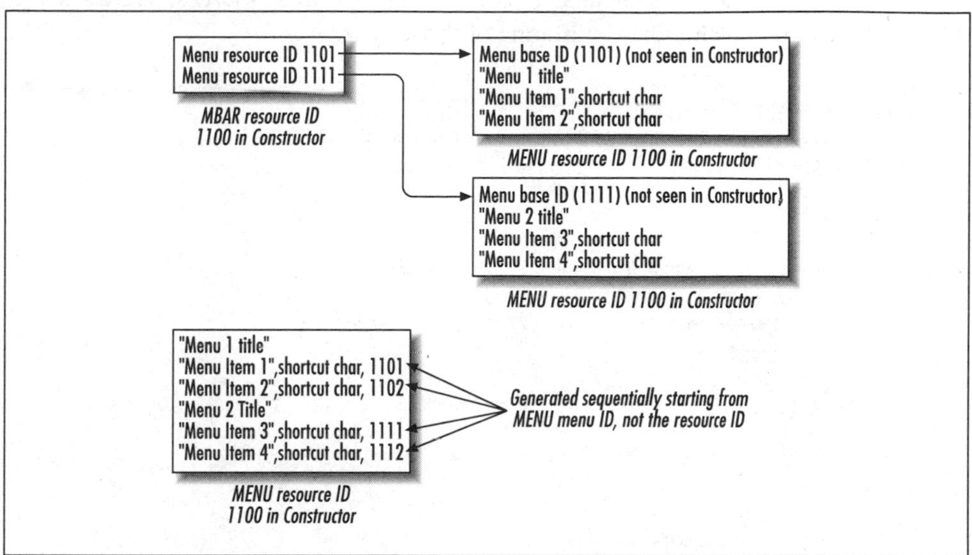


*Figure 7-6. Conceptual relationship between MENU and MBAR resources in Constructor and the MBAR resource in a .PRC file*

MENU in more than one MBAR. This is a bigger problem than you might at first imagine. For example, in our Sales application we have identical Edit menus in our Customer Details and Order forms (Figure 7-3). Even though they are the same, we still have to create two separate menus in Constructor. That means more code to maintain and the possibility of more mistakes.

The second problem has to do with the way base IDs are created. Constructor sets the base ID of a menu to the menu's resource ID. This makes it impossible in Constructor for different menus to share the same menu IDs.

If you have simple menus and menubars, with no need to have the same menu or menu items multiple times, Constructor works fine. Otherwise, switch to creating your menus textually.

### Creating your menus textually with PalmRez

PalmRez is a resource compiler like PilRC, but uses a different format for resources. PalmRez is based on the Macintosh Programmer's Workshop (MPW) Rez tool, which is designed to create Macintosh resources.

PalmRez compiles files with the *.r* extension. Instead of creating your menus and menubars in Constructor, you create a *.r* file that contains your menu and menubar definitions.

PalmRez has to be told the format of MENU and MBAR resources. Here's a file, *MenuDefs.r*, that contains the definitions of those types:

```
type 'MENU'
{
   integer SYS_EDIT_MENU = 10000;   // base menu ID
   fill byte[12];
   pstring;                    // menu title
   array
   {
      pstring SEPARATOR = "-";   // item text
      fill byte;
      char NONE = "\$00";        // Graffiti shortcut
      fill byte[2];
   };
   byte = 0;                   // terminator
};

type 'MBAR'
{
   integer = $$CountOf(menus);
   array menus
   {
      integer;                // menu ID
   };
};
```

Include *MenuDefs.r* in your resource file. Here's an example *MyMenus.r* file defining a menubar with two menus in it:

```
#include "MenuDefs.r"

resource 'MENU' (1001) {
   1001,      // base ID
   "Menu1",
   {
      "Item1", "I";
      "Item2", NONE;
   }
};

resource 'MENU' (1011) {
   1011,      // base ID
   "Menu2",
   {
      "Item3", NONE;
      "Item4", NONE;
   }
};

resource 'MBAR' (1000) {
   {1001, 1011}
};
```

## *Associating Menubars with Forms*

When you create a form, you specify the ID of a menubar to go along with it. A form with the value of 0 has no associated menubar. The Palm OS automatically uses the menubar of a form while the form is active. More than one form can use the same menubar.

### *Specifying the menubar of a form in Constructor*

If you look at Figure 7-7, you will see that you simply supply the resource value of a menubar ID that you want that form to use.

| Form | |
|---|---|
| Left Origin | 0 |
| Top Origin | 0 |
| Width | 160 |
| Height | 160 |
| Usable | [X] Usable |
| Modal | [ ] Modal |
| Save Behind | [ ] Save Behind |
| Form ID | 1000 |
| Help ID | 0 |
| Menu Bar ID | 1000 |

*Figure 7-7. Forms have a menubar ID; this one has a menubar ID of 1000*

### *Specifying the menubar of a form in PilRC*

Specifying a menubar ID for a particular form is just as simple in PilRC:

```
FORM ID 1000 at (0, 0, 160, 160)
MENUID 1000
BEGIN

END
```

# *Application Code for Menus*

There's not a lot of code that needs to be added to support menus. Further, what you do add is straightforward and in some cases standard from application to application. The three routines that have some responsibility for handling menus are:

- *MenuHandleEvent*
- *MyFormHandleEvent*
- *MyFormHandleMenuEvent*

There is some cookbook code to add that handles the Edit menu, and we need to handle the About menu, as well.

## *MenuHandleEvent*

This routine is responsible for handling menu-specific events. Chapter 4, *Structure of an Application*, contains a description of *MenuHandleEvent* and its role within your main event loop. Here is an example found in a main event loop:

```
do {
   EvtGetEvent(&event, evtWaitForever);
   if (! SysHandleEvent(&event))
      if (! MenuHandleEvent(0, &event, &error))
         if (! ApplicationHandleEvent(&event))
            FrmDispatchEvent(&event);
} while (event.eType != appStopEvent);
```

## *MyFormHandleEvent*

Your form's event handler receives an event of type **menuEvent** if a menu item is chosen. If you have more than one or two menu items handled by a form, it is customary to put the menu item dispatching in a separate routine, *MyFormHandle-MenuEvent*. Here is our event handler:

```
static Boolean MyFormHandleEvent(EventPtr event)
{
   Boolean     handled = false;

#ifdef __GNUC__
   CALLBACK_PROLOGUE
#endif
   switch (event->eType)
      {
         /* code removed */
      case menuEvent:
         handled = MyFormHandleMenuEvent(event->data.menu.itemID);
         break;
      /* code removed */
      }
#ifdef __GNUC__
   CALLBACK_EPILOGUE
#endif
   return handled;
}
```

## *MyFormHandleMenuEvent*

This is the routine that actually handles the menu items:

```
static Boolean MyFormHandleMenuEvent(Word menuID)
{
   Boolean handled = false;
   /* declarations removed */
   switch (menuID) {
   case MenuItem1:
```

```
        // code removed that handles MenuItem1
        handled = true;
        break;

    case MenuItem2:
        // code removed that handles MenuItem2
        handled = true;
        break;
    }
    return handled;
}
```

## *Handling Items in the Edit Menu*

The good news about the Edit menu is that there is a cookbook approach to handling each of the menu items. The bad news is that it takes a slight amount of work to avoid duplicating this cookbook code throughout your application. We show you how to avoid duplicated code in "A Procedure for Handling Common Menu Items" later in this chapter.

First, let's look at the cookbook code for handling each of the edit menu items:

```
// returns field that has the focus, if any, including in embedded tables
static FieldPtr GetFocusObjectPtr (void)
{
    FormPtr frm;
    Word focus;
    FormObjectKind objType;

    frm = FrmGetActiveForm ();
    focus = FrmGetFocus (frm);
    if (focus == noFocus)
        return (NULL);

    objType = FrmGetObjectType (frm, focus);

    if (objType == frmFieldObj)
        return (FrmGetObjectPtr (frm, focus));

    else if (objType == frmTableObj)
        return (TblGetCurrentField (FrmGetObjectPtr (frm, focus)));

    return NULL;
}

Boolean void MyFormHandleMenuEvent(Word menuID)
{
    FieldPtr    fld;

    switch (menuID) {
    /* code for other menu items removed */

    case EditUndo:
    case EditCut:
```

```
      case EditCopy:
      case EditPaste:
      case EditSelectAll:
         fld = GetFocusObjectPtr();
         if (!fld)
            return false;
         if (menuID == EditUndo)
            FldUndo(fld);
         else if (menuID == EditCut)
            FldCut(fld);
         else if (menuID == EditCopy)
            FldCopy(fld);
         else if (menuID == EditPaste)
            FldPaste(fld);
         else if (menuID == EditSelectAll)
            FldSetSelection (fld, 0, FldGetTextLength (fld));
         return true;

      case EditKeyboard:
         SysKeyboardDialog(kbdDefault);
         return true;

      case EditGrafitti:
         SysGraffitiReferenceDialog(referenceDefault);
         return true;
      }
      return false;
   }
```

The emphasized calls are standard Palm OS calls that you use to handle the Edit menu. The cookbook can be used with each of your menubars that contain an Edit menu.

## *The About Menu*

The Palm OS provides a routine, *AbtShowAbout*, that allows the display of an application name and icon (see Figure 7-8). As you can see, it isn't appropriate for anything but the built-in applications.*

It is more useful to handle the About menu item by creating a simple alert and displaying it with *FrmAlert* (see Figure 7-9):

```
   case OptionsAbout:
      FrmAlert(AboutBoxAlert);
      break;
```

This is fine if all you want is some text. If you have pictures, however, create a modal form and display it with *FrmDoDialog*. "Modal Dialogs" on page 101 describes how to do that.

---

* This is almost certain to change in future releases of the SDK. Check your version to see if Palm Computing has changed *AbtShowAbout* to support third-party About Boxes.

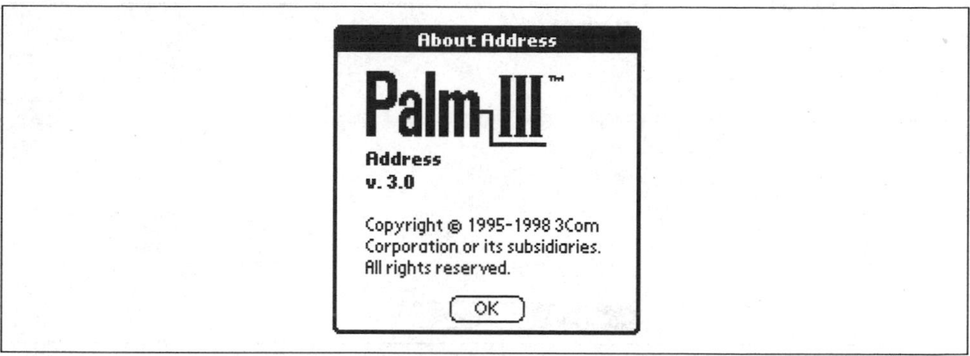


*Figure 7-8. AbtShowAbout shows a 3Com-specific About Box*

*Figure 7-9. An About Box displayed using FrmAlert*

## Menu Erase Status

There is a problem with menus and refreshing the display of the Palm screen that you should take into account in your applications. Before describing the fix to the problem, let us explain what the user does and when the problem occurs.

When the user chooses a menu item using a shortcut key, the Menu Manager displays the status of this task in the lower left of the display. First, the Menu Manager displays the word "Command" (see Figure 7-10) to indicate that a stroke has been noticed. If the user then writes a valid shortcut key, the Menu Manager displays the menu item name (see Figure 7-11) and dispatches the menu event for the application to handle.

This shortcut key status is shown on the screen for a couple of seconds: just enough time for the user to read it and get feedback that the Palm device has noticed the stroke. After this, the status update automatically goes away.

There is one case in which you need to clear the status yourself because a problem occurs. The Palm OS notes when the user chooses a menu item using a shortcut key and saves the screen bits underneath the area where the word "Command" is displayed. Once the timer goes off, the bits are restored. If you have changed the screen contents in the meantime, the bits that are restored are stale. Figure 7-12 shows the problem.

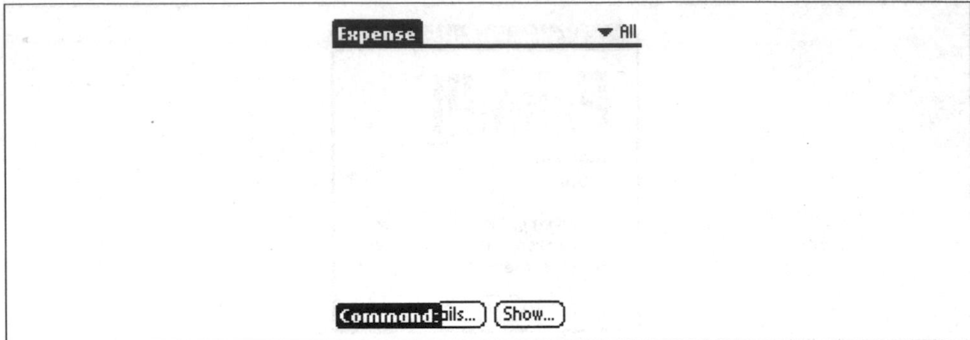


*Figure 7-10. Menu status after entering a shortcut character*

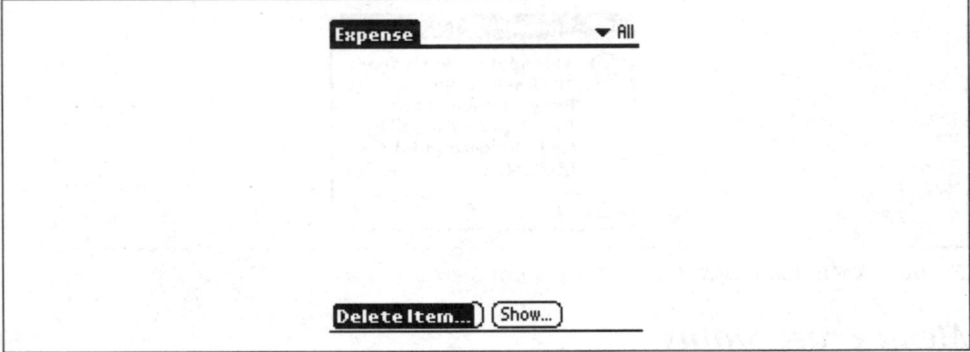


*Figure 7-11. Menu status after entering a shortcut character and then a menu shortcut key*

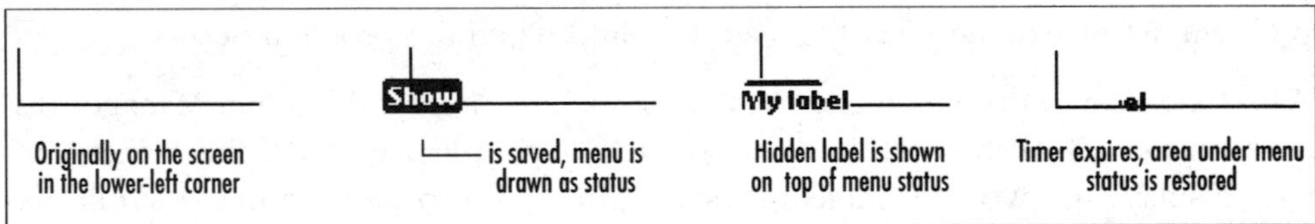


*Figure 7-12. Menu code changing contents of lower left of screen without calling MenuEraseStatus*

A common case where your menu code would change the screen contents is in an alert or another form. Nicely enough, the Palm OS catches this case automatically and erases the status for you. You will have trouble, however, when you change the contents of the current form. Here's some sample code that shows the problem in Figure 7-12 (the code shows a previously hidden form object):

```
case ShowLabelMenuItem:
   {
      Word      index;
      FormPtr   frm;
```

```
        frm = FrmGetActiveForm();
        index = FrmGetObjectIndex(frm, CustomersTestLabel);
        FrmShowObject(frm, index);
    }
    break;
```

Deal with this problem by doing your own erasing. The call to clear the status is *MenuEraseStatus*. The fix to the code that exhibits the problem is simply a call to *MenuEraseStatus* before modifying the screen:

```
case ShowLabelMenuItem:
    {
        Word        index;
        FormPtr    frm;

        MenuEraseStatus();
        frm = FrmGetActiveForm();
        index = FrmGetObjectIndex(frm, CustomersTestLabel);
        FrmShowObject(frm, index);
    }
    break;
```

You have to be careful with this fix, however, as it is a double-edged sword. You don't want to call *MenuEraseStatus* unnecessarily, as there is a price to pay. When you call it, the user gets only a very brief glimpse of the confirmed menu item. You wiped out the confirmed menu item when you restored the screen bits. This cure is still better than the problem, however, as a mess on the screen is worse than wiping out the status quickly.

A good way to ensure that you have implemented *MenuEraseStatus* when necessary is to use shortcut characters in your testing. This lets you determine when you need to make a call to *MenuEraseStatus* to clean up screen trash.

The folks at Palm Computing are getting wiser. Unfortunately, not until OS 2.0 did they fix this problem some of the time. The earlier 1.0 OS does not even erase the status before putting up another form. If you're supporting the 1.0 OS, you need to call *MenuErase-Status* in any menu-handling code that puts up a form or alert.

Forms that have buttons at the bottom that don't ever change are obviously not affected by this problem. For these forms, the menu status automatic timed erasing works just fine. It's only the few forms with changing data at the bottom left that are affected.

## Handling Unusable Menu Items

The Menu Manager APIs don't provide a mechanism for adding or deleting menu items dynamically. In addition, there's no way to visually disable them (by graying them). This, of course, immediately raises the question of what you should do if there are menus or menu items that can't be used in certain situations.

One possibility is to present an alert to the user explaining why it's not possible to do what was requested. That's the strategy used by the built-in Expense application when the user tries to delete an item and nothing is selected (see Figure 7-13).

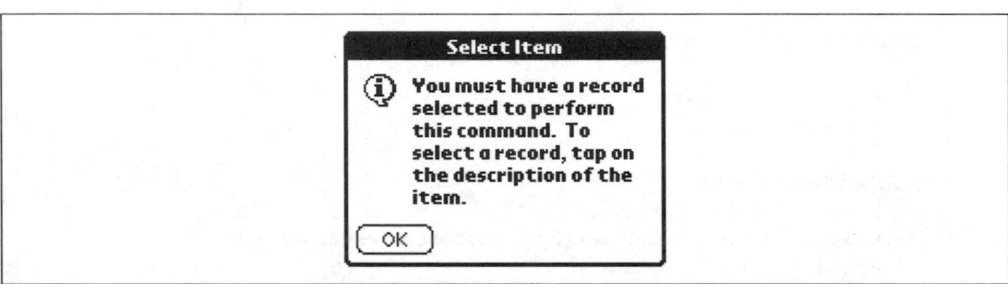


*Figure 7-13. Deleting an item in Expense when nothing is selected*

This is certainly better than having the menu item appear and disappear as an item is selected and deselected—a tactic guaranteed to make users foam at the mouth. Disappearing and reappearing things make many people doubt their sanity, as they often have absolutely no idea how to make a menu item reappear.

### *A good time to remove a menu item*

There are cases, however, where you do want to remove menu items. For example, you may have a menu item that will never be present on a user's device. An obvious case of this is beaming, which is available only if OS 3.0 is present. A well-designed application ought to figure out what OS it is running under and behave accordingly. It should have the Beam item show on 3.0 devices and disappear on pre-3.0 devices.

In order to implement this nice design, you actually use a rather simplistic solution—two menu bars, each with its own copy of the menus. One of the menus has a Beam item, the other doesn't.

Since applications built with CodeWarrior (Release 4, as of this writing) have their menu IDs automatically assigned, you should create these menus carefully. To make sure that menu items that are in both menubars remain in the same position, put the Beam menu item at the bottom of the 3.0 version.

Specify one menubar as the form's menubar as part of the resource (let's make it the one with the Beam item). You may need to change the menubar at runtime using *FrmSetMenu*, which changes the menubar ID of a form. Make the change when you open the form with code like this:

```
if (sysGetROMVerMajor(gRomVersion) < 3)
   FrmSetMenu(FrmGetActiveForm(), CustomersnobeamMenuBar);
```

#### *Tools for implementing duplicate menus*

If you want to have multiple menus that share the same menu IDs, you need to create your menus textually. If you use PilRC, you're doing that already (just make sure duplicate menu items share the same menu ID). If you use CodeWarrior, you need to create an *.r* file with the textual menus (duplicate menus should share the same base ID).

## *A Procedure for Handling Common Menu Items*

We have already noted that you often have more than one form with an Edit menu—especially in forms with text fields. It might also make sense to have your About menu item present often. In such cases, you should use some common method to handle these and other standard menu items.

You typically put the About menu in the Options menu. Because the Options menu can and does occur in more than one form, it makes a lot of sense to leave the About menu in every instance. It is less confusing to the user if it is always there.

Your first step is to use the same menu IDs for the shared menu items. Next, you need a function to handle the common menu items such as *HandleCommonMenuItems*. It should work for the standard Edit menu items, as well as the About menu item. Example 7-1 shows the code to use.

*Example 7-1. A Routine to Handle Menu Items Common to More than One Form*

```
static Boolean HandleCommonMenuItems(Word menuID)
{
   FieldPtr   fld;

   switch (menuID) {
   case EditUndo:
   case EditCut:
   case EditCopy:
   case EditPaste:
   case EditSelectAll:
      fld = GetFocusObjectPtr();
      if (!fld)
         return false;
      if (menuID == EditUndo)
```

*Example 7-1. A Routine to Handle Menu Items Common to More than One Form (continued)*

```
            FldUndo(fld);
        else if (menuID == EditCut)
            FldCut(fld);
        else if (menuID == EditCopy)
            FldCopy(fld);
        else if (menuID == EditPaste)
            FldCopy(fld);
        else if (menuID == EditSelectAll)
            FldSetSelection (fld, 0, FldGetTextLength (fld));
        return true;

    case EditKeyboard:
        SysKeyboardDialog(kbdDefault);
        return true;

    case EditGrafitti:
        SysGraffitiReferenceDialog(referenceDefault);
        return true;

    case OptionsAbout:
        FrmAlert(AboutBoxAlert);
        return true;

    default:
        return false;
    }
}
```

Call *HandleCommonMenuItems* from each of your menu-handling routines:

```
Boolean void MyFormHandleMenuEvent(Word menuID)
{
   if (HandleCommonMenuItems(menuID)
      return true;
   else switch (menuID) {
      // other items here
   }
}
```

# *Adding Menus to the Sample Application*

Now it is time to add the menus to our Sales application. The menubars are added first. Next, we set up our definitions for our menu items and menubars. Once that is in place, we can create our code to handle common menu items and the functions we need to handle our forms. Our last step is to make sure the main event loop in our application correctly calls our menu-handling function.

## *The Menubars*

The application has five menubars, the first of which is shown in Figure 7-14. This menubar is for the Order form, which contains the menus Record, Edit, and Options.

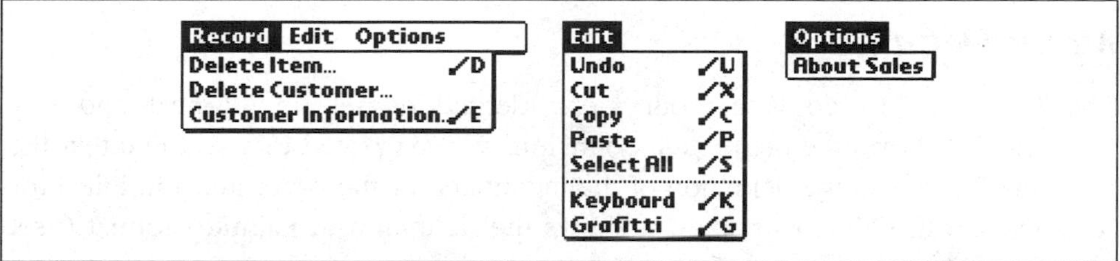


*Figure 7-14. The Order menubar on a pre-3.0 device*

The second menubar is like the first, but has a Beam Customer item at the end of the Record menu (see Figure 7-15).

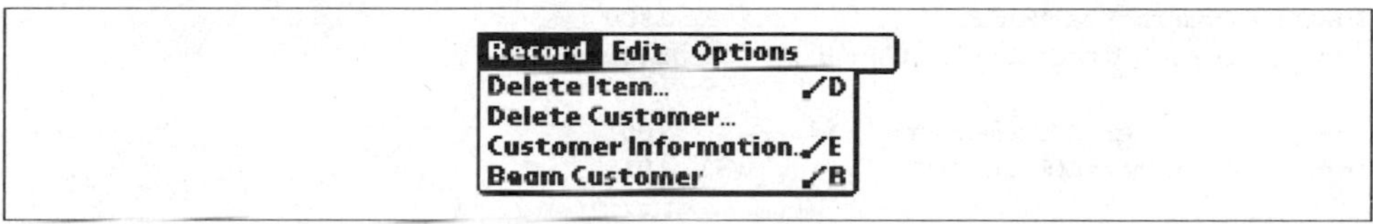


*Figure 7-15. The Order menubar on a 3.0 or later device*

The third menubar, *DialogWithInputField*, is used for dialogs that have textual input fields (see Figure 7-16).

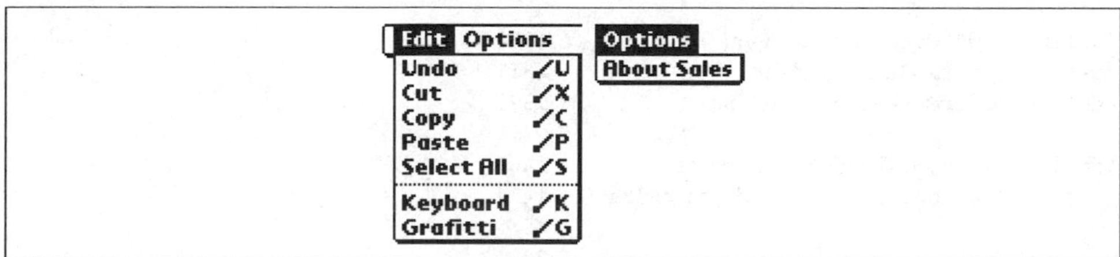


*Figure 7-16. The menus for dialogs with input fields*

The fourth and fifth bars are used separately, depending on whether the application is running on a 3.0 or earlier device. As you can see in Figure 7-17, the difference is whether beaming shows up as a menu item. We have different menus for different devices so that a pre-3.0 user doesn't get confused about either the application's or device's capability.

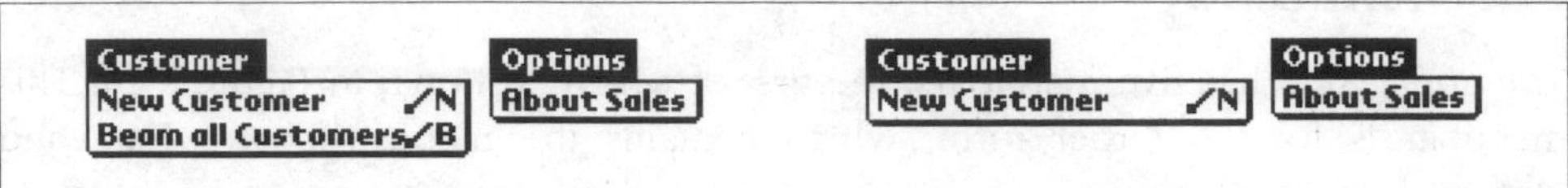


*Figure 7-17. The Customer menus for 3.0 and pre-3.0 devices*

## Menu Definitions

The first thing to do is get our menu definitions set up all neat and tidy. Example 7-2 shows the menu item definitions we've created in a separate text file. Example 7-3 shows the definition of the menubars for the order items in PilRC format (used with GCC). Example 7-4 shows the definition in PalmRez format (used with CodeWarrior).

*Example 7-2. SalesMenus.h, Defining Constants for Menus and Menubars*

```
#define CustomersMenuBar                    1000
#define CustomersNoBeamMenuBar              1100
#define OrderMenuBar                        1200
#define OrderNoBeamMenuBar                  1300
#define DialogWithInputFieldMenuBar         1400

#define CustomersCustomerMenu               1001
#define CustomersOptionsMenu                1011

#define CustomersNoBeamCustomerMenu         1101
#define CustomersNoBeamOptionsMenu          1111

#define OrderRecordMenu                     1201
#define OrderEditMenu                       1211
#define OrderOptionsMenu                    1221

#define OrderNoBeamRecordMenu               1301
#define OrderNoBeamEditMenu                 1311
#define OrderNoBeamOptionsMenu              1321

#define DialogWithInputFieldEditMenu        1401
#define DialogWithInputFieldOptionsMenu     1411

#define CustomerBase                        2001
#define CustomerNewCustomer                 2001
#define CustomerBeamAllCustomers            2002

#define OptionsBase                         2101
#define OptionsAboutSales                   2101

#define RecordBase                          2201
#define RecordDeleteItem                    2201
#define RecordDeleteCustomer                2202
#define RecordCustomerDetails               2203
#define RecordBeamCustomer                  2204
```

*Example 7-2. SalesMenus.h, Defining Constants for Menus and Menubars (continued)*

```
#define EditBase                        2301
#define EditUndo                        2301
#define EditCut                         2302
#define EditCopy                        2303
#define EditPaste                       2304
#define EditSelectAll                   2305
// separator
#define EditKeyboard                    2307
#define EditGrafitti                    2308
```

*Example 7-3. Part of Sales.rcp File, Used for Menus with GCC*

```
#include "SalesMenus.h"

MENU ID OrderMenuBar
BEGIN
   PULLDOWN "Record"
   BEGIN
      MENUITEM "Delete Item..." ID RecordDeleteItem "D"
      MENUITEM "Delete Customer..." ID RecordDeleteCustomer
      MENUITEM "Customer Information..." ID RecordCustomerDetails "E"
      MENUITEM "Beam Customer" ID RecordBeamCustomer "B"
   END

   PULLDOWN "Edit"
   BEGIN
      MENUITEM "Undo" ID EditUndo "U"
      MENUITEM "Cut" ID EditCut "X"
      MENUITEM "Copy" ID EditCopy "C"
      MENUITEM "Paste" ID EditPaste "P"
      MENUITEM "Select All" ID EditSelectAll "S"
      MENUITEM "-" AUTOID
      MENUITEM "Keyboard" ID EditKeyboard "K"
      MENUITEM "Grafitti " ID EditGrafitti "G"
   END

   PULLDOWN "Options"
   BEGIN
      MENUITEM "About Sales" ID OptionsAboutSales
   END
END

MENU ID OrderNoBeamMenuBar
BEGIN
   PULLDOWN "Record"
   BEGIN
      MENUITEM "Delete Item..." ID RecordDeleteItem "D"
      MENUITEM "Delete Customer..." ID RecordDeleteCustomer
      MENUITEM "Customer Information..." ID RecordCustomerDetails "E"
   END

   PULLDOWN "Edit"
   BEGIN
```

*Example 7-3. Part of Sales.rcp File, Used for Menus with GCC (continued)*

```
      MENUITEM "Undo" ID EditUndo "U"
      MENUITEM "Cut" ID EditCut "X"
      MENUITEM "Copy" ID EditCopy "C"
      MENUITEM "Paste" ID EditPaste "P"
      MENUITEM "Select All" ID EditSelectAll "S"
      MENUITEM "-" AUTOID
      MENUITEM "Keyboard" ID EditKeyboard "K"
      MENUITEM "Grafitti " ID EditGrafitti "G"
   END

   PULLDOWN "Options"
   BEGIN
      MENUITEM "About Sales" ID OptionsAboutSales
   END
END

MENU ID DialogWithInputFieldMenuBar
BEGIN
   PULLDOWN "Edit"
   BEGIN
      MENUITEM "Undo" ID EditUndo "U"
      MENUITEM "Cut" ID EditCut "X"
      MENUITEM "Copy" ID EditCopy "C"
      MENUITEM "Paste" ID EditPaste "P"
      MENUITEM "Select All" ID EditSelectAll "S"
      MENUITEM "-" AUTOID
      MENUITEM "Keyboard" ID EditKeyboard "K"
      MENUITEM "Grafitti " ID EditGrafitti "G"
   END

   PULLDOWN "Options"
   BEGIN
      MENUITEM "About Sales" ID OptionsAboutSales
   END
END

MENU ID CustomersMenuBar
BEGIN
   PULLDOWN "Customer"
   BEGIN
      MENUITEM "New Customer" ID CustomerNewCustomer "N"
      MENUITEM "Beam all Customers" ID CustomerBeamAllCustomers "B"
   END

   PULLDOWN "Options"
   BEGIN
      MENUITEM "About Sales" ID OptionsAboutSales
   END
END

MENU ID CustomersNoBeamMenuBar
BEGIN
```

*Example 7-3. Part of Sales.rcp File, Used for Menus with GCC (continued)*

```
   PULLDOWN "Customer"
   BEGIN
      MENUITEM "New Customer" ID CustomerNewCustomer "N"
   END

   PULLDOWN "Options"
   BEGIN
      MENUITEM "About Sales" ID OptionsAboutSales
   END
END
```

*Example 7-4. Sales.r, Used for Menus with CodeWarrior*

```
#include "MenuDefs.r"

#include "SalesMenus.h"

resource 'MENU' (OrderRecordMenu) {
   RecordBase,
   "Record",
   {
      "Delete Item...",        "D";
      "Delete Customer...",    NONE;
      "Customer Information...", "E";
      "Beam Customer",      "B";
   }
};

resource 'MENU' (OrderEditMenu) {
   EditBase,
   "Edit",
   {
      "Undo",   "U";
      "Cut",    "X";
      "Copy",   "C";
      "Paste", "P";
      "Select All",   "S";
      SEPARATOR, NONE;
      "Keyboard", "K";
      "Graffiti", "G";
   }
};

resource 'MENU' (OrderOptionsMenu) {
   OptionsBase,
   "Options",
   {
      "About Sales", NONE;
   }
};

resource 'MENU' (OrderNoBeamRecordMenu) {
   RecordBase,
```

*Example 7-4. Sales.r, Used for Menus with CodeWarrior (continued)*

```
    "Record",
    {
       "Delete Item...",       "D";
       "Delete Customer...",   NONE;
       "Customer Information...", "E";
    }
};

resource 'MENU' (OrderNoBeamEditMenu) {
    EditBase,
    "Edit",
    {
       "Undo",  "U";
       "Cut",   "X";
       "Copy",  "C";
       "Paste", "P";
       "Select All",  "S";
       SEPARATOR, NONE;
       "Keyboard", "K";
       "Graffiti", "G";
    }
};

resource 'MENU' (OrderNoBeamOptionsMenu) {
    OptionsBase,
    "Options",
    {
       "About Sales", NONE;
    }
};

resource 'MBAR' (OrderMenuBar) {
    {OrderRecordMenu, OrderEditMenu, OrderOptionsMenu}
};

resource 'MBAR' (OrderNoBeamMenuBar) {
    {OrderNoBeamRecordMenu, OrderNoBeamEditMenu, OrderNoBeamOptionsMenu}
};

resource 'MENU' (DialogWithInputFieldEditMenu) {
    EditBase,
    "Edit",
    {
       "Undo",  "U";
       "Cut",   "X";
       "Copy",  "C";
       "Paste", "P";
       "Select All",  "S";
       SEPARATOR, NONE;
       "Keyboard", "K";
       "Graffiti", "G";
    }
};
```

*Example 7-4. Sales.r, Used for Menus with CodeWarrior (continued)*

```
resource 'MENU' (DialogWithInputFieldOptionsMenu) {
   OptionsBase,
   "Options",
   {
      "About Sales", NONE;
   }
};

resource 'MBAR' (DialogWithInputFieldMenuBar) {
   {DialogWithInputFieldEditMenu, DialogWithInputFieldOptionsMenu}
};


resource 'MENU' (CustomersCustomerMenu) {
   CustomerBase,
   "Customer",
   {
      "New Customer...", "N";
      "Beam all Customers", "B";
   }
};

resource 'MENU' (CustomersOptionsMenu) {
   OptionsBase,
   "Options",
   {
      "About Sales", NONE;
   }
};

resource 'MENU' (CustomersNoBeamCustomerMenu) {
   CustomerBase,
   "Customer",
   {
      "New Customer...", "N";
   }
};

resource 'MENU' (CustomersNoBeamOptionsMenu) {
   OptionsBase,
   "Options",
   {
      "About Sales", NONE;
   }
};

resource 'MBAR' (CustomersMenuBar) {
   {CustomersCustomerMenu, CustomersOptionsMenu}
};

resource 'MBAR' (CustomersNoBeamMenuBar) {
   {CustomersNoBeamCustomerMenu, CustomersNoBeamOptionsMenu}
};
```

## Handling Common Menus

The Sales application has a *HandleCommonMenuItems*, as shown earlier in Example 7-1. The *ItemHandleEvent* routine calls *HandleCommonMenuItems* in case of a menu event:

```
static Boolean ItemHandleEvent(EventPtr event)
{
   Boolean     handled = false;

#ifdef __GNUC__
   CALLBACK_PROLOGUE
#endif
   switch (event->eType) {
      // code deleted that handles other kinds of events

      case menuEvent:
         handled = HandleCommonMenuItems(event->data.menu.itemID);
      }
#ifdef __GNUC__
   CALLBACK_EPILOGUE
#endif
   return handled;
}
```

*OrderHandleMenuEvent* is responsible for the menu items for the Order form:

```
static Boolean OrderHandleMenuEvent(Word menuID)
{
   Boolean handled = false;

   if (HandleCommonMenuItems(menuID))
      handled = true;
   else
      switch (menuID) {
      case RecordDeleteItem:
         if (!gCellSelected)
            FrmAlert(NoItemSelectedAlert);
         else
            // code deleted that deletes an item
         handled = true;
         break;

      case RecordCustomerDetails:
         // code deleted that opens customer details dialog
         handled = true;
         break;

      case RecordBeamCustomer:
         BeamCustomer(
            GetRecordNumberForCustomer(gCurrentOrder->customerID));
         handled = true;
         break;

      case RecordDeleteCustomer:
         // code deleted that deletes a customer
```

```
            break;
        }
    return handled;
}
```

It is called by *OrderHandleEvent* if a menu event occurs:

```
static Boolean OrderHandleEvent(EventPtr event)
{
   Boolean     handled = false;

#ifdef __GNUC__
   CALLBACK_PROLOGUE
#endif
   switch (event->eType)
      {
      // code deleted that handles other kinds of events

      case menuEvent:
         handled = OrderHandleMenuEvent(event->data.menu.itemID);
      }
#ifdef __GNUC__
   CALLBACK_EPILOGUE
#endif
   return handled;
}
```

The New Customer/Edit Customer dialog has an event handler that has to handle the common menu items:

```
static Boolean CustomerHandleEvent(EventPtr event)
{
#ifdef __GNUC__
   CALLBACK_PROLOGUE
#endif
   // code removed that handles other types of events
   } else if (event->eType == menuEvent) {
      if (HandleCommonMenuItems(event->data.menu.itemID))
         return true;
   }
#ifdef __GNUC__
   CALLBACK_EPILOGUE
#endif
   return false;
}
```

## Checking the OS Version Number

The Customers form has two different menubars, one with a Beam item. Here's where one is changed if we're running on a pre-3.0 system:

```
static void CustomersFormOpen(void)
{
   // code removed that initializes the customer list
```

```
    if (sysGetROMVerMajor(gRomVersion) < 3)
        FrmSetMenu(FrmGetActiveForm(), CustomersNoBeamMenuBar);
}
```

## The Customers Form

Here's the menu-handling code for the Customers form:

```
static Boolean CustomersHandleMenuEvent(Word menuID)
{
    Boolean handled = false;

    if (HandleCommonMenuItems(menuID))
        return true;
    else switch (menuID) {
    case CustomerNewCustomer:
        // code deleted that creates a new customer
        handled = true;
        break;

    case CustomerBeamAllCustomers:
        // code deleted that beams all customers
        handled = true;
        break;
    }
    return handled;
}

static Boolean CustomersHandleEvent(EventPtr event)
{
    Boolean     handled = false;

#ifdef __GNUC__
    CALLBACK_PROLOGUE
#endif
    switch (event->eType)
        {
        case menuEvent:
            handled = CustomersHandleMenuEvent(event->data.menu.itemID);
            break;

        // code deleted that handles other events
        }
#ifdef __GNUC__
    CALLBACK_EPILOGUE
#endif
    return handled;
}
```

This is all the code and definitions necessary to make our menus work. You saw that our strategy for menus included a design preference for making menu items completely disappear if the application is present on a device that doesn't use the feature (as in beaming). There were also a few problems you encountered when you create duplicate types of menus and when handling the display of the Graffiti shortcut status in the bottom left corner of the unit.

At this point, the Sales application is almost complete—you have all the essential UI elements and code in place. What is left are just a few bits, though they are important bits. You will add support for these features the next chapter for tables, find, and beaming.

# 8

*In this chapter:*
- *Tables*
- *Tables in the Sample Application*
- *Find*
- *Beaming*
- *Barcodes*

# *Extras*

This chapter is a grab bag of items that have no particular programmatic relationship to each other. We put them together here because they need to be discussed, and they had to go somewhere.

## *Tables*

In this section, we do three things. First, we talk in general about tables, the kinds of data they contain, what they look like, what features are automatically supported, and what you need to add yourself. Second, we create a small sample application that shows you how to implement all the available table data types. Third, we show you the implementation of a table in our Sales order application. We also discuss the problems that we encountered in implementing tables and offer you a variety of tips.

### *An Overview of Tables*

Tables are useful forms if you need to display and edit multiple columns of data. (Use a list to display a single column; see "List Objects" in Chapter 5, *Forms and Form Objects*, on page 91). Figure 8-1 contains three examples of tables from the built-in applications. As you can see, tables can contain a number of different types of data—everything from text to dates to numbers.

#### *Scrolling in tables*

While the List Manager automatically supports scrolling, the Table Manager does not. You have to add that support if you need it.

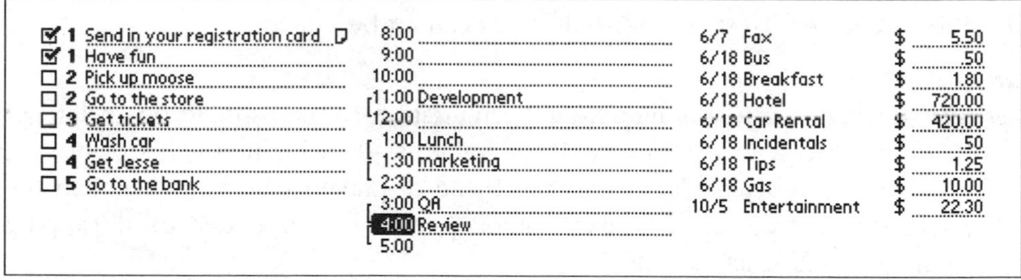


*Figure 8-1. Sample tables from the built-in applications; the first item in the To Do list has a note icon associated with it*

### *Adjusting width and height*

The height and width of table columns and rows are independently adjustable (in fact, editing a text field automatically makes a row change size).

### *Data types in tables*

The Palm OS Table Manager offers greater built-in support for displaying data than for editing it. The following sections list the data types and whether the Table Manager supports them for display purposes only or for editing as well.

***Display-only data types.*** The following are display-only data types:

- Numbers
- Dates
- Labels (non-editable text)

***Edit and display data types.*** The following are edit and display data types:

- Text (including an optional note icon; see Figure 8-1)
- Pop-up triggers
- Checkboxes

Unlike other controls, tables require some programming in order to work. The table stores data for each cell in two parts—an integer and a pointer. The data is used differently, depending on the type of the column. Because of this, you must specify a data type for each column. Here are the possible specifications you can make.

---

The source code for the 1.0 OS Table Manager can be found at *http://www.palmpilot.com/devzone.* Be aware that the Table Manager has changed since the 1.0 OS. It is still useful, however, as it gives you a good idea of how the manager works.

---

***Display-only data types.*** These are the actual names of data types supported by the Table Manager. These display-only types cannot be edited.

*dateTableItem*

This displays a date (as month/day). The data for a cell should be an integer that can be cast to a *DateType*. If the value is –1, a hyphen (–) is displayed; otherwise, the actual date is shown. If the displayed date is earlier than the handheld's current date, an exclamation point (!) is appended to it. Tapping on a date highlights the cell.

*labelTableItem*

This displays the text stored in the pointer portion of the cell with an appended colon (:). Tapping on a label highlights the cell.

*numericTableItem*

This displays the number stored in the integer portion of the cell. Tapping on a numeric cell highlights the cell.

***Editable data types.*** These are the types of data that the user can change or edit as necessary:

*checkboxTableItem*

This displays a checkbox with no associated label. The data for a particular cell should be an integer with a value of either 0 or 1. Clicking on the checkbox toggles the value. Tapping on a checkbox doesn't highlight the row.

*popupTriggerTableItem*

This displays an item from a pop-up list (with an arrow before it). The list pointer is stored in the pointer data of the cell; the item from the list is stored in the integer data of the cell. Tapping on a pop-up trigger displays the pop-up, allowing the user to change the value in the integer.

*textTableItem*

This displays a text cell that can be edited. The column that contains these cells needs a load routine that provides a handle. This handle has an offset and length that are used when editing the text cell. An optional save routine is called after editing.

*textWithNoteTableItem*

This is similar to *textTableItem*, but it also displays a note icon at the righthand side of the cell. Tapping on the note icon highlights the cell.

*narrowTextTableItem*

This is like *textTableItem*, but it reserves space at the righthand side of the cell. The number of pixel spaces reserved is stored in the integer data of the cell. This is often used for text fields that have 0 or more icons and need to reserve space for them.

*customTableItem*

This is used for a custom cell. A callback routine needs to be installed for the column; it will be called to draw the contents of each cell at display time. The callback routine can use the integer and pointer data in the cell for whatever it likes. Tapping on a custom table cell highlights the cell.

### *Initializing tables*

There are some difficulties with initializing tables. When you initialize a table, you should first set the types of each column. You can further mark each row and column as usable or unusable. By dynamically switching a column (or row) from unusable to usable (or usable to unusable), you can make it appear (or disappear).

Although *Table.h* defines a `timeTableItem` type, this type doesn't actually work.

If you make changes to the data in a cell, you need to mark that row invalid so that it will be redisplayed when the table is redrawn. For some mysterious reason, by default rows are usable, but by default columns are not. If you don't explicitly mark your columns as usable, they won't display.

You can set a two-byte ID and a two-byte data value, which are associated with each row. It's common to set the row ID to the record number of a record in a database.

## *Simple Table Sample*

The following sections describe a table sample in a simple application that shows you how to use all the table data types available in the Table Manager. Figure 8-2 shows the running application. You can see that it contains one table with nine columns and eight rows. Figure 8-3 contains the resource descriptions as they are created in Constructor. Note that the columns go from the easiest data types to code to the hardest.

TableSample
0 0: – 1:
2 2: 8/29! 3:
3 3: 8/29! 4:
4 4: 8/29 5:
5 5: 8/29 1:
6 6: 8/29 2:
7 7: 8/29 3:

*Figure 8-2. The table sample*

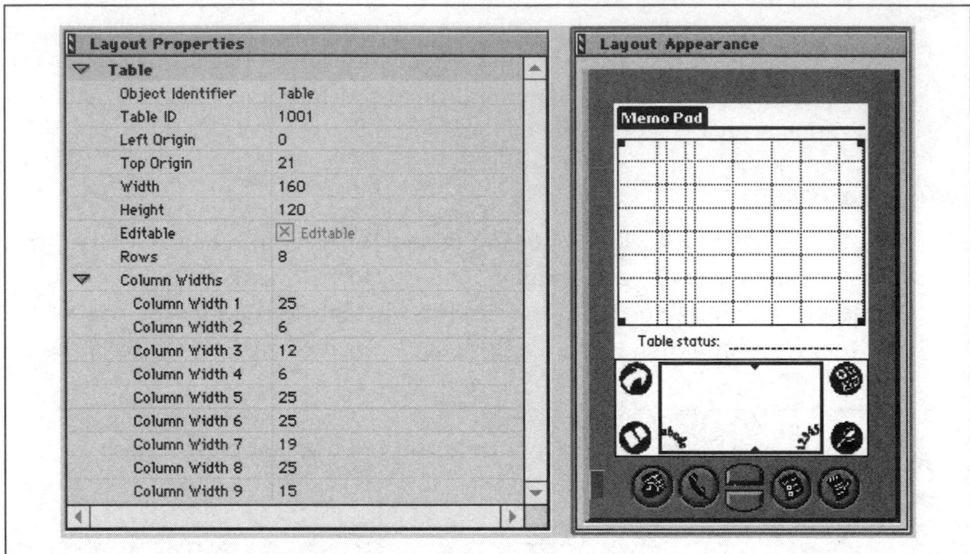


*Figure 8-3. The table resource in Constructor*

### *Initialization of the simple table sample*

Initializing this table requires initializing the style and data for each cell in the table. Example 8-1 shows you the entire initialization method. First, look at the entire block of code; then we discuss it, bit by bit.

*Example 8-1. Initialization of Table*

```
 void MainViewInit(void)
{
   FormPtr         frm;
   TablePtr        tableP;
   UInt            numRows;
   UInt            i;
   static char *   labels[] = {"0", "1", "2", "3", "4", "5", "6", "7"};
   DateType        dates[10];
   ListPtr         list;

   // we"ll have a missing date, and then some dates before and
   // after the current date
   * ((IntPtr) &dates[0]) = noTime;
   for (i = 1; i < sizeof(dates)/sizeof(*dates); i++) {
      dates[i].year = 1994 + i - 1904; // offset from 1904
      dates[i].month = 8;
      dates[i].day = 29;
   }
   // Get a pointer to the main form.
   frm = FrmGetActiveForm();

   tableP = FrmGetObjectPtr(frm,
```

*Example 8-1. Initialization of Table (continued)*

```
      FrmGetObjectIndex(frm, MemoPadMainTableTable));
   list = FrmGetObjectPtr(frm,
      FrmGetObjectIndex (frm, MemoPadMainListList));

   numRows = TblGetNumberOfRows (tableP);
   for (i = 0; i < numRows; i++) {
      TblSetItemStyle(tableP, i, 0, textWithNoteTableItem);

      TblSetItemStyle(tableP, i, 1, numericTableItem);
      TblSetItemInt(tableP, i, 1, i);

      TblSetItemStyle(tableP, i, 2, checkboxTableItem);
      TblSetItemInt(tableP, i, 2, i % 2);

      TblSetItemStyle(tableP, i, 3, labelTableItem);
      TblSetItemPtr(tableP, i, 3, labels[i]);

      TblSetItemStyle(tableP, i, 4, dateTableItem);
      TblSetItemInt(tableP, i, 4, DateToInt(dates[i]));

      TblSetItemStyle(tableP, i, 5, textTableItem);
      TblSetItemInt(tableP, i, 5, i * 2);

      TblSetItemStyle(tableP, i, 6, popupTriggerTableItem);
      TblSetItemInt(tableP, i, 6, i % 5);
      TblSetItemPtr(tableP, i, 6, list);

      TblSetItemStyle(tableP, i, 7, narrowTextTableItem);
      TblSetItemInt(tableP, i, 7, i * 2);

      TblSetItemStyle(tableP, i, 8, customTableItem);
      TblSetItemInt(tableP, i, 8, i % 4);
   }
   TblSetRowUsable(tableP, 1, false);  // just to see what happens

   for (i = 0; i < kNumColumns; i++)
      TblSetColumnUsable(tableP, i, true);

   TblSetLoadDataProcedure(tableP, 0, CustomLoadItem);
   TblSetLoadDataProcedure(tableP, 5, CustomLoadItem);
   TblSetSaveDataProcedure(tableP, 5, CustomSaveItem);
   TblSetLoadDataProcedure(tableP, 7, CustomLoadItem);

   TblSetCustomDrawProcedure(tableP, 8, CustomDrawItem);

   // Draw the form.
   FrmDrawForm(frm);
}
```

Let's look at the columns not in column order, but in terms of complexity.

### *Column 1—handling numbers*

The code starts with a numeric column that is quite an easy data type to handle. We use the row number as the number to display. Here's the code that executes for each row. As you can see, there is not a lot to it:

```
TblSetItemStyle(tableP, i, 1, numericTableItem);
TblSetItemInt(tableP, i, 1, i);
```

### *Column 2—a checkbox*

This second column displays a simple checkbox. We set the initial value of the checkbox to be on for even row numbers and off for odd row numbers:

```
TblSetItemStyle(tableP, i, 2, checkboxTableItem);
TblSetItemInt(tableP, i, 2, i % 2);
```

### *Column 3—a label*

This column displays a label that contains a piece of noneditable text. We set the text to successive values from a text array. The table manager appends a colon to the label:

```
static char *   labels[] = {"0", "1", "2", "3", "4", "5", "6", "7"};
// for each row:
   TblSetItemStyle(tableP, i, 3, labelTableItem);
   TblSetItemPtr(tableP, i, 3, labels[i]);
```

### *Column 4—a date*

In the date column, we create an array of dates that are used to initialize each cell. Note that the first date is missing, which is why the "–" is displayed instead of a date. The remaining dates range over successive years; some dates are before the current time, and others are after it:

```
DateType        dates[10];
ListPtr         list;

// we"ll have a missing date, and then some before and after
// the current date
* ((IntPtr) &dates[0]) = noTime;
for (i = 1; i < sizeof(dates)/sizeof(*dates); i++) {
   dates[i].year = 1994 + i - 1904; // offset from 1904
   dates[i].month = 8;
   dates[i].day = 29;
}
// for each row:
   TblSetItemStyle(tableP, i, 4, dateTableItem);
   TblSetItemInt(tableP, i, 4, DateToInt(dates[i]));
```

### *Column 6—a pop-up trigger*

As with any pop-up trigger, we've got to create a list in our resource. We've created one that has the values "1", "2", "3", "4", and "5". For each cell in the column, we set the pointer value to the list itself, then set the data value as the item number in the list:

```
ListPtr   list;
list = FrmGetObjectPtr(frm,
   FrmGetObjectIndex(frm, MemoPadMainListList));
// for each row:
   TblSetItemStyle(tableP, i, 6, popupTriggerTableItem);
   TblSetItemInt(tableP, i, 6, i % 5);
   TblSetItemPtr(tableP, i, 6, list);
```

### *Columns 0, 5, and 7—handling text*

Now let's look at the text columns. Notice that we use all three of the available text column types:

```
   TblSetItemStyle(tableP, i, 0, textWithNoteTableItem);
   TblSetItemStyle(tableP, i, 5, textTableItem);
   TblSetItemStyle(tableP, i, 7, narrowTextTableItem);
```

With the narrow text table item, we set the integer data as a pixel reserve on the righthand side. We give each row a different pixel reserve so that we can see the effect:

```
   TblSetItemInt(tableP, i, 7, i * 2);
```

Each of the text items requires a custom load procedure to provide the needed handle for the cell. Actually, we have the option of providing only a portion of the handle as well:

```
TblSetLoadDataProcedure(tableP, 0, CustomLoadItem);
TblSetLoadDataProcedure(tableP, 5, CustomLoadItem);
TblSetLoadDataProcedure(tableP, 7, CustomLoadItem);
```

We customize the saving of the second text column:

```
TblSetSaveDataProcedure(tableP, 5, CustomSaveItem);
```

We'll look at the custom load and save routines that we just called after we discuss the eighth column.

### *Column 8—handling custom content*

The final column is a custom column that displays a line at one of four angles. The angle is determined by the integer data in the cell. We initialize the integer data to a value between 0 and 3, depending on the row:

```
   TblSetItemStyle(tableP, i, 8, customTableItem);
   TblSetItemInt(tableP, i, 8, i % 4);
```

We set a custom draw procedure for that column:

```
TblSetCustomDrawProcedure(tableP, 8, CustomDrawItem);
```

### *Displaying the columns*

In order to make the columns display, we've got to mark them usable:

```
for (i = 0; i < kNumColumns; i++)
   TblSetColumnUsable(tableP, i, true);
```

Just as an exercise, we mark row 1 as unusable (now it won't appear in the table):

```
TblSetRowUsable(tableP, 1, false);    // just to see what happens
```

### *Custom load routines*

The custom load routines that we used with the text columns need to return three things:

- A handle
- An offset within it
- A length within it

The Table Manager calls on the Field Manager to display and edit the range within the handle. It's our job to allocate one (null-terminated) handle for every text cell:

```
#define  kNumTextColumns   3
Handle   gHandles[kNumTextColumns][kNumRows];
static Boolean StartApplication(void)
{
   int   i;
   int   j;

#ifdef __GNUC__
   CALLBACK_PROLOGUE
#endif
   for (i = 0; i < kNumTextColumns; i++)
      for (j = 0; j < kNumRows; j++) {
         CharPtr  s;
         gHandles[i][j] = MemHandleNew(1);
         s = MemHandleLock(gHandles[i][j]);
         *s = '\0';
         MemHandleUnlock(gHandles[i][j]);
      }
#ifdef __GNUC__
   CALLBACK_EPILOGUE
#endif
   return false;
}
```

A utility routine converts a table column number to an appropriate index in our handles array:

```
static int WhichTextColumn(int column)
{
   if (column == 0)
      return 0;
   else if (column == 5)
      return 1;
   else //column == 7
      return 2;
}
```

Once we have the handles for each text cell, we can set the offset and length within each one. We set our offset to 0 and the size to the appropriate length of data:

```
static Err CustomLoadItem(VoidPtr table, Word row, Word column,
   Boolean editable, VoidHand * dataH, WordPtr dataOffset,
   WordPtr dataSize, FieldPtr fld)
{
#ifdef __GNUC__
   CALLBACK_PROLOGUE
#endif
   *dataH = gHandles[WhichTextColumn(column)][row];
   *dataOffset = 0;
   *dataSize = MemHandleSize(*dataH);

#ifdef __GNUC__
   CALLBACK_EPILOGUE
#endif
return 0;
}
```

### *Custom save routine*

This save routine customizes the saving of the first cell in the second text column. If the text has been edited, the text converts from uppercase to lowercase. Note that the save routine returns true in this case to show that the table needs to be redrawn:

```
static Boolean CustomSaveItem(VoidPtr table, Word row, Word column)
{
   int textColumn;
   Boolean result = false;

#ifdef __GNUC__
   CALLBACK_PROLOGUE
#endif
   textColumn = WhichTextColumn(column);
   // the handle that we provided in CustomLoadItem has been modified
   // We could edit that (if we wanted).
```

```
   // If it's been edited, let's make the first row
   // convert to lower-case and redraw
   if (row == 0 && textColumn == 1) {
      FieldPtr field = TblGetCurrentField(table);
      if (field && FldDirty(field)) {
         VoidHand h = gHandles[textColumn][row];
         CharPtr        s;
         int            i;

         s = MemHandleLock(h);
         for (i = 0; s[i] != '\0'; i++)
            if (s[i] >= 'A' && s[i] <= 'Z')
               s[i] += 'a' - 'A';
         MemHandleUnlock(h);
         TblMarkRowInvalid(table, row);
         result = true;
      }
   }
#ifdef __GNUC__
   CALLBACK_EPILOGUE
#endif
   return result;  // should the table be redrawn
}
```

### *Custom draw routine*

We need a drawing routine that creates our rotating line:

```
// draws either \, |, /, or -
static void CustomDrawItem(VoidPtr table, Word row, Word column,
   RectanglePtr bounds)
{
   UInt  fromx, fromy, tox, toy;

#ifdef __GNUC__
   CALLBACK_PROLOGUE
#endif
   switch (TblGetItemInt(table, row, column)) {
   case 0:
      fromx = bounds->topLeft.x;
      fromy = bounds->topLeft.y;
      tox = fromx + bounds->extent.x;
      toy = fromy + bounds->extent.y;
      break;
   case 1:
      fromx = bounds->topLeft.x + bounds->extent.x / 2;
      fromy = bounds->topLeft.y;
      tox = fromx;
      toy = fromy + bounds->extent.y;
      break;
   case 2:
      fromx = bounds->topLeft.x + bounds->extent.x;
      fromy = bounds->topLeft.y;
      tox = bounds->topLeft.x;
      toy = fromy + bounds->extent.y;
```

```
        break;
    case 3:
        fromx = bounds->topLeft.x;
        fromy = bounds->topLeft.y + bounds->extent.y / 2;
        tox = fromx + bounds->extent.x;
        toy = fromy;
        break;
    default:
        fromx = tox = bounds->topLeft.x;
        fromy = toy = bounds->topLeft.y;
        break;
    }
    WinDrawLine(fromx, fromy, tox, toy);
#ifdef __GNUC__
    CALLBACK_EPILOGUE
#endif
}
```

### *Handling a table event*

If we tap on a cell in the custom column, we want the angle of the line to change. We do that by changing the integer value. The *tblSelectEvent* is posted to the event queue when a custom cell is successfully tapped (that is, the user taps on and releases the same cell).

While you might assume that the *tblSelectEvent* is where to change the value and redraw, this isn't the case. The Table Manager highlights the selected cell, and we overwrite the highlighting when we redraw. If we switch to a new cell, the Table Manager tries to unhighlight by inverting. As these are certainly not the results we want, we need to handle the call in another place.

We're going to handle the redraw in *tblEnterEvent*, looking to see whether the tapped cell is in our column:

```
static Boolean MainViewHandleEvent(EventPtr event)
{
    Boolean     handled = false;

#ifdef __GNUC__
    CALLBACK_PROLOGUE
#endif
    switch (event->eType)
    {
        // code deleted

        case tblSelectEvent:
            // handle successful tap on a cell
            // for a checkbox or popup, tblExitEvent will be
            // called instead of tblSelectEvent
```

```
            // if the user cancels the control
            break;

         case tblEnterEvent:
            {
               UInt  row = event->data.tblEnter.row;
               UInt  column = event->data.tblEnter.column;

               if (column == 8) {
                  TablePtr table = event->data.tblEnter.pTable;
                  int      oldValue = TblGetItemInt(table, row, column);

                  TblSetItemInt(table, row, column, (oldValue + 1) % 4);
                  TblMarkRowInvalid(table, row);
                  TblRedrawTable(table);
                  handled = true;
               }
            }
            break;
      }
   #ifdef __GNUC__
      CALLBACK_EPILOGUE
   #endif
      return handled;
   }
```

This is all that is worth mentioning in the simple example of a table. It should be enough to guide you in the implementation of these data types in your own tables.

# *Tables in the Sample Application*

In our sample application, we use a table in the Order form. There are three columns: the product ID, the product, and the quantity. Note that we don't use the numeric cell type for either the product ID or quantity, because we need editing as well as display.

We don't use the text cell type for the product ID or quantity, either. These are numbers that we want displayed as right-justified—the text cell type doesn't provide for right-justified text. Therefore, we don't use table's built-in types. We use the custom cell type to create our own data type, an editable numeric value, instead.

## *Tables with Editable Numeric Values*

If we ignore the Table Manager APIs and create our own data type, we have the advantage of having a preexisting model on which we can rely—the built-in applications for which source code is available use this approach. The major disadvantage to this approach is that we won't be able to rely on the Table Manager for help with all the standard little details (such as key events). For our application, all the Table Manager provides is some iterating through cells for drawing and indicating which cell has been tapped. Thus, we will need to write additional code for the following:

- Key events
- Selecting and deselecting an item in an Order form (a row in the table)
- Tapping on a product ID
- Tapping on an item quantity

### *Initialization*

Here's the code for the one-time initialization done when we load the Order form:

```
static void InitializeItemsList(void)
{
   TablePtr table = GetObjectFromActiveForm(OrderItemsTable);
   Word     rowsInTable;
   Word     row;

   ErrNonFatalDisplayIf(!gCurrentOrder, "nil gCurrentOrder");

   TblSetCustomDrawProcedure(table, kProductNameColumn,
      OrderDrawProductName);
   TblSetCustomDrawProcedure(table, kQuantityColumn, OrderDrawNumber);
   TblSetCustomDrawProcedure(table, kProductIDColumn, OrderDrawNumber);

   rowsInTable = TblGetNumberOfRows(table);
   for (row = 0; row < rowsInTable; row++) {
      TblSetItemStyle(table, row, kProductIDColumn, customTableItem);
      TblSetItemStyle(table, row, kProductNameColumn, customTableItem);
      TblSetItemStyle(table, row, kQuantityColumn, customTableItem);
   }
   TblSetColumnUsable(table, kProductIDColumn, true);
   TblSetColumnUsable(table, kProductNameColumn, true);
   TblSetColumnUsable(table, kQuantityColumn, true);

   LoadTable();
}
tblSelectEvent
```

### *Refreshing the form*

Since the contents of the rows change (as scrolling takes place or as items are added or deleted), we need a routine to update the contents of each row. *LoadTable* updates the scrollbars, sets whether each row is visible or not visible, and sets the global *gTopVisibleItem*:

```
static void LoadTable(void)
{
   TablePtr table = GetObjectFromActiveForm(OrderItemsTable);
   Word  rowsInTable = TblGetNumberOfRows(table);
```

```
    Word row;
    SWord lastPossibleTopItem = ((Word) gCurrentOrder->numItems) -
       rowsInTable;

    if (lastPossibleTopItem < 0)
       lastPossibleTopItem = 0;

    // If we have a currently selected item, make sure that it is visible
    if (gCellSelected)
       if (gCurrentSelectedItemIndex < gTopVisibleItem ||
          gCurrentSelectedItemIndex >= gTopVisibleItem + rowsInTable)
          gTopVisibleItem = gCurrentSelectedItemIndex;

    // scroll up as necessary to display an entire page of info
    gTopVisibleItem = min(gTopVisibleItem, lastPossibleTopItem);

    for (row = 0; row < rowsInTable; row++) {
       if (row + gTopVisibleItem < gCurrentOrder->numItems)
          OrderInitTableRow(table, row, row + gTopVisibleItem);
       else
          TblSetRowUsable(table, row, false);
    }
    SclSetScrollBar(GetObjectFromActiveForm(OrderScrollbarScrollBar),
       gTopVisibleItem, 0, lastPossibleTopItem, rowsInTable - 1);
}
```

### *Displaying the quantity and product data*

*OrderInitTableRow* actually makes the Table Manager calls to (1) mark this row usable, (2) set the row ID to the item number (so we can go from table row to an item), and (3) mark the row as invalid so that it will be redrawn:

```
static void OrderInitTableRow(TablePtr table, Word row, Word itemNum)
{
    // Make the row usable.
    TblSetRowUsable(table, row, true);

    // Store the item number as the row id.
    TblSetRowID(table, row, itemNum);

    // make sure the row will be redrawn
    TblMarkRowInvalid(table, row);
}
```

Instead of creating one field for each numeric cell, we create a field when it's time to draw the cell or when it's time to edit a numeric cell.

Using this programming strategy is a big win for memory use, which, you will remember, is quite tight on the handheld. Because we are creating a field for only one cell at a time, we need to allocate memory for only that one field. If we created all the fields all at once, we would have to reserve a great deal of precious memory, as well.

The custom draw routine for the quantity and product ID is *OrderDrawNumber*:

```
static void OrderDrawNumber(VoidPtr table, Word row, Word column,
   RectanglePtr bounds)
{
   FieldPtr field;
#ifdef __GNUC__
   CALLBACK_PROLOGUE
#endif
   field = OrderInitNumberField(table, row, column, bounds, true);

   FldDrawField(field);
   FldFreeMemory(field);

   OrderDeinitNumberField(table, field);
#ifdef __GNUC__
   CALLBACK_EPILOGUE
#endif
}
```

### *Dynamically adjusting number fields*

We want to dynamically adjust the number fields as an optimization of memory usage, as well. Unfortunately, there is no documented way prior to 3.0 to dynamically set aspects of a field (bounds, etc.). Therefore, like the built-in applications, we need a routine that fills in the fields of the structure by hand. On a 3.0 (or later) OS, there is a documented *FldNewField* routine to create a new field in the form (although there is still no way to modify an existing field).

---

The code that calls *FldNewField* and *FrmRemoveObject* (in *Order-DeInitNumberField*) can cause a runtime error (at least we found one in our Gremlins testing). Deadlines happen to everyone, and we had to go to press before finding the cause of this error. Check the code on the CD, as it might reflect a solution (the CD has a later deadline!).

Rather than not show you the code at all, we've defined a constant, `qUseDynamicUI`. If it's false, the code isn't actually used. In the event that we don't yet have a solution, we would be glad to hear from you if you find the answer (*neil@pobox.com*, *julie@pobox.com*).

---

We've provided code that uses *FldNewField*:

```
#define  qUseDynamicUI     0
#define  kDynamicFieldID   9999  // a field ID not present in the form

// WARNING, the form, and any controls, table, etc. on the form may change
// locations in memory after this call; don't keep pointers to them while
// calling this routine.
static FieldPtr OrderInitNumberField(TablePtr table, Word row,
   Word column, RectanglePtr bounds, Boolean temporary)
```

```
{
   VoidHand    textH;
   CharPtr  textP;
   char     buffer[10];
   ULong    number;
   UInt     itemNumber = TblGetRowID(table, row);
   FieldPtr fld;

   if (!qUseDynamicUI || sysGetROMVerMajor(gRomVersion) < 3) {
      if (temporary)
         fld = &gTempFieldType;
      else
         gCurrentFieldInTable = fld = TblGetCurrentField(table);

      MemSet(fld, sizeof(FieldType), 0);

      RctCopyRectangle(bounds, &fld->rect);

      fld->attr.usable = true;
      fld->attr.visible = !temporary;
      fld->attr.editable = true;
      fld->attr.singleLine = true;
      fld->attr.dynamicSize = false;
      fld->attr.underlined = true;
      fld->attr.insPtVisible = true;
      fld->attr.numeric = true;
      fld->attr.justification = rightAlign;

      fld->maxChars = kMaxNumericStringLength;
   } else {
      FormPtr  frm = FrmGetActiveForm();

      fld = FldNewField((VoidPtr) &frm, kDynamicFieldID,
         bounds->topLeft.x, bounds->topLeft.y, bounds->extent.x,
         bounds->extent.y, stdFont, kMaxNumericStringLength,
         true, true, true, false, rightAlign, false, false, true);
      if (!temporary)
         gCurrentFieldInTable = fld;
   }

   if (column == kQuantityColumn)
      number = gCurrentOrder->items[itemNumber].quantity;
   else
      number = gCurrentOrder->items[itemNumber].productID;

   buffer[0] = '\0';
   // 0 will display as empty string
   if (number)
      StrIToA(buffer, number);

   textH = MemHandleNew(StrLen(buffer) + 1);
   textP = MemHandleLock(textH);
   StrCopy(textP, buffer);
```

```
    MemPtrUnlock(textP);
    FldSetTextHandle(fld, (Handle) textH);

    if (temporary)
        return fld;
    else
        return NULL;
}
```

### *Deallocating number fields*

If the qUseDynamicUI macro is set to true, the deinitialization routine deallocates the field on a 3.0 or later OS:

```
// WARNING, the form, and any controls, table, etc. on the form may change
// locations in memory after this call; don't keep pointers to them while
// calling this routine.
static void OrderDeinitNumberField(TablePtr table, FieldPtr fld)
{
    if (qUseDynamicUI && sysGetROMVerMajor(gRomVersion) >= 3) {
        FormPtr  frm = FrmGetActiveForm();

        FrmRemoveObject(&frm, FrmGetObjectIndex(frm, kDynamicFieldID));
    }
    if (fld == gCurrentFieldInTable)
            gCurrentFieldInTable = NULL;
}
```

*FldNewField* and *FrmRemoveObject* both change the form pointer and can change the pointers to any objects in the form. Make sure not to reuse any pointer (like the table or the field) after calling either of these routines.

### *Adding product names*

Here's the routine that draws a product name (since it's called by the Table Manager, it must have the CALLBACK macros for GCC):

```
static void OrderDrawProductName(VoidPtr table, Word row, Word column,
    RectanglePtr bounds)
{
    VoidHand h = NULL;
    Product  p;
    UInt  itemNumber;
    ULong productID;
    CharPtr  toDraw;

#ifdef __GNUC__
    CALLBACK_PROLOGUE
```

```
#endif
   itemNumber = TblGetRowID(table, row);
   productID = gCurrentOrder->items[itemNumber].productID;
   if (productID) {
      h = GetProductFromProductID(productID, &p, NULL);
      toDraw = (CharPtr) p.name;
   } else
      toDraw = "-Product-";
   DrawCharsToFitWidth(toDraw, bounds);
   if (h)
      MemHandleUnlock(h);
#ifdef __GNUC__
   CALLBACK_EPILOGUE
#endif
}
```

### *Adding scrolling support*

We've got to handle scrolling if we want items to display properly. In the routine *OrderHandleEvent*, we look for a *sclRepeatEvent*:

```
case sclRepeatEvent:
   OrderDeselectRowAndDeleteIfEmpty();
   OrderScrollRows(event->data.sclRepeat.newValue -
      event->data.sclRepeat.value);
   handled = false;  // scrollbar needs to handle the event, too
   break;
```

*OrderScrollRows* is straightforward. It updates *gTopVisibleItem*, then reloads the table and redraws it:

```
static void OrderScrollRows(SWord numRows)
{
   TablePtr table = GetObjectFromActiveForm(OrderItemsTable);

   gTopVisibleItem += numRows;
   if (gTopVisibleItem < 0)
      gTopVisibleItem = 0;

   LoadTable();
   TblUnhighlightSelection(table);
   TblRedrawTable(table);
}
```

### *The table event handler*

We handle a great number of things in our code and rely on the Table Manager for very little. As a result, we've got quite a complex event handler. Here's how we handle the *tblEnterEvent*:

```
case tblEnterEvent:
{
   Word      row = event->data.tblEnter.row;
   Word      column = event->data.tblEnter.column;
```

```
TablePtr table = event->data.tblEnter.pTable;

// if the user taps on a new row, deselect the old row
if (gCellSelected && row != table->currentRow) {
   handled = OrderDeselectRowAndDeleteIfEmpty();
   // if we delete a row, leave everything unselected
   if (handled)
      break;
}
if (gCellSelected) {
   // if the user taps a prod in the currently selected row, edit it
   if (column == kProductNameColumn) {
      ListPtr list = GetObjectFromActiveForm(OrderProductsList);
      int      selection;
      UInt  index;
      UInt  attr;

      LstSetDrawFunction(list, DrawOneProductInList);

      if (gCurrentOrder->items[gCurrentSelectedItemIndex].productID) {
         // initialize the popup for this product
         GetProductFromProductID(
            gCurrentOrder->items[gCurrentSelectedItemIndex].productID,
            NULL, &index);
         DmRecordInfo(gProductDB, index, &attr, NULL, NULL);
         SelectACategory(list, attr & dmRecAttrCategoryMask);

         LstSetSelection(list,
            DmPositionInCategory(gProductDB, index, gCurrentCategory) +
            (gNumCategories + 1));
      } else
         SelectACategory(list, gCurrentCategory);

      do {
         selection = LstPopupList(list);
         if (selection >= 0 && selection < gNumCategories)
            SelectACategory(list, selection);
      } while (selection >= 0 && selection < (gNumCategories + 1));
      if (selection >= 0) {
         UInt  index = 0;
         VoidHand       h;
         PackedProduct  *packedProduct;
         Product        s;
         Int            oldSelectedColumn = table->currentColumn;

         gCurrentProductIndex = 0;
         DmSeekRecordInCategory(gProductDB, &gCurrentProductIndex,
            selection - (gNumCategories + 1), dmSeekForward,
            gCurrentCategory);
         ErrNonFatalDisplayIf(DmGetLastErr(), "Can't seek to product");
         h = DmQueryRecord(gProductDB, gCurrentProductIndex);
         gHaveProductIndex = true;

         ErrNonFatalDisplayIf(!h, "Can't get record");
```

```
            packedProduct = MemHandleLock(h);
            UnpackProduct(&s, packedProduct);

            DmWrite(gCurrentOrder,
               offsetof(Order,
               items[gCurrentSelectedItemIndex].productID),
               &packedProduct->productID,
               sizeof(packedProduct->productID));
            MemHandleUnlock(h);
            // Redraw current row. Can't have anything selected or the
            // table will highlight it.
            OrderSaveAmount(table);
            LoadTable();
            TblRedrawTable(table);
            OrderSelectNumericCell(NULL, OrderItemsTable, row,
               oldSelectedColumn);
         }
      } else {
         if (column == table->currentColumn) {
            // the user tapped in the current field
            OrderTapInActiveField(event, table);
         } else {
            // the user tapped in another field in the row
            OrderSaveAmount(table);
            OrderSelectNumericCell(event, OrderItemsTable, row, column);
         }
      }
   } else {
      // user tapped in a new row
      if (column == kQuantityColumn || column == kProductIDColumn) {
         OrderSelectNumericCell(event, OrderItemsTable, row, column);
      } else {
         OrderSelectRow(OrderItemsTable, row);
      }
   }
   handled = true;
}
break;
```

### *Handling taps*

We need to convert a *tblEnterEvent* (tap in a numeric cell) into a *fldEnterEvent* so that the Field Manager will handle the event and set the insertion point, or start drag-selecting. Here is how we do that:

```
static void OrderTapInActiveField(EventPtr event, TablePtr table)
{
   EventType   newEvent;
   FieldPtr    fld;

   fld = gCurrentFieldInTable;
   // Convert the table enter event to a field enter event.

   EvtCopyEvent(event, &newEvent);
```

```
    newEvent.eType = fldEnterEvent;
    newEvent.data.fldEnter.fieldID = fld->id;
    newEvent.data.fldEnter.pField = fld;

    FldHandleEvent(fld, &newEvent);
}
```

### *Handling key events*

We've got to handle scrolling when our table receives key-down events. If the user is writing in a cell, we filter to allow only arrows, backspace, and digits. If the user has no cell selected and writes a digit, we add a new item and insert the new digit in the quantity cell.

Note that the character we retrieve from the event is a two-byte `word`, not a one-byte `char`:

```
static Boolean OrderHandleKey(EventPtr event)
{
   Word  c = event->data.keyDown.chr;

   // bottom-to-top screen gesture can cause this, depending on
   // configuration in Prefs/Buttons/Pen
   if (c == sendDataChr)
      return OrderHandleMenuEvent(RecordBeamCustomer);
   else if (c == pageUpChr || c == pageDownChr) {
      SWord numRowsToScroll =
         TblGetNumberOfRows(GetObjectFromActiveForm(OrderItemsTable)) - 1;

      OrderDeselectRowAndDeleteIfEmpty();
      if (c == pageUpChr)
         numRowsToScroll = -numRowsToScroll;
      OrderScrollRows(numRowsToScroll);
   } else if (c == linefeedChr) {
      // The return character takes us out of edit mode.
      OrderDeselectRowAndDeleteIfEmpty();
   } else if (gCellSelected) {
      if ((c == backspaceChr) || (c == leftArrowChr) ||
         (c == rightArrowChr) || IsDigit(GetCharAttr(), c))
         FldHandleEvent(gCurrentFieldInTable, event);
   } else {
      // writing a digit with nothing selected creates a new item
      if (IsDigit(GetCharAttr(), c)) {
         UInt  itemNumber;

         OrderDeselectRowAndDeleteIfEmpty();
         if (AddNewItem(&itemNumber)) {
            OrderSelectItemNumber(itemNumber, kQuantityColumn);
            FldHandleEvent(gCurrentFieldInTable, event);
         }
      }
   }
   return true;
}
```

### *Handling numeric cell selection*

Here's how we handle the user's tapping on a numeric cell:

```
static void OrderSelectNumericCell(EventPtr event, Word tableID,
   Word row, Word column)
{
   TablePtr    table;

   table = GetObjectFromActiveForm(tableID);

   // make this cell selected, if it isn't already
   if (row != table->currentRow || column != table->currentColumn ||
      !table->attr.editing) {
      RectangleType  r;
      FormPtr        frm;

      table->attr.editing = true;
      table->currentRow = row;
      table->currentColumn = column;

      TblGetItemBounds(table, row, column, &r);
      OrderInitNumberField(table, row, column, &r, false);

      // reacquire the table, since OrderInitNumberField may have
      // made it invalid
      table = GetObjectFromActiveForm(tableID);

      gCurrentSelectedItemIndex = TblGetRowID(table, row);
      gCellSelected = true;
      OrderHiliteSelectedRow(table, true);

      frm = FrmGetActiveForm();
      FrmSetFocus(frm, FrmGetObjectIndex(frm, tableID));
      FldGrabFocus(gCurrentFieldInTable);
   }
   // if there's an event, pass it on
   if (event)
      OrderTapInActiveField(event, table);
}
```

We (like the built-in applications) modify the table fields **`attr.editing`**, **`currentRow`**, and **`currentColumn`** directly, since there is no API to change these values.

# *Find*

In this section, we discuss the Find feature of the Palm OS. First, we give you an overview of Find, the user interface, and its intended goals. Second, we walk through the entire Find process from the beginning to the end. Third, we implement Find in our sample application and discuss important aspects of the code.

## *Overview of Find*

The Palm OS user interface supports a global Find—a user can find all the instances of a string in all applications. The operating system doesn't do the work, however. Instead, it orders each application, in turn, to search through its own databases and return the results.

There is much to be said for this approach. The most obvious rationale is that the operating system has no idea what's inside the records of a database: strings, numbers, or other data. Therefore, it's in no position to know what's a reasonable return result and what's nonsense. Indeed, the application is uniquely positioned to interpret the Find request and determine the display of the found information to the user.

Find requests are sent from the OS by calling the application's *PilotMain* (see "Other Times Your Application Is Called" on page 88) with a specific launch code, `sysAppLaunchCmdFind`, along with parameters having to do with interpreting the Find.

### *The objectives of Find*

Remembering that speed on the handheld is essential, Find is intended to be a very quick process. Here are some of the things that the OS does to ensure this:

*No global variables*
: An application's global variables are not created when it receives the `sysAppLaunchCmdFind` launch code, as creating, initializing, and releasing every application's globals would be a time-consuming process.

*Only one screenful of items at a time*
: The Find goes on only long enough to fill one screen with items. If the user wants to see more results, the Find resumes where it left off until it has another screenful of found items, then stops again. This process continues until it runs out of return results.

*Long Finds are easy to stop*
: Applications check the event queue every so often to see whether an event has occurred. If so, the application prematurely quits the Find. Thus, a simple tap outside the Find prevents a long search of a large database that would otherwise lock up the handheld.

Another goal is to minimize the amount of memory used. Remember that the Find request could well occur while an application other than yours is running. In such cases, it would be very rude, indeed, to suck away the application's dynamic heap. To prevent such bad manners, memory use is minimized in the following ways:

*No global variables*
: No unopen application global variables are created.

*Minimal information about each found item is stored*
: An application doesn't save much about the items it finds. Rather, the application draws a summary of the found items and passes the Find Manager six bits of information: the database, the record number, the field number, the card number, the position within the field, and an additional integer.

*Only one screenful of items at a time*
: Only one screenful of found items is maintained in memory. If the user requests more, the current information is thrown out and the search continues where it left off.

## A Walkthrough of Finding Items

The following is a walkthrough of what happens when the user writes in a string to be found and taps Find. First, the current application is sent the launch code `sysAppLaunchCmdSaveData`, which requests that the application save any data that is currently being edited but not yet saved in a database. Then, starting with the open application, each application is sent the launch code `sysAppLaunchCmdFind`.

### The application's response to a Find request

Each application responds with these steps:

1. The application opens its database(s) using the mode specified in its Find parameters. This can be specified as read-only mode and may also (depending on the user's Security settings) specify that secret records should be shown.
2. The application draws an application header in the Find Results dialog. Figure 8-4 contains some examples of application headers as they appear in the dialog. The application uses *FindDrawHeader* to retrieve the application header from the application's resource database. If *FindDrawHeader* returns true, there is no more space in the Find Results dialog, and step 3 is skipped. If there is room in the dialog, it is on to step 3.
3. The application iterates through each of its records in the database. If it is sent a Find request and there is room to fit all of the found items on the screen, the application iterates through the records starting at record 0. If some records from the application have already been displayed, the application has the Find Manager store the record number of the last displayed record and continues the iteration with the next record when the user taps the More button.
    a. Most applications retrieve the next record by using *DmQueryNextInCategory*, which skips private records, if necessary. If an error occurs, the application exits the loop.

*Figure 8-4. Find results dialog showing application headers*

b. It looks for a string that matches. An application should normally ignore case while determining a match. The application can use *FindStrInStr* to determine whether there is a match and where the match occurs.

c. If the application finds a match, it saves information about the match using *FindSaveMatch*. If *FindSaveMatch* returns true, no more items can be drawn in the Find Results dialog. In this case, the application has finished iterating and goes to step 4. Otherwise, it draws to the Find Results dialog a one-line summary of the matching item (*FindGetLineBounds* returns the rectangle in which to draw). The summary should, if possible, include the searched-for string, along with other contextual information.

   In addition, the application increments the `lineNumber` field of the Find parameters.

d. The application should check the event queue every so often (using *EvtSysEventAvail*). If an event has occurred, the application should set the more field of the Find parameters to true and go to step 4.

4. The application closes any databases it has opened and returns.

When the Find Results dialog is displayed, the user can choose Find More. In this case, the Find Manager starts the process again, skipping any applications that have been completely searched.

In the documentation for Find that was current at the time of this book's writing, some Find functions and a field in the Find parameters are incorrectly documented as being for system use only. The following functions are necessary to correctly support Find: *FindDrawHeader*, *FindGetLineBounds*, *FindStrInStr*, *FindSaveMatch*. This Find parameter field is also necessary: `lineNumber`.

### *Handling a Find request with multiple databases*

If your application supports searching in multiple databases, you've got to carefully handle continuing a search (Find More). The Find parameters provide the last matched record number (as saved by *FindSaveMatch*), but not the last matched database. Because of this, your Find routine doesn't know which database was last searched.

Our recommendation is to use system preferences as a place to store the name of the last database. When you call *FindSaveMatch*, you can retrieve the information. When you receive the Find launch code, if the `continuation` field of the Find parameters is false, mark the last database as invalid and start the search with your first database. If the `continuation` field of the Find parameters is true, start your search with the saved database (if it is valid).

Remember that you can't store information in global variables, because when the `sysAppLaunchCmdFind` launch code is sent, your application's global variables don't get allocated.

Alternatively, you could use the record number field as a combination record number and database. You could store the indicated database (0, 1, 2, etc.) in the upper few bits, and the actual record number in the remaining bits.

### *Navigating to a found item*

When the user taps on an item in the Find Results dialog, that item's application is sent the `sysAppLaunchCmdGoTo` launch code. That application may or may not be the current application. If it is, the application just switches to displaying the found item. If it isn't, the application must call *StartApplication* and enter a standard event loop.

The Find parameters are sent, along with the `sysAppLaunchCmdGoTo` launch code. These parameters are all the items that were passed to *FindSaveMatch*, along with an additional one: the length of the searched-for string. Your application should then display the found item, highlighting the searched-for string within the found item.

### *Displaying a found item from a running application*

Here's the step-by-step process your open application will go through when it receives the `sysAppLaunchCmdGoTo` launch code:

1. Close any existing forms (using *FrmCloseAllForms*).
2. Open the form appropriate to display the found item (using *FrmGotoForm*).

3. Create a `frmGotoEvent` event record with fields initialized from the go to parameters, and post it to the event queue (using *EvtAddEventToQueue*).
4. Respond to the `frmGotoEvent` event in your form's event handler by navigating to the correct record and highlighting the found contents (using *FldSetScrollPosition* and *FldSetSelection*).

Note that we must find the unique ID of the specified `recordNumber` before we close all the forms. There are many cases that call for this, but, as an example, the user might be viewing a blank form immediately prior to the Find request. Before displaying the found item, the application needs to delete the blank Customer dialog and close the form. If this occurs, however, the records in the database may no longer be numbered the same. Therefore, we find the unique ID of the found record. After closing the forms, we then find the record based on its unchanging unique ID instead of the possibly compromised record number.

### *Displaying a found item from a closed application*

If your application is closed when it receives the `sysAppLaunchCmdGoTo` launch code, you need to do a few more things:

1. As specified by the *sysAppLaunchFlagNewGlobals* launch flag, call *StartApplication.*
2. Create a `frmGotoEvent` event record with fields initialized from the goto parameters and post it to the event queue (using *EvtAddEventToQueue*).
3. Enter your *EventLoop.*
4. Respond to the `frmGotoEvent` event in your form's event handler by navigating to the correct record and highlighting the found contents (using *FldSetScrollPosition* and *FldSetSelection*).
5. Call *StopApplication* after the *EventLoop* is finished.

## *Find in the Sales Application*

From the earlier description of Find, you can see that supporting it in your application, while straightforward, does require handling a number of steps and possible situations.

Let's look now at how we handle these steps in the Sales application.

### *Handling the Find request*

The *PilotMain* handles the save data and the Find launch codes. Here's the bit of code from *PilotMain* that shows the call to **sysAppLaunchCmdFind**:

```
// Launch code sent to running app before sysAppLaunchCmdFind
// or other action codes that will cause data searches or manipulation.
else if (cmd == sysAppLaunchCmdSaveData) {
   FrmSaveAllForms();
}
else if (cmd == sysAppLaunchCmdFind) {
   Search((FindParamsPtr)cmdPBP);
}
```

### *Searching for matching strings*

Here's the *Search* routine that actually handles the searching through our customer database. The part of the code that's specific to our application is emphasized; the remaining code is likely to be the standard for most applications:

```
static void Search(FindParamsPtr findParams)
{
   Err             err;
   Word            pos;
   UInt            fieldNum;
   UInt            cardNo = 0;
   UInt            recordNum;
   CharPtr         header;
   Boolean         done;
   VoidHand            recordH;
   VoidHand            headerH;
   LocalID         dbID;
   DmOpenRef           dbP;
   RectangleType       r;
   DmSearchStateType searchState;

   // unless told otherwise, there are no more items to be found
   findParams->more = false;

   // Find the application's data file.
   err = DmGetNextDatabaseByTypeCreator(true, &searchState,
      kCustomerDBType, kSalesCreator, true, &cardNo, &dbID);
   if (err)
      return;

   // Open the expense database.
   dbP = DmOpenDatabase(cardNo, dbID, findParams->dbAccesMode);
   if (! dbP)
      return;

   // Display the heading line.
   headerH = DmGetResource(strRsc, FindHeaderString);
   header = MemHandleLock(headerH);
   done = FindDrawHeader(findParams, header);
```

```
MemHandleUnlock(headerH);
if (done) {
   findParams->more = true;
}
else {
   // Search all the fields; start from the last record searched.
   recordNum = findParams->recordNum;
   for(;;) {
      Boolean match = false;
      Customer       customer;

      // Because applications can take a long time to finish a find
      // users like to be able to stop the find.  Stop the find
      // if an event is pending. This stops if the user does
      // something with the device.  Because this call slows down
      // the search we perform it every so many records instead of
      // every record.  The response time should still be short
      // without introducing much extra work to the search.

      // Note that in the implementation below, if the next 16th
      // record is secret the check doesn't happen.  Generally
      // this shouldn't be a problem since if most of the records
      // are secret then the search won't take long anyway!
      if ((recordNum & 0x000f) == 0 &&        // every 16th record
         EvtSysEventAvail(true)) {
         // Stop the search process.
         findParams->more = true;
         break;
      }

      recordH = DmQueryNextInCategory(dbP, &recordNum,
         dmAllCategories);
      // Have we run out of records?
      if (! recordH)
         break;

      // Search each of the fields of the customer

      UnpackCustomer(&customer, MemHandleLock(recordH));

      if ((match = FindStrInStr((CharPtr) customer.name,
         findParams->strToFind, &pos)) != false)
         fieldNum = CustomerNameField;
      else if ((match = FindStrInStr((CharPtr) customer.address,
         findParams->strToFind, &pos)) != false)
         fieldNum = CustomerAddressField;
      else if ((match = FindStrInStr((CharPtr) customer.city,
         findParams->strToFind, &pos)) != false)
         fieldNum = CustomerCityField;
      else if ((match = FindStrInStr((CharPtr) customer.phone,
         findParams->strToFind, &pos)) != false)
         fieldNum = CustomerPhoneField;

      if (match) {
```

```
            done = FindSaveMatch(findParams, recordNum, pos, fieldNum, 0,
               cardNo, dbID);
            if (done)
               break;

            //Get the bounds of the region where we will draw the results.
            FindGetLineBounds(findParams, &r);

            // Display the title of the description.
            DrawCharsToFitWidth(customer.name, &r);

            findParams->lineNumber++;
         }
         MemHandleUnlock(recordH);
         if (done)
            break;
         recordNum++;
      }
   }
   DmCloseDatabase(dbP);
}
```

### *Displaying the found item*

First, here's the code from *PilotMain* that calls *StartApplication*, *EventLoop*, and *StopApplication*, if necessary (if using GCC and the application was already running, the code must have the CALLBACK macros, since *PilotMain* was called as a subroutine from a system function):

```
// This launch code might be sent to the app when it's already running
   else if (cmd == sysAppLaunchCmdGoTo) {
      Boolean  launched;
      launched = launchFlags & sysAppLaunchFlagNewGlobals;

      if (launched) {
         error = StartApplication();
         if (!error) {
            GoToItem((GoToParamsPtr) cmdPBP, launched);
            EventLoop();
            StopApplication();
         }
      } else {
#ifdef __GNUC__
         CALLBACK_PROLOGUE
#endif
         GoToItem((GoToParamsPtr) cmdPBP, launched);
#ifdef __GNUC__
         CALLBACK_EPILOGUE
#endif
      }
   }
```

Here's the *GoToItem* function that opens the correct form and posts a `frmGotoEvent`:

```
static void GoToItem (GoToParamsPtr goToParams, Boolean launchingApp)
{
   EventType   event;
   UInt      recordNum = goToParams->recordNum;

   // If the current record is blank, then it will be deleted, so we'll use
   // the record's unique id to find the record index again, after all
   // the forms are closed.
   if (! launchingApp) {
      ULong    uniqueID;

      DmRecordInfo(gCustomerDB, recordNum, NULL, &uniqueID, NULL);
      FrmCloseAllForms();
      DmFindRecordByID(gCustomerDB, uniqueID, &recordNum);
   }

   FrmGotoForm(CustomersForm);

   // Send an event to select the matching text.
   MemSet (&event, 0, sizeof(EventType));

   event.eType = frmGotoEvent;
   event.data.frmGoto.formID = CustomersForm;
   event.data.frmGoto.recordNum = goToParams->recordNum;
   event.data.frmGoto.matchPos = goToParams->matchPos;
   event.data.frmGoto.matchLen = goToParams->searchStrLen;
   event.data.frmGoto.matchFieldNum = goToParams->matchFieldNum;
   event.data.frmGoto.matchCustom = goToParams->matchCustom;
   EvtAddEventToQueue(&event);
}
```

Remember that this code needs to take into account the possibility of records that change numbers in between closing open forms and displaying the found record. We do this using *DmRecordInfo* and *DmFindRecordByID*. The first takes the record and finds the unique idea associated with it; the second returns a record based on the unique idea.

Note also that we're opening the *CustomersForm*, even though we really want the *CustomerForm*. The reason we do this is that we can't get to the *CustomerForm* directly. It is a modal dialog that is displayed above the *CustomersForm*. Thus, the *CustomersForm* needs to be opened first, because it is that bit of code that knows how to open the *CustomerForm*. Here's the code from *CustomersHandleEvent* that opens the *CustomerForm*:

```
case frmGotoEvent:
   EditCustomerWithSelection(event->data.frmGoto.recordNum, false,
      &deleted, &hidden, &event->data.frmGoto);
   handled = true;
   break;
```

Here's the portion of *EditCustomerWithSelection* that scrolls and highlights the correct text:

```
static void EditCustomerWithSelection(UInt recordNumber, Boolean isNew,
   Boolean *deleted, Boolean *hidden, struct frmGoto *gotoData)
{
   // code deleted that gets the customer record and initializes
   // the fields

   // select one of the fields
   if (gotoData && gotoData->matchFieldNum) {
      FieldPtr selectedField =
         GetObjectFromActiveForm(gotoData->matchFieldNum);
      FldSetScrollPosition(selectedField, gotoData->matchPos);
      FrmSetFocus(frm, FrmGetObjectIndex(frm, gotoData->matchFieldNum));
      FldSetSelection(selectedField, gotoData->matchPos,
         gotoData->matchPos + gotoData->matchLen);
   }

   // code deleted that displays the dialog and handles updates
   // when the dialog is dismissed
}
```

That is all there is to adding support for Find to our application. Indeed, the trickiest part of the code is figuring out the type of situations you might encounter that will cause Find to work incorrectly. The two most important of these are searching applications with multiple databases correctly and making sure that you don't lose the record in between closing forms and displaying results.

# Beaming

In this section, we discuss beaming. First, we give you a general overview of beaming, describe the user interface, and offer you a few useful tips. Next, we provide a checklist that you can use to implement beaming in an application. Last, we implement beaming in the Sales application.

## Beaming and the Exchange Manager

The Exchange Manager is in charge of exchanging of information between Palm OS devices and other devices. This manager is new to Palm OS 3.0 and is built on industry standards.

Currently, the Exchange Manager works only over an infrared link, although it may be enhanced in the future to work over other links (such as TCP/IP or email). The exchange manager uses the ObEx Infrared Data Association (IrDA) standard to exchange information. As a result, it should be possible to exchange information between Palm OS devices and other devices that implement this ObEx standard.

For information on IrDA standards, see *http://www.irda.org*. For information on Multipurpose Internet Mail Extensions (MIME), see *http://www.mindspring.com/~mgrand/mime.html* or *http://www.cis.ohio-state.edu/hypertext/faq/usenet/mail/mime-faq/top.html*.

## *How Beaming Works*

Applications that support this feature usually allow beaming either a single item or an entire category. When the user chooses the Beam menu item, a dialog appears showing that the beam is being prepared. Then it searches for another device using infrared. Once it finds the other device, it beeps and starts sending the data. After the remote device receives all the data, it beeps and presents a dialog to the user, asking whether the user wants to accept the data. If the user decides to accept the data, it is put away; if not, it is thrown away. The creator type of the item is matched to an appropriate application on the receiving device, which then displays the newly received data.

Newly received items are always placed in the Unfiled category. This is true even when both sending and receiving units have the same categories. While problematic for a few users, this it the right solution for most situations. Users will have one consistent interface for receiving items. After all, who is to say that a user wants beamed items filed in the same name category that the sending handheld uses?

The user can also send an entire category. When a category is sent, private records are skipped (to avoid accidentally sending unintended records). Newly received items are placed in the Unfiled category.

## *Programming Tips*

The following sections present a set of miscellaneous tips to help you implement beaming. The first ones are optimization suggestions, the next will help you when debugging your code, and the last are a grab bag of helpful ideas.

### *Optimization tips*

- When calling *ExgSend*, don't make a lot of calls, each with only a few bytes in them. It is much better to allocate a buffer and send the entire buffer, if necessary. Throughput will be faster with larger, fewer calls.
- When a receive beam launch code is sent to your *PilotMain*, your application is not necessarily running. As a result, you can't allocate similarly large buffers for receiving data with *ExgReceive*. In fact, you should make as few and as

small a set of allocations as possible to avoid stressing the currently running application. It is quite proper, however, to allocate a large buffer if you are the currently running application when a receive beam takes place.

*Debugging tips*

- If you have textual data to send, you can send to the Memo Pad (set the name to end in *.TXT*) even before you've written your receive code. If the text doesn't appear, you know you've got problems in the sending portion of the code.
- Set `localMode` (in the `ExgSocketType`) to true to begin with. This gives you a loop of the data back to the same device. Or use the Graffiti shortcut in combination with two other characters to tell Exchange Manager to make all beams local. That combination is:

- See "Device Reset" on page 289 for more information.
- Use the Graffiti shortcut in combination with two other characters to tell Exchange Manager to use the serial port rather than IR. That combination is:

- This is a tricky way to use POSE (which doesn't support IR hardware) to test your code. See "Device Reset" in Chapter 10 for more information.

*General tips*

- If you set the `target` creator ID when sending, you prohibit any other application from receiving the data on the other end.
- You must call *ExgSend* in a loop, because it may not send all the bytes you instruct it to send. *ExgSend* stops when it can send a full packet; it doesn't continue sending the remaining data without further prompting.
- Call *ExgRegisterData* in your *PilotMain* when you receive the `sysAppLaunchCmdSyncNotify`. If you wait until you call your *StartApplication* routine to register with the system, a user won't be able to beam to your application after it has been installed until it has actually been run once.

- Don't call any Exchange Manager routines if your application is running on OS 2.0 or earlier. In fact, your code should specifically check for the version of the OS and take the proper precautions.
- Try running on a 3.0 device that lacks IR capability (like, for instance, POSE) to make sure that you fail gracefully. You should get the alert shown in Figure 8-5.

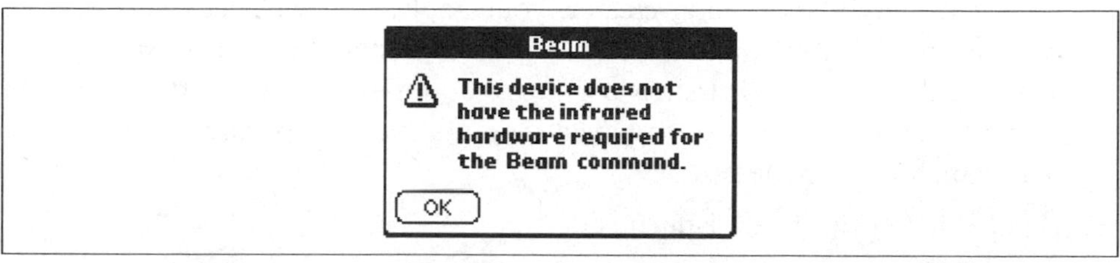


*Figure 8-5. Alert shown when user attempts to beam on a device that has the beaming APIs (3.0 OS or greater), but no IR hardware*

## Step-by-Step Implementation Checklist

Beaming lends itself well to a checklist approach of implementation. If you follow these steps in a cookbook-like fashion, you should get beaming up in a jiffy.

### Determine data interchange format

1. You first need to decide whether you'll use a file extension or MIME type (or both). You also have to determine the format of the transmitted data (for both a single entry and an category).

### Add beam user interface

2. Add a Beam menu item to beam the current entry.
3. Add a Beam Category item to the overview Record menu to beam the current category.

### Send an entry

4. Add `<ExgMgr.h>` to your include files.
5. Declare an `ExgSocketType` and initialize it to 0.
6. Initialize the `description` field of the `ExgSocketType`.
7. Initialize `type`, `target`, and/or `name`.
8. Initialize `localMode` to 1 (this is for testing with one device; it's optional).
9. Call *ExgPut* to begin the beam.
10. Call *ExgSend* in a loop to send the actual data.
11. Call *ExgDisconnect* to terminate the beam.

*Receive an entry*

12. Register for receiving based on the MIME type and/or file extension (optional) you set up in step 1.

    In *PilotMain*, when a `sysAppLaunchCmdSyncNotify` launch code occurs, call *ExgRegisterData* with `exgRegExtensionID` and/or call *ExgRegisterData* with `exgRegTypeID`. This setup is optional, however. If a sender beams data specifying your target application creator, your application will get sent a launch code even if it hasn't registered for a specific extension and/or MIME type. You should do this registration if you have a specific kind of data that you want to handle; senders of that data may not have a specific application in mind when they do the send.

13. Handle the receive beam launch code.

    In *PilotMain*, check for the `sysAppLaunchCmdExgReceiveData` launch code. You won't have global variables unless you happen to be the open application.

14. Call *ExgAccept*.
15. Call *ExgReceive* repeatedly and until *ExgReceive* returns 0. A zero is returned when no more data is being received or an error has occurred.
16. Call *ExgDisconnect* to hang up properly.
17. Set `gotoLaunchCode` and `gotoParams`.

    Set `gotoLaunchCode` to your creator's application. Set the following fields in `gotoParams` with the appropriate values: `uniqueID`, `dbID`, `dbCardNo`, `recordNum`.

*Display received item*

This feature is a free gift thanks to the work you did in supporting Find. If your application already correctly handles Find, displaying received items is no work.

*Send an entire category*

The code for sending an entire category is very similar to the code for sending one item (the actual data you send will be different, of course). You must make sure that your data format allows you to distinguish between one item and multiple items.

18. Declare an *ExgSocketType* and initialize it to 0.
19. Initialize the `description` field of the *ExgSocketType*.
20. Initialize `type`, `target`, and/or `name`.
21. Initialize `localMode` to `1` (this is for testing with one device; it's optional).

22. Call *ExgPut* to begin the beam.
23. Call *ExgSend* in a loop to send the actual data.
24. Call *ExgDisconnect* to terminate the beam.

***Receive an entire category***

Receiving an entire category is similar to receiving one item.

25. Call *ExgAccept.*
26. Call *ExgReceive* repeatedly.
27. Call *ExgDisconnect.*
28. Set `gotoLaunchCode` and `gotoParams`.

***Test all possibilities***

You need to run a gamut of tests to make sure you haven't forgotten any of the details. Test every one of the following combinations of sending and receiving and any other tests that come to mind.

29. Send a record while your application is open on the remote device.
30. Send a record while your application isn't open on the remote device.
31. Send a category with lots of records (so that the *ExgReceive* can't read all its data at one time).
32. Tap No when the Accept dialog is presented on the remote device.
33. Send a category with a private record. Verify that the private record isn't received.
34. Verify that beaming an empty category does nothing (doesn't try to send anything).
35. If you've registered a MIME type or extension, send using the *ExgSend* test application to make sure your application correctly receives (rather than relying strictly on the target).
36. Try the test on a 3.0 device that lacks IR capability (for example, POSE).

## Sales Application

The Sales application doesn't have categories, so we don't have a Beam Category menu item; instead, we support Beam all Customers for times when the user wants to beam all the customer information. We also support beaming a single customer.

We don't support beaming an entire order, although that would be a reasonable thing to add to the application, particularly if it were a commercial product. Our interests are pedagogical rather than commercial, so we are skipping that bit; adding this support would not teach you anything new.

When beaming a single customer, we send the customer record itself, with a name ending in *.CST*. When beaming all customers, we send:

- A two-byte record count indicating the number of total records we are beaming
- For each record:
  - A two-byte record length for the record
  - The customer record itself

Let's look at handling a single customer first and then turn to dealing with them all.

*Sending a single customer*

We add support for beaming to *OrderHandleMenuEvent*, where we add the Beam menu item:

```
case RecordBeamCustomer:
   BeamCustomer(GetRecordNumberForCustomer(gCurrentOrder->customerID));
   handled = true;
   break;
```

When the user selects the menu item, the *BeamCustomer* routine we have created gets called into play. *BeamCustomer* beams a single customer:

```
static void BeamCustomer(UInt recordNumber)
{
   ExgSocketType  s;
   Handle         theRecord = DmQueryRecord(gCustomerDB, recordNumber);
   PackedCustomer *thePackedCustomer = MemHandleLock(theRecord);
   Err            err;

   MemSet(&s, sizeof(s), 0);
   s.description = thePackedCustomer->name;
   s.name = "customer.cst";
   s.target = salesCreator;

   err = ExgPut(&s);
   if (!err)
      err = BeamBytes(&s, thePackedCustomer, MemHandleSize(theRecord));
   MemHandleUnlock(theRecord);
   err = ExgDisconnect(&s, err);
}
```

*BeamCustomer* relies on *BeamBytes* to actually send the data. Here is that code:

```
static Err BeamBytes(ExgSocketPtr s, void *buffer, ULong bytesToSend)
{
   Err err = 0;

   while (!err && bytesToSend > 0) {
      ULong bytesSent = ExgSend(s, buffer, bytesToSend, &err);
      bytesToSend -= bytesSent;
      buffer = ((char *) buffer) + bytesSent;
   }
   return err;
}
```

That is all the code for beaming one customer. Let's look at what we need to do to receive that information on the other end.

### *Receiving a record*

First, we need to register with the Exchange Manager in *PilotMain*. Note that we check to make sure we are running OS 3.0 or greater before setting to work:

```
} else if (cmd == sysAppLaunchCmdSyncNotify) {
   DWord    romVersion;

   FtrGet(sysFtrCreator, sysFtrNumROMVersion, &romVersion);
   if (sysGetROMVerMajor(romVersion) >= 3)
      ExgRegisterData(kSalesCreator, exgRegExtensionID, "cst");

   // code deleted that resorts our databases
}
```

Next, we've got to handle the receive data launch code, which we also put into our *PilotMain*:

```
} else if (cmd == sysAppLaunchCmdExgReceiveData) {
      DmOpenRef    dbP;

      // if our app is not active, we need to open the database
      // The subcall flag is used to determine whether we are active
      if (launchFlags & sysAppLaunchFlagSubCall) {
#ifdef __GNUC__
         CALLBACK_PROLOGUE
#endif
         dbP = gCustomerDB;

         // save any data we may be editing.
         FrmSaveAllForms();

         error = ReceiveBeam(dbP, (ExgSocketPtr) cmdPBP);
#ifdef __GNUC__
         CALLBACK_EPILOGUE
#endif
      } else {
         dbP = DmOpenDatabaseByTypeCreator(kCustomerDBType, kSalesCreator,
```

```
            dmModeReadWrite);
         if (dbP) {
            error = ReceiveBeam(dbP, (ExgSocketPtr) cmdPBP);

            DmCloseDatabase(dbP);
         }
      }
   }
```

We open the customer database if our application isn't already running. If our application is running, and if we're using GCC, we must use *CALLBACK_PROLOGUE* and *CALLBACK_EPILOGUE*, since *PilotMain* is being called as a subroutine call from the Palm OS (if we don't put in the callback macros, we'll crash if we try to access global variables like gCustomerDB). Then, we call *FrmSaveAllForms* to save any data currently being edited. *ReceiveBeam* handles much of this work. Note that since new customers need to have unique customer IDs, we assign a new customer ID to the newly received customer, just as we would if the user used the New Customer... menu item.

This version of *ReceiveBeam* doesn't receive all customers yet. See "Receiving all customers" on page 249 for the final version, which does.

```
// NB: First version that doesn't support receiving all customers yet
static Err ReceiveBeam(DmOpenRef db, ExgSocketPtr socketPtr)
{
   Err      err;
   UInt  index;
   SDWord   newCustomerID = GetLowestCustomerID() - 1;

   err = ExgAccept(socketPtr);
   if (!err) {
      err = ReadIntoNewRecord(db, socketPtr, 0xffffffff, &index);
      // must assign a new unique customer ID
         if (!err) {
            VoidHand h = DmGetRecord(db, index);
            DmWrite(MemHandleLock(h), offsetof(Customer, customerID),
               &newCustomerID, sizeof(newCustomerID));
            MemHandleUnlock(h);
            DmReleaseRecord(db, index, true);
         }
   }
   err = ExgDisconnect(socketPtr, err);

   if (!err) {
      DmRecordInfo(db, index, NULL, &socketPtr->goToParams.uniqueID,
         NULL);
      DmOpenDatabaseInfo(db, &socketPtr->goToParams.dbID,
         NULL, NULL, &socketPtr->goToParams.dbCardNo, NULL);
      socketPtr->goToParams.recordNum = index;
      socketPtr->goToCreator = salesCreator;
   }
   return err;
}
```

*ReadIntoNewRecord* reads until there is no more to read (or the number of bytes specified, a feature we use when reading all customers). It returns the new record number in the **indexPtr** parameter:

```
// read at most numBytes into a new record.
// Don't use very much dynamic RAM or stack space--another app is running
static Err ReadIntoNewRecord(DmOpenRef db, ExgSocketPtr socketPtr,
   ULong numBytes, UInt *indexPtr)
{
   char  buffer[100];
   Err      err;
   UInt  index = 0;
   ULong bytesReceived;
   VoidHand recHandle = NULL;
   CharPtr  recPtr;
   ULong recSize = 0;
   Boolean  allocatedRecord = false;

   do {
      ULong numBytesToRead;

      numBytesToRead = min(numBytes, sizeof(buffer));
      bytesReceived = ExgReceive(socketPtr, buffer, numBytesToRead,
         &err);
      numBytes -= bytesReceived;
      if (!err) {
         if (!recHandle)
            recHandle = DmNewRecord(db, &index, bytesReceived);
         else
            recHandle = DmResizeRecord(db, index,
               recSize + bytesReceived);
         if (!recHandle) {
            err = DmGetLastErr();
            break;
         }
         allocatedRecord = true;
         recPtr = MemHandleLock(recHandle);
         err = DmWrite(recPtr, recSize, buffer, bytesReceived);
         MemHandleUnlock(recHandle);
         recSize += bytesReceived;
      }
   } while (!err && bytesReceived > 0 && numBytes > 0);

   if (recHandle) {
      DmReleaseRecord(db, index, true);
   }
   if (err && allocatedRecord)
      DmRemoveRecord(db, index);

   *indexPtr = index;
   return err;
}
```

That is all there is to sending and receiving a single customer. Next, let's look at what additional changes you need to make to beam or receive them all at once.

### *Sending all customers*

Once again, we add something to our *CustomersHandleMenuEvent* that handles sending all customers:

```
case CustomerBeamAllCustomers:
   BeamAllCustomers();
   handled = true;
   break;
```

It calls *BeamAllCustomers* which beams the number of records, then the size of each record and the record itself:

```
#define kMaxNumberLength   5

static void BeamAllCustomers(void)
{
   DmOpenRef    dbP = gCustomerDB;
   UInt      mode;
   LocalID      dbID;
   UInt      cardNo;
   Boolean      databaseReopened;
   UInt      numCustomers;

   // If the database was opened to show secret records, reopen it to not
   // see secret records.  The idea is that secret records are not sent
   // when a category is sent.  They must be explicitly sent one by one.
   DmOpenDatabaseInfo(dbP, &dbID, NULL, &mode, &cardNo, NULL);
   if (mode & dmModeShowSecret) {
      dbP = DmOpenDatabase(cardNo, dbID, dmModeReadOnly);
      databaseReopened = true;
   } else
      databaseReopened = false;

   // We should send  because there's at least one record to send.
   if ((numCustomers = DmNumRecordsInCategory(dbP, dmAllCategories)) > 0)
   {
      ExgSocketType  s;
      VoidHand recHandle;
      Err      err;
      UInt  index = dmMaxRecordIndex;

      MemSet(&s, sizeof(s), 0);
      s.description = "All customers";
      s.target = kSalesCreator;
      s.localMode = 1;

      err = ExgPut(&s);
      if (!err)
         err = BeamBytes(&s, &numCustomers, sizeof(numCustomers));
```

```
        while (!err && numCustomers-- > 0) {
            UInt  numberToSeekBackward = 1;

            if (index == dmMaxRecordIndex)
                numberToSeekBackward = 0;  // we want the last one
            err = DmSeekRecordInCategory(dbP, &index, numberToSeekBackward,
                dmSeekBackward, dmAllCategories);
            if (!err) {
                UInt recordSize;

                recHandle = DmQueryRecord(dbP, index);
                ErrNonFatalDisplayIf(!recHandle, "Couldn't query record");
                recordSize = MemHandleSize(recHandle);
                err = BeamBytes(&s, &recordSize, sizeof(recordSize));
                if (!err) {
                    PackedCustomer *theRecord = MemHandleLock(recHandle);

                    err = BeamBytes(&s, theRecord, MemHandleSize(recHandle));
                    MemHandleUnlock(recHandle);
                }
            }
        }
        err = ExgDisconnect(&s, err);
    } else
        FrmAlert(NoDataToBeamAlert);

    if (databaseReopened)
        DmCloseDatabase(dbP);
}
```

*BeamAllCustomers* uses *BeamBytes*, which we've already seen.

### *Receiving all customers*

In order to receive all customers, *ReceiveBeam* must change just a bit (changes are in bold):

```
static Err ReceiveBeam(DmOpenRef db, ExgSocketPtr socketPtr)
{
    Err      err;
    UInt     index;
    Boolean  nameEndsWithCst = false;
    SDWord   newCustomerID = GetLowestCustomerID() - 1;

    // we have a single customer if it has a name ending
    // in ".cst". Otherwise, it's all customers. "All customers"
    //  will have a name
    // because the exchange manager provides one automatically.
    if (socketPtr->name) {
        CharPtr  dotLocation = StrChr(socketPtr->name, '.');
        if (dotLocation && StrCaselessCompare(dotLocation, ".cst") == 0)
            nameEndsWithCst = true;
    }
    err = ExgAccept(socketPtr);
```

```
        if (!err) {
            if (nameEndsWithCst || socketPtr->type) {
                // one customer
                err = ReadIntoNewRecord(db, socketPtr, 0xffffffff, &index);

                // must assign a new unique customer ID
                if (!err) {
                    VoidHand h = DmGetRecord(db, index);
                    DmWrite(MemHandleLock(h), offsetof(Customer, customerID),
                        &newCustomerID, sizeof(newCustomerID));
                    MemHandleUnlock(h);
                    DmReleaseRecord(db, index, true);
                }
            } else {
                // all customers
                UInt  numRecords;

                ExgReceive(socketPtr, &numRecords, sizeof(numRecords), &err);
                while (!err && numRecords-- > 0) {
                    UInt recordSize;

                    ExgReceive(socketPtr, &recordSize, sizeof(recordSize), &err);
                    if (!err) {
                        err = ReadIntoNewRecord(db, socketPtr, recordSize, &index);
                        // must assign a new unique customer ID
                        if (!err) {
                            VoidHand h = DmGetRecord(db, index);
                            DmWrite(MemHandleLock(h),
                            offsetof(Customer, customerID),
                            &newCustomerID, sizeof(newCustomerID));
                            newCustomerID--;
                            MemHandleUnlock(h);
                            DmReleaseRecord(db, index, true);
                        }
                    }
                }
            }
        }
        err = ExgDisconnect(socketPtr, err);

        if (!err) {
            DmRecordInfo(db, index, NULL, &socketPtr->goToParams.uniqueID,
                NULL);
            DmOpenDatabaseInfo(db, &socketPtr->goToParams.dbID,
                NULL, NULL, &socketPtr->goToParams.dbCardNo, NULL);
            socketPtr->goToParams.recordNum = index;
            socketPtr->goToCreator = kSalesCreator;
        }
        return err;
    }
```

That is all the code needed to support beaming. Use the checklist to make sure you take care of all the little details, and review the sample application if you have any further questions. Otherwise, it's on to another topic.

# Barcodes

The Symbol SPT 1500 has a built-in barcode scanner (see Figure 8-6). The two buttons at the top of the device start the scan, and the barcode scanner runs along the top of the device. As you might imagine, for some vertical applications, this can be quite useful (for example, salespeople could have a catalog with barcoded items; warehouse workers could read barcodes from boxes).

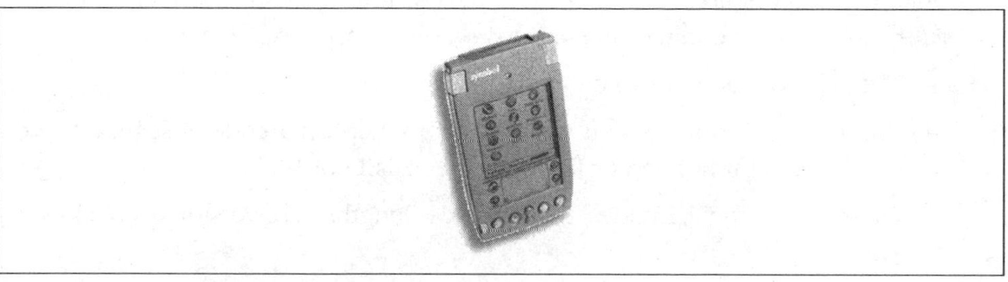

*Figure 8-6. Symbol SPT 1500 with barcode scanner*

If you want to implement barcode scanning in an application, there are some special requirements and APIs from Symbol to use. First, let's look at some of the API calls that barcode reading brings to the Palm 3.0 OS. Then we do a code walk-through of a sample application that scans barcodes.

For more information on the Symbol APIs or the SDK, contact Symbol Technologies (*http://www.symbol.com/palm*). Symbol also has a neat utility program that lets you turn the SPT 1500 device into a unit dedicated to your application. The utility allows you to reflash the device ROM to include or dedicate it to your application. For more information on this, contact Symbol.*

## Handling Scanning in an Application

There are some minor additions to the Palm 3.0 OS. The basic support for scanning barcodes requires these simple steps:

1. Your code needs to make sure you have a Symbol device by calling the function *ScanIsPalmSymbolUnit*. If it isn't a Symbol device, make no further Symbol calls. This routine is provided as part of a library; thus, you can call it whether or not you are on a Symbol device. You should normally call this once at the beginning of your program and store its result in a global.

* If you are new to barcode technologies, there is an excellent reference work available: *The Bar Code Book*, by Roger C. Palmer, 1995, Third Ed. (Helmers, ISBN: 0-91126-109-5).

2. The next step is to load the Symbol library with *ScanOpenDecoder*. Once you've done this, the scanner provides power to the scanning hardware. To save battery life, you usually don't do this at the start of your application, where scanning is inappropriate (for instance, only some forms may allow scanning, so you may enable scanning when such a form opens). After calling this routine, the scan hardware has power, but the user still can't press the buttons to do a scan.
3. Once the Symbol library is open, you have a few optional alternatives to consider. These involve initializing various scanning options, such as:
   - The type of barcodes to be recognized.
   - The feedback options you want to give when a barcode is scanned—you can have the unit beep or flash the green LED or both.
   - Options on the barcodes that include lengths, conversions, checksums, etc.
4. When you are actually ready for the user to scan, call *ScanCmdScanEnable*. Don't just blindly call this routine after opening the scanning library. Enable scanning only when it actually makes sense for the user to scan (for example, when the user enters a particular field). Otherwise, the user might accidentally press one of the two built-in scan buttons, which will:
   - Cause the laser to activate while the unit isn't pointing at a barcode. Activating lasers that are pointing at random locations is a bad idea (think lawsuit).
   - Unnecessarily drain the battery.
5. Your application needs to respond to two new events while scanning is enabled:
   - `scanDecodeEvent`. This is sent when a scan (successful or unsuccessful) has occurred. In response to such an event, call *ScanGetDecodedData*. You get the scanned ASCII data from this call as well as what kind of barcode (there are many different symbologies) was scanned.
   - `scanBatteryErrorEvent`. This event is sent when the battery is too low to do a scan. As a scan requires more power from the battery than simply running the handheld, there may be enough battery life to run the handheld, but not enough to do the scan. This event is sent so that you can alert the user to the problem.

It is very important that you handle `scanBatteryErrorEvent` correctly in your application. Without a proper alert, the user will have no idea why the scan did not occur.

6. When scanning is no longer appropriate (for instance, the user leaves a field in which they are allowed to scan), call *ScanCmdScanDisable.*
7. When you're ready to shut down the scanner, call *ScanCloseDecoder.* This may be at the end of your application for an application that allows scanning everywhere. It may be as a form closes, if you've got some forms that allow scanning and others that don't.

## *A Scanning Sample*

Some applications might be written so that any field could be written into with Graffiti or, alternatively, scanned into with the barcode scanner. The code we've written is designed to retrofit an existing application to allow input to any field from the scanner. A successful scan takes the scanned data and inserts it in the field that contains the insertion point.

### *Starting up the application*

In *AppStart*, we check to make sure we're running on a Symbol unit. If so, we initialize the library, set parameters so that we can scan every type of barcode and enable scanning (remember that this application allows scanning anywhere):

```
static Boolean gScanManagerInitialized = false;

static Err AppStart(void)
{
   // other initialization code deleted

   if (ScanIsPalmSymbolUnit()) {
      Err err = ScanOpenDecoder();  // load the scanner library
      if (err == 0) {
         int i;
         // we want to be able to scan everything we can get our hands on
         // If we just wanted the default types, we could jump directly
         // to calling ScanCmdScanEnable
         BarType allTypes[] = {
            barCODE39, barUPCA, barUPCE, barEAN13, barEAN8, barD25,
            barI2OF5, barCODABAR, barCODE128, barCODE93, barTRIOPTIC39,
            barUCC_EAN128, barMSI_PLESSEY, barUPCE1, barBOOKLAND_EAN,
            barISBT128, barCOUPON};
         for (i = 0; i < sizeof(allTypes) / sizeof(*allTypes); i++)
            err = ScanSetBarcodeEnabled(allTypes[i], true);
         err = ScanCmdSendParams(No_Beep); // send all the accumulated
                                           // settings to scanner
```

```
            // allow scanning as of now (uses some battery life)
            err = ScanCmdScanEnable();
            gScanManagerInitialized = true;
        }
    }
    return 0;
}
```

### The application shutdown

In *AppStop*, we disable scanning and close the library:

```
static void AppStop(void)
{
   // other termination code deleted

   if (gScanManagerInitialized) {
      ScanCmdScanDisable();   // turn scanner off
      ScanCloseDecoder();
   }
}
```

### Event handling

In *AppHandleEvent*, we put up an alert (see Figure 8-7) if the battery is too low to scan.

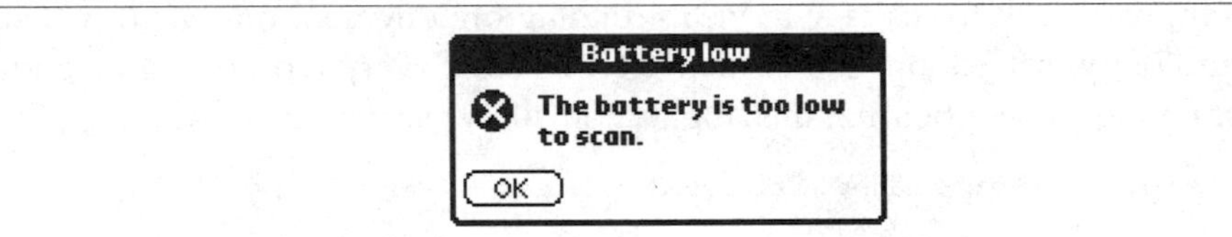


*Figure 8-7. The application's alert that is posted when a scanBatteryErrorEvent occurs*

Here is the code that accomplishes this task:

```
if (eventP->eType == scanBatteryErrorEvent) {
     FrmAlert(LowScanBatteryAlert);
     return true;
}
```

Also in *AppHandleEvent*, we need to handle a scan event:

```
if (eventP->eType == scanDecodeEvent) {
   MESSAGE decodeDataMsg;

   int status = ScanGetDecodedData( &decodeDataMsg );
   // if we successfully got the decode data from the API...
if( status == STATUS_OK ) {
     FormPtr form = FrmGetActiveForm();
```

```
        // a response of NR means no scan happened. If so, ignore it
        if (decodeDataMsg.length == 2 && decodeDataMsg.data[0] == 'N' &&
           decodeDataMsg.data[1] == 'R')
           return true;

        // find the focused field and insert there
        if (form) {
           Word     focusedIndex = FrmGetFocus(form);

           //focusedIndex is documented to return -1 but is also documented
           // to return a (unsigned) Word. Instead of returning -1, then,
           // it returns 65536
           if (focusedIndex >= 0 && focusedIndex < 65535) {
              if (FrmGetObjectType(form, focusedIndex) == frmFieldObj) {
                 FieldPtr focusedField =
                    (FieldPtr) FrmGetObjectPtr(form, focusedIndex);

                 if (focusedField->attr.editable)
                    FldInsert(focusedField, (CharPtr) decodeDataMsg.data,
                       decodeDataMsg.length);
              }
           }
        }
     }
     return true;
  }
```

This is all there is to supporting barcode reading in an application. With a dandy device like the Symbol SPT 1500 and such an easy set of changes required to support barcode scanning, you should expect to see a variety of applications.

# 9

# Communications

*In this chapter:*
- *Serial*
- *TCP/IP*

In this chapter, we discuss the types of communication available on the Palm OS. Next we go into detail about two of these types and show you how to write code to use them.

Palm OS supports three kinds of communication: IrDA, serial, and TCP/IP:

*IrDA*
: This is an industry-standard hardware and software protocol. We won't discuss the details of communicating using IrDA. We will, however, show you how to use the Exchange Manager to implement beaming (see the section entitled "Beaming" on page 238). Beaming is a data exchange method built on top of IrDA.

*Serial*
: Serial communication occurs between the handheld and other devices using the cradle port. This is the most common form of communication on the Palm OS, and as an example we develop a special serial application that communicates (indirectly) with satellites.

*TCP/IP*
: Currently, this communication standard is available only via a serial or modem connection. The future has no boundaries, however, so you might expect to see built-in Ethernet or devices using wireless TCP/IP appear some day. To show you how to use TCP/IP, we create a small application that sends email to a server.

# *Serial*

The Serial Manager is fairly straightforward. There are routines to do all of the following:

- Open and close the serial port
- Read and write data
- Query how many bytes are ready to be read
- Set options

Serial I/O is synchronous, so there's no notification when data gets received. Instead, your code must poll to see whether data has arrived.

## *Tips for Using the Serial Manager*

Here are a bunch of miscellaneous tips that will help you when it's time to add serial functionality to an application:

*Open port error*
: If your code calls *SerOpen* and it returns the error `serErrAlreadyOpen`, your open has succeeded, but some other code already opened the port. Although it's possible to share the port, a sane person wouldn't normally want to do so. Sharing reads and writes with some other code is a recipe for mangled data. If you get this error, you should notify the user that the port is in use and gracefully call *SerClose*.

*Open the serial port only for short periods of time*
: Don't leave the serial port open any longer than absolutely necessary. If your application reads data from the serial port every five minutes, don't leave it open for that entire time. Instead, close the port, and reopen it after five minutes. *As a rule of thumb, leave the serial port open for no longer than 30 seconds if it is not in use.*

: Similar advice is often given to drivers about stopped cars. If you will move again within a few minutes, leave the car idling; otherwise, shut the car off and restart it when you are ready to go. Just as an idling car wastes gas, an idle serial port wastes batteries by providing power to the serial chip. Such behavior will really annoy your users, who don't want an application that sucks all the life out of their batteries. Don't have sloppy serial code.

*Preventing automatic sleep*
: If you don't want the Palm OS device to sleep while you are communicating, call *EvtResetAutoOffTimer* at least once a minute. This prevents the automatic sleep that happens when no user input occurs. If you have communication

that shouldn't be interrupted, you certainly should do this, as you will lose the serial data when the device goes to sleep.

*Adjusting the receiving buffer size*

The default receive buffer is 512 bytes. Think of this receiving buffer as similar to a reservoir. The incoming data flows into the buffer, and reads from the buffer drain the data out the other side. Just as with a reservoir, if you get too much incoming data, the buffer overflows, and data spills out and is lost. The error you get is `serLineErrorSWOverrun`.

If you expect a lot of data, it's best to adjust your buffer to accommodate greater inflows. You can set the size using *SerSetReceiveBuffer*. When you're done, make sure to release the buffer before you close the port; do so by calling *SerSetReceiveBuffer* with a size of `0`. *SerClose* won't release the buffer, so if you don't do it yourself, you'll leak memory.

*Knowing when there is data in the receive buffer*

When reading data, it is best to do it in two steps. The first step is to call *SerReceiveWait*, which blocks until the specified number of bytes are available in the buffer. To provide a timeout mechanism, *SerReceiveWait* takes as a parameter an interbyte tick timeout. This timeout is used for a watchdog timer that is reset on every received byte. If the timer expires, the function returns with `serErrTimeOut`. Once *SerReceiveWait* returns, the second step is to call *SerReceive* to actually read the data from the receive buffer.

The timeout measures the time between successive bytes, not the time for all bytes. For example, if you call *SerReceiveWait* waiting for 200 bytes with a 50-tick timeout, *SerReceiveWait* returns either when 200 bytes are available, or when 50 ticks have passed since the last received byte. In the slowest case, if bytes come in one every 49 ticks, *SerReceiveWait* won't time out.

*SerReceiveWait* is the preferred call, because it can put the processor into a low-power state while waiting for incoming data—another battery-saving technique that will make your users happy.

*Handling user input during a serial event*

Don't ignore user input while communicating. Wherever possible, you need to structure your application so that it deals with serial communication when the user isn't doing other stuff. Practically, this means you can do one of two things. Your application could communicate every so often by calling *EvtGetEvent* with a timeout value. Or, if your communication code is in a tight loop that doesn't call *EvtGetEvent*, you can call *SysEventAvail* every so often (certainly no less than once a second). This allows you to see whether there's a user event to process. If there are user events, return to your event loop to process the event before attempting any more serial communication.

A user who can't cancel is an unhappy user.

*Receiving error messages*

If *SerReceive*, *SerReceiveWait*, or *SerReceiveCheck* return `serErrLineErr`, you need to clear the error using *SerClearErr*. Alternatively, you should use *SerReceiveFlush* if you also need to flush the buffer, since it will call *SerClearErr*.

*Palm OS version differences*

*SerSend* and *SerReceive* have been enhanced in Palm OS 2.0. In this OS, they return the number of bytes sent or received. If you are running on Palm OS 1.0, you need to use *SerSend10* and *SerReceive10*, which have different parameters. Make sure your code does the right thing for each OS version.

*Serial to a state machine*

Often, serial protocols are best written as though they are going to a state machine. You can do this by defining various states and the transitions that cause changes from one state to another. You use a global to contain information on the current state. While it might sound complicated, writing your serial code this way often makes it simpler and easier to maintain.

For example, if you use your Palm device to log into a Unix machine, you might send <CR><CR> and then enter the "Waiting for login:" state. In this state, you'd read until you got the characters "`login:`". You would then send your account name and enter the "Waiting for password:" state. In that state, you'd read until you got the characters "`password:`". Then you would send the password and enter yet another state.

## Sample Serial Application

Our Sales application doesn't have serial code in it. Instead, we've written a small application that communicates with a Global Positioning System (GPS) device. A GPS device reads information sent by orbiting satellites; from that data it determines the location of the device. In addition to the location (latitude, longitude, and altitude), the device obtains the Universal Time Coordinate (UTC) time.

### *Features of the sample application*

Our sample application communicates with this GPS device using the industry-standard National Marine Electronics Association (NMEA) 0183 serial protocol.

The application's startup screen is shown in Figure 9-1. As you can see, it is blank except for telling the user that it has no GPS information. The state changes as soon as the handheld has established communication with the GPS device and has acquired a satellite. Now it displays the time, latitude, and longitude, as shown in Figure 9-2. The application updates these values every five seconds to make sure the location and time are up-to-date. If the GPS device loses contact with the satellite (as might happen when the user enters a building), the sample application promptly warns the user (as shown in Figure 9-3).

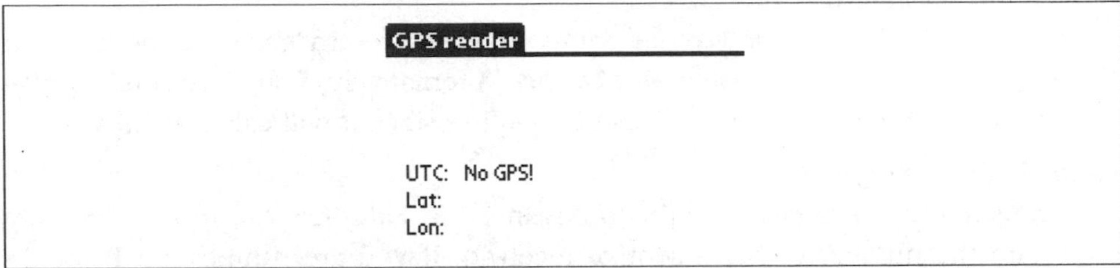


*Figure 9-1. The GPS application when it is has not recently heard from the GPS device*

*Figure 9-2. The GPS application displaying the current time, latitude, and longitude*

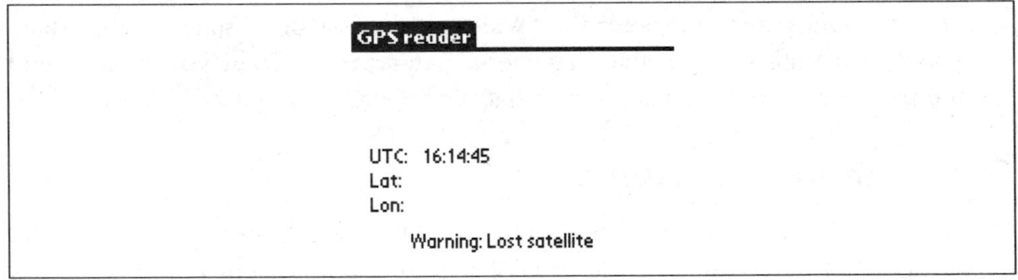


*Figure 9-3. The GPS application warning that the satellite has been lost*

A GPS device hooked to a Palm OS handheld is a compact and useful combination. Imagine the versatile and convenient applications you could create that would use information augmented with exact location and precision time-stamping. For example, a nature specialist could create a custom trail guide that other people could use to retrace the guide's path.

### *The GPS device*

We're using a Garmin 12 GPS device purchased for under $200 from the sporting goods section of a discount store. The serial connector on this device is custom, so we bought a Garmin-to-DB-9 serial cable. (A DB-9 connector is a nine-pin connector commonly used for serial connections.) Connected to the Palm device is a HotSync cable. Between the two devices is a null-modem converter. The Garmin is configured to send NMEA 0183 2.0 at 9600 baud. Figure 9-4 shows the setup.*

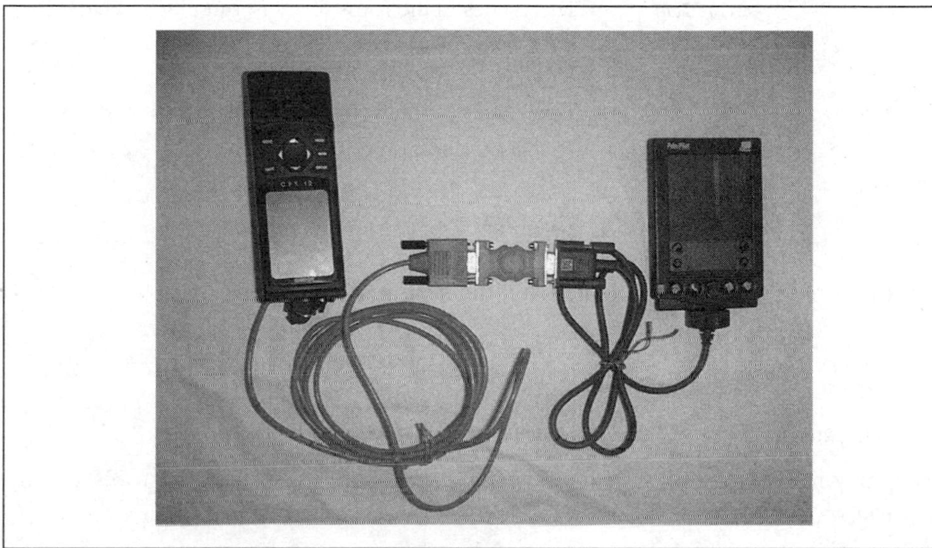

*Figure 9-4. The GPS device and handheld setup*

### *The NMEA protocol*

In our application, we want to update the time, latitude, and longitude every 5 seconds. Updating more often seems unnecessary and would reduce the battery life of the Palm OS device. The GPS device sends 10 lines of information every second; of the 50 that are sent over a 5-second period, we simply parse out the information we need. The rest we ignore. As a result, we don't have to understand the entire NMEA 0183 protocol, but just the bit that pertains to our one line of interest.†

If we have valid satellite data, the relevant part will look similar to this string:

```
$GPRMC,204700,A,3403.868,N,11709.432,W,001.9,336.9,170698,013.6,E*6E
```

* Had we been willing to sacrifice a HotSync cable, we could have cut off the DB-9 end and soldered on a replacement Garmin end. However, we weren't willing to make the sacrifice (although Figure 9-4 would certainly have looked less cluttered).

† The NMEA 0183 protocol is a document that is available only in hard copy form. It can be ordered from NMEA at (252) 638-2626.

Let's look more closely at this example to see what each part means. Note that we care about only the first seven pieces of data. In Table 9-1 the important parts of the string are laid out with the definitions beside each item.

*Table 9-1. NMEA String from GPS Device*

| Sample String Value | NMEA 0183 Protocol | Description |
|---|---|---|
| $GPRMC | | GPS Recommended Minimum data. |
| 204700 | *UTC_TIME* | This comes in the form of a 24-hour clock, where the time uses HHMMSS as the format. |
| A | `A or V` | `A` means the data is OK; `V` is a warning. |
| 3403.868 | *LAT* | This comes in the form of a number like *####.###* |
| N | *LAT_DIR* | This isV (N)orth or (S)outh. |
| 11709.432 | *LON* | *#####.###* |
| W | *LON_DIR* | This is (W)est or (E)ast. |

If we aren't receiving valid satellite data, the string is of the form:

```
$GPRMC,UTC_TIME,V,...
```

And here's a typical example:

```
$GPRMC,204149,V,,,,,,,170698,,*3A
```

Now that you have an idea of what we want to accomplish and the tools we are going to use, it is time to look at the code for the sample application.

### *The sample application serial code*

We are going to open the serial port in our *StartApplication* routine:

```
UInt  gSerialRefNum;
char  gSerialBuffer[900];  // should be more than enough for one second of
                           // data--10 lines @ 80 chars per line

static Boolean StartApplication(void)
{
   Err   err;

   err = SysLibFind("Serial Library", &gSerialRefNum);
   ErrNonFatalDisplayIf(err != 0, "Can't find serial library");

   err = SerOpen(gSerialRefNum, 0, 9600);
   if (err != 0) {
      if (err == serErrAlreadyOpen) {
         FrmAlert(SerialInUseAlert);
         SerClose(gSerialRefNum);
      } else
         FrmAlert(CantopenserialAlert);
      return true;
```

```
    }
    err = SerSetReceiveBuffer(gSerialRefNum, gSerialBuffer,
       sizeof(gSerialBuffer));
    return false;
}
```

We set our own receive buffer so that we can hold an entire second's worth of data. We don't want to risk losing any data, so we give ourselves ample room.

In *StopApplication*, we close the port (after resetting the buffer to the default):

```
static void StopApplication(void)
{
   // restore the default buffer before closing the serial port
   SerSetReceiveBuffer(gSerialRefNum, NULL, 0);
   SerClose(gSerialRefNum);
}
```

We need to create some globals to store information about timing:

```
// tickCount of last time we read data from GPS
ULong    gLastSuccessfulReception = 0;

// tickCount of last time we displayed GPS data on the Palm device
ULong    gLastTimeDisplay = 0;

// tickCount of the next scheduled read
ULong    gNextReadTime = 0;

Boolean  gFormOpened = false;

// if we go this long without updating the time
// then update as soon as we get a valid time
// (without waiting for an even 5-second time)
#define  kMaxTicksWithoutTime (6 * sysTicksPerSecond)

// if we go this long without communicating with GPS,
// we've lost it and need to notify the user
#define  kTicksToLoseGPS (15 * sysTicksPerSecond)
```

We initialize gFormOpened in *MainViewInit*. We keep track of this because we don't want to start receiving nil events until the form has been opened and displayed:

```
static void MainViewInit(void)
{
   FormPtr        frm = FrmGetActiveForm();

   // Draw the form.
   FrmDrawForm(frm);
   gFormOpened = true;
}
```

In our event loop, instead of calling *EvtGetEvent* with no timeout, we call the function *TimeUntilNextRead* to obtain a timeout when we need it. Here's our *EventLoop*:

```
static void EventLoop(void)
{
   EventType    event;
   Word         error;

   do
      {
      // Get the next available event.
      EvtGetEvent(&event, TimeUntilNextRead());
      if (! SysHandleEvent(&event))
         if (! MenuHandleEvent(0, &event, &error))
            if (! ApplicationHandleEvent(&event))
               FrmDispatchEvent(&event);
      }
   while (event.eType != appStopEvent);
}
```

*EvtGetEvent*, like *SerReceiveCheck*, enters a low-power processor mode if possible.

Note that *TimeUntilNextRead* returns the number of ticks until the next scheduled read:

```
static long TimeUntilNextRead(void)
{
   if (!gFormOpened)
      return evtWaitForever;
   else {
      Long  timeRemaining;

      timeRemaining = gNextReadTime - TimGetTicks();

      if (timeRemaining < 0)
         timeRemaining = 0;
      return timeRemaining;
   }
}
```

The guts of the application are in the event handler, *MainViewHandleEvent*:

```
case nilEvent:
   handled = true;
   SerReceiveFlush(gSerialRefNum, 1);  // throw away anything in the,
                                       // buffer-- we want fresh data
   // we loop until an event occurs, or until
   // we update the display
```

```
do {
   ULong numBytesPending;
      // is the lost satellite label currently displayed
   static Boolean showingLostSatellite = false;
   ULong now = TimGetTicks();
   char     theData[165];  // two lines (80 chars with <CR><LF>
                           //  + one for null byte

   // if we've gone too long without hearing from the GPS
   // tell the user
   if ((now - gLastSuccessfulReception) > kTicksToLoseGPS) {
      FormPtr  frm = FrmGetActiveForm();

      FrmCopyLabel(frm, GPSMainTimeLabel, "No GPS!");
      FrmCopyLabel(frm, GPSMainLatitudeLabel, "");
      FrmCopyLabel(frm, GPSMainLongtitudeLabel, "");
   }

   // We'll fill our read buffer, or 1/2 second between
   // bytes, whichever comes first.
   err = SerReceiveWait(gSerialRefNum, sizeof(theData) - 1, 30);
   if (err == serErrLineErr) {
      SerReceiveFlush(gSerialRefNum, 1);  // will clear the error
      continue;          // go back and try reading again
   }
   if (err != serErrTimeOut)
      ErrFatalDisplayIf(err != 0, "SerReceiveWait");
   err = SerReceiveCheck(gSerialRefNum, &numBytesPending);
   if (err == serErrLineErr) {
      SerReceiveFlush(gSerialRefNum, 1);  // will clear the error
      continue;          // go back and try reading again
   }
   ErrFatalDisplayIf(err != 0, "SerReceiveCheckFail");
   if (numBytesPending > 0) {
      ULong    numBytes;
      char     *startOfMessage;

      // read however many bytes are waiting
      numBytes = SerReceive(gSerialRefNum, theData,
         numBytesPending, 0, &err);
      if (err == serErrLineErr) {
         SerReceiveFlush(gSerialRefNum, 1);  // will clear the error
         continue;       // go back and try reading again
      }
      theData[numBytes] = '\0';  // null-terminate theData

      // look for our magic string
      if ((startOfMessage = StrStr(theData, "$GPRMC")) != NULL) {
         char  s[10];
         gLastSuccessfulReception = now;  // we successfully read
         if (GetField(startOfMessage, 1, s)) {
            // even multiple of five seconds OR it's been at
            // least kMaxTicksWithoutTime seconds since a display
            // That way, if we lose 11:11:35, we won't have the
```

```
// time go from 11:11:30 to 11:11:40. Instead, it'll go
// 11:11:30, 11:11:36, 11:11:40
if (s[5] == '0' || s[5] == '5' ||
   (now - gLastTimeDisplay) > kMaxTicksWithoutTime) {
   FormPtr  frm = FrmGetActiveForm();

   updatedTime = true;
   // change from HHMMSS to HH:MM:SS
   s[8] = '\0';
   s[7] = s[5];
   s[6] = s[4];
   s[5] = ':';
   s[4] = s[3];
   s[3] = s[2];
   s[2] = ':';

   // Most of the time, we'll be on a multiple of five.
   // Thus, we want to read in four more seconds.
   // Otherwise, we want to read immediately
   if (s[5] == '0' || s[5] == '5')
      gNextReadTime = gLastSuccessfulReception +
         4*sysTicksPerSecond;
   else
      gNextReadTime = 0;

   // update the time display
   FrmCopyLabel(frm, GPSMainTimeLabel, s);
   gLastTimeDisplay = gLastSuccessfulReception;

   if (GetField(startOfMessage, 2, s)) {
      // update "Lost satellite" label
      if (s[0] == 'V' && !showingLostSatellite) {
         showingLostSatellite = true;
         FrmShowObject(frm, FrmGetObjectIndex(frm,
            GPSMainLostSatelliteLabel));
      } else if (s[0] == 'A' && showingLostSatellite) {
         showingLostSatellite = false;
         FrmHideObject(frm, FrmGetObjectIndex(frm,
            GPSMainLostSatelliteLabel));
      }

      // update Lat & Lon
      if (s[0] != 'V')  {
         // 4 is N or S for Lat direction, 3 is lat
         if (GetField(startOfMessage, 4, s) &&
            GetField(startOfMessage, 3, s + StrLen(s)))
            FrmCopyLabel(frm, GPSMainLatitudeLabel, s);

         // 5 is E or W for Lat direction, 6 is lon
         if (GetField(startOfMessage, 6, s) &&
            GetField(startOfMessage, 5, s + StrLen(s)))
            FrmCopyLabel(frm, GPSMainLongtitudeLabel, s);
      }
   }
```

```
                    }
                }
            }
        }
    } while (!updatedTime && !EvtSysEventAvail(false));
    break;
```

Remember that the GPS device is spewing out data once a second. We are not going to update that often; we've settled on updating every five seconds as a happy medium. Normally when we receive an idle event, we have just been in the event loop, dozing for four seconds. Thus, our receive buffer could have old data in it or could have overflowed. In the previous code, we first flush our buffer (we don't want any stale information from the buffer) and then read in two lines of data.

Next, we look for our string by searching for `$GPRMC`. If we find it, we know we've communicated with the GPS device. `gLastSuccessfulReception` then gets updated.

Next, we parse out the time from the string. If it is a multiple of five or we've gone too long without updating the display, we do all of the following:

1. Set the next time to read.
2. Parse out the remaining information.
3. Update our display with the new information (the current position or an indication that the link to the satellite is lost).
4. Return to the event loop.

Otherwise, we continue in a loop until we do successfully read or until a user event occurs.

Last, we need a small utility routine, *GetField*, to parse out a comma-delimited field:

```
// returns n'th (0-based) comma-delimeted field within buffer
// true if field found, false otherwise
static Boolean GetField(const char *buffer, UInt n, char *result)
{
   int   i;

   // skip n commas
   for (i = 0; i < n; i++) {
      while (*buffer && *buffer != ',')
         buffer++;
      if (*buffer == '\0')
         return false;
      buffer++;
   }
   while (*buffer && *buffer != ',')
```

```
        *result++ = *buffer++;
    if (*buffer != ',')
        return false;
    *result = '\0';
    return true;
}
```

That is all there is to our application. But as you can see from the discussion prior to the code, the difficulty with serial is not in the actual calls but in configuring your application to do the right thing. Much of the complexity is in being responsive to the user while doing communications and in conserving battery life by idling with *EvtGetEvent* and *SerReceiveWait*.

# TCP/IP

In this section, we show you how to use TCP/IP on a Palm device. To accomplish this, we discuss the API for networking on a Palm device, we give you some programming tips for implementing TCP/IP, and last we create a small sample application that sends email to a Simple Mail Transfer Protocol (SMTP) server.

## Network API

The Palm SDK (Version 2.0 or later) contains a net library that provides network services, like TCP/IP, to applications. With this library, an application on the Palm device can connect to any other machine on a network using standard TCP/IP protocols. The API for this library is a socket interface, modeled very closely on the Berkeley Sockets API.

Sockets are a communication mechanism. Information is sent into a socket on one machine and comes out of a socket on a remote machine (and vice versa). With a connection-oriented socket interface, you can establish the connection between the two machines prior to sending data. The connection stay opens whether or not data is sent. A good example of this is TCP. Sockets also allow a connectionless mode for sending datagrams. These can be sent to an address without any prior connection using a protocol like User Datagram Protocol (UDP).

For a brief introduction to Berkeley Sockets and socket programming, see *http://www.ibrado.com/sock-faq/*. For a more detailed discussion, see *Unix Network Programming*, by W. Richard Stevens (Prentice Hall; ISBN: 0-13-949876-1).

The similarity between the Berkeley Sockets API and the net library is so close that you can compile Berkeley Sockets code for the Palm OS with minor—and sometimes no—changes. As a result, porting networking code to the Palm OS is very simple.

The ported code works so nicely because the net library includes header files with macros that convert Berkeley Sockets calls to Palm OS calls. The main difference between the two is that calls to the net library accept three additional parameters. These are:

*A networking reference number*
: All calls to the net library need to use an integer reference to the net library. The Berkeley Sockets macros pass the global *AppNetRefnum* as their first parameter. The default value for this global is two seconds, which may not be enough for communicating over a modem to busy servers; if necessary, increase this value.

*An error code pointer*
: The Berkeley Sockets macros pass the address of the global variable `errno`.

*A timeout*
: The net library routines return if they haven't finished before the timeout. The Berkeley Sockets macros pass the global `AppNetTimeout`. Note that the default timeout (two seconds) may be too short for communicating by modem to busy servers.

## *Tips for Using TCP/IP*

*Use Berkeley Sockets*
: Use the Berkeley Sockets interface in preference to the Palm OS API. This gives you two advantages. Your networking code is portable to other platforms, and programmers who are new to the Palm OS will find your code easier to read.

*Use the Palm OS API if necessary*
: If you need to call networking code when your application globals aren't available, you must use the Palm OS API. You can't use the Berkeley Sockets API (which relies on the global variables `errno`, `AppNetRefnum`, and `AppNetTimeout`). Indeed, the only choice available to you is the Palm OS API, which allows, but doesn't require, globals.

*Write and test the code on another platform*
: Consider writing and testing your networking code on another platform, perhaps Unix or Linux. Debugging tools for networking for the Palm OS are very primitive at the time of this book's writing (although POSE can make a dial-up connection on some machines, it's not able to do so reliably on all configurations). Much more sophisticated debugging tools are available in the Unix/Linux world.

Even if source-level debugging were available, the need to dial up a remote machine still makes this a choice of last resort. As debugging would require a dial-up connection, the test portion of the edit/compile/download/test cycle would be tediously long. On a Unix/Linux machine, you can probably test without a dial-up connection, as your machine might be on Ethernet. Single-machine testing is also possible via the loopback interface (an interface enabling a machine to make a network connection to itself).

*Don't immediately close the connection*

When you close the net library with *NetLibClose*, pass `false` as the `immediate` parameter; the net library then remains open until the user-specified timer expires. As a result of the clever design of *NetLibClose*, the user can switch to another application that makes networking calls without having to redial. If you pass `true` as the `immediate` parameter, the dial-up connection closed immediately, and the connection must be reestablished when the user switches to another application.

---

Imagine the situation of a user with three different network applications on the Palm device. The user might first check email with one application, next read a newsgroup, and last look at a few web sites. This is so common a situation that you should account for it in your code. If the emailer, newsreader, and web browser each closed the network connection when they closed, the user would be fairly annoyed at the unnecessary waits to reestablish a connection.

A better solution is to let the user determine when to close the network connection using the Preferences application. While it is true that the net library, when open, sucks up an enormous amount of memory and should be closed when not needed, it is also true that users often handle network tasks during discrete periods of time. Letting the network close after a user-specified time seems the best solution to both conditions. In your network application documentation, you can direct the user to the Preferences dialog, explain the situation concerning the network connection, and guide the choice of setting.

---

*When to open a network connection*

Consider carefully when to open the net library and establish a connection. Your *StartApplication* routine is probably not a very good choice, as the Palm device would dial-up for a connection as soon as the user tapped the application icon. A better way to handle this is to wait for some explicit user request to make the connection; such a request could be put in a menu.

## *Sample Network Application*

Our Sales application does not use network services, so we've created a custom sample application to show you how to use the net library and communicate over a network. Our example sends email to an SMTP server. The user fills in:

- SMTP host name (the host that's running the SMTP server)
- A From email address
- A To email address
- Subject
- Body of the message

When the user taps Send, we connect to the SMTP server and send the email message using the SMTP protocol.

---

The SMTP protocol is documented in RFC 821. Various sites contain the RFC documents; see *http://www.yahoo.com/Computers_and_Internet/Standards/RFCs/* for a list.

---

#### *The sample on Linux*

Following our own advice, we first created this sample application on another platform and then ported it to the Palm OS. The application was originally written on a Linux machine and tested with a simple command-line interface. Here's the header file that describes the interface to *sendmail*:

```
typedef void    (*StatusCallbackFunc)(char *status);
typedef void    (*ErrorCallbackFunc)(char *problem, char *extraInfo);

int sendmail(char *smtpHost, char *from, char *to, char *subject,
   char *data, StatusCallbackFunc statusFunc,
   ErrorCallbackFunc errorFunc);
```

The `data` parameter is the body of the mail message, with individual lines separated by newline characters (`'\n'`). The *StatusCallbackFunc* and *ErrorCallbackFunc* are used to provide status (although *sendmail* doesn't currently provide status) and error information to the caller. These are abstracted from the *sendmail* routine itself to make porting the program easier. A Linux command-line program has very different error reporting than a Palm OS application.

#### *The Linux main program*

Here's the Linux main program that operates as a test harness for *sendmail*:

```
#include "sendmail.h"
#include <stdio.h>
```

```
void MyStatusFunc(char *status)
{
   printf("status: %s\n", status);
}

void MyErrorFunc(char *err, char *extra)
{
   if (extra)
      printf("error %s: %s\n", err, extra);
   else
      printf("error %s\n", err);
}

char    gMailMessage[5000];

int main(int argc, char **argv)
{
   if (argc != 5) {
      fprintf(stderr,
         "Usage: TestSendMail smtpServer fromAddress toAddres subject\n");
         exit(1);
   }
   fread(gMailMessage, sizeof(gMailMessage), 1, stdin);
   sendmail(argv[1], argv[2], argv[3],
      argv[4], gMailMessage,
      MyStatusFunc, MyErrorFunc);
   return 0;
}
```

### *Linux include files and global definitions*

Here are the include files and global definitions from *sendmail.c*:

```
#include <sys/socket.h>
#include <netdb.h>
#include <netinet/in.h>
#include <arpa/inet.h>

// Application headers

#include "sendmail.h"


static const int kLinefeedChr = '\012';
static const int kCrChr = '\015';

static StatusCallbackFunc gStatusFunc;
static ErrorCallbackFunc  gErrorFunc;
```

### *Sending the mail*

Here's the *sendmail* function, where we send data:

```
#define  kOK         '2'
#define  kWantMore   '3'
```

```
int sendmail(char *smtpHost, char *from, char *to, char *subject,
   char *data, StatusCallbackFunc statusFunc,
   ErrorCallbackFunc errorFunc)
{
   int success = 0;
   int   fd        = -1;      // socket file descriptor

   gErrorFunc = errorFunc;
   gStatusFunc = statusFunc;

   // open connection to the server
   if ((fd = make_connection("smtp", SOCK_STREAM, smtpHost)) < 0 )
   {
      (*errorFunc)("Couldn't open connection", NULL);
      goto _Exit;
   }

   // send & receive the data
   if (!GotReply(fd, kOK))
      goto _Exit;

   if (!Send(fd, "HELO [", "127.0.0.1", "]"))
      goto _Exit;
   if (!GotReply(fd, kOK))
      goto _Exit;

   if (!Send(fd, "MAIL from:<", from, ">"))
      goto _Exit;
   if (!GotReply(fd, kOK))
      goto _Exit;

   if (!Send(fd, "RCPT to:<", to, ">"))
      goto _Exit;
   if (!GotReply(fd, kOK))
      goto _Exit;

   if (!Send(fd, "DATA", NULL, NULL))
      goto _Exit;
   if (!GotReply(fd, kWantMore))
      goto _Exit;

   if (!Send(fd, "Subject: ", subject, NULL))
      goto _Exit;

// need empty line between headers and data
   if (!Send(fd, NULL, NULL, NULL))
      goto _Exit;

   if (!SendBody(fd,data))
      goto _Exit;
   if (!Send(fd, ".", NULL, NULL))
      goto _Exit;

   if (!GotReply(fd, kOK))
      goto _Exit;
```

```
    if (!Send(fd, "QUIT", NULL, NULL))
       goto _Exit;


    success = 1;
    // cleanup the mess...

_Exit:

    if ( fd >= 0 ) close( fd );

    return success;
}
```

We make a connection to the SMTP server and alternate receiving status information and sending data. The entire conversation is in ASCII; every response from the SMTP server has a numeric code as the first three digits. We look at the first digit to determine whether a problem has occurred. A digit of "2" signifies that everything is fine. A digit of "3" signifies that more data is needed (the expected response when we send the **DATA** command; it's asking us to send the body of the email). Any other digit (for our purposes) represents an error.

The protocol specifies that each sent line ends with <CRLF> and that the body of the email ends with a period (.) on a line by itself. Any lines beginning with a period must have the period duplicated (for instance, ".xyz" is sent as "..xyz"); the SMTP server strips the extra period before processing the email.

### *Connecting to the server*

The function *make_connection* actually makes the connection to the SMTP server:

```
/* This is a generic function to make a connection to a given server/port.
   service is the port name/number,
   type is either SOCK_STREAM or SOCK_DGRAM, and
   netaddress is the host name to connect to.
   The function returns the socket, ready for action.*/
static int make_connection(char *service, int type, char *netaddress)
{
  /* First convert service from a string, to a number... */
  int port = -1;
  struct in_addr *addr;
  int sock, connected;
  struct sockaddr_in address;

  if (type == SOCK_STREAM)
    port = atoport(service, "tcp");
  if (type == SOCK_DGRAM)
    port = atoport(service, "udp");
  if (port == -1) {
   (*gErrorFunc)("make_connection:  Invalid socket type.\n", NULL);
    return -1;
  }
```

```
    addr = atoaddr(netaddress);
    if (addr == NULL) {
      (*gErrorFunc)("make_connection:  Invalid network address.\n", NULL);
      return -1;
    }

    memset((char *) &address, 0, sizeof(address));
    address.sin_family = AF_INET;
    address.sin_port = (port);
    address.sin_addr.s_addr = addr->s_addr;

    sock = socket(AF_INET, type, 0);

    if (type == SOCK_STREAM) {
      connected = connect(sock, (struct sockaddr *) &address,
        sizeof(address));
      if (connected < 0) {
       (*gErrorFunc)("connect", NULL);
        return -1;
      }
      return sock;
    }
    /* Otherwise, must be for udp, so bind to address. */
    if (bind(sock, (struct sockaddr *) &address, sizeof(address)) < 0) {
     (*gErrorFunc)("bind", NULL);
      return -1;
    }
    return sock;
  }
```

This function uses the Berkeley Sockets API calls *socket* and *connect* (*bind* is used only for datagram sockets). Note that *connect* returns a file descriptor that is used in later *read*, *write*, and *close* calls.

### *Getting a port*

To connect, we have to specify an address consisting of an IP address and a port number. We use *atoport* to convert a well-known service name to a port number:

```
/* Take a service name, and a service type, and return a port number.  The
   number returned is byte ordered for the network. */
static int atoport(char *service, char *proto)
{
  int port;
  struct servent *serv;

  /* First try to read it from /etc/services */
  serv = getservbyname(service, proto);
  if (serv != NULL)
    port = serv->s_port;
  else {
      return -1; /* Invalid port address */
  }
  return port;
}
```

*atoport* uses the Berkeley Sockets API function *getservbyname*. Then *atoaddr* converts a hostname (or string of the form "aaa.bbb.ccc.ddd") to an IP address:

```
/* Converts ascii text to in_addr struct.  NULL is returned if the address
   can not be found. */
static struct in_addr *atoaddr(char *address)
{
  struct hostent *host;
  static struct in_addr saddr;

  /* First try it as aaa.bbb.ccc.ddd. */
  saddr.s_addr = inet_addr(address);
  if (saddr.s_addr != -1) {
    return &saddr;
  }
  host = gethostbyname(address);
  if (host != NULL) {
    return (struct in_addr *) *host->h_addr_list;
  }
  return NULL;
}
```

Note also that *atoaddr* uses the Berkley Sockets *gethostbyname* call.

### *Reading data character by character*

Once the connection has been made, we need to start sending and receiving data. We use a utility routine, *sock_gets*, to read an entire <CRLF>-delimited line (note that it reads one character at a time):

```
/* This function reads from a socket, until it receives a linefeed
   character.  It fills the buffer "str" up to the maximum size "count".
   This function will return -1 if the socket is closed during the read
   operation.

   Note that if a single line exceeds the length of count, the extra data
   will be read and discarded!  You have been warned. */
static int sock_gets(int sockfd, char *str, size_t count)
{
  int bytes_read;
  int total_count = 0;
  char *current_position;
  char last_read = 0;
  const char kLinefeed = 10;
  const char kCR = 13;

  current_position = str;
  while (last_read != kLinefeed) {
    bytes_read = read(sockfd, &last_read, 1);
    if (bytes_read <= 0) {
      /* The other side may have closed unexpectedly */
      return -1; /* Is this effective on other platforms than linux? */
    }
    if ( (total_count < count) && (last_read != kLinefeed) &&
        (last_read != kCR) )
```

```
        {
          current_position[0] = last_read;
          current_position++;
          total_count++;
        }
      }
      if (count > 0)
        current_position[0] = 0;
      return total_count;
    }
```

The *sendmail* protocol specifies that the server may send us multiple lines for any reply. The last line will start with a three-digit numeric code and a space (### ); any previous lines will have a – instead of the space (###–). We need to keep reading until we read the last line. *ReadReply* does that:

```
#define IsDigit(c) ((c) >= '0' && (c) <= '9')

// reads lines until we get a non-continuation line
static int ReadReply(int fd, char *s, unsigned int sLen)
{
   int       numBytes;
   do {
      numBytes = sock_gets(fd, s, sLen);
   } while (numBytes >= 0 && !(strlen(s) >= 4 && s[3] == ' ' &&
      IsDigit(s[0]) && IsDigit(s[1]) && IsDigit(s[2])));
   if (numBytes < 0)
         return numBytes;
   else
      return 0;
}
```

We use *ReadReply* in *GotReply*, which takes an expected status character and returns true if we receive that character and false otherwise:

```
#define kMaxReplySize 512

static int GotReply(int fd, char expectedLeadingChar)
{
   int       err;
   char  reply[kMaxReplySize];

   err = ReadReply(fd, reply, sizeof(reply));
   if (err != 0) {
      (*gErrorFunc)("Read error", NULL);
      return 0;
   }
   if (*reply != expectedLeadingChar) {
      (*gErrorFunc)("Protocol error", reply);
      return 0;
   }
   return 1;
}
```

The SMTP protocol specifies that no reply will exceed 512 characters (including the trailing <CRLF> characters); that's why we can safely define **kMaxReplySize** as we did. If the digit we read doesn't match the expected character, we call the error function, passing the line itself. This works well because the server usually provides a reasonable English error message with the numeric code. As a result, the user gets more than "Protocol error" for error information. This is all there is to reading data.

### *Sending data character by character*

Having taken care of reading data, now we need to deal with sending it. *Send* sends one line of data (and tacks on a <CRLF> pair at the end):

```
// sends s1 followed by s2 followed by s3 followed by CRLF
static int Send(int fd, char *s1, char *s2, char *s3)
{

   if (s1 && nwrite(fd, s1, strlen(s1)) < 0)
      goto error;
   if (s2 && nwrite(fd, s2, strlen(s2)) < 0)
      goto error;
   if (s3 && nwrite(fd, s3, strlen(s3)) < 0)
      goto error;
   if (nwrite(fd, "\015\012", 2) < 0)
      goto error;
   return 1;

error:
   (*gErrorFunc)("Write error", NULL);
   return 0;
}
```

*SendBody* sends the body of the email:

```
static int SendBody(int fd, char *body)
{
   char  *lineStart = body;
   int   result = 0;

   // send all the newline-terminated lines
   while (*body != '\0' && result == 0) {
      if (*body == '\n') {
         result = SendSingleBodyLine(fd, lineStart,
            body - lineStart);
         lineStart = body + 1;
      }
      body++;
   }

   // send the last partial line
   if (lineStart < body && result == 0)
      result = SendSingleBodyLine(fd, lineStart,
```

```
            body - lineStart);
    return result;
}
```

It relies on *SendSingleBodyLine*, which converts \n chars to <CRLF> and doubles "." characters that occur at the beginning of lines:

```
// sends aLine which is length chars long
static int SendSingleBodyLine(int fd, char *aLine, int length)
{
    if (*aLine == '.') // double-up on '.' lines
        if (nwrite(fd, ".", 1) < 0)
            goto error;
    if (nwrite(fd, aLine, length) < 0)
        goto error;
    if (nwrite(fd, "\015\012", 2) < 0)
        goto error;
error:
    (*gErrorFunc)("Write error", NULL);
    return 0;
```

Both these sending routines use *nwrite*, a utility routine that does our writing:

```
static unsigned int nwrite(int fd, char *ptr, unsigned int nbytes)
{
    unsigned int    nleft;
    int             chunk;
    int             nwritten;

    nleft = nbytes;
    while (nleft > 0) {

        if (nleft > 0x7000) chunk = 0x7000;
        else chunk = nleft;

        nwritten = write(fd, ptr, chunk);
        if (nwritten <= 0)
            return(nwritten);    /* error */

        nleft -= nwritten;
        ptr   += nwritten;
    }
    return(nbytes - nleft);
}
```

This routine loops through, calling write over and over until all the data is sent. For sockets, the write routine may not send all the data you request. A lesser amount may be all that will fit in a packet.

### *Testing the Linux application*

Testing was simplified because the Linux machine is on a network with a full-time connection to the Internet. Therefore, we have no time delays in making a connection. (If it hadn't had a full-time connection, we could have run an SMTP server on the Linux machine and run standalone, with no connection to the Internet.)

We used the Linux source-level debugger, GDB, to step through the original code. We also fixed some errors in our original attempt.

### *Porting the Linux application to Palm OS*

Now let's take a look at what it will take to port the Linux application to the Palm OS world. The *sendmail.c* requires only one small change in order to work under the Palm OS. Another couple of changes need to be made to the include files for the Palm OS, as they are slightly different. We use *sys_socket.h* instead of *sys/socket.h*. No other changes to the guts of the application, *sendmail.c*, are necessary:

```
#ifdef linux
#include <sys/socket.h>
#include <netdb.h>
#include <netinet/in.h>
#include <arpa/inet.h>
#else
#include <sys_socket.h>
#endif
```

We need to handle the user interface of a Palm OS application. We won't use the command-line interface of the Linux application. In our main source file, *Pilot-Send.c*, we must include *NetMgr.h*, declare *AppNetRefnum*, and define `errno`:

```
#include <NetMgr.h>
extern Word AppNetRefnum;
Err   errno;                // needed for Berkely socket interfaces
```

We have fairly primitive *error* and *status* routines; all they do is put up an alert:

```
static void MyErrorFunc(char *error, char *additional)
{
   FrmCustomAlert(ErrorAlert, error, additional ? additional : "", NULL);
}

static void MyStatusFunc(char *status)
{
   FrmCustomAlert(StatusAlert, status, NULL, NULL);
}
```

We also need a new utility routine that returns the text in a field:

```
// returns (locked) text in a field object
static char *GetLockedPtr(Word objectID)
{
   FormPtr  frm = FrmGetActiveForm();
   FieldPtr fld = FrmGetObjectPtr(frm, FrmGetObjectIndex(frm, objectID));
   Handle   h = FldGetTextHandle(fld);

   if (h)
      return MemHandleLock(h);
```

```
    else
        return 0;
}
```

Here's the guts of the sending portion of our event-handling routine. Just as in the Linux version of the application, we still call *sendmail* to send the data:

```
if (event->data.ctlEnter.controlID == SendmailMainSendButton) {
   if (SysLibFind( "Net.lib", &AppNetRefnum) == 0) {
      Word  interfaceError;
      Err   error;
      char  *smtpServer = GetLockedPtr(SendmailMainSmtpHostField);
      char  *to = GetLockedPtr(SendmailMainToField);
      char  *from = GetLockedPtr(SendmailMainFromField);
      char  *subject = GetLockedPtr(SendmailMainSubjectField);
      char  *body = GetLockedPtr(SendmailMainBodyField);

      if (!smtpServer)
         MyErrorFunc("Missing smtpServer", NULL);
      else if (!to)
         MyErrorFunc("Missing to", NULL);
      else if (!from)
         MyErrorFunc("Missing from", NULL);
      else if (!body)
         MyErrorFunc("Missing body", NULL);
      else  {
         error = NetLibOpen(AppNetRefnum, &interfaceError);
         if (interfaceError != 0) {
            MyErrorFunc("NetLibOpen: interface error", NULL);
            NetLibClose(AppNetRefnum, true);
         } else if (error == 0 || error == netErrAlreadyOpen) {
            if (sendmail(smtpServer, from, to,
               subject, body, MyStatusFunc, MyErrorFunc))
               MyStatusFunc("Completed successfully");
            NetLibClose(AppNetRefnum, false);
         } else
            MyErrorFunc("netLibOpen error", NULL);
      }
         if (smtpServer)
            MemPtrUnlock(smtpServer);
         if (to)
            MemPtrUnlock(to);
         if (from)
            MemPtrUnlock(from);
         if (subject)
            MemPtrUnlock(subject);
         if (body)
            MemPtrUnlock(body);
  }
   else
      MyErrorFunc("Can't SysLibFind", NULL);
}
handled = true;
break;
```

The only additional networking code we need is a call to open the net library (*NetLibOpen*) and a call to close it (*NetLibClose*). Note that *NetLibClose* does not immediately close the network connection, but relies on the user's preferences for when to do so.

## TCP/IP Summary

You can see from this example that writing code that uses network services on the Palm OS is fairly simple. A distinct advantage of Palm's implementation of the Berkeley Sockets API is that you can easily have code that ports to many platforms. This also made it possible to write the data-sending portion of the email program, the *sendmail* function, on another platform where testing was easier. Very little was required to get that email program up and running on the Palm platform after the Linux version was tested. We simply had to give the Palm application a user interface, including error information, and put a new shell around the data-sending portion of the code.

*In this chapter:*

- *Using POSE*
- *Device Reset*
- *Graffiti Shortcut Characters*
- *Source-Level Debugging with CodeWarrior*
- *Source-Level Debugging with GNU PalmPilot SDK*
- *Using Simulator on Mac OS*
- *Gremlins*

# 10

# *Debugging Palm Applications*

There are a variety of useful tools to help you debug your Palm application. The best by far is the Palm OS Emulator (POSE). With it you can code, build, and test your handheld application, without ever leaving the comfort of your desktop. Another useful tool is the strategic use of the reset buttons. There are a couple of different forms that we discuss. There are also a number of hidden Graffiti shortcut characters that offer you debugging aids and shortcuts.

Source-level debugging is available for both CodeWarrior and GNU PalmPilot SDK. This goes a long way toward making your debugging job easier. Using the Simulator on Mac OS is also worth a brief discussion for those of you who will work on that platform.

Last, we discuss Gremlins—the useful testing creatures that bear not the slightest resemblance to fanciful beings. Gremlins in the Palm world are little monkeys who bash about randomly on your code looking for problems. You may not like them, but you will find them very helpful for catching bugs you might otherwise have missed.

## *Using POSE*

POSE emulates, at the hardware level, a Palm handheld. It emulates a Motorola Dragonball processor, a display, and so on. Actual Palm OS handhelds also contain ROM—the emulator requires ROM, as well (actually, a file containing a ROM image). POSE can emulate a 1.0, 2.0, or 3.0 OS device, depending on the ROM you provide.

POSE is based on Copilot, an application written by Greg Hewgill. POSE is supported by Palm Computing for both Windows and Mac (XPilot, a port of Copilot running under X Windows on Unix/Linux, also exists). Better yet, source code is provided. You are free to make changes, but if you do, please contribute them to Palm Computing. Your enhancements may be incorporated in the main code base, making life better for everybody.

POSE can be downloaded from *http://www.palm.com/devzone*. You should always check Palm's web site for the most recent version, as this tool evolves rapidly. It also comes with the Metrowerks CodeWarrior for Palm OS. Versions of Copilot are available, though not officially supported by Palm, for Unix and Linux. The Linux port is available at Red Hat Software (*http://www.redhat.com*).

Debug versions of 2.0 and 3.0 ROMs can be downloaded from Palm's web site (*http://www.palm.com/devzone*). These versions do extra sanity checking on calls; each can catch some problems that would cause a crash on a nondebug ROM (or problems that don't cause an error today but are still wrong).

## *Major Advantages to POSE*

In our programming, we use POSE almost exclusively. Every once in a while, we download to an actual device for testing, but all the following reasons should make it clear why this is a less attractive alternative:

*POSE provides source-level debugging*
: If you have ever tried to work on a platform that did not have tools for source-level debugging (we have!), you know how useful this is.

*POSE doesn't need batteries*
: We don't have to buy AAA batteries nearly as often.

*POSE doesn't need cables to download an application*
: It can download an application directly from your desktop machine without a cable. (If you want to HotSync with POSE, however, you need a cable.)

*POSE can use the keyboard*
: You can use the keyboard as an alternative to Graffiti.

*POSE on a laptop is a self-contained environment*
: We've done development and testing at the beach, in the car, poolside, and in many other places where it would have been very inconvenient to also have had a Palm OS device and associated cabling.

*POSE detects bad programming practices*

Though we personally don't need to worry about this, since there are never bugs in *our* code, POSE is great for finding all sorts of violations. It lets you know if you are trying to access low memory, system globals, screen memory, hardware registers, and unimplemented functions (okay, this one gets us occasionally).

*Screenshots are a snap*

It's easy to take screenshots (for product manuals or books!).

*You can use POSE to demonstrate a Palm OS application*

With an LCD projector, hundreds of people can see your application being demonstrated. If you don't know that this is an advantage, try displaying a Palm application running on an actual handheld to even two people.

## Future POSE Features

POSE is a heavily revised application, and you should always check Palm's web site for a current version. This also means new features are in the works for POSE if they haven't already been added. Here are some of the forthcoming features that will be even more helpful for debugging:

*Profiling*

You'll be able to profile your code to determine where it is spending its time; almost a necessity for effective optimizing.

*Illegal access checking*

You can check for an application's accessing of any of the following memory locations:

- Low memory
- System globals
- LCD screen buffer
- Hardware registers
- Areas outside a heap block or the stack

*Stack space*

The emulator will check to make sure that the stack pointer doesn't exceed the space allocated for the stack.

*Logging events*

You will be able to keep a log of events, whether they are events in the event queue, a log of system or application functions that are called, or CPU opcodes that get executed.

*Memory block checking*

Soon POSE should be able to do all the following:

- Track memory leaks in an application
- Check for locked or busy database records when the application closes
- Fill newly allocated memory blocks with garbage to catch applications that don't properly initialize their allocated memory
- Fill disposed memory with garbage to catch applications that attempt to reuse disposed memory
- Fill stack space with garbage when leaving a routine to catch applications that keep pointers to stack variables that don't exist any longer

## Minor Disadvantages to POSE

Though we hate to admit it, POSE is bad for certain things:

*The speed isn't the same as on an actual device*

POSE can be faster or much slower than an actual device, depending on the particulars of the desktop machine on which it is running. (This makes optimizing wickedly difficult.)

*This isn't the ROM on which your final application will run*

As a result, you still need to test with the nondebug version of the ROM from an actual handheld unit. While nondebug versions of the ROMs aren't available from Palm's web site, you can use POSE to copy the (nondebug) ROM from your handheld. POSE comes with a handheld application that lets you upload a ROM copy from your handheld to POSE. Even after testing with a nondebug ROM under POSE, you still want to test on an actual handheld device.

*Graffiti is harder to use*

It's much harder to use Graffiti with a mouse (or touchpad) than it is with a stylus. (Though, as we said, you should see some improvement in future revisions.)

*POSE doesn't contain support for infrared*

This means that all beaming functionality must be tested with actual handheld devices.

*Some current versions of POSE can't reliably do serial communication*

We've had problems with 2.0b3 on both Windows and Mac OS on all machine configurations. A good test for serial communication is to hook up a modem and attempt a dial-up TCP/IP connection; if POSE cannot do this on your machine, it will have problems with the serial communication code that you write. If you happen to be a serial communication wizard, please check to see if this has been fixed; if not, consider fixing it and giving back the changes!

## *Cross-Platform Capabilities*

POSE is available for both Macintosh and Windows and both platforms share quite a range of capabilities. POSE on Mac and Windows can:

- Reset
- HotSync
- Load an application or PDB file
- Upload a copy of the ROM from a device
- Save a copy of the screen as a file (the Windows version saves in *.BMP* format; the Mac version saves in PICT format)
- Do automated testing with Gremlins (see Figure 10-9)

There are settings that control the following:

*RAM size*
: Emulate the 128K of the original PalmPilot, or be the first on your block to run with 8MB of RAM!

*Screen doubling*
: You can run with one pixel stretched to two pixels in either direction. This can make it easier to see little bitty controls and edges of things that aren't refreshing properly.

*Communications port settings*
: This controls the emulator's connection to the available desktop ports.

## *Mac OS-Specific Commands*

The Mac version has all commands in a menubar (see Figure 10-1).

## *Windows-Specific Commands*

The Windows version has all commands in a pop-up menu. Right-click on the POSE window to pop-up the menu (see Figure 10-2).

Once you have used POSE for a while, we think you will find it hard to imagine how you could have done handheld development without it. It is a very useful development and debugging tool.

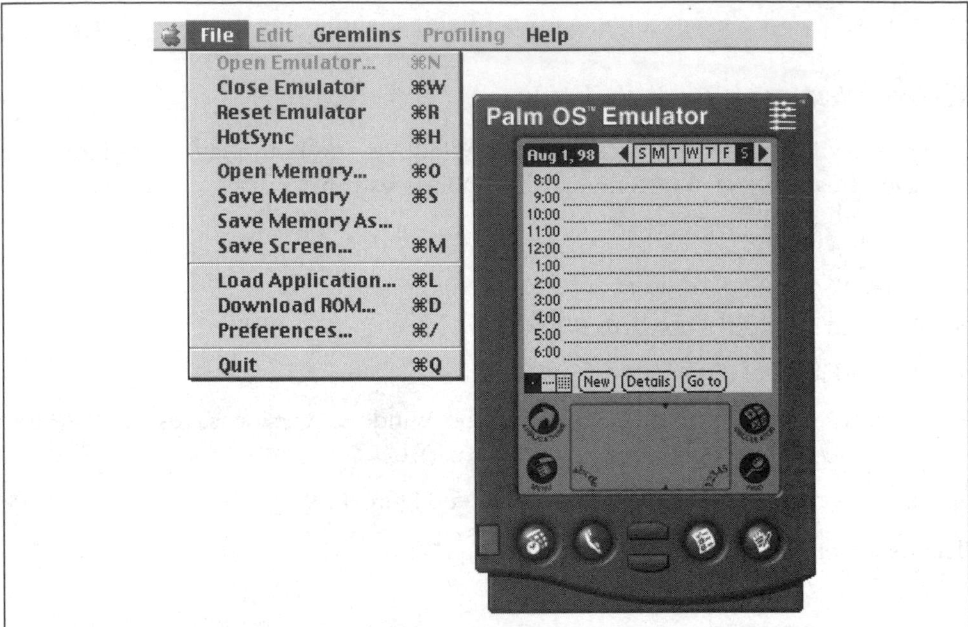


*Figure 10-1. Palm OS Emulator on Mac OS with commands in menu*

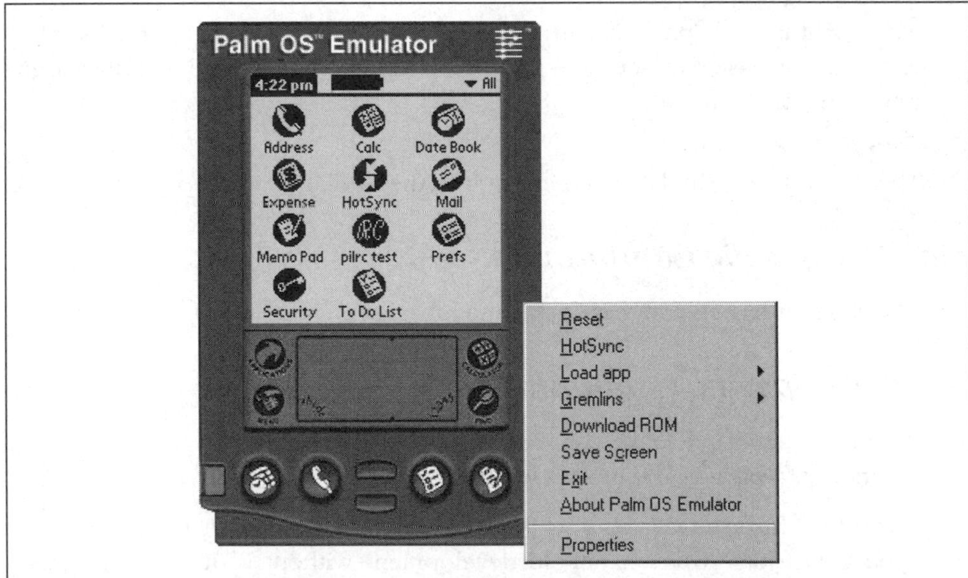


*Figure 10-2. Palm OS Emulator on Windows with commands in pop-up menu*

# *Device Reset*

Now it is time to move back to a discussion of things on the handheld. There are a couple of different kinds of resets that can be done to your Palm device:

*Soft reset*
: This is done by pressing the reset button with a blunt instrument, like an unfolded paper clip. This resets the dynamic heap but not the storage heaps, so no data is lost. Each installed application receives the `sysAppLaunchCmd-SystemReset` launch code.

*Hard reset*
: You do this by pressing the reset button while holding down the power key. You are provided with the option to erase everything in RAM. If you choose it, everything in RAM is erased, including all your data.

*Debug reset*
: By pressing the reset button while pushing the down-arrow key, you get a debug reset. This puts the Palm device into debug mode. You see a flashing box in the upper left.

*No-notify reset*
: This happens we you press the reset button while holding down the up-arrow key. The OS boots without sending reset launch codes to each application. This is essential to use if you've got a bug in your *PilotMain* (like trying to access globals without checking the launch code).

It's not uncommon to accidentally access globals when you shouldn't in your *PilotMain* (typically by not checking the launch code, for example). You can get into a vicious cycle in such cases. After a reset, your application is sent the `sysAppLaunchCmdSystem-Reset` launch code, at which point you access globals, at which point you crash and cause a reset, and so on, and so on, and so on.

The solution to this vexing problem is to use the no-notify reset, which allows the device to successfully boot. Now you can delete your application, fix the *PilotMain*, and download a new version. Of course, a hard reset would also solve the problem, but the cure would be worse than the disease.

# *Graffiti Shortcut Characters*

There are a number of hidden debugging aids that you can access using the Graffiti shortcut mechanism.

These debugging mechanisms can drain your battery quickly or cause the loss of all your data. Use them judiciously.

The Graffiti shortcuts are accessed by writing the Graffiti shortcut character (a cursive lowercase L) followed by two taps (the two taps generate a dot, or period), followed by a specific character or number. It's common to open the Find dialog before writing them. (Find has a text field that's available in all applications, and it's nice to have the feedback of seeing the characters as you write them.) Here is a complete list of these shortcuts:

ℓ *.1*
: Enters debugger mode. The device opens the serial port and listens for a low-level debugger to connect to it (for example, the unsupported Palm Debugger application). Do a soft reset to exit this mode.

ℓ *.2*
: Enters console mode. The device opens the serial port and listens for a high-level debugger like CodeWarrior to connect to it. Do a soft reset to exit this mode.

ℓ *.3*
: Turns off the power auto-off feature. The device does not power off after idle time (although the power key still works). Do a soft reset to exit this mode.

ℓ *.4*
: Displays the user's name and random number.

ℓ *.5*
: Erases the user's name and random number. On the next HotSync, this device appears to be a never-before-synced device. Syncing to an existing user recognizes all the records on the device as new; thus, they are all duplicated for the existing user on the desktop and handheld.

ℓ *.6*
: Displays the ROM build date and time.

ℓ *.7*
: Switches battery profiles from alkaline to NiCad (theoretically to adjust when the battery warning alerts appear). We didn't find this to be very effective.

ℓ *.t*
: Toggles loopback mode on and off for the Exchange Manager. This allows loopback mode testing even for applications that haven't set the `localMode` field to true in the `ExgSocketType` structure (like the built-in applications, for instance). See "Send an entry" on page 241 for information on initializing the `ExgSocketType` structure.

ℓ *.s*
: Toggles between serial and IR modes on the device. In serial mode, information that would normally be sent via infrared is sent via the serial port. This works on a Palm III device with a built-in IR port, but may or may not work on an OS 3.0 upgraded unit that has an IR port on the memory card.

# *Source-Level Debugging with CodeWarrior*

CodeWarrior can do source-level debugging either with a handheld (attached via a serial cable) or with POSE.

In either case, you've got to enable source-level debugging with Enable Debugger from the Project menu. (This is a toggle menu item, so if it says Disable Debugger, debugging is on.)

## *Choosing a Target*

You need to tell CodeWarrior whether you are using POSE or the handheld; then it needs to acquire its target.

### *Using POSE*

To use POSE, select Palm OS Emulator from the Target pop-up menu in the Preferences dialog box (see Figure 10-3).

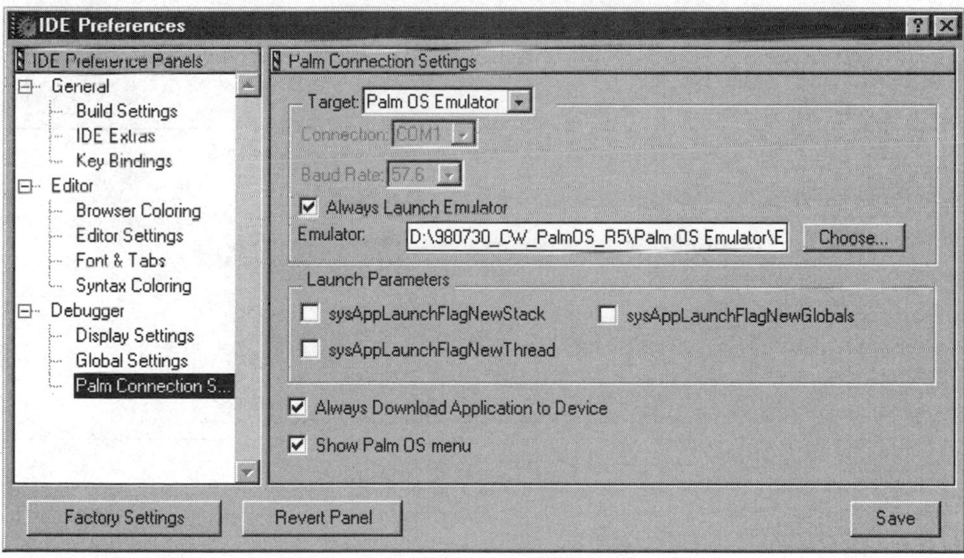


*Figure 10-3. Selecting options for debugging using POSE*

In order to debug, POSE has to be running. When you choose Debug from the Project menu, CodeWarrior automatically downloads the PRC file to the Emulator and stops at the first line of the program.

### *Using a handheld*

To use the handheld, specify the target as Palm OS Device in the Preferences dialog box (see Figure 10-4). When you choose Debug from the Project menu,

CodeWarrior prompts you to enter console mode (see Figure 10-5). At that point, use shortcut .2 on the handheld, and click OK in the CodeWarrior dialog box. CodeWarrior then automatically downloads the PRC file to the device and stops at the first line of the program.

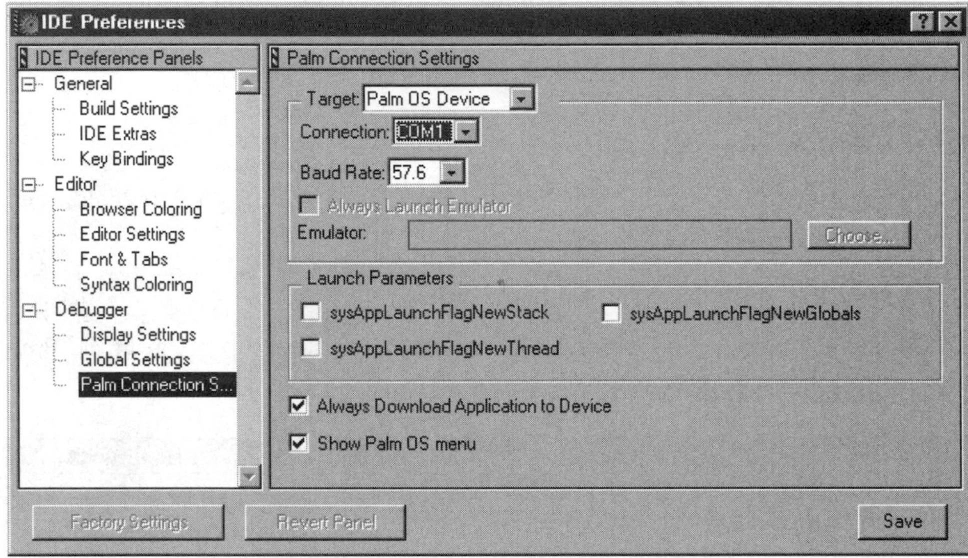


*Figure 10-4. Specifying the device as the target in the Preferences dialog box*

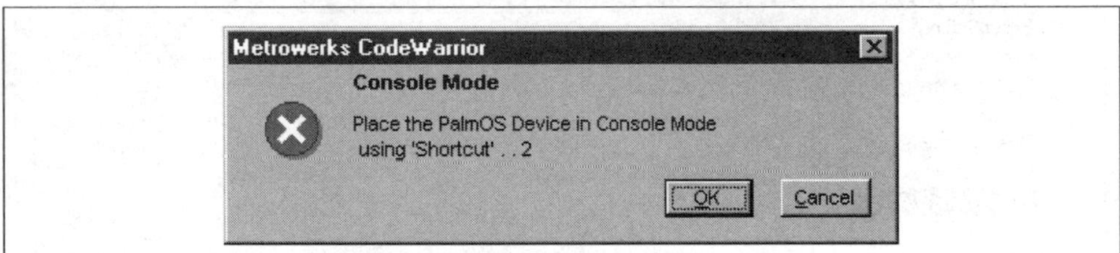


*Figure 10-5. CodeWarrior prompting to enter console mode*

## *Debugging Commands*

Figure 10-6 shows CodeWarrior source-level debugging in action. With it you can do all of the following.

- Control execution of the program
  - Set and remove breakpoints
  - Single-step (step into and step over)
  - Step out
- View variables and memory

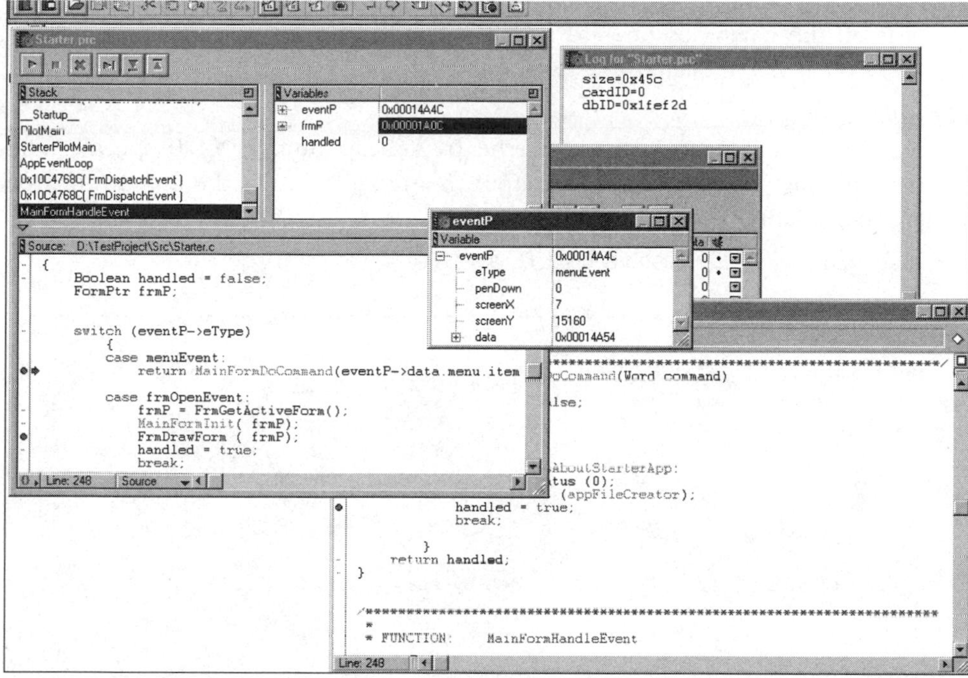

*Figure 10-6. Debugging in CodeWarrior*

## Console Window

While you are debugging, a console window is available to you. From the Palm OS menu, choose the Open Debug Console menu item to open this window. In this command-line-oriented window, you can issue commands to the device (or emulator) in order to obtain information about memory and databases and to export databases.

To execute lines in the console window, use the Enter key on the numeric keypad, not the Enter key on the main keyboard area.

Common debugger commands are:

*help*
    Displays a list of all commands.

*help command*
    Displays help for the specified command.

*dir 0*
: Lists all the databases on card 0. This is useful to see whether your application's database or databases exist.

*ht heapNumber*
: Displays a summary of the given heap. A heap number of 0 specifies the dynamic heap. Here's example output (note that it shows the amount of free space available):

```
Displaying Heap ID: 0000, mapped to 00001480

-------------------------------------------------------------------

Heap Summary:

  flags:              8000

  size:               016B80

  numHandles:         #40

  Free Chunks:        #7       (01204A bytes)

  Movable Chunks:     #4       (0004E4 bytes)

  Non-Movable Chunks: #39      (0045A2 bytes)
```

*hd heapNumber*
: Displays not just a summary, but all the chunks in a heap. A heap number of 0 specifies the dynamic heap. This allows you to see which chunks are where, which are locked, which are unlocked, etc. It's not necessary to see the heap in such detail very often, however.

## Source-Level Debugging with GNU PalmPilot SDK

The GNU tools can't debug an application running on the handheld. You only have POSE available to you. To debug:

1. Compile and link your application with the `-g` flag.
2. Run POSE and load your application.
3. Run an intermediary application called *gdbplug*, which communicates via TCP/IP to GDB. It communicates with POSE using a POSE debugging protocol. See *http://www.tiac.net/users/thomas/pilot-gdbplug.html* for documentation and the latest version.

   In a separate DOS window, run:

   ```
   gdbplug -port 2000 -enable
   ```

4. Run GDB. Pass as a command-line argument your linked file, not the PRC (if your application is *foo*, pass *foo* as the parameter, not *foo.prc*):

   ```
   m68k-palmos-coff-gdb your_linked_app
   ```

5. Within GDB, specify the PalmPilot as a target by executing:

   ```
   target pilot localhost:2000
   ```

6. Within POSE, start your application. GDB stops at the first line.

Here are the most important commands that GDB supports:

*print expressionToPrint1, ..., expressionToPrintN*
: Use the print command to look at the values of variables. Here's an example:

```
print *myStructPtr, theString[5], myOtherStruct.x
```

*backtrace*
: Prints a stack crawl, showing each function in the stack, including parameter names and values.

*step*
: Single-steps, stepping into functions.

*next*
: Single-steps, stepping over functions.

*cont*
: Continues running the program until it reaches a breakpoint, causes an error, or exits.

*break funcNameOrLineNumber*
: Sets a breakpoint. You can break at a function:

```
break MyFunction
```

Or you can set a breakpoint at a specific line number in a file:

```
break MyFile.c:16
```

*quit*
: Quits the program. If the program is still running, you are prompted for GDB to automatically quit it (by resetting POSE).

*help*
: There are, of course, many other functions. Use help to find out more about them all.

GDB is a text-oriented debugger, where commands and responses to commands are interleaved (Figure 10-7 shows an example of GDB running). GNU PalmPilot SDK comes with the Emacs text editor. Emacs can be used as an Integrated Development Environment (IDE) that can control the debugging process. As you debug, Emacs makes sure that the source file with the current line is always displayed, and it provides some menu commands that can be used instead of typing into GDB.

```
33                                  if (MenuHandleEvent((void *)0, &e, &err))
(gdb) step
36                                  switch (e.eType)
(gdb) break 33
Breakpoint 1 at 0x10012ad4: file pilrctst.c, line 33.
(gdb) cont
Continuing.

Program received signal SIGTRAP, Trace/breakpoint trap.
PilotMain (cmd=0, cmdPBP=0x0, launchFlags=142) at pilrctst.c:33
33                                  if (MenuHandleEvent((void *)0, &e, &err))
(gdb) list
28                      while(1)
29                                  {
30                                  EvtGetEvent(&e, 100);
31                                  if (SysHandleEvent(&e))
32                                          continue;
33                                  if (MenuHandleEvent((void *)0, &e, &err))
34                                          continue;
35
36                                  switch (e.eType)
37                                          {
(gdb) print e.eType
$3 = winEnterEvent
(gdb)
```

*Figure 10-7. GDB debugging an application*

# *Using Simulator on Mac OS*

CodeWarrior running on the Mac OS has a feature not found on the Windows version: the Simulator. The Simulator consists of some libraries that contain a subset of the Palm OS. These libraries are hosted so that they run on the Mac OS. When you create a Simulator version of your application, you actually build a Mac OS application that simulates a Palm OS application. It does not simulate the entire Palm OS, only your application—no other applications are present. Figure 10-8 shows a Simulator application running.

Before POSE was available, the Simulator was an almost indispensable tool. Like POSE, the Simulator doesn't require a Palm device to be connected. It also allows debugging applications that use serial communications (tough to do if you're debugging with the device itself and have the one-and-only serial port connected to the debugger).

Now that POSE is available, however, the Simulator is much less useful. In fact, we don't use it anymore. We can think of only one advantage that the Simulator has compared to POSE—it is faster. On a reasonably fast Mac OS machine, POSE is quick enough, so the speed isn't much of an issue.

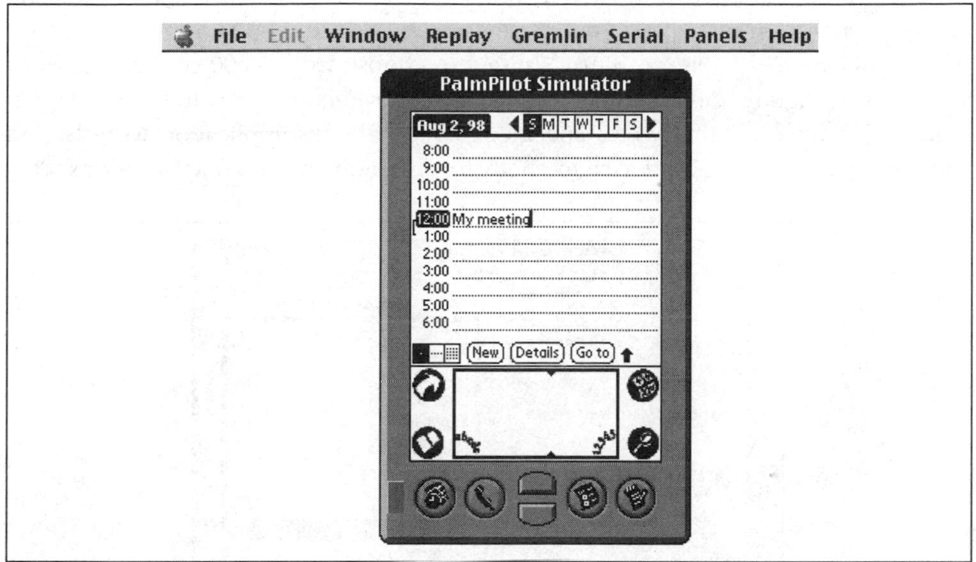


*Figure 10-8. Datebook running as a Simulator application on Mac OS*

# *Gremlins*

There are two approaches to testing software, which can often be used in a complementary fashion:

- Functionality testing—careful systematic testing on a feature-by-feature basis, making sure everything works as advertised.
- Bashing on it—an almost random use of the software to make sure it doesn't break when stressed.

Gremlins does the second sort of testing. Imagine, if you will, a very inquisitive monkey given a Palm OS device with your application on it. The monkey grabs the stylus and starts tapping away. Let's look at some characteristics of the monkey:

- It's especially attracted to buttons, pop-ups, and other active items on the screen. It taps in nonactive areas on the screen but not very often; it likes active areas.
- It's a literate monkey that knows Graffiti. It inputs Graffiti characters—sometimes garbage runs of characters but occasionally fragments of Shakespeare.
- It's hyperactive. On one of our machines, it can do 1,000 events in 30 seconds.
- It's well-behaved. If told to debug a certain application, it won't switch out of that application.

You start a Gremlin from the Gremlins dialog of POSE by selecting New from the Gremlins menu. In this dialog you specify which Gremlin you want to use and on what application (see Figure 10-9). You get to choose from 1,000 of them, each of which acts slightly differently in terms of the events it generates. Looking at Figure 10-9, you see that we've specified our own Sales application to test. You can also specify the entire device to check for problems between applications.

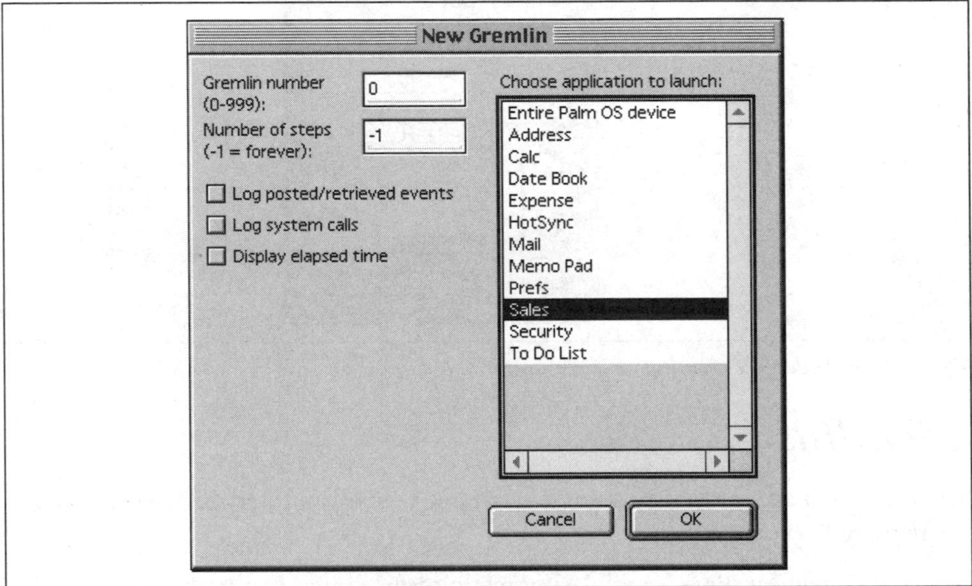


*Figure 10-9. Gremlins dialog box, where you select the application and Gremlin number*

Gremlins goes to work by generating events and causing your application to respond to them. It generates pen-downs (mostly on active areas), inputs keys, and does everything a user could do. You'll find, however, that it will end up exercising parts of your program you'd never tested: fields with more characters than you'd anticipated or more records than you'd planned for (to the extent that the entire data heap will probably be filled).

Here are the various things you can specify for Gremlins:

- You can choose a Gremlin number (each does the same thing every time you run it).
- You can choose an application (from among those installed), and the Gremlin will not exit that application.
- You can specify the number of events to run (it's not uncommon to have a bug that shows up only after hundreds of thousands of events).

Figure 10-10 shows the dialog that occurs after the Gremlins run is over. You have to request it, however, in the initial-run dialog box by selecting "Display elapsed time."

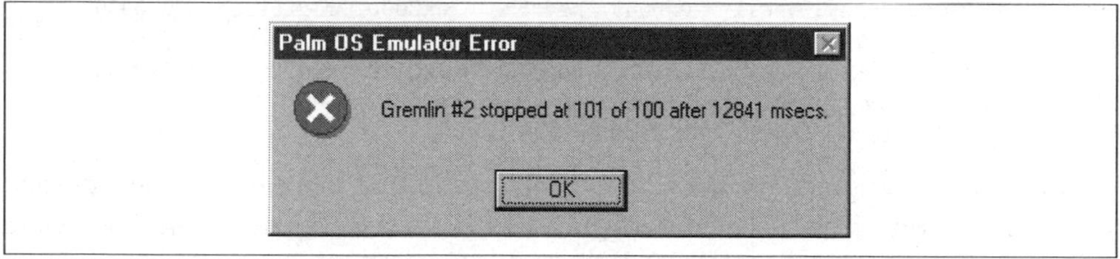


*Figure 10-10. Dialog shown after a Gremlins run with "Displays elapsed time" chosen*

If you encounter an error while running Gremlins (as is often the case), the dialog box shown in Figure 10-11 tells you about the problem.

*Figure 10-11. Gremlin error dialog failing on the 971st event; clicking the Debug button drops you into the debugger*

If you choose to "Log posted/retrieved events" (see Figure 10-9), POSE creates a file (named *Event Log #n.txt*, where n increments on every run). This is useful if you want to know how far Gremlins got before an error occurred, or to find out events that happened before the error. Here's an example output:

```
Gremlin #2 started, 10 steps.
>>> EvtEnqueueKey: ascii = 0x007C, keycode = 0x0000, modifiers = 0x0000.
<<< 0: keyDownEvent    Key:'|' 0x7c,  Modifiers: 0x0000
>>> EvtEnqueuePenPoint: pen->x=99, pen->y=150.
<<< 1: penDownEvent    X:97   Y:136
<<< 1: ctlEnterEvent   ID: 10307
>>> EvtEnqueuePenPoint: pen->x=91, pen->y=157.
<<< 2: EvtGetPen: screenX=89, screenY=143, penDown=1.
>>> EvtEnqueuePenPoint: pen->x=156, pen->y=87.
<<< 3: EvtGetPen: screenX=154, screenY=73, penDown=1.
>>> EvtEnqueuePenPoint: pen->x=-1, pen->y=-1.
<<< 4: EvtGetPen: screenX=154, screenY=73, penDown=0.
<<< 4: ctlExitEvent
<<< 4: penUpEvent      X:154   Y:73
>>> KeyHandleInterrupt: periodic=0, status=0x00000020.
>>> EvtEnqueueKey: ascii = 0x0069, keycode = 0x0000, modifiers = 0x0000.
```

```
<<< 6: keyDownEvent    Key:'i' 0x69,  Modifiers: 0x0000
>>> EvtEnqueueKey: ascii = 0x0079, keycode = 0x0000, modifiers = 0x0000.
<<< 7: keyDownEvent    Key:'y' 0x79,  Modifiers: 0x0000
>>> EvtEnqueueKey: ascii = 0x0044, keycode = 0x0000, modifiers = 0x0000.
<<< 8: keyDownEvent    Key:'D' 0x44,  Modifiers: 0x0000
>>> EvtEnqueueKey: ascii = 0x0065, keycode = 0x0000, modifiers = 0x0000.
<<< 9: keyDownEvent    Key:'e' 0x65,  Modifiers: 0x0000
>>> EvtEnqueueKey: ascii = 0x0020, keycode = 0x0000, modifiers = 0x0000.
<<< 10: keyDownEvent    Key:' ' 0x20,  Modifiers: 0x0000
Gremlin #2 stopped at 11 of 10 after 378 msecs.
```

If you request "Log system calls," the system calls that are executed are output. Here's a portion of output where logging was requested (some of the lines were removed for brevity):

```
Gremlin #2 started, 5 steps.
--- System Call 0xA2C9: SysEvGroupSignal.
--- System Call 0xA08D: SysDoze.
--- System Call 0xA23F: HwrDoze.
...
--- System Call 0xA2C9: SysEvGroupSignal.
--- System Call 0xA0A5: SysDisableInts.
--- System Call 0xA0A6: SysRestoreStatus.
--- System Call 0xA12E: EvtDequeueKeyEvent.
--- System Call 0xA23A: AlmDisplayAlarm.
--- System Call 0xA2CB: SysEvGroupWait.
>>> EvtEnqueueKey: ascii = 0x007C, keycode = 0x0000, modifiers = 0x0000.
--- System Call 0xA2C9: SysEvGroupSignal.
--- System Call 0xA0A5: SysDisableInts.
--- System Call 0xA0A6: SysRestoreStatus.
--- System Call 0xA12E: EvtDequeueKeyEvent.
--- System Call 0xA272: PenRawToScreen.
--- System Call 0xA20D: WinDisplayToWindowPt.
```

Logs are verbose; it's not uncommon to have an average of 10K per event when both types of logging are enabled. Rather than growing the log without bounds, POSE reuses log files that reach 128K. Thus, only the last 128K of log information is saved. A nice refinement, we think.

## *Gremlins and Gadgets*

Gremlins generate pen taps almost exclusively on active areas of the screen: buttons, fields, lists, places where there are form objects. This also means that areas of the screen where there are no form objects are almost completely ignored. You can take advantage of this behavior in your application if you wish. A good testing technique can be to place an empty gadget in an area of your screen where tapping does something; this way, you will grab the Gremlin's attention, and it will do some tapping there.

## *Using Gremlins Repeatedly*

One very nice thing about Gremlins is that even though each Gremlin (of the 1,000 different ones) has its own sequence of events that it generates, a specific Gremlin always generates the *same* sequence of events. Thus, if you run Gremlin 5 and find that, on a fresh POSE with your application just loaded on it, your application crashes after event 3006, every time you run that Gremlin with the same starting configuration, the crash happens. We're sure you'll appreciate the ability to reproduce the bug easily.

## *Other Advice*

Make sure you start your Gremlins run in a known configuration. Have a known amount of memory available (best done by starting with a fresh RAM file with POSE by deleting the old RAM file). Let Gremlins launch your application (so that from the beginning your application is receiving events from Gremlins).

Test your application with Gremlins set to generate one million events (start it before you go home at night). That's enough to catch almost anything. You certainly don't need to try each of the 1,000 different Gremlins. Start with just numbers 0 and 1.

Run Gremlins while your source-level debugger is active. That way, if and when your application crashes, you can drop into the debugger and see what's going on. If you can't tell what's going on at the error, Gremlins does provide the ability to step event by event. The log shows the event number at which the error occurs. You can run Gremlins until 5 or 10 events before the error. Then you can step event by event until the error occurs. This may give you a better context to figure out what's going on.

# III

# *Designing Conduits*

You get a detailed look at conduits in this section—everything from a complete description of the parts of a conduit to development platforms for conduits and code walkthroughs. Chapter 11, *Getting Started with Conduits*, starts with the big picture and ends with the code for the shell of a conduit. Chapter 12, *Uploading and Downloading Data with a Conduit*, takes this a step further; you see how to upload and download data between the desktop and the conduit. Chapter 13, *Two-Way Syncing*, shows you a conduit that uses full-blown data syncing, with exchange of data depending on where it has last been modified. The chapter covers two very different ways of creating this type of conduit. Chapter 14, *Debugging Conduits*, shows you how to debug the conduit you just finished creating. Last, in the appendix, *Where to Go From Here*, we tell you about some useful resources for Palm programming.

*In this chapter:*

- *Overview of Conduits*
- *Registering and Unregistering a Conduit*
- *Conduit Entry Points*
- *The HotSync Log*
- *When the HotSync Button Gets Pressed*
- *Using the Backup Conduit*
- *Creating a Minimal Sales Conduit*

# 11

# *Getting Started with Conduits*

It is time to discuss conduits—what they do, how to create them, what's involved in getting a minimal conduit working. It would also help if you understood (code-wise) what happens when a Palm device is plopped into a cradle and the user pushes the HotSync button.

This is useful if you want a detailed understanding of what happens when your conduit code is called, and how it interacts with the Sync Manager to perform its tasks.

We take a brief detour to discuss the types of applications that can profitably use the Backup conduit (a conduit that simply archives application data on the desktop). We also show you the code changes required to do this. Last, we create an actual conduit. As you might imagine, we build a conduit for the Sales application using Visual C++. This conduit doesn't do much; it just writes a message to the log file. However, it's still quite useful. You can see very easily what is involved in creating a minimal conduit and what it takes to get to the point where syncing is ready to begin.

## *Overview of Conduits*

A conduit can be simple or complex, depending on the job it has to do. Regardless of its complexity, you create it in the same way—a conduit is a desktop plug-in made in a desktop development environment. This isn't code that runs on the Palm handheld, but an executable library that runs during the HotSync synchronization.

## *What Does a Conduit Do?*

A conduit is responsible for the application's data during a synchronization between the handheld and a desktop computer. The conduit needs to:

- Open and close databases on the Palm device.
- Determine whether data should be uploaded only, downloaded only, or some combination of both.
- Appropriately add, delete, and modify records on the handheld and on the desktop.
- Be able to work within a multiuser environment where more that one Palm handheld may be syncing to the same network or desktop computer (though not necessarily at the same time).
- Convert the data in the application's database records to appropriate data structures on the desktop computer.
- Optionally, though usually recommended, compare records so that only modified records are synced.

Your conduit is responsible for saving the data on the desktop in whatever way makes sense. If your conduit syncs to a file for a desktop application, it needs to read and write data in that application's file format. Your conduit may read and write records from a database on the desktop or some database on the network. As a result, each conduit handles storing and retrieving desktop data differently.

There are three broad categories of conduits:

*Upload- or download-only*
: Conduits that just copy a database to or from the handheld.

*Mirror-image record synchronization*
: Conduits that do a two-way synchronization. The conduits for Address Book, Memo Pad, and To Do are examples.

*Transaction processing*
: Conduits that do some sort of processing of records but aren't doing a mirror-image synchronization. A good example might be an order entry application on the handheld that sends transactions out the conduit to be processed on the desktop.

## *Conduit Development on Windows*

At the current time, conduit development is only possible on Windows 95/98/NT. Releases of the Conduit Development Kit (CDK) in the very near future will see this change, but for now we are discussing only Windows.

### *CDK 3.0*

At the time this book was written, the final version of CDK 3.0 had not yet been released. We, of course, did the logical thing and used the beta version. As a result, our information is based on that and on the planned content of the final version.

The final version should include the following important features:

- A wizard for creating conduits
- The ability to use languages other than C++ (C rather than C++ or Visual Basic, for example)
- The ability to use compilers other than Visual C++ (Borland C++, for example)

---

Conduits developed using the older 2.1 version of the CDK work with both the PalmPilot Desktop 2.0 (shipped with the PalmPilot and PalmPilot Pro) and the Pilot Desktop 1.1 (shipped with various versions of the Pilot 1000 and 5000). 2.1-based conduits are also upward compatible with Palm Desktop 3.0 (shipped with the Palm III).

---

Certain new features of Palm Desktop 3.0 are only supported for conduits created with CDK 3.0. The major new feature is File Linking, which provides a way to copy information from an external file to a separate category. An example of this would be as part of syncing to a user's personal address book on the desktop, to copy entries from a company-wide address book to a special category on the handheld. There are some other slight API changes in 3.0.

Conduits created with CDK 3.0 are generally backward-compatible with older versions of the desktop software, although the new API calls can't be called in earlier versions (your application can make a call to find out what version of the APIs is available).

### *Using Visual C++*

The beta version of CDK 3.0 requires Visual C++ 5.0 or later running on Windows 95/NT or later. We use Visual C++ 5.0 to create our Sales conduit.

### *Using Java*

Using the CDK Java Edition you can also create a conduit using everyone's favorite caffeinated development language.

This CDK supports development using Visual J++ or Symantec Visual Cafe for Java.

We don't cover creating Java conduits in this book.

Although other Java development environments aren't officially supported, it seems to us that they should work. Remember, however, this is advice coming from people who haven't actually used these products.

## Conduit Development on Macintosh

As the time of this book's writing, the CDK C/C++ version for Macintosh was still in its infancy (read: an almost unusable alpha version). When Palm finishes the Mac OS HotSync Manager and this development kit, you will be able to create conduits on Macintosh using CodeWarrior for Macintosh, developing in C/C++. Hopefully, by the time this book is in your hands, it will be out. See *http://www.palm.com/devzone* for the status of this project.

## Required Elements in a Minimal Conduit

In a little while, we will show you how to create a minimal conduit. That conduit will contain a few essential elements that we want to tell you about now:

*A mechanism for installation and uninstallation*
: Different versions of the CDK require different mechanisms for registering and unregistering your application.

*Three C entry points*
: One entry point registers the conduit's name, another its version number, and the last serves as an entryway into the conduit.

*Log messages*
: You need to provide log messages to the user. Among other things, you must tell the user whether the sync was successful or not.

We first look at installation and uninstallation issues and then discuss the entry points. Last, we discuss log messages.

# Registering and Unregistering a Conduit

Before the conduit can be used, it needs to be registered. This is how the HotSync Manager application knows that it exists and knows which databases the conduit is responsible for syncing. Depending on which version of the CDK you have, there are differences in what you do to register. We talk about the old, difficult way and then the new improved methods.

## The Old, Ugly Way

In version 2.1 (and earlier versions) of the CDK, this registration was done by adding entries to the Windows Registry. Unregistration required removing entries from the Registry (and possibly renaming existing entries). Further, this process for adding entries was fragile—one developer modifying the registry incorrectly could cause some or all of the other conduits to fail.

These troubles only increased during the acquisition frenzy, when the keys used for the Windows Registry by various versions of HotSync Manager and the Desktop Manager changed from Palm Computing to U.S. Robotics.*

Conduits then needed to be aware of various registry keys and needed to perform a careful set of steps when registering and an even more careful set when unregistering.

The time was ripe for a better approach to registration.

## The New, Sleek Way

The Conduit Manager, provided as part of Palm Desktop 3.0 and as part of the 3.0 version of the CDK, contains an API for registration and unregistration. It knows about the various versions of HotSync, the different keys used in the Windows Registry, and the careful steps needed for registering and unregistering.

The Conduit Manager functionality is provided in a DLL that ships with the new version of the Palm Desktop. As we discuss later in "Finding the Correct Conduit Manager DLL," you also need to include the DLL as part of your installer.

The 3.0 version of HotSync Manager continues to use the Windows Registry for the sake of older conduits that don't use the Conduit Manager. You should expect, however, that future versions of HotSync may not use the Windows Registry at all.

As long as you use the Conduit Manager, you'll be shielded from any such changes to the underlying registry mechanism.

## CDK 3.0—Information Needed to Register

There are different types of entries that you need to have in order to register a conduit. Some are required; others are optional.

* Palm Computing was acquired by U.S. Robotics, which was in turn acquired by 3Com.

### Required conduit entries

The following entries are required to register a conduit:

*Conduit*
: The name of the conduit DLL. If this entry doesn't include a directory, the name must be found in the HotSync directory or current PATH; otherwise, it should include the full pathname to the DLL. (Generally, you keep your DLLs in the HotSync directory.) If your conduit is written using Java, this entry should be "JSync.DLL", a C++ shim that translates between C++ and Java.

*Creator*
: The four-character creator ID of the database(s) your conduit is responsible for. Your conduit will be called during a HotSync only if an application with this creator ID exists on the handheld.

*Directory*
: In the HotSync directory, each user has a subdirectory. Within each user's directory, each conduit has its own directory where it can store files. This string specifies the conduit's directory name.

### Optional entries

The optional entries are more numerous. They include the following:

*File*
: A string specifying a file (if the string doesn't include a directory, it is assumed to be within the conduit's directory). This is intended to be the local file that the conduit will sync the handheld against. However, your conduit is not restricted to using only this file (some conduits may need to read/write multiple files on the desktop).

*Information*
: A string that provides information about your conduit. This string can be used to resolve conflicts. If more than one conduit wants to handle the same creator ID, an installation tool could display this string and ask the user which conduit should be used for syncing.

*Name*
: A string that is the user-visible name of the conduit.

*Priority*
: A value between 0 and 4, this controls the relative order in which conduits run. Conduits registered with a lower priority run before conduits registered with higher priorities. If you don't set this value, the HotSync Manger uses a default value of 2 for your application.

*Remote DB*
: A string specifying a database name on the handheld. This string is provided for you to use in your conduit when it runs; your conduit isn't required to use it, however.

*Username*
: The name of the user for which this conduit is installed. Note that this entry is not currently used.

#### *Java-only entries*

Finally, there are entries relevant only if the conduit is written in Java:

*Class name*
: The name of the Java conduit class (including package).

*Class path*
: The directory that contains all the classes used by the Java conduit.

*VM*
: Specify "Sun" for the Sun Java Virtual Machine or "MS" for the Microsoft Java Virtual Machine. This is provided since some Java code is, unfortunately, sensitive to the virtual machine on which it runs.

## *Registering and Unregistering Manually Using CondCfg*

Along with the Conduit Manager DLL is an application, *CondCfg*, that uses the Conduit Manager (see Figure 11-1). This application displays all the registered conduits and allows you to register conduits, change registered information, and delete conduits.

Your end users won't use or even see *CondCfg*, however, as you automate the conduit registration process as part of installing and uninstalling it on the desktop.

## *Automatically Installing and Uninstalling a Conduit*

A small command-line program (*ConduitInstall.exe*) is going to install and register our conduit. We use a separate one (*ConduitDeinstall.exe*) to uninstall.

#### *Installing the conduit*

As *ConduitInstall.exe* executes, it makes calls to the Conduit Manager API to install and register our conduit. It also needs to make calls to the three required entry points of the conduit (`Conduit`, `Creator`, `Directory`) and to any of the optional entry points we want to set.

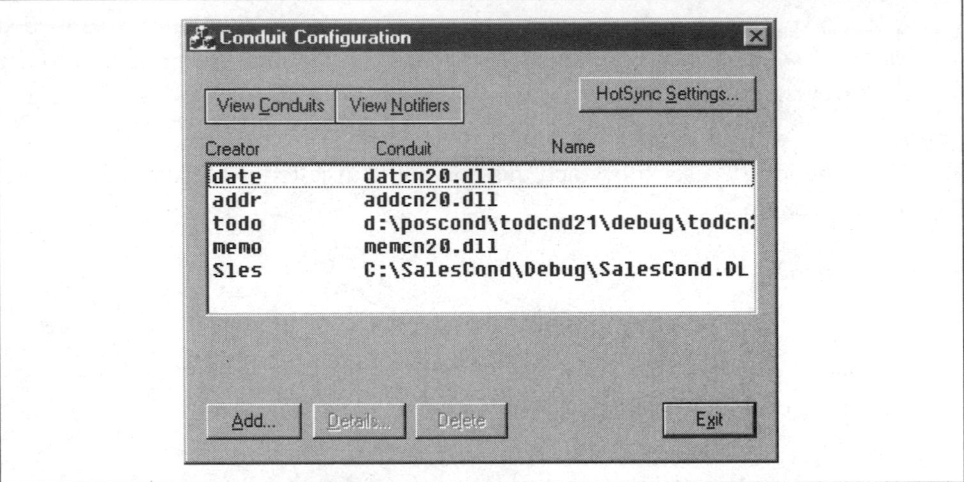


*Figure 11-1. CondCfg—a developer utility for registering and unregistering conduits*

We use *ConduitInstall.exe*, a simple command-line program, to avoid clouding the relevant issues with a lot of technical details concerning Windows application programming. We couldn't possibly cover all the available methods. You could fold your installation into a program that handles other installations, as well. You could be using the popular installer utility *InstallShield* (the CDK contains a sample that shows how to use this). In any event, we keep things simple so that you can understand exactly what is necessary to install and register a conduit.

The first call you make is one that registers the `Creator` entry point of the conduit:

```
int CmInstallCreator(const char *creatorString, int conduitType);
```

If that succeeds, you call a different *CmSetCreator* routine for all the rest of your entry points. Most of the *CmSetCreator* routines match the entry point name and are easy to figure out (the two exceptions are *CmSetCreatorName* and *CmSetCreatorTitle*). Here are the routines we use and the entry points they register:

*CmSetCreatorName*
: Sets the required `Conduit` entry point

*CmSetCreatorDirectory*
: Sets the required `Directory` entry point

*CmSetCreatorFile*
: Sets the `file` entry point

*CmSetCreatorPriority*
: Sets the `priority` entry point

*CmSetCreatorTitle*
: Sets the `name` entry point

### *ConduitInstall.exe*

Here's our command-line program, *ConduitInstall.exe*, that registers a conduit:

```
#include <Windows.h>
#include "CondMgre.h"
#include <stdio.h>

int main(int argc, char **argv)
{
   const char *kCreator = "Sles";

   err = CmInstallCreator(kCreator, CONDUIT_APPLICATION);
   if (err == 0)
      err = CmSetCreatorName(kCreator,
            "C:\\SalesCond\\Debug\\SalesCond.DLL");
   if (err == 0)
      err = CmSetCreatorDirectory(kCreator, "Sales");
   if (err == 0)
      err = CmSetCreatorFile(kCreator, "Sales");
   if (err == 0)
      err = CmSetCreatorPriority(kCreator, 2);
   if (err == 0)
      printf("Registration succeeded\n");
        else
      printf("Registration failed %d\n", err);
   return err;
}
```

### *Automatically uninstalling a conduit*

Uninstalling is just as simple. Our application, *ConduitDeinstall.exe*, uses *CmRemoveConduitByCreatorID*, which removes all the conduits registered with a particular creator ID. It returns with the number of conduits removed (or a negative number in the case of an error). The application prints the number of conduits it unregistered.

### *ConduitDeinstall.exe*

```
#include <Windows.h>
#include "CondMgre.h"

int main(int argc, char **argv)
{
   const char *kCreator = "Sles";
   int numConduitsRemoved = CmRemoveConduitByCreatorID(kCreator);
```

```
    if (numConduitsRemoved >= 0)
        printf("Unregistration succeeded for %d conduits\n",
            numConduitsRemoved);
    else
        printf("Unregistration failed %d\n", numConduitsRemoved);
}
```

## Finding the Correct Conduit Manager DLL

The Conduit Manager calls that our installation program relies on are in a DLL, specifically the *CondMgr.DLL*. This is quite useful, as we are not required to recompile if the underlying registration architecture changes. A new DLL could register in a different way, and our code won't need to know about it.

There is a problem, however, and it doesn't have a very simple workaround. You might wonder how it is that your installation code could use a new version of the conduit manager DLL. You might assume that Palm Computing would help you out here and ensure that *CondMgr.DLL* would always be found in the same place. For example, if *CondMgr.DLL* were installed in the system directory, it would be part of the path that the system searched to load DLLs and would be automatically found and loaded when your installation program ran. Well, things are not that simple.

*CondMgr.DLL* is not (currently) installed in the system directory when the user installs the Palm Desktop software. Instead, it is put in the same directory as the Palm Desktop software. You might say that this is no big deal; you just need to know where the Palm Desktop software is. The folks at Palm Computing are happy to provide that information—they tell you the path to that directory in the Windows Registry.

Here is the problem. You may remember how we get into the Registry. Yep—using the Conduit Manager APIs that are in the Conduit Manager DLL. It's a chicken-and-egg problem. Fortunately, we have a solution.

### The solution to finding CondMgr.DLL

Here's the solution:

1. Check to see if the *CondMgr.DLL* is in the system path. If so, use it (it was probably installed by a later version of the Palm Desktop software).
2. If not, use a copy of *CondMgr.DLL* that you ship with your installation program to find the directory containing the Palm Desktop software (*CmGetCorePath* returns the directory). Check in that directory for *CondMgr.DLL*. If it's there, use it (it may be newer than the version you are shipping in your installation program).

3. If there's no *CondMgr.DLL* in the system path, and no *CondMgr.DLL* in the Palm Desktop software, revert to using the *CondMgr.DLL* that you ship along with your installation program (Palm Desktop software prior to version 3.0 didn't have *CondMgr.DLL*).

#### *Implementing the solution*

We use a separate program that checks for which *CondMgr.DLL* to use. Once this program finds that slippery little DLL, it changes the current directory to that location. This location is one of the following:

- A subdirectory containing a version of *CondMgr.DLL* that we ship.
- The Palm Desktop directory.
- If we're using *CondMgr.DLL* from the system path, we won't change the directory.

Then this program launches our real installation program, which automatically loads the *CondMgr.DLL* from the current directory.

An alternative approach would have been to have one program and call *LoadLibrary* to explicitly load the *CondMgr.DLL* we wanted. We didn't go this route because it's not as simple to call routines in an explicitly loaded DLL as it is in an implicitly loaded DLL.

#### *The elements in our installation*

Our installation directory contains:

*Install.exe*
: This is the program that figures out which *CondMgr.DLL* to use. It then changes the current directory and runs *ConduitInstall.exe.*

*ConduitInstall.exe*
: This application just makes Conduit Manager API calls and is blissfully unaware of the trouble of finding the correct *CondMgr.DLL.* It implicitly loads *CondMgr.DLL* (that is, the system loads it when the application starts; if the system can't find *CondMgr.DLL*, it produces an error—*Install.exe* sets things up to guarantee the system can find *CondMgr.DLL*).

*CondMgr*
: A subdirectory containing one file:

  *CondMgr.DLL*
  : The Palm DLL that we ship with our installation. We use it to find the Palm Desktop directory. In the case that *Install.exe* can't find an installed *CondMgr.DLL*, we also use this DLL for our registration.

Here's the entire code for *Install.exe* (*LoadLibrary*, *GetProcAddress*, *FreeLibrary*, *_getcwd*, *_chdir*, and *system* are all calls provided by the Windows OS):

```
#include <Windows.h>
#include <Condmgre.h>
#include <stdio.h>
#include <direct.h>
#include <process.h>

typedef int (WINAPI *CmGetCorePathPtr)(TCHAR *pPath, int *piSize);

int main(int argc, char **argv)
{
    int result = 0;
    char    conduitExecutable[_MAX_PATH];

   /* Get the current working directory: */
    if( _getcwd( conduitExecutable, _MAX_PATH ) == NULL ) {
        fprintf(stderr, "_getcwd error" );
        result = 3;
    }
    else
        strcat(conduitExecutable, "\\ConduitInstall.exe");

   if (LoadLibrary("Condmgr.dll"))
        printf("loaded library using normal path\n");
    else {
        printf("didn't find library in normal path\n");

        HINSTANCE lib;
        if ((lib = LoadLibrary(".\\CondMgr\\CondMgr.dll")) != NULL) {
            printf("loaded my version of condmgr\n");
            char    buffer[512];
            int     size = sizeof(buffer);
            CmGetCorePathPtr corePathFunc;

            corePathFunc = (CmGetCorePathPtr) GetProcAddress(
                lib, "CmGetCorePath");
            if (corePathFunc) {
                if ((*corePathFunc)(buffer, &size) == 0) {
                    char    fullPathnameConduitMgr[512];
                    printf("path = \"%s\"\n", buffer);
                    FreeLibrary(lib);

                    strcpy(fullPathnameConduitMgr, buffer);
                    strcat(fullPathnameConduitMgr, "\\CondMgr.dll");
                    HINSTANCE full = LoadLibrary(fullPathnameConduitMgr);
                    if (full != NULL) {
                        printf("Found %s\n", fullPathnameConduitMgr);
                        FreeLibrary(full);
                        result = _chdir(buffer);
                    } else {
                        printf("must use our conduit mgr\n");
                        result = _chdir(".\\CondMgr");
                    }
                }
```

```
            } else {
                fprintf(stderr, "couldn't load CmGetCorePath\n");
                result = 1;
            }
        } else {
            fprintf(stderr, "Couldn't load .\\CondMgr\\CondMgr.dll\n");
            result = 2;
        }
    }
    if (result == 0) {
        // we found a library and we've changed directories,
        // if necessary
        fprintf(stderr, "running \"%s\"\n", conduitExecutable);
        result = system(conduitExecutable);
        if (result != 0)
            fprintf(stderr, "Calling ConduitInstall failed\n");
    }
    return result;
}
```

As it runs, it prints a commentary of what is happening. When it's complete, it returns 0 in case of success; a nonzero result indicates an error.

# Conduit Entry Points

We told you before that a conduit has three required entry points. There are also some optional ones (including some that are only for CDK 3.0), which we look at next.

## Required Entry Points

The required entry points are as follows:

*GetConduitName*
: This returns the conduit's name.

*GetConduitVersion*
: This function returns the version of the conduit as a four-byte value. The minor version is in the low byte. The major version is in the next byte. The upper two bytes are unused. A conduit with Version 2.1 would return 0x21.

*OpenConduit*
: It is from this entry point that the conduit actually does its work. This point passes a parameter that is a class object with information about the sync. The information includes:

- The username
- Remote database and filename
- The type of synchronization to be performed—copy handheld to desktop, copy desktop to PC, fast sync, slow sync, or do nothing

## Optional Entry Points

The optional entry points have to do with customization (and File Linking in 3.0):

*ConfigureConduit (CfgConduit is a newer version of this)*

This is called when the user wants to customize the conduit by pressing Change in the Custom Hotsync dialog (see Figure 11-2). The conduit is responsible for displaying a dialog and saving user choices. A mirror-image synchronization conduit is responsible for displaying the dialog shown in Figure 11-3. The user chooses what action should happen when a sync occurs (unchecking the permanent checkbox in the dialog specifies that the dialog setting should occur only on the next sync).

Specific conduits may also have different things the user can configure. In any case, conduit configuration should always allow the user the option to do nothing. This way, the user can pick and choose which conduits are active (for example, to expedite syncing just the address book before rushing to a meeting).

If this entry point isn't present in your conduit, pressing the Change button does nothing—an action guaranteed to be confusing and annoying to users. Even if you are unwilling to provide a way for the user to configure your conduit to do nothing, you should provide this entry point and have it tell the user that the conduit can't be configured.

Our reasoning relies on an age-old adage of good design: every allowable user action should produce a visible effect. Words to warm a designer's heart.

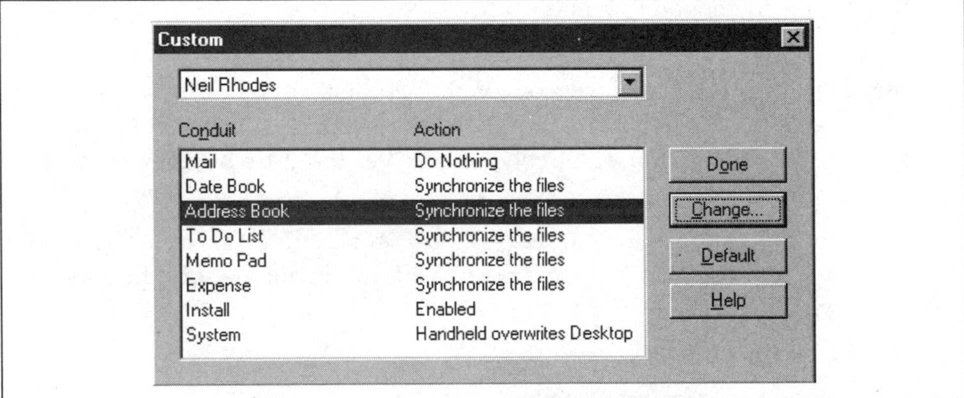


*Figure 11-2. HotSync dialog for customizing conduits*

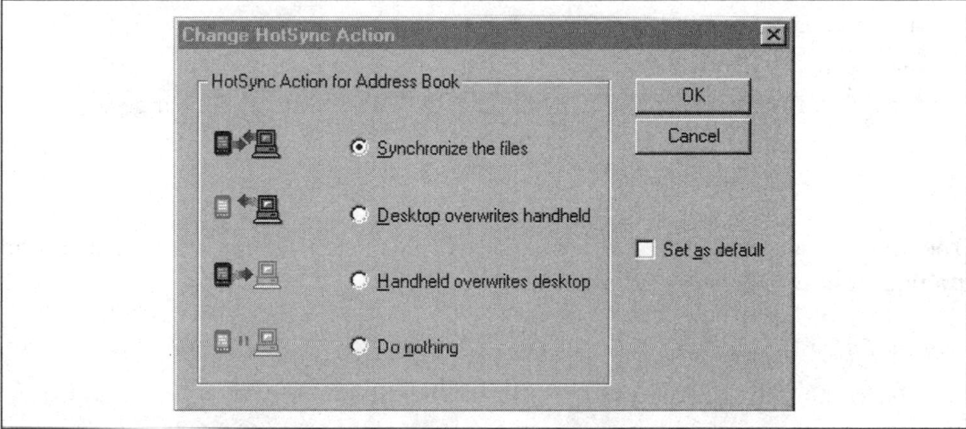


*Figure 11-3. A conduit's configuration dialog*

*CfgConduit*

This is a newer entry point that replaces *ConfigureConduit*. Its purpose is the same as that of *ConfigureConduit*, but it receives more information when called. Because it is extensible (due to a variable-size argument block), even more information will probably be provided in the future.

It's called by HotSync Manager 3.0 and later. If this entry point isn't there, HotSync Manager 3.0 reverts to calling *ConfigureConduit*.

Support for calling *ConfigureConduit* may be phased out in future versions of the HotSync Manager.

*GetConduitInfo*

This is called by the HotSync Manager to return the name of the conduit (as an alternative to *GetConduitName*), the version of Microsoft Foundation Classes (MFC) used to build the conduit, and the default action of the conduit (the choices being: no action, sync, handheld overwrites desktop, or desktop overwrites handheld).

These are the entry points used only for File Linking. (File Linking is provided in HotSync 3.0 or later and is not covered in this book):

*SubscriptionSupported*

If this entry point exists and returns 0, File Linking is supported by this conduit.

*ConfigureSubscription*

Called to provide information necessary for File Linking.

*ImportData*
  Imports data from a linked file and displays it to the user.

*UpdateTables*
  Called to update desktop files when File Linking information changes.

# The HotSync Log

The CDK provides routines that add to a HotSync log. There are several useful routines, but the main one to use is *LogAddEntry*.

### LogAddEntry

Use this routine to add entries to the HotSync all the time.

***LogAddEntry(logString, activity, timestamp)***

`timestamp`
  This is a boolean. True means that the log entry will be timestamped.

`activity`
  This is an enumerated type. There are many different enumeration constants available for your use.

The enumerated types used most often as a value for `activity` are:

*slSyncStarted*
  Tells the log that your conduit is beginning synchronization. Call the following when you begin the sync process:

```
LogAddEntry("", slSyncStarted, false)
```

*slSyncAborted*
  Tells the log that your conduit is done and that there was an error. Call:

```
LogAddEntry(your conduit name, slSyncAborted, false)
```

  when you finish syncing with an error.

*slSyncFinished*
  Tells the log that your conduit is done without errors. Call:

```
LogAddEntry(your conduit name, slSyncFinished, false)
```

  when you finish syncing without an error.

*slWarning*
  Adds the specified `logString` to the log and tells the user at the end of the HotSync that there are messages in the log.

  `slText`

  Adds the specified `logString` to the log, but doesn't tell the user about the message.

### *LogAddFormattedEntry*

Another useful routine is *LogAddFormattedEntry*. It acts as a combination of `sprintf` and *LogAddEntry* and helps if you need to construct the log string from numbers or other strings. Here's an example of its use:

```
LogAddFormattedEntry(slText, false, "The number (%d) is bad", myNumber)
```

This is all that you need to know about installation, entry points, and log messages. Next, we discuss the events that occur when the user does a sync.

## *When the HotSync Button Gets Pressed*

It is worth going through a step-by-step sequence of the events that occur when the user pops a Palm device into the cradle and pushes the HotSync button. From this sequence (started here and continued in the next chapter), you can see exactly when and how the code in your conduit interacts with the desktop, the Palm device, and the Sync Manager.

For the purposes of this example, you should assume that our sample application has been successfully installed and contains no problems. Table 11-1 contains a description on the left of what the user does or what activity is occurring; the right column indicates what's going on programmatically in your conduit or on the desktop.

For now, we are just going to wave our hands around when we get to a description of data up/downloading, and exporting and importing. We fill in these gaps in the next chapter. The whole grand system should be clear by that point.

*Table 11-1. What Happens When a Synchronization Occurs*

| Action (by the User or by the System) | What Is Happening Programmatically |
|---|---|
| User pushes the HotSync Button. | The handheld sends an "Are you there" message out the serial port until the HotSync Manger on the desktop notices that someone is knocking. |
| HotSync synchronizing starts. | The HotSync Manager negotiates a baud rate with the handheld and begins communication. It reads the user ID and name from the handheld and tries to find a corresponding HotSync user. If it doesn't find one, it prompts on the desktop for the user to select one or to create a new one. |

*Table 11-1. What Happens When a Synchronization Occurs (continued)*

| Action (by the User or by the System) | What Is Happening Programmatically |
|---|---|
| The user gets the message: *Connecting with the desktop*. HotSync retrieves from the handheld a list of all databases and their creators. | For each database on the handheld, the HotSync Manager tries to find a conduit registered for that creator.<br>Databases that don't have a corresponding conduit but that have the backup bit set get added to the list to be backed up by the Backup conduit. Remaining databases are ignored completely. |
| **3.0 or later—Sync Manager installs new databases.** | **The Install conduit gets called to install databases.** |
| The HotSync Manager determines whether a fast sync is possible (if this is the same desktop machine last synced with) or whether a slow sync is required (if it is different). | Conduits can take advantage of a fast sync by only reading from the handheld records marked as modified; nonmarked records won't have changed since the last sync. |
| The user gets notified that syncing has now started. | Install conduit gets run and new applications are installed.<br>The HotSync Manager starts the iteration through its list of conduits based on their priority code (as specified when the conduit was registered). |
| The HotSync Manager finishes with the conduit prior to ours. | |
| The HotSync Manager prepares to sync. | Our conduit gets loaded. |
| The HotSync Manager checks the conduit's version number. | *GetConduitVersion* is called and returns the conduit's version number. |
| The HotSync Manager gets the conduit name so that is can display information in the Status dialog. | *GetConduitName* is called and returns the name of the conduit. |
| The HotSync Manager prepares to sync by passing the synchronization off to the conduit. | *OpenConduit* gets called, and the conduit's DLL gets loaded into memory. It is told whether to do a fast sync, a slow sync, a copy from handheld to desktop, a copy from desktop to handheld, or nothing. When *OpenConduit* returns, it has completed the task. |
| **The HotSync Manager runs the remaining conduits.** | |
| The HotSync Manager backs up modified databases that don't have a corresponding conduit but do have the backup bit set. | The Backup conduit gets called. |
| **2.0 or earlier—Sync Manager installs new databases.** | **The Install conduit gets called to install databases.** |

*Table 11-1. What Happens When a Synchronization Occurs (continued)*

| Action (by the User or by the System) | What Is Happening Programmatically |
|---|---|
| Handheld notifies applications whose conduits have run that their database(s) have been synced. | Your handheld application gets a `sysAppLaunchCmdSyncNotify` launch code if any of its databases have been modified during the sync. |
| Syncing is complete. | |

# *Using the Backup Conduit*

You may have an application that doesn't require its own conduit. In such cases, you can rely on the Backup conduit. First, let's discuss the types of applications that can profitably use this approach and then tell you what you need to do to your application.

The Backup conduit works on any application's database that:

- Has no other conduit
- Has the backup flag set
- Has been modified since the last sync

Whenever the Backup conduit is used, the data in the database is completely copied from the Palm device to the desktop and saved as a PDB (database) or PRC (application) file. This type of backup occurs during every sync, which is why you don't want to use this as a solution for large databases or most applications.

## *Applications That Might Use the Backup Conduit*

The Backup conduit is well suited to the following types of applications:

*Games*
: Where you save top score information

*Utilities*
: Where you save some user settings

*Alarm clocks or other timers*
: Where you save world clock information or other types of alarm settings

*Electronic books*
: Where you save display information, bookmarks, or the books themselves

*Newsreaders*
: Where you save newsgroup lists

## *Using System Prefs Instead*

Another approach for these types of applications is to use the System Prefs database. This database contains a record for each application that stores preferences. These preferences are automatically backed up because the Systems Prefs database has the backup bit set.

Actually, when you create system preferences, you can specify whether you want them to be backed up or not (a true value for the `saved` parameter to *PrefSetAppPreferences* means you want the preferences backed up). If you've got some information that you want to save between calls to your application but that you don't need backed up, you'll use the nonbacked-up preferences (a false value for the `saved` parameter).

A game might want the 512 bytes of high scores backed up (heaven forbid *they* get lost!), but not the 6K of information about what level the user was on, what weapons were in what hands, etc.

## *Setting the Backup Bit for a Database*

To set the backup bit, you can use the *DmSetDatabaseInfo* call on the handheld to change the attributes of a database. Here's code for the handheld that changes the open database *myDB*:

```
LocalID     theLocalID;
UInt        theCardNum;
UInt        theAttributes;

DmOpenDatabaseInfo(myDB, &theLocalID, NULL, NULL, &theCardNum, NULL);
DmDatabaseInfo(theCardNum, theLocalID, NULL, &theAttributes, NULL,
   NULL, NULL, NULL, NULL, NULL, NULL, NULL, NULL);
theAttributes |= dmHdrAttrBackup;
DmSetDatabaseInfo(theCardNum, theLocalID, NULL, &theAttributes, NULL,
   NULL, NULL, NULL, NULL, NULL, NULL, NULL, NULL);
```

Note that the backup bit isn't reset automatically after a backup. With devices running versions of the Palm OS prior to 2.0, as long as the backup bit of a database is set—and there is no conduit installed for it—the database is backed up every time the user syncs. With Palm OS 2.0 and later, the database is backed up only if it has been modified since the last sync.

# *Creating a Minimal Sales Conduit*

Using Visual C++ and the development kit, only a few steps are required to create a minimal conduit. We assume that you've installed the CDK on your C: drive in the *\CDK* folder. Let's walk through the steps.

The final 3.0 version of the CDK promises a Conduit Wizard, which may make this creation process even easier.

1. Create a new project of type *MFC AppWizard (dll)* (see Figure 11-4).
2. Specify that the project is a regular DLL using the MFC shared library as shown in Figure 11-5.
3. Add the Conduit SDK's include directory to the list of places the compiler searches for include files. To do this, after you've created the project, open the Project Settings dialog and, in the C/C++ settings panel (see Figure 11-6), add the following to the Project Options area:

   ```
   /I "C:\CDK\INCLUDE"
   ```

4. Add needed libraries to the project in the Link panel of the same dialog (see Figure 11-7). For this minimal conduit, you need to add three libraries, one containing entry points for logging, one containing entry points for the HotSync dialog, and the last containing entry points for the Sync Manager initialization/deinitialization:

   ```
   C:\CDK\lib\hslog20d.lib
   C:\CDK\lib\pdcmn21d.lib
   C:\CDK\lib\sync20d.lib
   ```

If you edit the Win32 version of your DLL, link with the nondebug versions of the libraries (*hslog20.lib*, *pdcmn21.lib*, and *sync20.lib*).

## *Code for the Sales Conduit*

As we said before, this is a conduit that does very little. It considers itself successful if it writes a message to the log file. It's great, however, at distilling the process you use for creating the outer shell of the conduit. We first cover the code and then look at registering and testing the conduit.

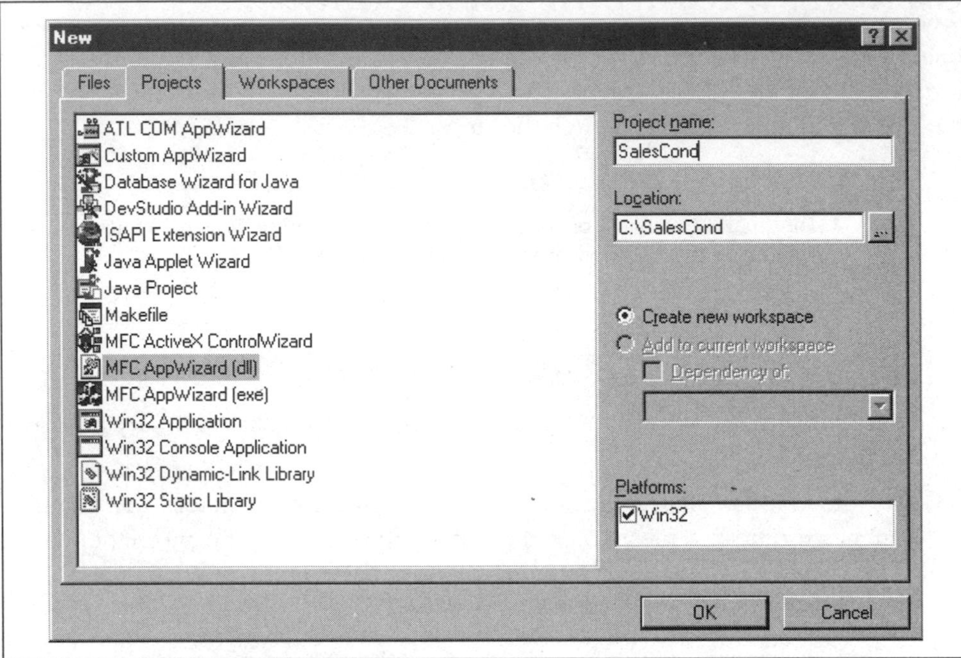


*Figure 11-4. A new MFC AppWizard project for our do-nothing minimal conduit*

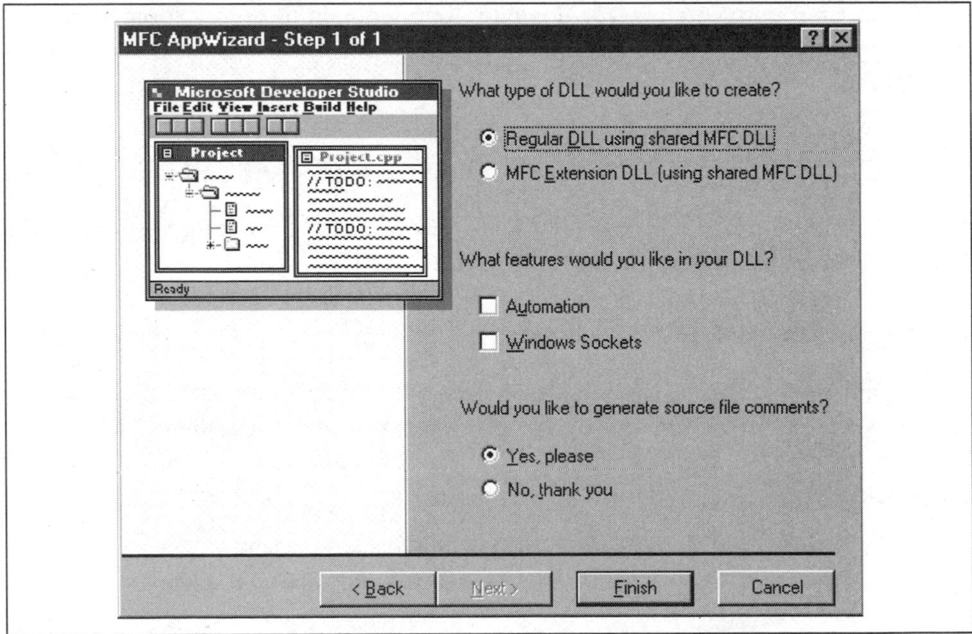


*Figure 11-5. Selecting the type of MFC DLL*

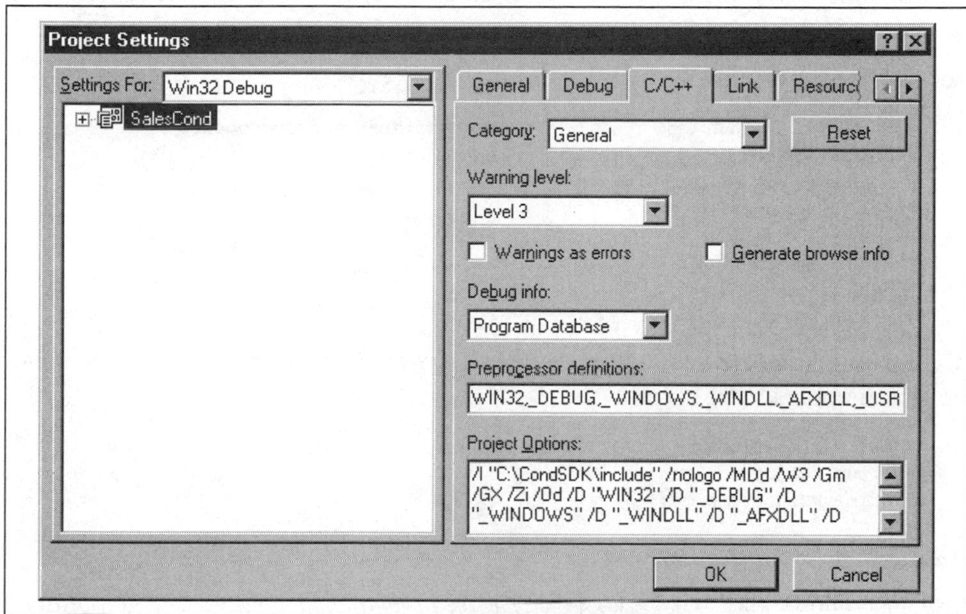


*Figure 11-6. C/C++ Project Settings to add to the include search path*

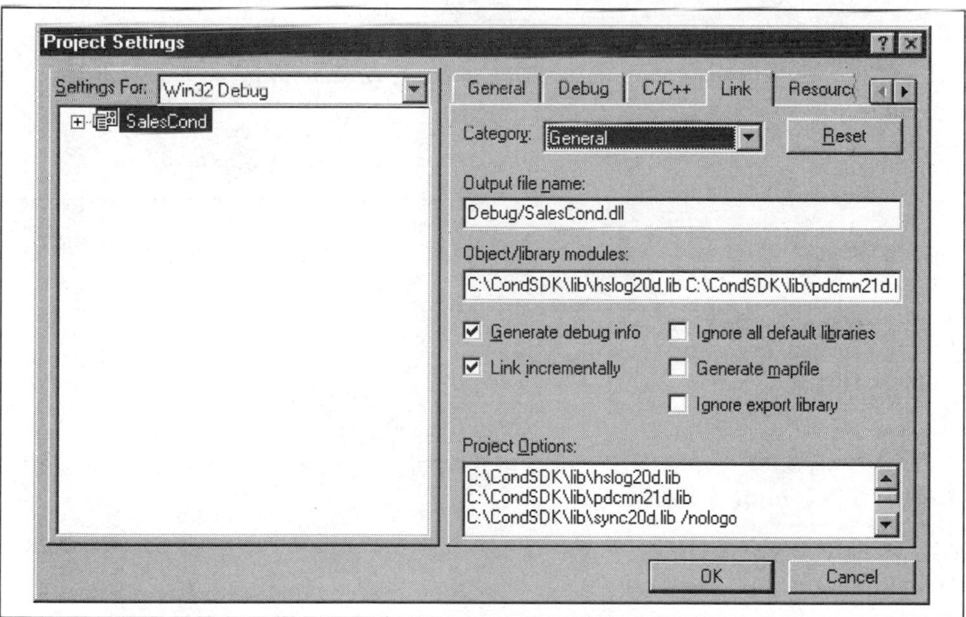


*Figure 11-7. Adding libraries to link with*

The *SalesCond.cpp* file already contains the shell of a DLL as created by the MFC DLL wizard.

Let's add some include files we need:

```
#include <afxwin.h>         // MFC core and standard components
#include <HSLog.h>          // for LogAddEntry
#include <SyncMgr.h>
#include <CondAPI.h>

#include <pdcmnDll.h>       // for the dialogs
#include <cmnres.h>
#include <ActDlg.h>
```

We'll create some constants that define the conduit name and major and minor version numbers:

```
#define kConduitName    "Sales"
#define kMajorVersion   1
#define kMinorVersion   0
```

### *Adding GetConduitName*

The first entry point we look at is *GetConduitName*. It gets passed a buffer in which it writes the name and the length of that name. It returns 0 in the case of no error.

Like all the entry points of the conduit, *GetConduitName* must call the **AFX_MANAGE_STATE** macro before doing anything else (this is a requirement of these types of MFC DLLs). All the entry points must also be declared with the **__declsepc(dllexport)** type modifiers.

```
__declspec(dllexport) long GetConduitName(char *name, WORD maxLen)
{
    AFX_MANAGE_STATE(AfxGetStaticModuleState());
    memset(name, 0, maxLen);
    strncpy(name, kConduitName, maxLen-1);

    return 0;
}
```

### *Adding GetConduitVersion*

Here is *GetConduitVersion*, whose low byte is the minor version and whose next higher byte is the major version:

```
__declspec(dllexport) DWORD GetConduitVersion()
{
    AFX_MANAGE_STATE(AfxGetStaticModuleState());
    return (kMajorVersion << 8) | kMinorVersion;
}
```

### *Adding OpenConduit*

*OpenConduit* is passed a class, `CSyncProperties`, which contains information about the sync that will take place. We're interested in the `m_SyncType` field of that class. This tells us what type of sync we have. The only type of sync we can handle is `eDoNothing`. In that case, we write an appropriate message to the log and then return.

For any other type of sync, we begin the sync process by calling *SyncRegisterConduit* (if that fails, we return the error) then we write to the log that we've begun. When we finish, we write to the log that we've finished (or, if an error had occurred, that we've aborted). We call *SyncUnRegisterConduit* and return any error:

```
__declspec(dllexport) long OpenConduit(PROGRESSFN progress,
   CSyncProperties &sync)
{
    AFX_MANAGE_STATE(AfxGetStaticModuleState());
    long err = 0;

    if (sync.m_SyncType == eDoNothing) {
        LogAddEntry("Sales - sync configured to Do Nothing", slText,
           false);
        return 0;
    }

    CONDHANDLE myConduitHandle;
    if ((err = SyncRegisterConduit(myConduitHandle)) != 0) {
        return err;
    }

    LogAddEntry("", slSyncStarted, false);

    // this is where we'll actually sync

    LogAddEntry(kConduitName, err ? slSyncAborted : slSyncFinished,
       false);
    SyncUnRegisterConduit(myConduitHandle);

    return err;
}
```

### *Adding ConfigureConduit*

Although these three functions, *GetConduitName*, *GetConduitVersion*, and *OpenConduit*, are the only required entry points, we also provide *ConfigureConduit*, so that the user can change what happens in our conduit on a sync:

```
__declspec(dllexport) long ConfigureConduit(CSyncPreference& pref)
{
    AFX_MANAGE_STATE(AfxGetStaticModuleState());
    long nRtn = -1;
    CHotSyncActionDlg actDlg;
```

```
        pref.m_SyncPref = eNoPreference;
        actDlg.m_csGroupText = kConduitName;

        switch (pref.m_SyncType)
        {
            case eFast:
            case eSlow:
                actDlg.m_nActionIndex = 0;
            break;
            case ePCtoHH:
                actDlg.m_nActionIndex = 1;
            break;
            case eHHtoPC:
                actDlg.m_nActionIndex = 2;
            break;
            case eDoNothing:
            default:
                actDlg.m_nActionIndex = 3;
        }

        if (actDlg.DoModal() == IDOK)
        {

            switch (actDlg.m_nActionIndex)
            {
                case 0:
                    pref.m_SyncType = eFast;
                break;
                case 1:
                    pref.m_SyncType = ePCtoHH;
                break;
                case 2:
                        pref.m_SyncType = eHHtoPC;
                break;
                case 3:
                default:
                        pref.m_SyncType = eDoNothing;
                    break;
            }

            pref.m_SyncPref = (actDlg.m_bMakeDefault) ? ePermanentPreference :
                eTemporaryPreference;

            nRtn = 0;
        }

        return nRtn;
    }
```

The code gets a standard HotSync dialog, putting the conduit's name and current sync type setting in it. After the dialog is dismissed, it updates the sync type.

We use *ConfigureConduit* instead of *CfgConduit* because we want our conduit to work on versions of HotSync earlier than 3.0. Plus, we really don't need the additional information that *CfgConduit* provides.

The dialog that *ConfigureConduit* uses is provided by the pdcmn DLL. In order to use it, our DLL must initialize the pdcmn DLL. We'll do that when our DLL starts.

### *DLL doings*

Here's our DLL's class declaration (as created by the Visual C++ automatically) to which we've overridden *InitInstance* and *ExitInstance*:

```
class CSalesCondDll : public CWinApp
{
public:
    //CSalesCondDll();
    virtual BOOL InitInstance(); // Initialization
    virtual int ExitInstance();  // Termination

// Overrides
    // ClassWizard generated virtual function overrides
    //{{AFX_VIRTUAL(CSalesCondDll)
    //}}AFX_VIRTUAL

    //{{AFX_MSG(CSalesCondDll)
        // NOTE - the ClassWizard will add/remove member functions here.
        //    DO NOT EDIT what you see in these blocks of generated code !
    //}}AFX_MSG
    DECLARE_MESSAGE_MAP()
};
```

We define a global count to keep track of how many instances of our DLL are active:

```
static int ClientCount = 0;
```

Our *InitInstance* will increment the `ClientCount` and initialize the pdcmn DLL:

```
BOOL CSalesCondApp::InitInstance()
{
    // DLL initialization
    TRACE0("SalesCond.DLL initializing\n");

    if (!ClientCount ) {

        // add any extension DLLs into CDynLinkLibrary chain
        InitPdcmn5DLL();
    }

    ClientCount++;

    return TRUE;
}
```

Our *ExitInstance* will decrement the ClientCount:

```
int CSalesCondApp::ExitInstance()
{
    TRACE0("UpDownCond.DLL Terminating!\n");

    // Check for last client and clean up potential memory leak.
    if (--ClientCount <= 0)
    {

    }

    // DLL clean up, if required
    return CWinApp::ExitInstance();
}
```

### *Adding GetConduitInfo*

We also provide *GetConduitInfo*. It can return the name of the conduit, the default action of the conduit, as well as the version of MFC used by the conduit:

```
__declspec(dllexport) long GetConduitInfo(ConduitInfoEnum infoType,
   void *pInArgs, void *pOut, DWORD *pdwOutSize)
{
    AFX_MANAGE_STATE(AfxGetStaticModuleState());

    if (!pOut)
        return CONDERR_INVALID_PTR;
    if (!pdwOutSize)
        return CONDERR_INVALID_OUTSIZE_PTR;

    switch (infoType) {
        case eConduitName:

             if (!pInArgs)
                return CONDERR_INVALID_INARGS_PTR;
            ConduitRequestInfoType *pInfo;
            pInfo = (ConduitRequestInfoType *)pInArgs;
            if ((pInfo->dwVersion != CONDUITREQUESTINFO_VERSION_1) ||
                (pInfo->dwSize != SZ_CONDUITREQUESTINFO))
                return CONDERR_INVALID_INARGS_STRUCT;

            strncpy((TCHAR*) pOut, kConduitName, (*pdwOutSize) - 1);
            break;
        case eDefaultAction:
            if (*pdwOutSize != sizeof(eSyncTypes))
                return CONDERR_INVALID_BUFFER_SIZE;
            (*(eSyncTypes*)pOut) = eFast;
            break;
        case eMfcVersion:
            if (*pdwOutSize != sizeof(DWORD))
                return CONDERR_INVALID_BUFFER_SIZE;
            (*(DWORD*)pOut) = MFC_VERSION_50;
            break;
```

```
            default:
                return CONDERR_UNSUPPORTED_CONDUITINFO_ENUM;
        }
        return 0;
    }
```

## *Registering the Conduit*

We run *CondCfg* and add a new entry. Figure 11-8 shows the settings we use.

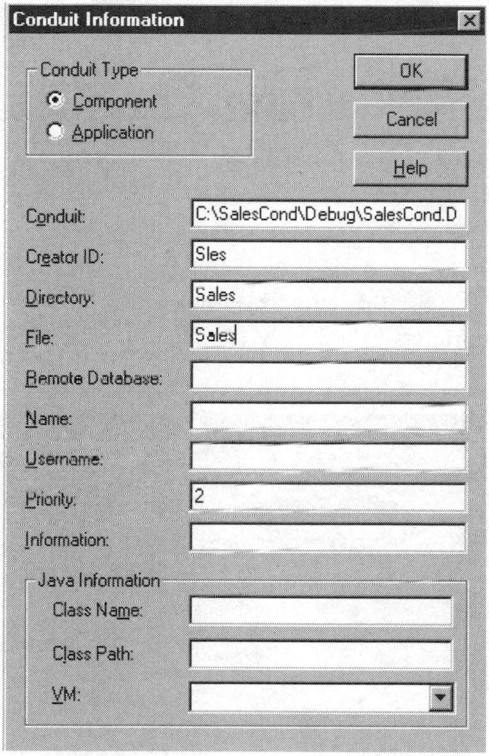

*Figure 11-8. Registering the Sales conduit in CondCfg*

## *Testing*

Once you've registered the conduit, start the HotSync Manager (quit it first if it is already running so that the registry gets properly updated). If you've registered a debug version of your conduit, make sure you start the debug version of HotSync Manager. Then choose Custom from the HotSync menu. You should see the Sales conduit in the list of conduits (see Figure 11-9).

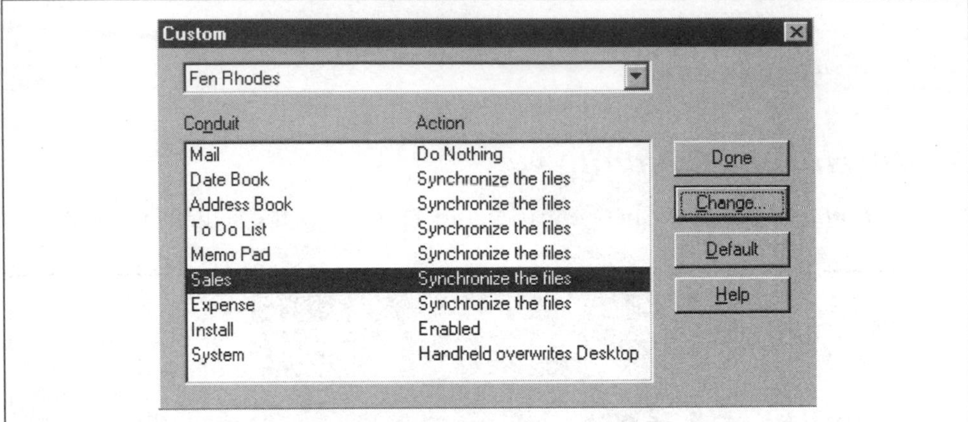


*Figure 11-9. The Custom dialog of HotSync showing the list of registered conduits*

### *Proving ChangeConduit works*

Select the Sales application and click the Change button. You should see the dialog shown in Figure 11-10. Bringing this dialog up proves that your conduit's *ChangeConduit* function gets called.

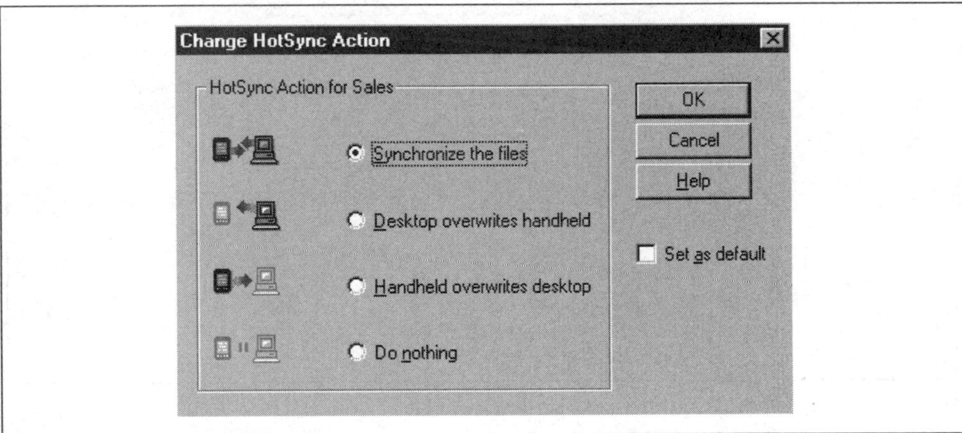


*Figure 11-10. Changing the HotSync settings of the Sales conduit*

Next, it's time to test syncing. First, make sure that the Sales application has been installed on the handheld (otherwise, a database with the correct creator won't exist on the handheld, and the Sales conduit won't be invoked).

### *Seeing the conduit in the HotSync log*

When you sync, you should see the message "Synchronizing Sales" as part of the process. Once a sync has been completed, open the HotSync log for that device.

You should see information that includes a line about the Sales conduit. For example:

```
HotSync started 07/30/98 11:59:53
OK Date Book
OK Address Book
OK To Do List
OK Memo Pad
OK Sales
OK Expense
```

### *Setting the conduit to Do Nothing*

Now change the HotSync settings for the Sales conduit to Do Nothing. After you sync, the log should show the following:

```
HotSync started 07/30/98 12:02:37
OK Date Book
OK Address Book
OK To Do List
OK Memo Pad
Sales - sync configured to Do Nothing
OK Expense
```

If you run into any problems getting the conduit to work, see Chapter 14, *Debugging Conduits.*

Now that you have a conduit shell that has been tested and works correctly, we can continue adding functionality to it. Let's start in the next chapter by uploading and downloading data.

# 12

# *Uploading and Downloading Data with a Conduit*

*In this chapter:*


Now we are going to show you how to move data back and forth from the desktop to the handheld. To do this, we need to discuss quite a few Sync Manager functions. We show you the functionality required in a conduit to support data transfers and some useful additional features as well. After we discuss these topics, we return to our walkthrough of what happens after the HotSync button gets pressed.

Next we discuss portability issues. Knowing that you are breathless with anticipation by this point, we return to the Sales application conduit. We walk through the code that handles uploading and downloading. We show how to upload the sales orders and customers from the handheld, and download the products and customers from the desktop. We also handle deleted records in the customer database.

## *Conduit Requirements*

At a bare minimum, a conduit that handles data uploading and downloading has to do all of the following:

- Register and unregister the conduit with the Sync Manager
- Open and close databases
- Read and write records
- Deal with categories (if the application supports categories)

## *Where to Store Data*

There is an important demarcation to remember when deciding where to store data on the desktop. Data specific to a particular user should be stored in a private location, whereas data shared among many users should be stored in a group location. For example, in our Sales Application each salesperson has her or his own list of customers but gets the product list from a general location. The first set of data is specific to a particular user; the second type is general. They should be stored in separate locations.

*Specific data*
: Store this data in your conduit folder in the user's folder in the HotSync folder.

*General data*
: Store this data in your application's desktop folder.

Also keep in mind that data doesn't necessary need to be stored locally. While it may be stored on a particular desktop, it is just as likely to be stored on a server or a web site.

## *Creating, Opening, and Closing Databases*

Database management during synchronization is handled completely by the conduit.

### *Creating a Database*

There is a standard database call used by the Sync Manger to create a database:

```
SyncCreateDB(CDbCreateDB& rDbStats)
```

*SyncCreateDB* creates a new record or resource database on the handheld and then opens it. You have the same control over database creation from within the conduit that you have on the handheld. The `rDbStats` parameter is of type `CDb-CreateDBClass` and contains the following important fields:

`m_FileHandle`
: Output field. On a successful return, this contains a handle to the created database with read/write access.

`m_Creator`
: Database creator ID. This should match the creator ID of the application.

`m_Flags`
: The database attributes. Choose one of the following: `eRecord` for a standard database, `eResource` for a resource database. Another flag is `eBackupDB`, which you set for the backup bit.

`m_Type`
: The four-byte database type.

`m_CardNo`
: Memory card where the database is located. Use 0, since no Palm OS device currently has more than one memory card.

`m_Name`
: The database name.

`m_Version`
: The version of the database.

`m_dwReserved`
: Reserved for future use. Must be set to 0.

## *Opening a Database*

The Sync Manager call to open a remote database is:

```
SyncOpenDB(char *pname, int nCardNum, Byte& rHandle, Byte openMode)
```

The values for the four parameters are:

`pName`
: Name of the database.

`nCardNum`
: Memory card where database is located. Use 0, since no Palm OS device currently has more than one memory card.

`rHandle`
: Output parameter. On a successful return, this contains a handle to the open database.

`openMode`
: Use (*dbRead* | *dbShowSecret*) to read all records, including private ones. Use (*dbRead* | *dbWrite* | *dbShowSecret*) to be able to write and/or delete records.

You need to close any database you open; only one can be open at a time. An error results if you try to open a new database without closing the prior one.

### *Closing the Database*

The Sync Manager call to close a remote database should come as no surprise. It is *SyncCloseDB*, and it takes only one parameter, the handle you created when you opened or created a database:

```
SyncCloseDB(Byte fHandle)
```

Slightly more sophisticated results can be had from *SnycCloseDBEx*. This function also allows you to modify the database's backup and modification date. Both functions close databases that were opened with either *SyncCreateDB* or *SyncOpenDB*.

## *Downloading to the Handheld*

As we discussed earlier, there are several different ways that you might want to move data around during a synchronization. Let's look at what is involved in moving data from the desktop to the handheld. This is commonly done with databases that are exclusively updated on the desktop and are routinely downloaded to handhelds where they aren't modified. Or you may do this in the case that the user chooses "Desktop overwrites handheld" in the HotSync settings dialog (see Figure 11-3 on page 319).

You need to create the database if it doesn't yet exist. You should also delete any existing records before downloading the ones from the desktop. This is necessary because you don't want the old ones; all you want are the newly downloaded ones.

### *Deleting Existing Records*

There are a few different routines to choose from for deleting records:

*SyncDeleteRec*
    Deletes one specific record

*SyncPurgeAllRecs*
    Deletes all records

*SyncPurgeAllRecsInCategory*
    Deletes all records from the specified category

*SyncPurgeDeletedRecs*
    Deletes all records that have been marked as deleted or archived

In our particular case, *SyncPurgeAllRecs* is the call we want to use.

## *Writing Records*

Once you have a nice, empty database, you can fill it up with fresh records from the desktop. You do this with the Sync Manager call *SyncWriteRec*.

```
SyncWriteRec (CRawRecordInfo &rInfo)
```

The parameter `rInfo` (of class `CRawRecordInfo`) contains several important fields:

`m_FileHandle`
: Handle to the open database.

`m_RecId`
: Input/output field; the record's unique ID. To add a new record, set this field to 0; on return, the field contains the new record's unique ID. To modify an existing record, set this field to the unique ID of one of the records in the database. An error occurs if this field doesn't match an existing unique record ID. Note that when you add a new record, it's the handheld that assigns the unique record ID.

`m_Attribs`
: The attributes of the record. See "Working with Records" on page 146 for a complete discussion.

`m_CatId`
: The record's category index. Use values from 0 to 14.

`m_RecSize`
: The number of bytes in the record.

`m_TotalBytes`
: The number of bytes of data in the `m_pBytes` buffer. It should be set to the number of bytes in the record, however, to work around bugs in some versions of the Sync Manager.

---

Unique record IDs are not perfect. A record maintains its unique ID unless a hard reset happens. Prior to HotSync 3.0, after a hard reset HotSync would generate new unique IDs for the records when it restored the database. Only HotSync 3.0 or later restores the unique record IDs correctly.

---

On the handheld, when you create a database record you specify the location in the database of that record. When using a conduit, on the other hand, you have no way to specify the record's exact location. Although it could change in the future, *SyncWriteRec* currently adds new records at the end of the database.

This lack of control over the order of records can be a problem for databases that need to have a specific order. For example, you may have a database sorted by date. The question then becomes, "How can the conduit create the database in sorted order?"

The answer is that unfortunately it can't.

There is a workaround with existing versions of the Sync Manager. If your conduit is writing records to an empty database, it should add them in sorted order. With existing versions of the Sync Manager, the records will then be in the correct order. Be careful, however, as future versions of the Sync Manager may cause the records not to be in sorted order.

In such cases, the `sysAppLaunchCmdSyncNotify` launch code for Palm OS applications comes to the rescue. After a sync occurs for a database with a specific creator, that database's application is called with the `sysAppLaunchCmdSyncNotify` launch code. This launch code tells the application that its database has changed, and gives the application a chance to sort it.

## *Writing the AppInfo Block*

You commonly use the `AppInfo` block of a database to store categories and other information relevant to the database as a whole. The Sync Manager call that you use to write the AppInfo block is:

```
SyncWriteDBAppInfoBlock (BYTE fHandle, CDbGenInfo &rInfo)
```

The parameter `rInfo` is an object of type `CdbGenInfo` and contains the following fields:

`m_pBytes`
: A pointer to the data you want copied to the app info block.

`m_TotalBytes`
: The number of bytes of data in the `m_pBytes` buffer. This should be set to the number of bytes in the record to work around bugs in some versions of the Sync Manager.

`m_BytesRead`
: To work around bugs in some versions of the Sync Manager, set this to `m_TotalBytes`.

`m_dwReserved`
: Reserved for the future. Set this field to 0.

# Uploading to the Desktop

When you need to send data from the handheld to the desktop you have to read through the records of the remote database and translate them into appropriate structures on the desktop. Here is the process, a step at a time, starting with the choices you have in how you read through the records.

## Finding the Number of Records

*SyncGetDBRecordCount* finds the number of records in a database:

```
long SycnGetDBRecordCount(BYTE fHandle, Word &rNumRecs);
```

Call it with:

```
Word numRecords;
err = SyncGetDBRecordCount(rHandle, numRecords);
```

## Reading Records

You can read records in a remote database using any of the following strategies:

- Iterate through each record, locating the next altered record
- Look up exact records via unique record ID
- Read the *nth* record in the database

We employ the last strategy for reading the records from our Sales order databases and the first strategy when we fully synchronize our customer list. There are a few points worth mentioning about each strategy.

### Iterating through each record stopping only for altered ones

If you want to iterate through the records and stop only on the ones that have been modified, use *SyncReadNextModifiedRec*. It retrieves a record from the remote database if the dirty bit in the record has been set.

A variation of this routine is *SyncReadNextModifiedRecInCategory*, which also filters based on the record's category. This function takes the category index as an additional parameter.

### Looking up exact records via unique record ID

Sometimes you want to read records based on their unique record IDs. In such cases, use *SyncReadRecordByID*.

### *Iterating through the records of a database from beginning to end*

Use *SyncReadRecordByIndex* to get a record based on the record number. Use this when you want to read through a database from beginning to end. This function takes one parameter, `rInfo`, which has the record index as one of its fields.

### *The CRawRecordInfo class*

Each of these read routines takes as a parameter an object of the `CRawRecordInfo` class. The needed fields in the class are:

`m_FileHandle`
: This is a handle to the open database.

`m_pBytes`
: A pointer that you allocate into which the record will be copied.

`m_TotalBytes`
: The size of the `m_pBytes` pointer. This is the number of bytes that can be copied into `m_pBytes` without overflowing it.

`m_BytesRead`
: Output field; the number of bytes read. If `m_BytesRead` is greater than `m_TotalBytes`, the record is too large. Sync Manager 2.1 or later copies the first `m_totalBytes` of record data to `m_pBytes`. Previous versions of the Sync Manager copy nothing.

`m_catId`
: Input field for *SyncReadNextRecInCategory* and *SyncReadNextModifiedRecInCategory*. Output field for the other read routines. This contains the category, as a number between 0 and 14.

`m_RecIndex`
: Input field for *SyncReadRecordByIndex*. Output field for other read routines for Sync Manager 2.1 or later (earlier versions of Sync Manager don't write to this field).

`m_Attribs`
: The attributes of the record.

`m_dwReserved`
: Reserved for the future. Set this field to 0.

Beware of modifying the records in a database while iterating with *SyncReadNextModifiedRec* or *SyncReadNextModifiedRecInCatgegory*. In pre-2.0 versions of the Palm OS, the iteration routines don't work right. In Palm OS 2.0, a modified record is read again by the iteration routines. In Palm OS 3.0, the modified record isn't reread.

If the record you read is larger than you've allocated space for, the Sync read routines will not return an error. You need to explicitly check for this problem. If, after the read, `m_BytesRead` is greater than `m_TotalBytes`, you haven't allocated enough space. For Palm OS 3.0 and earlier, no record can be more than 65,505 bytes.

## Reading the AppInfo Block

There are times when you need to read information from the AppInfo block. For example, if the AppInfo block contains category names, you'll need to read it to get them. The Sync Manager call to use is *SyncReadDBAppInfoBlock*.

This function takes two parameters, a handle to the open record or database on the handheld, and the object, `rInfo`, that contains information about the database header.

The parameter `rInfo` is an object of type `CdbGenInfo` with the following fields:

`m_pBytes`
: A pointer to memory you've allocated into which you are going to copy the AppInfo block.

`m_TotalBytes`
: The number of bytes allocated for the `m_pBytes` field.

`m_BytesRead`
: Output field; the number of bytes read. If `m_BytesRead` is greater than `m_TotalBytes`, the AppInfo block is too large. Sync Manager 2.1 or later copies the first `m_totalBytes` of AppInfo block data to `m_pBytes`. Previous versions of the Sync Manager copy nothing.

`m_dwReserved`
: Reserved for the future. Set this field to 0.

## Deleted/Archived Records

For databases that will be two-way synced, the handheld application doesn't completely remove a deleted record; it marks it as deleted, instead. When a sync occurs, those marked records need to be deleted from the desktop database.

There are a couple of ways that you can delete marked records and a few pitfalls to avoid. First, note that you have two different ways in which records might be removed from a database. They can be either completely deleted or just archived. Figure 12-1 shows you the two possible dialog settings that a user can select when given the option to delete a record. Choosing "Save archive copy on PC" means the record is marked as deleted until the next sync, at which point it is saved in an archive file and then deleted from the database. Not choosing "Save archive copy on PC" means the record is marked as deleted until the next sync and then completely deleted from the database. See "Deleting a Record" on page 153 for further details.

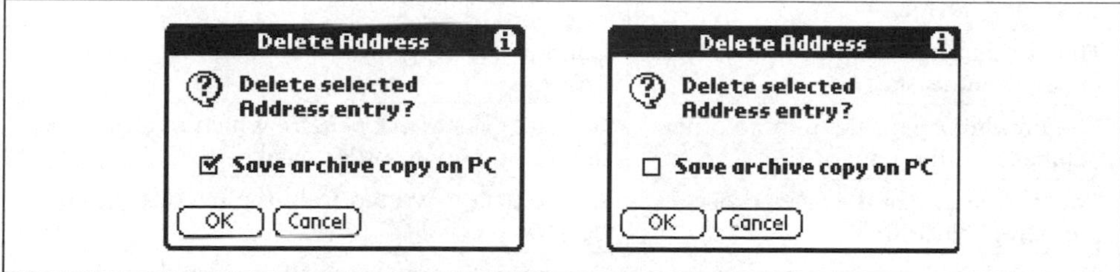


*Figure 12-1. Saving or not saving an archive copy when deleting a record*

### *Archiving records*

You should create a separate archive file and append archived records there. This is for situations in which the user doesn't want the records cluttering up the handheld or the normal desktop application, but does want the record available if needed. It's customary to create a separate archive file for each category.

### *Deleting records*

Once any archived records have been archived, and any deleted records have been removed from the corresponding desktop file, those records should be completely deleted from the handheld. *SyncPurgeDeletedRecs* is the call you should use:

```
err = SyncPurgeDeletedRecs(rHandle);
```

# *When the HotSync Button Gets Pressed*

We left off in the previous discussion at the point where we are ready to exchange information between the conduit on the desktop and the handheld unit. Let's continue now walking through the chain of events (see Table 12-1).

*Table 12-1. When the HotSync Button Gets Pressed*

| Action (by the User or by the System) | What Is Happening Programmatically |
|---|---|
| The HotSync Manager gets the conduit name so that it can display information in the status dialog. | *GetConduitName* is called and returns. |
| The HotSync Manager prepares to sync by passing the synchronization off to the conduit. | *OpenConduit* gets called and the conduit's DLL gets loaded into memory. It is told whether to do a fast sync, a slow sync, a copy from handheld to desktop, a copy from desktop to handheld, or to do nothing. When *OpenConduit* returns, it will have completed the task. |
| The conduit registers with the HotSync Manager. | *SyncRegisterConduit* returns a handle. |
| The conduit notifies the log that syncing is about to start. | Conduit calls *LogAddEntry("", slSyncStarted, false)*. |
| The conduit opens the remote order database on the handheld. | Conduit calls *SyncOpenDB*, which returns a handle to the remote order database. |
| The user sees that the Sales orders are being synced. | All the data is written from the handheld to the desktop. |
| The conduit closes the remote database. | Conduit calls *SyncCloseDB* to close the Sales order database. |
| The user sees that the Sales application product list is being synced. | Conduit calls *SyncOpenDB*, which returns a handle to the product database. |
| The conduit closes the remote database. | Conduit calls *SyncCloseDB*, which destroys the handle opened earlier for that database. |
| *The user sees that the Customer List is being synced.* | |
| Close up the conduit after syncing is finished. | The application calls *SyncUnRegisterConduit* to dispose of the handle that was set in *SyncRegisterConduit*. |
| The HotSync Manager backs up other stuff. | The Backup conduit gets called. |

# Portability Issues

There are two important portability issues that you need to take into account when moving data back and forth from the handheld to the desktop. They are byte ordering and structure packing.

## Byte Ordering

The Palm OS runs on a Motorola platform, which stores bytes differently from Windows running on an Intel platform. This crucial difference can royally mess up data transfers if you are not careful.

On the handheld, the 16-bit number 0x0102 is stored with the high byte, 0x01, first, and the low byte, 0x02, second. In the conduit on Windows, the same number is stored with the low byte, 0x02, first, and the high byte, 0x01, second. As a result, any two-byte values stored in your records or in your AppInfo block must be swapped when transferred between the two systems. (If you fail to swap, a simple request for 3 boxes of toys on the handheld would be processed on the desktop as a request for 768 boxes!) A similar problem occurs with four-byte values; they are also stored in switched forms (see Table 12-2).

*Table 12-2. Comparison of Byte Orderings for the Four-Byte Value 0x01020304*

| Palm Handheld Byte Order | Wintel Byte Order |
|---|---|
| 0x01 | 0x04 |
| 0x02 | 0x03 |
| 0x03 | 0x02 |
| 0x04 | 0x01 |

Strings are not affected by this byte ordering. On both platforms, the string "abc" is stored in the order "a", "b", "c", "\0".

The HotSync Manager provides routines for converting two- and four-byte values from the handheld to host byte ordering:

```
Word SyncHHtoHostWord(Word value)
DWord SyncHHToHostDWord(DWord value)
```

and for the opposite conversion:

```
Word SyncHostToHHWord(Word value)
DWord SyncHostToHHDWord(DWord value)
```

Here are the return values:

- `SyncHHtoHostWord(0x0102)` returns `0x0201`
- `SyncHostToHHWord(0x0201)` returns `0x0102`
- `SyncHHToHostDWord(0x01020304)` returns `0x04030201`
- `SyncHostToHHDWord(0x04030201)` returns `0x012020304`

## *Structure Packing*

Sometimes the compiler leaves holes in structures between successive fields. This is done in order for fields to begin on specific byte/word/double-word boundaries. As a result, you need to lay out the structures, defining your records and/or

AppInfo block in the same way for both the compiler you use for creating your handheld application and the compiler you use to create your conduit.

For Visual C++, we've found that the pack pragma can be used to change the packing rules to match that of CodeWarrior:

```
#pragma pack(2)

structure declarations for structures that will be read from the handheld

#pragma pack
```

# The Sales Conduit

We extend the Sales conduit so that our shell from the previous chapter also supports "Desktop overwrites handheld" and "Handheld overwrites desktop." We postponing syncing until Chapter 13, *Two-Way Syncing*.

For our conduit, we've got to define what it means to do each of these types of overwriting. Here's the logic that we think makes sense for the Sales application:

*Desktop overwrites handheld*
: The products database and the customers database are completely overwritten from the desktop; nothing happens to the orders database.

*Handheld overwrites database*
: The products are ignored (since they can't have changed on the handheld). The customers and orders databases are copied to the desktop. Any archived customers are appended to a separate file; deleted customers are removed from the handheld.

## Format Used to Store Data on the Desktop

We store data on the desktop as tab-delimited text files.

The customers will be stored in a file named *Customers.txt* in the user's directory within the Sales conduit directory. Each line in the file is of the form:

```
Customer ID<tab>Name<tab>Address<tab>City<tab>Phone
```

The orders will be stored in a file named *Orders.txt* in the same directory. Each order is stored as:

```
ORDER Customer ID
quantity<tab>Product ID
quantity<tab>Product ID
...
qauntity<tab>Product ID
```

Orders follow one another in the file.

The products are stored in a *Products.txt* file and start with the categories, followed by the products:

```
Name of Category 0
Name of Category 1
...
Name of last Category
<empty line>
Product ID<tab>Name<tab>Category Number<tab>Price in dollars and cents
...
Product ID<tab>Name<tab>Category Number<tab>Price in dollars and cents
```

## *Modifying OpenConduit*

We modify *OpenConduit* to handle copying from handheld to desktop (`eHHtoPC`) and from desktop to handheld (`ePCtoHH`):

```
__declspec(dllexport) long OpenConduit(PROGRESSFN progress,
                                       CSyncProperties &sync)
{
    AFX_MANAGE_STATE(AfxGetStaticModuleState());
    long err = 0;

    if (sync.m_SyncType == eDoNothing) {
        LogAddEntry("Sales - sync configured to Do Nothing", slText,
            false);
            return 0;
    }

    CONDHANDLE myConduitHandle;
    if ((err = SyncRegisterConduit(myConduitHandle)) != 0) return err;

    LogAddEntry("", slSyncStarted, false);

    if (sync.m_SyncType == eHHtoPC) {
        if ((err = CopyOrdersFromHH(sync)) != 0)
            goto exit;
        if ((err = CopyCustomersFromHH(sync)) != 0)
            goto exit;
    } else if (sync.m_SyncType == ePCtoHH) {
        if ((err = CopyProductsAndCategoriesToHH(sync)) != 0)
            goto exit;
        if ((err = CopyCustomersToHH(sync)) != 0)
            goto exit;
    } else if (sync.m_SyncType == eFast || sync.m_SyncType == eSlow) {
    }

exit:
    LogAddEntry(kConduitName, err ? slSyncAborted : slSyncFinished,
        false);
    SyncUnRegisterConduit(myConduitHandle);

    return err;
}
```

## General Code

We have some other code to add, as well. We need to define our databases, create a global variable, and add some data structures.

### *Database defines*

We've got defines for the databases (these can be copied directly from the code for the handheld application):

```
#define salesCreator      'Sles'
#define salesVersion      0
#define customerDBType    'cust'
#define customerDBName    "Customers_Sles"
#define orderDBType       'Ordr'
#define orderDBName       "Orders_Sles"
#define productDBType     'Prod'
#define productDBName     "Products_Sles"
```

### *Globals*

We read and write records using a global buffer. We size it to be bigger than any possible record (at least on Palm OS 3.0 or earlier):

```
#define kMaxRecordSize  66000
char    gBigBuffer[kMaxRecordSize];
```

### *Data structures*

We have structures that need to correspond exactly to structures on the handheld (thus, we use the pack pragma). We then use these structures to read and write data on the handheld:

```
// on the Palm handheld, the items array in PackedOrder starts at offset 6
// Natural alignment on Windows would start it at offset 8
#pragma pack(2)

struct Item {
    unsigned long   productID;
    unsigned long   quantity;
};

struct PackedOrder {
    long            customerID;
    unsigned short  numItems;
    Item            items[1];
};

struct PackedCustomer{
    long customerID;
    char name[1];
};
```

```
struct PackedProduct {
    unsigned long   productID;
    unsigned long   price;  // in cents
    char    name[1];
};

#define kCategoryNameLength 15
typedef char    CategoryName[kCategoryNameLength + 1];

struct PackedCategories {
    unsigned short  numCategories;
    CategoryName    names[1];
};

#pragma pack()
```

Next, we've got some structures that we use to store data in memory in the conduit. Since we're using C++, we have constructors and destructors to make our lives easier:

```
struct Customer {
    Customer() { name = address = city = phone = 0;}
    ~Customer() {delete [] name; delete [] address; delete [] city;
        delete [] phone; };
    long customerID;
    char *name;
    char *address;
    char *city;
    char *phone;
};

struct Categories {
    Categories(int num) { numCategories = num;
        names = new CategoryName[num];}
    ~Categories() {delete [] names;};
    unsigned short numCategories;
    CategoryName *names;
};

struct Order {
    Order(unsigned short num) { numItems = num;
       items = new Item[numItems];};
    ~Order() { delete [] items;};
    long            customerID;
    unsigned short  numItems;
    Item            *items;
};

struct Product {
    Product() {name = 0;};
    ~Product() {delete [] name;};

    unsigned long   productID;
    unsigned long   price;  // in cents
```

```
    unsigned char   category:4;
    char    *name;
};
```

## Downloading to the Handheld

To download data to the handheld, we have to take care of a number of things. First, we need to copy the customers to the handheld. If the database doesn't exist, we need to create it. Once the database is open, we need to read through the records. When we finish with customers, we need to do the same things for products.

### Downloading customers

We've got to copy the customers to the handheld. We do this in *CopyCustomersToHH*:

```
int CopyCustomersToHH(CSyncProperties &sync)
{
    FILE *fp = NULL;
    BYTE rHandle;
    int err;
    bool dbOpen = false;

    if ((err = SyncOpenDB(customerDBName, 0, rHandle, eDbWrite | eDbRead
      | eDbShowSecret)) != 0) {
        LogAddEntry("SyncOpenDB failed", slWarning, false);
        if (err == SYNCERR_FILE_NOT_FOUND)
        {
            CDbCreateDB dbInfo;
            memset(&dbInfo, 0, sizeof(dbInfo));
            dbInfo.m_Creator    = salesCreator;
            dbInfo.m_Flags      = eRecord;
            dbInfo.m_CardNo     = 0;
            dbInfo.m_Type       = customerDBType;
            strcpy(dbInfo.m_Name, customerDBName);

            if ((err = SyncCreateDB(dbInfo)) != 0)
            {
                LogAddEntry("SyncCreateDB failed", slWarning, false);
                goto exit;
            }
            rHandle = dbInfo.m_FileHandle;
        } else
            goto exit;
    }
    dbOpen = true;

    char    buffer[BIG_PATH *2];
    strcpy(buffer, sync.m_PathName);
    strcat(buffer, "Customers.txt");
```

```
    if ((fp = fopen(buffer, "r")) == NULL) {
        err = 1;
        LogAddFormattedEntry(slWarning, false, "fopen(%s) failed",
            buffer);
        goto exit;
    }

    if ((err = SyncPurgeAllRecs(rHandle)) != 0) {
        LogAddEntry("SyncPurgeAllRecs failed", slWarning, false);
        goto exit;
    }

    Customer *c;
    while (c = ReadCustomer(fp)) {
        CRawRecordInfo recordInfo;
        recordInfo.m_FileHandle = rHandle;
        recordInfo.m_RecId = 0;
        recordInfo.m_pBytes = (unsigned char *) gBigBuffer;
        recordInfo.m_Attribs = 0;
        recordInfo.m_CatId = 0;
        recordInfo.m_RecSize = CustomerToRawRecord(gBigBuffer,
            sizeof(gBigBuffer), c);
        recordInfo.m_dwReserved = 0;

        if ((err = SyncWriteRec(recordInfo)) !=0) {
            delete c;
            LogAddEntry("SyncWriteRec failed", slWarning, false);
            goto exit;
        }

        delete c;
    }

exit:
    if (fp)
        fclose(fp);
    if (dbOpen)
        if ((err = SyncCloseDB(rHandle)) != 0)
            LogAddEntry("SyncDBClose failed", slWarning, false);
    return err;
}
```

We try to open the customers database on the handheld. If it doesn't exist, we create it. Next, we open *Customers.txt*, the file with the customers. We delete all the existing records from the customers database on the handheld and then start reading each customer (using *ReadCustomer*) and writing the customer to the database with *SyncWriteRec*.

We added a couple of log entries in this code, as well. These were not intended for users, but to help in our debugging. We get notified via the log if the code failed to properly open *Customers.txt* or if we failed to delete all the existing records.

*ReadCustomer* reads a customer from a text file, returning 0 if there are no more customers:

```
Customer *ReadCustomer(FILE *fp)
{
    const char *separator = "\t";
    if (fgets(gBigBuffer, sizeof(gBigBuffer), fp) == NULL)
        return 0;
    char *customerID = strtok(gBigBuffer, separator);
    char *name = strtok(NULL, separator);
    char *address = strtok(NULL, separator);
    char *city = strtok(NULL, separator);
    char *phone = strtok(NULL, separator);

    if (!address)
        address = "";
    if (!city)
        city = "";
    if (!phone)
        phone = "";
    if (customerID && name) {
        Customer *c = new Customer;
        c->customerID = atol(customerID);
        c->name = new char[strlen(name) + 1];
        strcpy(c->name, name);
        c->address = new char[strlen(address) + 1];
        strcpy(c->address, address);
        c->city = new char[strlen(city) + 1];
        strcpy(c->city, city);
        c->phone = new char[strlen(phone) + 1];
        strcpy(c->phone, phone);
        return c;
    } else
        return 0;
}
```

*CustomerToRawRecord* writes a customer to the passed-in buffer in the format the handheld expects. It returns the number of bytes it has written. Note that it must swap the four-byte `customerID` to match the byte ordering on the handheld:

```
int CustomerToRawRecord(void *buf, int bufLength, Customer *c)
{
    PackedCustomer *cp = (PackedCustomer *) buf;
    cp->customerID = SyncHostToHHDWord(c->customerID);
    char *s = cp->name;
```

```
        strcpy(s, c->name);
        s += strlen(s) + 1;
        strcpy(s, c->address);
        s += strlen(s) + 1;
        strcpy(s, c->city);
        s += strlen(s) + 1;
        strcpy(s, c->phone);
        s += strlen(s) + 1;
        return s - (char *) buf;
    }
```

### *Downloading products*

The *CopyProductsAndCategoriesToHH* function updates the products database on the handheld from the *Products.txt* file on the PC:

```
int CopyProductsAndCategoriesToHH(CSyncProperties &sync)
{
    FILE *fp = NULL;
    BYTE rHandle;
    int err;
    bool dbOpen = false;

    char    buffer[BIG_PATH *2];
    strcpy(buffer, sync.m_PathName);
    strcat(buffer, "Products.txt");

    if ((fp = fopen(buffer, "r")) == NULL) {
        err = 1;
        LogAddFormattedEntry(slWarning, false, "fopen(%s) failed",
            buffer);
        goto exit;
    }

    if ((err = SyncOpenDB(productDBName, 0, rHandle,
        eDbWrite | eDbRead | eDbShowSecret)) != 0) {
        if (err == SYNCERR_FILE_NOT_FOUND)
        {
            CDbCreateDB dbInfo;
            memset(&dbInfo, 0, sizeof(dbInfo));
            dbInfo.m_Creator  = salesCreator;
            dbInfo.m_Flags    = eRecord;
            dbInfo.m_CardNo   = 0;
            dbInfo.m_Type     = productDBType;
            strcpy(dbInfo.m_Name, productDBName);

            if ((err = SyncCreateDB(dbInfo)) != 0)
            {
                LogAddEntry("SyncCreateDB failed", slWarning, false);
                goto exit;
            }
            rHandle = dbInfo.m_FileHandle;
        } else
            goto exit;
```

```
    }
    dbOpen = true;

    if ((err = SyncPurgeAllRecs(rHandle)) != 0) {
        LogAddEntry("SyncPurgeAllRecs failed", slWarning, false);
        goto exit;
    }

    Categories *c;
    if (c = ReadCategories(fp)) {
        CDbGenInfo  rInfo;

        rInfo.m_pBytes = (unsigned char *) gBigBuffer;
        rInfo.m_TotalBytes = CategoriesToRawRecord(gBigBuffer,
            sizeof(gBigBuffer), c);
        rInfo.m_BytesRead = rInfo.m_TotalBytes; // Because older versions
                  // of the sync manager looked in the wrong field for
                  // the total size, the documented API of
                  // SyncWriteDBAppInfoBLock is that both m_TotalBytes
                  // and m_BytesRead should be filled in with the total
        rInfo.m_dwReserved = 0;
        if ((err = SyncWriteDBAppInfoBlock(rHandle, rInfo)) !=0) {
            delete c;
            LogAddEntry("SyncWriteDBAppInfoBlock failed", slWarning,
              false);
            goto exit;
        }
        delete c;
    }

    Product *p;
    while (p = ReadProduct(fp)) {
        CRawRecordInfo recordInfo;
        recordInfo.m_FileHandle = rHandle;
        recordInfo.m_RecId = 0;
        recordInfo.m_pBytes = (unsigned char *) gBigBuffer;
        recordInfo.m_Attribs = 0;
        recordInfo.m_CatId = p->category;
        recordInfo.m_RecSize = ProductToRawRecord(gBigBuffer,
            sizeof(gBigBuffer), p);
        recordInfo.m_dwReserved = 0;

        if ((err = SyncWriteRec(recordInfo)) !=0) {
            delete p;
            LogAddEntry("SyncWriteRec failed", slWarning, false);
            goto exit;
        }
        delete p;
    }

exit:
    if (fp)
        fclose(fp);
```

```
    if (dbOpen)
        if ((err = SyncCloseDB(rHandle)) != 0)
            LogAddEntry("SyncDBClose failed", slWarning, false);
    return err;
}
```

This routine has almost exactly the same structure as *CopyCustomersToHH*. The categories are written to the AppInfo block using *SyncWriteDBAppInfoBlock* instead. It uses *ReadCategories* to read the categories from the *Products.txt* file. The function continues reading categories, one per line, until it reaches an empty line:

```
#define kMaxCategories  15
Categories *ReadCategories(FILE *fp)
{
    const char *separator = "\n";
    int numCategories = 0;
    Categories *c = new Categories(kMaxCategories);
    for (int i = 0; i < kMaxCategories ; i++) {
        if (fgets(gBigBuffer, sizeof(gBigBuffer), fp) == NULL)
            break;
        // strip newline
        if (gBigBuffer[strlen(gBigBuffer) - 1] == '\n')
            gBigBuffer[strlen(gBigBuffer) - 1] = '\0';
        if (gBigBuffer[0] == '\0')
            break;
        // copy it
        strncpy(c->names[i], gBigBuffer, kCategoryNameLength);
        c->names[i][kCategoryNameLength] = '\0';
    }

    c->numCategories = i;
    return c;
}
```

*ReadProduct* reads the products that follow in the file:

```
Product *ReadProduct(FILE *fp)
{
    const char *separator = "\t";
    if (fgets(gBigBuffer, sizeof(gBigBuffer), fp) == NULL)
        return 0;

    char *productID = strtok(gBigBuffer, separator);
    char *name = strtok(NULL, separator);
    char *categoryNumber = strtok(NULL, separator);
    char *price = strtok(NULL, separator);

    if (productID && name && categoryNumber) {
        Product *p = new Product;
        p->productID = atol(productID);
        p->name = new char[strlen(name) + 1];
        strcpy(p->name, name);
        p->category = (unsigned char) atoi(categoryNumber);
```

```
        p->price = (long) (atof(price) * 100);  // convert to cents
        return p;
    } else
        return 0;
}
```

*CategoriesToRawRecord* writes the categories in the format expected by the handheld (therefore, the `numCategories` two-byte field must be swapped):

```
int CategoriesToRawRecord(void *buf, int bufLength, Categories *c)
{
    PackedCategories *pc = (PackedCategories *) buf;
    pc->numCategories = SyncHostToHHWord(c->numCategories);
    char *s = (char *) pc->names;
    for (int i = 0; i < c->numCategories; i++) {
        memcpy(s, c->names[i], sizeof(CategoryName));
        s += sizeof(CategoryName);
    }
    return s - (char *) buf;
}
```

*ProductToRawRecord* is similar, but must swap both the `productID` and the `price`:

```
int ProductToRawRecord(void *buf, int bufLength, Product *p)
{
    PackedProduct *pp = (PackedProduct *) buf;
    pp->productID = SyncHostToHHDWord(p->productID);
    pp->price = SyncHostToHHDWord(p->price);
    strcpy(pp->name, p->name);
    return offsetof(PackedProduct, name) + strlen(pp->name) + 1;
}
```

That completes the conduit code for downloading. Remember, however, that the order in which *SyncWriteRec* adds new records to the database isn't defined. As a result, the handheld must re-sort the databases (to be sorted by ID). Here's the code in our *PilotMain* handheld function that does this:

```
} else if (cmd == sysAppLaunchCmdSyncNotify) {
    DmOpenRef   db;

    // code for beaming removed

// After a sync, we aren't guaranteed the order of any changed databases.
// We'll just resort the products and customer which could have changed.
// we're going to do an insertion sort because the databases
// should be almost completel sorted (and an insertion sort is
// quicker on an almost-sorted database than a quicksort).
// Since the current implementation of the Sync Manager creates new
// records at the end of the database, our database are probably sorted.
    db= DmOpenDatabaseByTypeCreator(customerDBType, salesCreator,
        dmModeReadWrite);
    if (db) {
        DmInsertionSort(db, (DmComparF *) CompareIDFunc, 0);
        DmCloseDatabase(db);
```

```
        } else
            error = DmGetLastErr();
        db= DmOpenDatabaseByTypeCreator(productDBType, salesCreator,
            dmModeReadWrite);
        if (db) {
            DmInsertionSort(db, (DmComparF *) CompareIDFunc, 0);
            DmCloseDatabase(db);
        } else
            error = DmGetLastErr();
}
```

## Uploading to the Desktop

We need to handle the same sorts of things when we are uploading instead of downloading data. First, we copy orders from the handheld to the desktop by opening the database, reading the records, doing the proper conversion, and sending them along their merry way to the desktop. Then we do the same for customers.

### Uploading orders

We've got to copy the orders from the handheld to the desktop:

```
int CopyOrdersFromHH(CSyncProperties &sync)
{
    FILE *fp = NULL;
    BYTE rHandle;
    int err;
    bool dbOpen = false;
    int i;

    if ((err = SyncOpenDB(orderDBName, 0, rHandle,
        eDbRead | eDbShowSecret )) != 0) {
        LogAddEntry("SyncOpenDB failed", slWarning, false);
        goto exit;
    }
    dbOpen = true;

    char    buffer[BIG_PATH *2];
    strcpy(buffer, sync.m_PathName);
    strcat(buffer, "Orders.txt");

    if ((fp = fopen(buffer, "w")) == NULL) {
        LogAddFormattedEntry(slWarning, false, "fopen(%s) failed",
            buffer);
        goto exit;
    }

    WORD recordCount;
    if ((err = SyncGetDBRecordCount(rHandle, recordCount)) !=0) {
        LogAddEntry("SyncGetDBRecordCount failed", slWarning, false);
        goto exit;
    }
```

```
    CRawRecordInfo recordInfo;
    recordInfo.m_FileHandle = rHandle;

    for (i = 0; i < recordCount; i++) {
        recordInfo.m_RecIndex = i;
        recordInfo.m_TotalBytes = (unsigned short) sizeof(gBigBuffer);
        recordInfo.m_pBytes = (unsigned char *) gBigBuffer;
        recordInfo.m_dwReserved = 0;

        if ((err = SyncReadRecordByIndex(recordInfo)) !=0) {
            LogAddEntry("SyncReadRecordByIndex failed", slWarning, false);
            goto exit;
        }

        Order *o = RawRecordToOrder(recordInfo.m_pBytes);
        if ((err = WriteOrderToFile(fp, o)) != 0) {
            LogAddEntry("WriteOrderToFile failed", slWarning, false);
            delete o;
            goto exit;
        }
        delete o;
    }
exit:
    if (fp)
        fclose(fp);

    if (dbOpen)
        if ((err = SyncCloseDB(rHandle)) != 0)
            LogAddEntry("SyncDBClose failed", slWarning, false);
    return err;
}
```

The code opens the orders database (read-only, since it won't change the database). Then it creates the *Orders.txt* file. It finds the number of records in the database with *SyncGetDBRecordCount*. Then it reads record by record using *SyncReadRecordByIndex*. *RawRecordToOrder* reads the raw record and converts it to an in-memory record. Finally, the order is written to the file with *WriteOrderToFile*.

Here's the code that converts a record to an order (again, byte-swapping is necessary):

```
Order *RawRecordToOrder(void *p)
{
    PackedOrder *po = (PackedOrder *) p;
    unsigned short numItems = SyncHHToHostWord(po->numItems);
    Order *o = new Order(numItems);
    o->customerID = SyncHHToHostDWord(po->customerID);
    for (int i = 0; i < o->numItems; i++) {
        o->items[i].productID = SyncHHToHostDWord(po->items[i].productID);
        o->items[i].quantity = SyncHHToHostDWord(po->items[i].quantity);
    }
    return o;
}
```

Last, here's the code that writes the order to the file:

```
int WriteOrderToFile(FILE *fp, const Order *o)
{
    int result;

    if ((result = fprintf(fp, "ORDER %ld\n", o->customerID)) < 0)
        return result;
    for (int i = 0; i < o->numItems; i++) {
        if ((result = fprintf(fp, "%ld %ld\n", o->items[i].quantity,
            o->items[i].productID)) < 0)
            return result;
    }
    return 0;
}
```

### *Uploading customers*

Here's the routine that uploads the customers database:

```
int CopyCustomersFromHH(CSyncProperties &sync)
{
    FILE *fp = NULL;
    FILE *archivefp = NULL;
    BYTE rHandlc;
    int err;
    bool dbOpen = false;
    int i;

    if ((err = SyncOpenDB(customerDBName, 0, rHandle,
        eDbWrite | eDbRead | eDbShowSecret)) != 0) {
        LogAddEntry("SyncOpenDB failed", slWarning, false);
        goto exit;
    }
    dbOpen = true;

    char    buffer[BIG_PATH *2];
    strcpy(buffer, sync.m_PathName);
    strcat(buffer, "Customers.txt");

    if ((fp = fopen(buffer, "w")) == NULL) {
        LogAddFormattedEntry(slWarning, false, "fopen(%s) failed",
            buffer);
        goto exit;
    }

    strcpy(buffer, sync.m_PathName);
    strcat(buffer, "CustomersArchive.txt");

    if ((archivefp = fopen(buffer, "a")) == NULL) {
        LogAddFormattedEntry(slWarning, false, "fopen(%s) failed",
            buffer);
        goto exit;
    }
```

```
    WORD recordCount;
    if ((err = SyncGetDBRecordCount(rHandle, recordCount)) !=0) {
        LogAddEntry("SyncGetDBRecordCount failed", slWarning, false);
        goto exit;
    }

    CRawRecordInfo recordInfo;
    recordInfo.m_FileHandle = rHandle;

    for (i = 0; i < recordCount; i++) {
        recordInfo.m_RecIndex = i;
        recordInfo.m_TotalBytes = (unsigned short) sizeof(gBigBuffer);
        recordInfo.m_pBytes = (unsigned char *) gBigBuffer;
        recordInfo.m_dwReserved = 0;

        if ((err = SyncReadRecordByIndex(recordInfo)) !=0) {
            LogAddEntry("SyncReadRecordByIndex failed", slWarning, false);
            goto exit;
        }

        FILE *fileToWriteTo;
        if (recordInfo.m_Attribs & eRecAttrArchived)
            fileToWriteTo = archivefp;
        else if (recordInfo.m_Attribs & eRecAttrDeleted)
            continue;    // skip deleted records
        else
            fileToWriteTo = fp;

        Customer *c = RawRecordToCustomer(recordInfo.m_pBytes);
        if ((err = WriteCustomerToFile(fileToWriteTo, c)) != 0) {
            delete c;
            LogAddEntry("WriteCustomerToFile failed", slWarning, false);
            goto exit;
        }
        delete c;
    }

    if ((err = SyncPurgeDeletedRecs(rHandle)) != 0)
        LogAddEntry("SyncPurgeDeletedRecs failed", slWarning, false);

exit:
    if (fp)
        fclose(fp);

    if (archivefp)
        fclose(archivefp);

    if (dbOpen)
        if ((err = SyncCloseDB(rHandle)) != 0)
            LogAddEntry("SyncDBClose failed", slWarning, false);
    return err;
}
```

Uploading customers is slightly more complicated than uploading orders, because the handheld supports deleting and archiving customers (see "Editing Customers" on page 170).

After reading each record with *SyncReadRecordByIndex*, we examine the record attributes (`m_Attribs`). If the archive bit is set, we write the record to a different file (appending to *CustomersArchive.txt*). If the delete bit is set, we skip this record.

Once we're done iterating through the records, we remove the deleted and archived records from the handheld (using `SyncPurgeDeletedRecs`). In order to change the database in this way, we had to open the database with write permission (`eDbWrite`).

With this code in place, we have a conduit that can upload and download data as needed. Now we are ready to tackle full two-way data syncing.

# 13

*In this chapter:*
- *The Logic of Syncing*
- *The Conduit Classes*
- *Sales Conduit Sample Based on the Classes*
- *Generic Conduit*
- *Sales Conduit Based on Generic Conduit*

# *Two-Way Syncing*

You can implement two-way syncing using two different methods. While both methods rely on Palm sample code, that is where the similarity ends. The first is based on the conduit classes (commonly referred to as *basemon* and *basetabl*) and the second on new code called Generic Conduit. Before delving into either approach, however, we need to discuss the logic involved in two-way, mirror image syncing.

## *The Logic of Syncing*

There are two forms of syncing that occur between the desktop and the handheld. The quicker method is appropriately named "fast sync" and the other is likewise aptly named "slow sync." A fast sync occurs when the handheld is being synced to the same desktop machine that it was synced to the previous time. Because handhelds can be synced to multiple desktops, this is not the only possibility. As a result, there are quite a few logic puzzles that need sorting out when records don't match. Let's start with the easier, fast scenario.

### *Fast Sync*

A fast sync occurs when a handheld syncs to the same desktop as it last did, so you can be assured that the delete/archive/modify bits from the handheld are accurate. In such cases, the conduit needs to do the following:

#### *Examine the desktop data*

The conduit reads the current desktop data into a local database.

### *Examine the handheld data*

For each changed record on the handheld, the conduit does the following:

- If the record is archived, it adds the record to an archived database on the desktop and marks it in the local database as a pending delete. It deletes the archived record from the handheld.
- If deleted, it marks it in the local database as a pending delete and removes it from the handheld. (Remember, user-deleted records aren't actually deleted until a sync occurs; the user may not see them, but your application keeps them around for this very occasion.)
- If modified, it modifies it in the local database.
- If new—if the record doesn't exist in the local database—the conduit adds it.

### *Examine the local data*

It is necessary to handle modified records in the local database by comparing them to the handheld records:

- If archived, it removes the record from the handheld, puts it in the archived database, and marks it as a pending delete in the local database.
- If a record is deleted, the conduit removes it from the handheld and marks it as a pending delete in the local database.
- If modified, it copies the modifications to the handheld and clears the modification flag from the record in the local database.
- If new, it copies the record to the handheld and clears the added flag from the record in the local database.

### *Dispose of the old data*

Now the conduit deletes all records in the local database that are marked for deletion. At this point, all the records in the local database should match those on the handheld.

### *Write local database to desktop database*

Finally, all the data is moved from the temporary local database back to permanent storage; the archive database is written out first and then the local database. A copy of the local database is also saved as a backup database—you will use this for slow sync.

## Thorny Comparisons—Changes to the Same Records on Both Platforms

There are some very thorny cases of record conflicts we have to consider. When you give users the capability of modifying a record in more than one location, some twists result. The problem occurs when you have a record that can be changed simultaneously on the handheld and on the local database, but in different ways. For example, a customer record in our Sales application has its address changed on the handheld database and its name changed on the local database. Or a record was deleted on one platform and changed on another. The number of scenarios is so great that we require some formal rules to govern cases of conflict.

The Palm philosophy concerning such problems is that no data loss should occur, even at the price of a possible proliferation of records with only minor differences. Thus, in the case of a record with a name field of "Smith" on the handheld and "Smithy" on the local database, the end result is two records, each present in both databases. Here are the various possibilities and how this philosophy plays out into rules for actual conflicts.

***A record is deleted on one database and modified on the other***

The deleted version of the record is done away with, and the changed version is copied to the other platform.

***A record is archived on one database and changed on the other***

The archived version of the record is put in the archive database, and the changed version is copied to the other platform. Exception: if the archived version has been changed in exactly the same way, we do the right thing and end up with only one archived record.

***A record is archived on one database and deleted on the other***

The record is put in the archive database.

***A record is changed on one database and changed differently on the other***

The result is two records. This is true for records with the same field change, such as our case of "Smith" and "Smithy." It is also true for a record where the name field is changed on one record and the address field on the other. In this case, you also end up with two records. Thus these initial records:

| Handheld Database | Local Database |
|---|---|
| Name: Smith | Name: Smithy |
| Address: 120 Park Street | Address 100 East Street |
| City: River City | City: River City |

yield the following records in fully synced mirror image databases:

| Handheld Database | Local Database |
|---|---|
| Name: Smith | Name: Smith |
| Address: 120 Park Street | Address: 120 Park Street |
| City: River City | City: River City |
| | |
| Name: Smithy | Name: Smithy |
| Address 100 East Street | Address 100 East Street |
| City: River City | City: River City |

#### *A record is changed on one database and changed identically on the other*

If a record is changed in both places in the same way (the same field contains the same new value in both places), the result is one record in both places.

This can get tricky, however. While it may be clear that "Smith" is not "Smithy", it is not so obvious that "Smith" is not "smith". Depending on the nature of your record fields, you may need to make case-by-case decisions about the meaning of *identical.*

## Slow Sync

A slow sync takes place when the last sync of the handheld was not with this desktop. Commonly, this occurs when the user has more recently synced to another desktop machine. Less frequently, this happens because this is the first sync of a handheld. If the last sync of the handheld was not with this desktop, the modify/archive/delete bits are not accurate with respect to this desktop. They may be accurate with the desktop last synced to, but this doesn't help with the current sync scenario.

Since the modify/archive/delete bits aren't accurate, we've got to figure out how the handheld database has changed from the desktop database since the last sync. In order to do this, we need an accurate copy of the local database at the time of the last sync. This is complicated by the possibility that the local database may have changed since the last sync. The solution to this problem is to use the backup copy that we made after the last sync between these two machines—the last point at which these two matched.

Since this backup, both the handheld and the desktop database may have diverged. While it is true that all the changes to the desktop have been marked (changes, new, deleted, archived), it is not true for the handheld. Some or all of the changes to the handheld data were lost when the intervening sync took place;

the deleted/archived records were removed, and the modified records were unmarked.

To deal with this problem, we need to use a slow sync. As the name implies, a slow sync looks at every record from the handheld. It copies them to an in-memory database on the desktop called the remote database and compares them to the backup database records. Here are the possibilities that need to be taken into account:

- The remote record matches a record in the backup database—nothing has changed.
- The remote record isn't present in the backup database—the record is new and is marked as modified.
- The backup record isn't present in the remote database—the remote record has been deleted (it could have been archived, in which case it has been archived on a different desktop). The record is marked as deleted.
- The backup record and the remote record are different—the remote record has been modified. The record is marked as changed.

At this point, we've got a copy of the remote database where each record has been left alone, marked as modified (due to being new or changed), or marked as deleted. Now the conduit can carry out the rest of the sync. Thus, the difference between the two syncs is the initial time required to mark records so that the two databases agree. It is a slow sync because every record from the handheld had to be copied to the desktop.

Now that you know what to do with records during a sync, let's discuss how to do it.

## The Conduit Classes

You may be apprehensive about tackling two-way syncing using the conduit classes provided by Palm (sometimes called *basemon* and *basetabl* because of the filenames in which they are located). The implementation may seem murky and the examples quite complicated. If you looked over the samples, you certainly noted that there is no simple example showing how to do what you want to do. Things get even more formidable if you don't want to save your data in the format the base classes provide.

We had all these same apprehensions—many of them were well deserved. At the time this book was written, the documentation wasn't clear concerning the definitions and tasks of each class, nor was it clear what you specifically needed to do to write your own conduit (what methods you are required to override, for instance). The good news is that a detailed examination shows that the architecture of the conduit classes is sound; they do quite a lot for you, and it's not hard to support other file formats once you know what you have to change.

After diving in and working with the conduit classes, we figured out how to use them effectively. In a moment, we will show you their architecture and describe each class and its responsibilities. After that, we show you what is required on your part—what methods you must override and what data members you must set. Next, we show you the code for a complete syncing conduit that supports its own file format.

## *The Classes and Their Responsibilities*

The classes you use to create the conduit are:

*CBaseConduit Monitor*
: Runs the entire sync

*CBaseTable*
: Creates a table that holds all the records

*CBaseSchema*
: Defines the structure of a record in the table

*CBaseRecord*
: Creates an object used to read and write each record to the table

*CDTLinkConverter*
: Converts the Palm OS record format into a CBaseRecord and vice versa

## *CBaseConduitMonitor*

The CBaseConduitMonitor class is responsible for directing syncing from the start to the end. It does the logging, initializes and deinitializes the sync manager, creates tables, populates them, and decides what records should go where. It is the administrator of the sync. It is also within CBaseConduitMonitor that we add all of the code from the previous chapters that handle the uploading and downloading of data.

CBaseConduitMonitor contains five functions that you need to override:

- *CreateTable*
- *ConstructRecord*
- *SetArchiveFileExt*
- *LogRecordData*
- *LogApplicationName*

At this point, we give you a brief description of each function. Later, we'll look at actual code when examining our conduit sample.

### *CreateTable*

You override this to create your class derived from CBaseTable. Here's the function declaration:

```
long CreateTable(CBaseTable*& pBase);
```

### *ConstructRecord*

This routine creates your own class derived from CBaseRecord. Here is the function:

```
long ConstructRecord(CBaseRecord*& pBase,
          CBaseTable& rtable,  WORD wModAction);
```

If the incoming `wModAction` parameter is equal to `MODFILTER_STUPID`, the newly created CBaseRecord object should check any attempted changes to its fields. If the change attempts to set a new value equal to the old value, the CBaseRecord object should just ignore the change, not marking the record as having changed.

### *SetArchiveFileExt*

This function simply sets the filename extension used for archive files. Here is the override call:

```
void SetArchiveFileExt();
```

Your override should set the `m_ArchFileExt` data member of CBaseConduitMonitor to a string that will be appended to the category name and used as the filename of the archive.

### *LogRecordData*

This function writes a summary of a record to the log. Here is the function you override:

```
void LogRecordData(CBaseRecord&rRec, char *errBuf);
```

Here are the values of the parameters:

`rRec`
: The record to summarize

`errBuff`
: The buffer to write the summary to

This routine is called when the monitor is going to add a log entry for a specific record (for example, when a record has been changed on both the desktop and the handheld). It writes a succinct description of the record, one that enables the user to identify the record.

### *LogApplicationName*

This is the function that returns the name of the conduit:

```
void LogApplicationName(char* appName, WORD len);
```

The conduit name is returned into `appName` (the `appName` buffer is `len` bytes long).

### *CBaseConduitMonitor data member*

This class contains one data member that you must initialize:

`m_wRawRecSize`
: Initialize this to the maximum size of a record in your handheld database. It is used as the size of the `m_pBytes` field of the CRawRecordInfo (see "The CRawRecordInfo class" on page 343). It is used to read and write handheld database records.

## *CBaseTable*

This class is used to create a table that contains field objects for each record. The whole thing is stored in a large array. Every record contains the same number of fields in the same order. The number of rows in the array is the number of records in the table. The number of columns is the number of fields per record. You should imagine a structure similar to that shown in Figure 13-1.

**CBaseTable**

| | | | | | | |
|---|---|---|---|---|---|---|
| **Record 1** | Field 1 | Field 2 | Field 3 | Field 3 | Field 4 | *Field...N* |
| **Record 2** | Field 1 | Field 2 | Field 3 | Field 3 | Field 4 | *Field...N* |
| **Record 3** | Field 1 | Field 2 | Field 3 | Field 3 | Field 4 | *Field...N* |
| **Record 4** | Field 1 | Field 2 | Field 3 | Field 3 | Field 4 | *Field...N* |
| **Record 5** | Field 1 | Field 2 | Field 3 | Field 3 | Field 4 | *Field...N* |

*Figure 13-1. Record structure in CBaseTable*

This is not an array of arrays, but a single large one. The fields are stored in a single-dimensional array, where the fields for the first record are followed by those of the second record and so on. When it's necessary to retrieve the values in a row, a CBaseRecord is positioned at the appropriate fields in the array. It can then read from and write to the fields to effect a change to the row. The table is responsible for reading itself from a file and writing itself out. The default format is an MFC archive format.

This type of programming is a bit startling after months of handheld programming, where every byte of memory is precious. It's refreshing to be in an environment where memory is less limited. How profligate to just allocate a field object for every field in every row—all we can say is that its a good thing conduits aren't required to run in 15K of dynamic memory.

A conduit actually has several CBaseTables: one for the records on the handheld, one for the records on the desktop, one for the backup database during a slow sync, and one containing archived records.

Within a table, the data is handled in a straightforward manner and records are frequently copied from one table to another during a sync. While records can be individually deleted, they are normally marked as deleted and then all purged at once.

#### *Functions you must override*

This class has only one function to override:

```
virtual long  AppendDuplicateRecord (
    CBaseRecord&rFrom, CBaseRecord&rTo, BOOL bAllFlds = TRUE);
```

Here are the parameters and their values:

`rFrom`
: The record that contains the fields that are copied from.

`rTo`
: A record that contains the fields that get copied to.

`bAllFlds`
: If this is true, the record ID and status should be copied with all the other fields.

This adds a new row of fields.

#### *CBaseTable functions you can't override, but wish you could*

There are two other functions that you will often wish to override. The problem is that you can't, given the flawed design of the class. These functions are:

```
long  OpenFrom (CString& rTableName, long openFlag);
long  ExportTo (CString& rTableName, CString & csError);
```

These are the routines responsible for reading a table from and writing a table to disk. Thus, any time you want to use a different file format, you should override these.

Unfortunately, these routines aren't declared virtual in the original Palm class and can't easily be overridden. Since you can't accomplish what you need to in a standard way, you have to use a far less appealing method. See "The problem—virtual reality beats nonvirtual reality" later in this chapter for a description of the unpalatable measures we suggest.

## *CBaseSchema*

This class is responsible for defining the number, the order, and the type of the fields of each record.

### *Functions you must override*

This class contains only one function to override:

```
virtual long  DiscoverSchema(void);
```

This routine specifies each of the fields and marks which ones store the record ID, attributes, category ID, etc.

### *CBaseSchema data members*

There are several data members that you need to initialize in *DiscoverSchema*:

`m_FieldsPerRow`
: Initialize to the number of fields in each record.

`m_Fields`
: Call this object's *SetSize* member function to specify the number of fields in each record. Call the object's *SetAt* member function for every field from `0` to `m_FieldsPerRow-1` to specify the type of the field.

`m_RecordIdPos`
: Initialize to the field number containing the record ID.

`m_RecordStatusPos`
: Initialize to the field number containing the status byte.

`m_CategoryIdPos`
: Initialize to the field number containing the category ID.

`m_PlacementPos`
: Initialize to the field number containing the record number on the handheld. If you don't keep track of record numbers, you'll initialize to an empty field.

Most conduits do not need the record numbers from the handheld and therefore have a dummy field that the `m_PlacementPos` refers to. Occasionally, a conduit needs to know the ordering of the records on the handheld. For example, the Memo Pad conduit wants records on the desktop to be displayed in the same order as on the handheld and has no key on which to determine the order. Its solution is to use the ordering of the records in the database as the sort order (no other conduits for the built-in applications use record numbers).

A conduit that needs record numbers would do the following:

1. Override *ApplyRemotePositionMap* (which does nothing by default) to read the record IDs in the order in which they are stored on the handheld.
2. Store each record number in the field referenced by `m_PlacementPos`.

## *CBaseRecord*

A CBaseRecord is a transitory object that you use to access a record's fields. The fields are stored within the table itself; use the CBaseRecord to read and write data from a specific row within the table. Your derived class should contain utility routines to read and write the data in the record.

### *Functions you must override*

This class contains a couple of functions that you must override:

```
virtual BOOL  operator==(const CBaseRecord&r);
```

This function compares two records to determine whether they are the same. It should not just compare record IDs or attributes, but should use all the relevant fields in the records. Note that the parameter `r` is actually your subclass of CBaseRecord.

Whenever this function is called, the two records are in different tables:

```
virtual long Assign(const CBaseRecord&r);
```

This routine copies the contents of `r` to this record, including the record ID and attributes. Note that the parameter `r` is actually a subclass of CBaseRecord. The two records are in different tables.

### *Useful functions*

There are also several functions that you can use to set the record ID, get or set individual attributes of the record, and so on. Here they are:

```
long  SetRecordId      (int  nRecId);
long  GetRecordId      (int& rRecId);
long  SetStatus        (int  nStatus);
long  GetStatus        (int& rStatus);
```

```
long  SetCategoryId    (int  nCatId);
long  GetCategoryId    (int& rCatId);
long  SetArchiveBit    (BOOL bOnOff);

BOOL  IsDeleted        (void);
BOOL  IsModified       (void);
BOOL  IsAdded          (void);
BOOL  IsArchived       (void);
BOOL  IsNone           (void);
BOOL  IsPending        (void);
```

The first set of routines returns information about the record ID, its status, the category ID, and whether the record should be archived. The second set of routines tells you the modified status of the record.

### *CBaseRecord data members*

There are a couple of data members that are available for you to use:

`m_fields`
: This data member is an array of fields for this specific record. It is initialized by the table when the table is focused (so to speak) on the record. Only one record within a table can be focused at a time.

`m_Positioned`
: This specifies whether the table is positioned on this particular record. It starts out false, but when the table focuses on a record, it is set to true.

## *CDTLinkConverter*

This class is responsible for converting from Palm record format to your subclass of CBaseRecord and vice versa.

### *Functions you must override*

```
long ConvertToRemote(CBaseRecord &rRec, CRawRecordInfo &rInfo);
```

You use this function to convert from your subclass of CBaseRecord to the CRawRecordInfo. The `rInfo.m_pBytes` pointer has already been allocated for you. You must write into the buffer and update `rInfo.m_RecSize`:

```
long ConvertFromRemote(CBaseRecord &rRec, CRawRecordInfo &rInfo);
```

Convert from the CRawRecordInfo to your subclass of CBaseRecord. The `rRec` parameter is the subclass of CBaseRecord created by your CBaseTable::CreateRecord. You need to initialize `rRec` based on the values in `rInfo`.

# Sales Conduit Sample Based on the Classes

Now that you have an idea what each of the classes does and which functions you override, it is time to use this information to add syncing to the Sales application conduit. We use these new sync classes for syncing the customer database. We continue to use our own routines that we created in Chapter 12 to upload the orders database and download the products database.

There is also a problem in the implementation of two of the classes: CBaseConduitMonitor and CBaseTable. We use an unorthodox approach, which involves circumventing normal inheritance and copying the classes by hand. We talk about this as part of our discussion of each of these classes in the sample conduit. Other classes are used normally.

## CSalesConduitMonitor—Copying the Class

This is the class that is based on CBaseConduitMonitor. Let's look at a problem we have before going any further.

### A virtual conundrum

Our customer database doesn't use categories, but CBaseConduitMonitor expects them to exist. CBaseConduitMonitor's *ObtainRemoteCategories* function reads the app info block of the handheld database and causes an error if the AppInfo block doesn't exist. In the original class, there were two functions that expected information about categories. The first was *SynchronizeCategories,* which is responsible for syncing the categories. We overrode this routine to do nothing. Unfortunately, a second function dealing with categories was not declared virtual in the original class and thus could not be overridden. Here is the unseemly bit of code that caused our problem:

```
long  ObtainRemoteCategories (void); // acquire HH Categories
```

Because of this code, our function *ObtainRemoteCategories* never gets called, and our conduit fails with an error. After a bit of nail biting, our solution was to re-sort to copy and paste—we copy the *basemon.cpp* and *basemon.h* files to our conduit source directory and change the declaration of CBaseConduitMonitor so that *ObtainRemoteCategories* is virtual.

In a perfect world, you would never have to concern yourself with the following code. It would remain invisible to you. Doing this type of code copy is an action fraught with difficulty. If Palm Computing changes this class, you'll have to reapply this change (unless one of the changes was to add the needed **virtual**, in which case you could throw away your changes).

### *Code we wish you never had to see*

Here is the class that you need to copy into your conduit source directory (note that the line of code we change is in bold):

```
class CBaseConduitMonitor
{
protected:
    // code deleted that declares lots of data members

    virtual long  CreateTable    (CBaseTable*& pBase);
    virtual long  ConstructRecord (CBaseRecord*& pBase,
                                   CBaseTable& rtable,
                                   WORD wModAction);
    virtual void  SetArchiveFileExt();

    // Moved to Base class.
    virtual long  ObtainRemoteTables(void);// get HH real & archive tables
    virtual long  ObtainLocalTables (void);// get PC real & archive tables
    virtual long  AddRecord              (CBaseRecord& rFromRec,
                                          CBaseTable&  rTable);
    virtual long  AddRemoteRecord        (CBaseRecord& rRec);
    virtual long  ChangeRemoteRecord     (CBaseRecord& rRec);
    virtual long  CopyRecordsHHtoPC (void); // copy records from HH to PC
    virtual long  CopyRecordsPCtoHH (void); // copy records from PC to HH
    virtual long  FastSyncRecords (void); // carries out 'Fast' sync
    virtual long  SlowSyncRecords        (void); // carries out 'Slow' sync

    // deleted function
    // virtual  long  CreateLocArchTable    (CBaseTable*& pBase);

    virtual long  SaveLocalTables        (const char*);
    virtual long  PurgeLocalDeletedRecs (void);
    virtual long  GetLocalRecordCount    (void);
    virtual long  SendRemoteChanges      (CBaseRecord& rLocRecord);
    virtual long  ApplyRemotePositionMap(void);
    virtual long  SynchronizeCategories (void);
    virtual long  FlushPCRecordIDs       (void);
    virtual long  ArchiveRecords         (void);

    // file link related functions
    virtual long  ProcessSubscription    (void);
    virtual int GetFirstRecord (CStringArray*& pSubRecord );
```

```
    virtual int GetNextRecord(CStringArray*& );
    virtual int DeleteSubscTableRecs(CString& csCatName,
        CBaseTable* pTable, WORD wDeleteOption);
    virtual int AddCategory(CString& csCatName, CBaseTable* pTable);
    virtual long LogModifiedSubscRec(CBaseRecord* pRecord,
        BOOL blocalRec);
    virtual long SynchronizeSubscCategories(CCategoryMgr* catMgr);
    virtual long CheckFileName(CString& csFileName);
    virtual int  GetSubData (CString& csfilename, CString csFldOrder );
    virtual void  AddSubDataToTable( int subCatId);


    // Audit trail notifications (optional override)
    virtual long  AuditAddToPC          (CBaseRecord& rRec, long rowOffset);
    virtual long  AuditUpdateToPC       (CBaseRecord& rRec, long rowOffset);
    virtual long  AuditAddToHH          (CBaseRecord& rRec, long rowOffset);

    // Overload with care !!
    virtual long  EngageStandard        (void);
    virtual long  EngageInstall         (void);
    virtual long  EngageBackup          (void);
    virtual long  EngageDoNothing           (void);
```

*Code changed here:*

```
    // ObtainRemoteCategories changed to virtual Neil Rhodes 8/6/98
    virtual long  ObtainRemoteCategories (void); // acquire HH Categories
    virtual long  SaveRemoteCategories          (CCategoryMgr *catMgr);
    long  SaveLocalCategories           (CCategoryMgr *catMgr);
    long  ClearStatusAddRecord          (CBaseRecord& rFromRec,
                                         CBaseTable&  rTable);
    long  AllocateRawRecordMemory       (CRawRecordInfo& rawRecord, WORD);
    void  SetDirtyCategoryFlags         (CCategoryMgr* catMgr);
    void  UpdatePCCategories            (CUpdateCategoryId *updCatId);
    BOOL  IsRemoteMemError              (long);
    BOOL  IsCommsError                  (long);


    // Used by FastSync and SlowSync.
    virtual long  SynchronizeRecord      (CBaseRecord & rRemRecord,
                                          CBaseRecord & rLocRecord,
                                          CBaseRecord & rBackRecord);

    // code deleted that declares lots of log functions
    virtual BOOL IsFatalConduitError(long lError, CBaseRecord
         *prRec=NULL);

public:
             CBaseConduitMonitor        (PROGRESSFN pFn,
                                         CSyncProperties&,
                                         HINSTANCE hInst = NULL);
    virtual ~CBaseConduitMonitor        ();

    long  Engage                        (void);
    void  SetDllInstance                (HINSTANCE hInst);
```

```
    void  SetFilelinkSupport (long lvalue){ m_lFilelinkSupported = lvalue; }

    // file link public functions
    long UpdateTablesOnSubsc(void);
    int GetCategories(char  categoryNames[][CAT_NAME_LEN] );
};
```

There seems to be no rhyme or reason as to which functions are declared virtual and which aren't in CBaseConduitMonitor. These are not routines that get called hundreds of thousands of times a sync that never need to be overridden. We can't see any optimization that would warrant making them virtual. There's no excuse for this oversight.

Luckily, that's all that needs to be done; *basemon.cpp* will need to be recompiled, but that is uncomplicated.

## CSalesConduitMonitor

Now we can move on to a discussion of changes we would normally make to our code and standard modifications we make to this class.

### CSalesConduitMonitor Class Definition

Within this class, we do a few things. We override the category functions to do nothing. We also override *EngageStandard*. We insert the calls to our uploading and downloading databases. We also need to override the class functions that every conduit must override. Here is the class definition:

```
class CSalesConduitMonitor : public CBaseConduitMonitor
{
protected:
// required
    long CreateTable     (CBaseTable*& pBase);
    long ConstructRecord(CBaseRecord*& pBase,
            CBaseTable& rtable,  WORD wModAction);
    void SetArchiveFileExt();
    void LogRecordData           (CBaseRecord&, char*);
    void LogApplicationName      (char* appName, WORD);

//overridden to do nothing because we don't have categories
    virtual long  SynchronizeCategories (void);
    virtual long  ObtainRemoteCategories(void);
// ovverriden so we can upload and download our other databases
    virtual long  EngageStandard(void);

public:
    CSalesConduitMonitor(PROGRESSFN pFn, CSyncProperties&,
                HINSTANCE hInst = NULL);
};
```

### *CSalesConduitMonitor constructor*

Our constructor allocates a *DTLinkConverter* and sets the maximum size of handheld records:

```
CSalesConduitMonitor::CSalesConduitMonitor(
    PROGRESSFN pFn,
    CSyncProperties& rProps,
    HINSTANCE hInst
) : CBaseConduitMonitor(pFn, rProps, hInst)
{
    m_pDTConvert = new CSalesDTLinkConverter(hInst);
    m_wRawRecSize = 1000;    // no record will exceed 1000 bytes
}
```

### *Functions that require overriding*

There are five functions that we need to override:

*CreateTable*

This function simply creates a CSalesTable:

```
long CSalesConduitMonitor::CreateTable(CBaseTable*& pBase)
{
    pBase = new CSalesTable();

    return pBase ? 0 : -1;
}
```

*ConstructRecord*

This routine creates a new CSalesRecord:

```
long CSalesConduitMonitor::ConstructRecord(CBaseRecord*& pBase,
                                           CBaseTable& rtable ,
                                           WORD wModAction)
{
    pBase = new CSalesRecord((CSalesTable &) rtable, wModAction);

    return pBase ? 0 : -1;
}
```

*SetArchiveFileExt*

Next, we set the suffix for our archive files as *ARC.TXT* in *SetArchiveFileExt*. Our archive file is called *UnfiledARC.TXT* (all our records are category 0, the Unfiled category):

```
void  CSalesConduitMonitor::SetArchiveFileExt()
{
    strcpy(m_ArchFileExt, "ARC.TXT");
}
```

*LogRecordData*

Our *LogRecordData* summarizes a CSalesRecord to a log:

```
void CSalesConduitMonitor::LogRecordData(CBaseRecord& rRec,
    char * errBuff)
```

```
{
    // return something of the form " city name, "
    CSalesRecord    &rLocRec = (CSalesRecord&)rRec;
    CString     csStr;
    int         len = 0;

    rLocRec.GetCity(csStr);
    len = csStr.GetLength() ;
    if (len > 20)
        len = 20;

    strcpy(errBuff, "        ");
    strncat(errBuff, csStr, len);
    strcat(errBuff, ", ");

    rLocRec.GetName(csStr);
    len = csStr.GetLength() ;
    if (len > 20)
        len = 20;

    strncat(errBuff, csStr, len);
    strcat(errBuff, ", ");
    strncat(errBuff, csStr, len);
}
```

*LogApplicationName*

Last, but not least, we need to override the routine *LogApplicationName*. It returns our conduit's name:

```
void CSalesConduitMonitor::LogApplicationName(char* appName, WORD len)
{
    strncpy(appName, "Sales", len-1);
}
```

This ends the required routines. There are a few others we override.

### *The two category routines*

We override the two category routines to do nothing. This prevents CBaseConduit-Monitor from reading the app info block from the handheld and from actually trying to synchronize categories between the handheld and the desktop:

```
long CSalesConduitMonitor::ObtainRemoteCategories()
{
    return 0;
}

long CSalesConduitMonitor::SynchronizeCategories()
{
    return 0;
}
```

### *Modifying EngageStandard*

Next, we override *EngageStandard* so that we can call the routines we defined in Chapter 12 for copying orders from the handheld and copying products from the desktop. We have physically copied the inherited code, since we have to place our code in the middle of it. We place it after the conduit is registered with the Sync Manager and the log is started, but before the log is finished and the Sync Manager is closed.

Example 13-1 shows the entire function in all its complexity. We wanted you to see the complexity you avoid by using CBaseConduitMomitor for syncing instead of writing all of this from scratch.

*Example 13-1. EngageStandard*

```
long CSalesConduitMonitor::EngageStandard(void)
{
    CONDHANDLE  conduitHandle = (CONDHANDLE)0;
    long        retval = 0;
    char        appName[40];
    long        pcCount = 0;
    WORD        hhCount = 0;
    Activity    syncFinishCode = slSyncFinished;


    // Register this conduit with SyncMgr.DLL for communication to HH
    if (retval = SyncRegisterConduit(conduitHandle))
        return(retval);

    // Notify the log that a sync is about to begin
    LogAddEntry("", slSyncStarted,FALSE);

    memset(&m_DbGenInfo, 0, sizeof(m_DbGenInfo));

    //  Loop through all possible 'remote' db's
    for (; m_CurrRemoteDB < m_TotRemoteDBs && !retval; m_CurrRemoteDB++)
    {
        // Open the Remote Database
        retval = ObtainRemoteTables();

        // Open PC tables and load local records && local categories.
        if (!retval && !(retval = ObtainLocalTables()))
        {
            #ifdef _FILELNK
// Process Subscriptions
// This needs to be done first before desktop records are affected
// by other calls.
// (e.g.) FlushPCRecordIDs()... which will set all recStatus to Added
// for a  hard reset HH
            // (m_firstDevice = eHH)
            if (!retval)
                if (m_rSyncProperties.m_SyncType != eHHtoPC)
```

*Example 13-1. EngageStandard (continued)*

```
            {
                retval = ProcessSubscription();
            }
        #endif
        if( !(retval) )
        {
            FlushPCRecordIDs();

            if (!(retval = ObtainRemoteCategories()))
            {
// Synchronize the AppInfoBlock Info excluding the categories
                m_pDTConvert->SynchronizeAppInfoBlock(m_DbGenInfo,
                                    *m_LocRealTable,
                                    m_rSyncProperties.m_SyncType,
                                    m_rSyncProperties.m_FirstDevice);

                // Synchronize the categories
                retval = SynchronizeCategories();
            }
        }

    }

    // Synchronize the records
    if (!retval)
    {
        #ifdef  FILELNK
        // path for subsc info
        CString csSubInfoPath(m_rSyncProperties.m_PathName);
        csSubInfoPath =csSubInfoPath + SUBSC_FILENAME;
        SubError subErr = SubLoadInfo(csSubInfoPath);
        #endif

        if (m_rSyncProperties.m_SyncType == eHHtoPC)
            retval = CopyRecordsHHtoPC();
        else if (m_rSyncProperties.m_SyncType == ePCtoHH)
            retval = CopyRecordsPCtoHH();
        else if (m_rSyncProperties.m_SyncType == eFast)
            retval = FastSyncRecords();
        else if (m_rSyncProperties.m_SyncType == eSlow)
            retval = SlowSyncRecords();

        #ifdef _FILELNK
        SubSaveInfo(csSubInfoPath);
        #endif
    }

    // If the number of records are not equal after a FastSync or
    // SlowSync: If the PC has more records, then do a PCtoHH Sync.
    // If the HH has more records, then do a HHtoPC Sync.
    if (!retval && ((m_rSyncProperties.m_SyncType == eFast) ||
                    (m_rSyncProperties.m_SyncType == eSlow)))
```

*Example 13-1. EngageStandard (continued)*

```
        {
            // Get the record counts
            pcCount = GetLocalRecordCount();
            if (!(retval = SyncGetDBRecordCount(m_RemHandle, hhCount)))
            {
                if (pcCount > (long)hhCount)
                    retval = CopyRecordsPCtoHH();

                else if (pcCount < (long)hhCount)
                {
                    m_LocRealTable->PurgeAllRecords();
                    retval = CopyRecordsHHtoPC();
                }
            }
        }
        if (!retval || !IsCommsError(retval))
        {
         // Re-check the record counts, only if we've obtained rem tables
            pcCount = GetLocalRecordCount();
            hhCount = 0;
            retval  = SyncGetDBRecordCount(m_RemHandle, hhCount);

         // If the record counts are not equal, send message to the log.
            if (pcCount < (long)hhCount)
            {
                LogRecCountMismatch(pcCount, (long)hhCount);
                syncFinishCode = slSyncAborted;
            }
            else if (pcCount > (long)hhCount)
            {
                LogPilotFull(pcCount, (long)hhCount);
                syncFinishCode = slSyncAborted;
            }
        }


    // This allows exact display order matching with the remote device.
        if (!retval || !IsCommsError(retval))
            if (ApplyRemotePositionMap())
                LogBadXMap();

        if (!retval || IsRemoteMemError(retval))
        {
            // Save all records to be archived to their appropriate files
            if (ArchiveRecords())
                LogBadArchiveErr();

            // Copy PC file to Backup PC file
            CString backFile(m_rSyncProperties.m_PathName);
            CString dataFile(m_rSyncProperties.m_PathName);
            backFile += m_rSyncProperties.m_LocalName;
            dataFile += m_rSyncProperties.m_LocalName;
```

*Example 13-1. EngageStandard (continued)*

```
            int nIndex = backFile.ReverseFind(_T('.'));
            if (nIndex != -1)
                backFile = backFile.Left(nIndex);
            backFile += BACK_EXT;

            // Save synced records to PC file
            if (!SaveLocalTables((const char*)dataFile))
            {
                // Clear HH status flags
                if (SyncResetSyncFlags(m_RemHandle))
                {
                    LogBadResetSyncFlags();
                    syncFinishCode = slSyncAborted;
                }
                remove(backFile);
                CopyFile(dataFile, backFile, FALSE);
            }
            else
                syncFinishCode = slSyncAborted;
        }
        if (!IsCommsError(retval))
            SyncCloseDB(m_RemHandle);
    }

// added here for sales conduit
    if (retval == 0 && m_rSyncProperties.m_SyncType == eHHtoPC ||
        m_rSyncProperties.m_SyncType == eFast ||
        m_rSyncProperties.m_SyncType == eSlow)
        retval = CopyOrdersFromHH(m_rSyncProperties);
    if (retval == 0 && m_rSyncProperties.m_SyncType == ePCtoHH ||
        m_rSyncProperties.m_SyncType == eFast ||
        m_rSyncProperties.m_SyncType == eSlow)
        retval = CopyProductsAndCategoriesToHH(m_rSyncProperties);
// done added here for sales conduit

    if (retval)
        syncFinishCode = slSyncAborted;


    // Get the application name
    memset(appName, 0, sizeof(appName));
    LogApplicationName(appName, sizeof(appName));

    LogAddEntry(appName, syncFinishCode,FALSE);

    if (!IsCommsError(retval))
        SyncUnRegisterConduit(conduitHandle);

    return(retval);
}
```

These are all the changes to the CSalesConduitMonitor class. As you can see, there was very little complexity to the added code, especially when you realize that most of the difficulty occurs in the last routine, where we have to fold our code into a fairly large routine.

Now that we have dealt with the administration portion of the code, it is time to create the tables that hold the data.

## CBaseTable—Copying the Class

We need to create the class that is based on CBaseTable. Before we can define our table structure, however, we need to deal with another class problem. Once again, the solution is to resort to copying the class as a whole, and it is for just as unsatisfying a set of reasons.

### The problem—virtual reality beats nonvirtual reality

We want to store our tables in comma-delimited text files rather than in the default MFC archived file format. This is certainly a reasonable wish on our part. It is an even more attractive alternative when you realize that MFC archived files are very hard to read from anything but MFC-based code. We have no desire to create an MFC application just to read our data files, when a text-based system gives us such enormous versatility. Good reasoning on our part is unfortunately difficult to act on.

For example, if we attempt to override *CBaseTable::SaveTo* and *CBaseTable::OpenFrom*, we don't get very far. As you might have guessed, those two member functions are not declared `virtual` in the original CBaseTable class. We are stuck then with seeking a workaround. The solution to this problem is to copy the *basetabl.cpp* and *basetabl.h* files to our conduit's source folder.

### The CBaseTable code you have to copy

We need to modify the declaration of CBaseTable to add the `virtual` keywords. Here is the code we copy and the two changes we make:

```
class TABLES_DECL CBaseTable : public CObject
{
protected:
    friend              CBaseIterator;
    friend              CRepeateEventIterator;
    friend              CBaseRecord;
    CString             m_TableName;
    CString             m_TableString;
    CBaseSchema*        m_Schema;
    CBaseFieldArray*    m_Fields;
    CCategoryMgr*       m_pCatMgr;
    DWORD               m_dwVersion;
    BOOL                m_bOnTheMac;
```

```
//  CPtrArray           m_OpenIts;       // List of open  CBaseIterator(s)
//  long    AddIterator             (long& ItPos, CBaseIterator *);
//  long    RemoveIterator          (long  ItPos, CBaseIterator *);

    BOOL  SubstCRwithNL        (CString &);
    BOOL  SubstNLwithCR        (CString &);
    void  Serialize            (CArchive &);
    long  WipeOutRow           (long RecPos);
    long  ReadInFields         (CArchive &ar);
    long  DestroyAllFields     (void) ;
    void  DeleteContents       (void) ;
    virtual long  ConstructProperField (eFieldTypes, CBaseField**);


public:
    DECLARE_SERIAL(CBaseTable)

    CBaseTable             ();
    CBaseTable             (DWORD dwVersion);
    virtual ~CBaseTable          ();
// change OpenFrom to virtual
    virtual long  OpenFrom (CString& rTableName, long openFlag);
    long  ExportTo (CString& rTableName, CString & csError);
// change SaveTo to virtual
    virtual long  SaveTo               (CString& rTableName);
    virtual long  Save                 (void);
    virtual long  GetRecordCount       (void);
    virtual long  GetFieldCount        (void);
    virtual BOOL  AtEof                (long nRecPos);
    virtual long  AlignFieldPointers   (long RecPos, CBaseRecord&);
    virtual long  GetMySchema          (const CBaseSchema*& pSchema);
    virtual long  PurgeDeletedRecords  (void);
    virtual long  ClearPlacementField  (void);
    virtual long  PurgeAllRecords      (void);
    virtual long  AppendBlankRecord     (CBaseRecord&);
    virtual long  AppendDuplicateRecord (CBaseRecord&,
                                        CBaseRecord&,
                                        BOOL bAllFlds = TRUE);

    virtual long  GetTableString           (CString& rTableString);
    virtual long  SetTableString           (CString& rTableString);
    virtual CCategoryMgr* GetCategoryManager     (void);

    virtual void DumpRecords(LPCSTR lpPathName,BOOL bAppend=TRUE);
};
```

Don't breathe a sigh of relief just yet—we have a complication. This isn't like the straightforward copying we did with *basemon.cpp* for CBaseConduitMonitor—copy, link, recompile, and everything works greats. This is a horse of an entirely different color—unlike *basemon.cpp*, this isn't code that is normally added to your project and linked with your remaining code. Therein lies the wrinkle. This is code that is found in a DLL in the folder with HotSync. Since the DLL is already compiled without the virtual keyword, the DLL won't cooperate by calling our derived class's *OpenFrom* and *SaveTo*.

Our solution was to statically link the *basetabl.cpp* code into our application and not use the table DLL at all. This also required adding the define of the symbol `_TABLES` to our project—thereby ensuring that the `TABLES_DECL` define was no longer defined as `__declspec(import)`. This caused *basemon.h* to no longer declare the class as being imported from a DLL. Note that the only other choice besides imported for the `TABLES_DECL` define was `__declspec(export)`. We took what was offered. Unfortunately, the result is that our conduit DLL unnecessarily exports the functions in the CBaseTable class. On the positive side, by these various machinations, we avoid having to change the contents of *basetabl.cpp* at all.

That is all of the unusual stuff we need to do. Now we can move to more normal overriding.

### *CSalesTable*

We need to handle a number of things in our CBaseTable class. In our definitions, we override the two functions. We also add a couple of new routines to handle the read and write functions.

#### *Class definition*

Here's our actual class definition (with *OpenFrom* and *SaveTo* overridden). We also include *ReadCustomer* and *WriteRecord*, which are utility functions used by *OpenFrom* and *SaveTo*:

```
class CSalesTable : public CBaseTable
{
public:
     CSalesTable  () ;

// required
    virtual long  AppendDuplicateRecord (
        CBaseRecord&,
        CBaseRecord&,
        BOOL bAllFlds = TRUE
    );
// optional overridden
    long OpenFrom(CString& rTableName, long openFlag);
    long SaveTo(CString& rTableName);
// useful
    CSalesRecord *ReadCustomer(CStdioFile &file);
    long WriteRecord(HANDLE hFile, CSalesRecord& rRec);
};
```

#### *CSalesTable constructor*

The constructor creates the schema and initializes it:

```
CSalesTable::CSalesTable()
             : CBaseTable()
```

```
{
    m_Schema = new CSalesSchema;
    if (m_Schema)
        m_Schema->DiscoverSchema();

}
```

### *CSalesTable functions*

*AppendDuplicateRecord* creates a new row and copies `rFrom` to `rTo`. Note that `rFrom` and `rTo` are actually CSalesRecord objects:

```
long CSalesTable::AppendDuplicateRecord(CBaseRecord& rFrom,
                   CBaseRecord& rTo, BOOL bAllFlds)
{
    int     tempInt;
    CString tempStr;
    long    retval = -1;

    CSalesRecord& rFromRec = (CSalesRecord&)rFrom;
    CSalesRecord& rToRec   = (CSalesRecord&)rTo;

    // Source record must be positioned at valid data.
    if (!rFromRec.m_Positioned)
        return -1;
    if ((retval = CBaseTable::AppendBlankRecord(rToRec)) != 0)
        return retval;
    if (bAllFlds) {
        retval = rFromRec.GetRecordId(tempInt) ||
            rToRec.SetRecordId(tempInt);
        if (retval != 0)
            return retval;

        if ((retval = rFromRec.GetStatus(tempInt)) != 0)
            if ((retval = rToRec.SetStatus(tempInt)) != 0)
                return retval;

        if ((retval = rToRec.SetArchiveBit(rFromRec.IsArchived())) != 0)
            return retval;
    }

    if ((retval = rToRec.SetPrivate(rFromRec.IsPrivate())) != 0)
        return retval;

    retval = rFromRec.GetID(tempInt) || rToRec.SetID(tempInt);
    if (retval != 0)
        return retval;

    retval = rFromRec.GetName(tempStr) || rToRec.SetName(tempStr);
    if (retval != 0)
        return retval;

    retval = rFromRec.GetAddress(tempStr) || rToRec.SetAddress(tempStr);
    if (retval != 0)
        return retval;
```

```
    retval = rFromRec.GetCity(tempStr) || rToRec.SetCity(tempStr);
    if (retval != 0)
        return retval;

    retval = rFromRec.GetPhone(tempStr) || rToRec.SetPhone(tempStr);
    if (retval != 0)
        return retval;

    return 0;
}
```

This is the only required function. There are also two other functions we override.

### *SaveTo*

Here's our version of *SaveTo*. We use it to save in a comma-delimited format:

```
long CSalesTable::SaveTo(CString& rTableName)
{
    CSalesRecord     locRecord(*this, 0);
    CBaseIterator    locIterator(*this);
    long             err;

    CString tdvFile(rTableName);
    HANDLE tdvFileStream = CreateFile(
        tdvFile,
        GENERIC_READ | GENERIC_WRITE,
        FILE_SHARE_READ | FILE_SHARE_WRITE,
        NULL,
        CREATE_ALWAYS,
        FILE_ATTRIBUTE_NORMAL | FILE_FLAG_SEQUENTIAL_SCAN,
        NULL
    );

    // generate the file
    if (tdvFileStream != (HANDLE)INVALID_HANDLE_VALUE) {

        SetFilePointer(tdvFileStream, 0, NULL, FILE_BEGIN);
        SetEndOfFile(tdvFileStream);

        err = locIterator.FindFirst(locRecord, FALSE);
        while (!err) {
            WriteRecord(tdvFileStream, locRecord);
            err = locIterator.FindNext(locRecord, FALSE);
        }
        if (err == -1)  // we reached the last record
            err = 0;

        CloseHandle(tdvFileStream);
    }
    return err;
}
```

It creates the file, opens it, calls *WriteRecord* to do the actual writing of one record, and then closes the file.

### *WriteRecord*

Note that *WriteRecord* doesn't write the attributes (modified, deleted, etc.) to a record, because it isn't necessary. By the time we write a table to disk, all deleted records should be deleted, all modified records will be synced, all archived records will be archived, and all added records will be synced. Thus, the attribute information is not relevant:

```
long CSalesTable::WriteRecord(HANDLE hFile, CSalesRecord& rRec)
{
    int             customerID;
    CString         csName, csAddress, csCity, csPhone;
    int             recId;
    DWORD           dwPut;
    unsigned long   len;
    const int       kMaxRecordSize = 1000;
    char            buf[kMaxRecordSize];

    // Get the record ID
    rRec.GetRecordId(recId);

    // Get the customer ID, name, address, city & phone.
    // Replace any tabs with spaces in all.
    rRec.GetID(customerID);
    rRec.GetName(csName);
    rRec.GetAddress(csAddress);
    rRec.GetCity(csCity);
    rRec.GetPhone(csPhone);
    ReplaceTabs(csName);
    ReplaceTabs(csAddress);
    ReplaceTabs(csCity);
    ReplaceTabs(csPhone);

    // Write the record to the file as (if private):
    // <customerID>\t<name>\t<address>\t<city>\t<phone>\tP\t<recID>
    //    or, if not private:
    // <customerID>\t<name>\t<address>\t<city>\t<phone>\t\t<recID>
    sprintf(
        buf,
        "%d\t%s\t%s\t%s\t%s\t%s\t%d\r\n",
        customerID,
        csName.GetBuffer(csName.GetLength()),
        csAddress.GetBuffer(csAddress.GetLength()),
        csCity.GetBuffer(csCity.GetLength()),
        csPhone.GetBuffer(csPhone.GetLength()),
        rRec.IsPrivate() ? "P": "",
        recId
    );
    len = strlen(buf);
    WriteFile(
        hFile,
        buf,
        len,
```

```
        &dwPut,
        NULL
    );
    ASSERT(dwPut == len);

    // Release the string buffers
    csName.ReleaseBuffer();
    csAddress.ReleaseBuffer();
    csCity.ReleaseBuffer();
    csPhone.ReleaseBuffer();

    return 0;
}
```

For each of the strings that will be written (name, address, city, phone), *WriteRecord* replaces any tabs or newlines with spaces by using *ReplaceTabs.* This is necessary because it would ruin our tab-delimited format if a tab or newline occurred within a field.

### ReplaceTabs

Here's the code for *ReplaceTabs*:

```
static long ReplaceTabs(CString& csStr)
{
    char *p;

    p = csStr.GetBuffer(csStr.GetLength());

    // Scan and replace all tabs or newlines with blanks
    while (*p) {
        if (*p == '\t' || *p == '\r' || *p == '\n')
            *p = ' ';
        ++p;
    }

    csStr.ReleaseBuffer();

    return 0;
}
```

This is all that needs to be done to handle writing to the file.

### OpenFrom

We now need to take care of reading one of these files. *OpenFrom* does that. It checks for the existence of the file, opens and closes it, and handles any exceptions that are thrown:

```
long CSalesTable::OpenFrom(CString& rTableName, long openFlag)
{
    char *pszName ;
```

```
    CFileStatus fStat;
    CStdioFile  *file = 0;

    pszName = rTableName.GetBuffer(rTableName.GetLength());

    // Check for the presence of the disk file, if not here get out
    // *without* invoking any of the reading code.
    if (!CStdioFile::GetStatus(pszName, fStat))
        return DERR_FILE_NOT_FOUND;

    TRY
    {
        file = new CStdioFile(pszName, CFile::modeReadWrite |
                              CFile::shareDenyWrite);
        rTableName.ReleaseBuffer(-1);
    }
    CATCH_ALL(e)
    {
        rTableName.ReleaseBuffer(-1);
        if (file)
            file->Abort();
        delete file;
        return ((CFileException*)e)->m_cause;
    }
    END_CATCH_ALL

    // Get rid of current contents (if any)
    DestroyAllFields();

    CSalesRecord *newRecord = 0;
    TRY
    {
        while ((newRecord = ReadCustomer(*file)) != 0) {

            delete newRecord;
            newRecord = 0;
        }
        file->Close();
    }
    CATCH_ALL(e)
    {
        file->Abort();
        delete file;
        delete newRecord;
        return DERR_INVALID_FILE_FORMAT;
    }
    END_CATCH_ALL
    delete file;

    return 0;
}
```

### ReadCustomer

*ReadCustomer* has quite a lot of work to do. It creates a new CSalesRecord for each line in the file. It returns 0 when there are no more lines:

```
CSalesRecord *CSalesTable::ReadCustomer(CStdioFile &file)
{
    static char gBigBuffer[4096];
    int retval;
    if (file.ReadString(gBigBuffer, sizeof(gBigBuffer)) == NULL)
        return false;
    char *p = gBigBuffer;
    char *customerID = FindUpToNextTab(&p);
    char *name = FindUpToNextTab(&p);
    char *address = FindUpToNextTab(&p);
    char *city = FindUpToNextTab(&p);
    char *phone = FindUpToNextTab(&p);
    char *priv = FindUpToNextTab(&p);
    char *uniqueID = FindUpToNextTab(&p);
    char *attributes = FindUpToNextTab(&p);

    if (!address)
        address = "";
    if (!city)
        city = "";
    if (!phone)
        phone = "";
    if (!priv)
        priv = "";
    if (!attributes)
        attributes = "c";
    if (!uniqueID)
        uniqueID = "0";
    if (customerID && name) {
        CSalesRecord *rec = new CSalesRecord(*this, 0);

        if (AppendBlankRecord(*rec)) {
            // should throw an error here!
            return 0;
            // return(CONDERR_BAD_REMOTE_TABLES);
        }
        retval = rec->SetRecordId(atol(uniqueID));
        retval = rec->SetCategoryId(0);

        retval = rec->SetID(atol(customerID));
        retval = rec->SetName(CString(name));
        retval = rec->SetAddress(CString(address));
        retval = rec->SetCity(CString(city));
        retval = rec->SetPhone(CString(phone));
        retval = rec->SetPrivate(*priv == 'P');

        int attr = 0;
        // 'N' -- new, 'M' -- modify, 'D'-- delete, 'A' -- archive
        // if it's Add, it can't be modify
```

```
            if (strchr(attributes, 'N'))
                attr |= fldStatusADD;
            else if (strchr(attributes, 'M'))
                attr |= fldStatusUPDATE;
            if (strchr(attributes, 'D'))
                attr |= fldStatusDELETE;
            if (strchr(attributes, 'A'))
                attr |= fldStatusARCHIVE;
            rec->SetStatus(attr);

            return rec;
        } else
            return 0;
    }
```

Although *WriteRecord* doesn't write any attributes, *ReadCustomer* must handle the possibility of reading them. You might wonder how attributes could have gotten into the file. The answer is simple—the user of the desktop application that edits our comma-delimited file may have changed this record. Since we support desktop editing of records, we need to know if a modification has occurred (for the next sync).

In such instances, the routine appends a value to the end of the record. *ReadCustomer* adds an `M` as a field at the end. If the record has been deleted, it doesn't remove the record line from the file; instead, it adds a `D` in the last field. If the record is archived, it adds an `A`, and new records get marked with an `N`. On the next sync, all these newly marked records are dealt with by the sync code. Note that the marking is almost completely analogous to the marking done on the handheld side.

## *CSalesSchema*

The schema class defines the number, ordering, and type of the fields. We also declare a number of constants and create one function.

### *Constants*

These constants define the field ordering within a row for the record information we save:

```
#define slFLDRecordID       0
#define slFLDStatus         1

#define slFLDCustomerID     2
#define slFLDName           3
#define slFLDAddress        4
#define slFLDCity           5
#define slFLDPhone          6

#define slFLDPrivate        7
```

```
#define slFLDPlacement       8
#define slFLDCategoryID      9

#define slFLDLast            slFLDCategoryID
```

### CSalesSchema class definition

This is very straightforward, with only one function to define:

```
class CSalesSchema : public CBaseSchema
{
public:
    virtual long  DiscoverSchema      (void);

};
```

### CSalesSchema functions

The *DiscoverSchema* function must set the number of fields per record, set the type of each record, and mark which fields contain the record ID, the attributes, and the category ID. Even though our Sales application keeps its records sorted by customer number, we are still required to reserve a field for the record number:

```
long CSalesSchema::DiscoverSchema(void)
{
    m_FieldsPerRow = slFLDLast + 1;

    m_FieldTypes.SetSize(m_FieldsPerRow);
    m_FieldTypes.SetAt(slFLDRecordID,        (WORD)eInteger);
    m_FieldTypes.SetAt(slFLDStatus,          (WORD)eInteger);

    m_FieldTypes.SetAt(slFLDCustomerID,      (WORD)eInteger);
    m_FieldTypes.SetAt(slFLDName,            (WORD)eString);
    m_FieldTypes.SetAt(slFLDAddress,         (WORD)eString);
    m_FieldTypes.SetAt(slFLDCity,            (WORD)eString);
    m_FieldTypes.SetAt(slFLDPhone,           (WORD)eString);
    m_FieldTypes.SetAt(slFLDPrivate,         (WORD)eBool);
    m_FieldTypes.SetAt(slFLDPlacement,       (WORD)eInteger);
    m_FieldTypes.SetAt(slFLDCategoryID,      (WORD)eInteger);

    // Be sure to set the 4 common fields' position
    m_RecordIdPos      = slFLDRecordID;
    m_RecordStatusPos = slFLDStatus;
    m_CategoryIdPos    = slFLDCategoryID;
    m_PlacementPos     = slFLDPlacement;

    return 0;
}
```

## CSalesRecord

CSalesRecord is based on the CBaseRecord class. This is the class that deals with records in the table. We have routines that get and set appropriate fields in the record.

### *CSalesRecord class definition*

The constructor takes a **wModAction** parameter, which it uses to initialize its base class. Other routines just get and set the values of a customer record:

```
class CSalesRecord : public CBaseRecord
{
protected:
    friend          CSalesTable;

public:
    CSalesRecord                (CSalesTable &rTable,
                                    WORD wModAction);

    long SetID                  (int ID);
    long SetName                (CString &csName);
    long SetAddress             (CString &csAddress);
    long SetCity                (CString &csCity);
    long SetPhone               (CString &csPhone);

    long SetPrivate             (BOOL bPrivate);

    long GetID                  (int &ID);
    long GetName                (CString &csName);
    long GetAddress             (CString &csAddress);
    long GetCity                (CString &csCity);
    long GetPhone               (CString &csPhone);

    BOOL IsPrivate              (void);

// required overrides
    virtual BOOL  operator==(const CBaseRecord&r);
    virtual long Assign(const CBaseRecord&r);
};
```

### *Class constructor*

The constructor doesn't do much:

```
CSalesRecord::CSalesRecord(
    CSalesTable &rTable,
    WORD wModAction
) : CBaseRecord(rTable, wModAction)
{
}
```

### *CSalesRecord functions*

There are a number of functions, all of which involve getting or setting records fields. There are routines that get or set the customer ID, name, address, city, and ZIP Code. There are also routines that compare records and assign the values of one record to another.

#### *Getting the customer ID*

Here's the routine that gets the value of the customer ID. It gets the appropriately numbered field (checking first to make sure the table is positioned at this record) and asks the field for the current value:

```
long CSalesRecord::GetID(int &customerID)
{
    CIntegerField* pFld;

    if (m_Positioned &&
        (pFld = (CIntegerField*) m_Fields.GetAt(slFLDCustomerID)) &&
        pFld->GetValue(customerID) == 0)
        return 0;
    else
        return DERR_RECORD_NOT_POSITIONED;
}
```

#### *Setting the customer ID*

Here's the routine that sets the customer ID. Note that if `m_wModAction` is equal to `MODFILTER_STUPID`, the code checks the value being set to see if it is equal to the current value—if it is, the update (modified) attribute of the status isn't set:

```
long CSalesRecord::SetID(int customerID)
{
    BOOL autoFlip    = FALSE;
    int  currStatus = 0;
    long retval      = DERR_RECORD_NOT_POSITIONED;
    CIntegerField* pFld = NULL;

    if (m_Positioned &&
        (pFld = (CIntegerField*) m_Fields.GetAt(slFLDCustomerID)))
    {
        if (m_wModAction == MODFILTER_STUPID)
        {
            GetStatus(currStatus);
            if (currStatus != fldStatusADD)
            {
                CIntegerField tmpFld(customerID);
                if (pFld->Compare(&tmpFld))
                    autoFlip = TRUE;
            }
        }
        if (!pFld->SetValue(customerID))
```

```
            {
                if (autoFlip)
                    SetStatus(fldStatusUPDATE);
                retval = 0;
            }
        }
        return retval;
    }
```

Because the routines to get and set the name, address, city, and ZIP, and private value are so similar to those for the customer ID, we are not bothering to show them.

### *Assigning one record to another*

We need an assign function that assigns one CSalesRecord to another. It copies all fields, including the record ID and attributes:

```
    long CSalesRecord::Assign(const CBaseRecord& rSubj)
    {
        if (!m_Positioned)
            return -1;
        for (int x=slFLDRecordID; x <= slFLDLast; x++)
        {
            CBaseField* pMyFld    = (CBaseField*) m_Fields.GetAt(x);
            CBaseField* pSubjFld =
                (CBaseField*) ((CSalesRecord&)rSubj).m_Fields.GetAt(x);
            if (pMyFld && pSubjFld)
                pMyFld->Assign(*pSubjFld);
        }
        return 0;
    }
```

### *Comparing one record to another*

The comparison routine (== operator) checks to see whether one CSalesRecord is equal to another (ignoring record ID and attributes):

```
    BOOL CSalesRecord::operator==(const CBaseRecord& rSubj)
    {
        if (!m_Positioned)
            return FALSE;
        for (int x=slFLDCustomerID; x <= slFLDLast; x++)
        {
            CBaseField* pMyFld    = (CBaseField*) m_Fields.GetAt(x);
            CBaseField* pSubjFld =
                (CBaseField*) ((CSalesRecord&)rSubj).m_Fields.GetAt(x);
            if (!pMyFld || !pSubjFld)
                return FALSE;
            if (pMyFld->Compare(pSubjFld) != 0)
                return FALSE;
        }
        return TRUE;
    }
```

## CSalesDTLinkConverter

This is the last class that we have in our conduit. It is the one responsible for converting a record from one format to another and vice versa. We have one function that converts a Palm OS handheld record into a CBaseRecord format, and another does the opposite.

### CSalesDTLinkConverter class definition

The definition is simple with just two functions:

```
class CSalesDTLinkConverter : public CBaseDTLinkConverter
{
public:
    CSalesDTLinkConverter(HINSTANCE hInst);

    long ConvertToRemote(CBaseRecord &rRec, CRawRecordInfo &rInfo);
    long ConvertFromRemote(CBaseRecord &rRec, CRawRecordInfo &rInfo);

};
```

The `HINSTANCE` parameter in the constructor is there so that the converter can obtain strings from the DLL resource file, if it needs to.

### CSalesDTLinkConverter constructor

Here's the constructor:

```
CSalesDTLinkConverter::CSalesDTLinkConverter(HINSTANCE hInst)
                         : CBaseDTLinkConverter(hInst)
{
}
```

### Converting to Palm record format

Here's the code that converts to a handheld record. Note that it must set the record ID, the category ID, and the attributes as well as write the record contents. We use a utility routine, *SwapDWordToMotor*, to swap the customer ID:

```
long CSalesDTLinkConverter::ConvertToRemote(CBaseRecord& rRec,
                                            CRawRecordInfo& rInfo)
{
    long            retval = 0;
    char            *pBuff;
    CString         tempStr;
    int             destLen, tempInt;
    char            *pSrc;
    int             customerID;

    CSalesRecord& rExpRec = (CSalesRecord &)rRec;
    rInfo.m_RecSize = 0;
```

```
// Convert the record ID and Category ID
retval = rExpRec.GetRecordId(tempInt);
rInfo.m_RecId = (long)tempInt;
retval = rExpRec.GetCategoryId(tempInt);
rInfo.m_CatId = tempInt;

// Convert the attributes
rInfo.m_Attribs = 0;
if (rExpRec.IsPrivate())
    rInfo.m_Attribs |= PRIVATE_BIT;
if (rExpRec.IsArchived())
    rInfo.m_Attribs |= ARCHIVE_BIT;
if (rExpRec.IsDeleted())
    rInfo.m_Attribs |= DELETE_BIT;
if (rExpRec.IsModified() || rExpRec.IsAdded())
    rInfo.m_Attribs |= DIRTY_BIT;

pBuff = (char*)rInfo.m_pBytes;

// customer ID
retval = rExpRec.GetID(customerID);
*((DWORD *)pBuff) = SwapDWordToMotor(customerID);
pBuff += sizeof(DWORD);
rInfo.m_RecSize += sizeof(DWORD);

// name
retval = rExpRec.GetName(tempStr);
    // Strip the CR's (if present) places result directly into pBuff
pSrc     = tempStr.GetBuffer(tempStr.GetLength());
destLen = StripCRs(pBuff, pSrc, tempStr.GetLength());
tempStr.ReleaseBuffer(-1);
pBuff += destLen;
rInfo.m_RecSize += destLen;

// address
retval = rExpRec.GetAddress(tempStr);
    // Strip the CR's (if present) places result directly into pBuff
pSrc     = tempStr.GetBuffer(tempStr.GetLength());
destLen = StripCRs(pBuff, pSrc, tempStr.GetLength());
tempStr.ReleaseBuffer(-1);
pBuff += destLen;
rInfo.m_RecSize += destLen;

// city
retval = rExpRec.GetCity(tempStr);
    // Strip the CR's (if present) places result directly into pBuff
pSrc     = tempStr.GetBuffer(tempStr.GetLength());
destLen = StripCRs(pBuff, pSrc, tempStr.GetLength());
tempStr.ReleaseBuffer(-1);
pBuff += destLen;
rInfo.m_RecSize += destLen;

// phone
retval = rExpRec.GetPhone(tempStr);
```

```
        // Strip the CR's (if present) places result directly into pBuff
    pSrc    = tempStr.GetBuffer(tempStr.GetLength());
    destLen = StripCRs(pBuff, pSrc, tempStr.GetLength());
    tempStr.ReleaseBuffer(-1);
    pBuff += destLen;
    rInfo.m_RecSize += destLen;

    return retval;
}
```

### *Converting to CBaseRecord format*

Here's the code that converts from a handheld record to a CBaseRecord format. Note that it must read the record ID, the category ID, the attributes, and the record contents. We use a utility routine, *SwapDWordToIntel*, to swap the customer ID. If the record is deleted, there are no record contents. We don't try to read the record contents in such cases.

```
long CSalesDTLinkConverter::ConvertFromRemote(
    CBaseRecord& rRec,
    CRawRecordInfo& rInfo)
 {
    long                retval = 0;
    char                *pBuff;
    CString             aString;

    CSalesRecord& rExpRec = (CSalesRecord &)rRec;

    retval = rExpRec.SetRecordId(rInfo.m_RecId);
    retval = rExpRec.SetCategoryId(rInfo.m_CatId);
    if (rInfo.m_Attribs & ARCHIVE_BIT)
        retval = rExpRec.SetArchiveBit(TRUE);
    else
        retval = rExpRec.SetArchiveBit(FALSE);

    if (rInfo.m_Attribs & PRIVATE_BIT)
        retval = rExpRec.SetPrivate(TRUE);
    else
        retval = rExpRec.SetPrivate(FALSE);

    retval = rExpRec.SetStatus(fldStatusNONE);
    if (rInfo.m_Attribs & DELETE_BIT) // Delete flag
        retval = rExpRec.SetStatus(fldStatusDELETE);
    else if (rInfo.m_Attribs & DIRTY_BIT) // Dirty flag
        retval = rExpRec.SetStatus(fldStatusUPDATE);

    // Only convert body if remote record is *not* deleted..
    if (!(rInfo.m_Attribs & DELETE_BIT))
    {
        pBuff = (char*)rInfo.m_pBytes;

        //  Customer ID
        long customerID = SwapDWordToIntel(*((DWORD*)pBuff));
```

```
        retval = rExpRec.SetID(customerID);
        pBuff += sizeof(DWORD);

        // Name
        AddCRs(pBuff, strlen(pBuff));
        aString = m_TransBuff;
        retval = rExpRec.SetName(aString);
        pBuff += strlen(pBuff) + 1;

        // Address
        AddCRs(pBuff, strlen(pBuff));
        aString = m_TransBuff;
        retval = rExpRec.SetAddress(aString);
        pBuff += strlen(pBuff) + 1;

        // City
        AddCRs(pBuff, strlen(pBuff));
        aString = m_TransBuff;
        retval = rExpRec.SetCity(aString);
        pBuff += strlen(pBuff) + 1;

        // Phone
        AddCRs(pBuff, strlen(pBuff));
        aString = m_TransBuff;
        retval = rExpRec.SetPhone(aString);
        pBuff += strlen(pBuff) + 1;
    }
    return retval ;
}
```

## The DLL

The one remaining piece in our puzzle is the DLL where the CSalesConduitMonitor actually gets created.

### DLL OpenConduit

DLL's *OpenConduit* is where we put the conduit creation code:

```
__declspec(dllexport) long OpenConduit(PROGRESSFN pFn,
    CSyncProperties& rProps)
{
    AFX_MANAGE_STATE(AfxGetStaticModuleState());

    long retval = -1;

    rProps.m_DbType = 'Cust';// in case it needs to be created
    if (pFn) {
        CSalesConduitMonitor* pMonitor;

        pMonitor = new CSalesConduitMonitor(pFn, rProps, myInst);
        if (pMonitor)
        {
            retval = pMonitor->Engage();
```

```
                delete pMonitor;
            }
        }
        return retval;
    }
```

Note that we set the `m_DbType` field of `rProps`. We do this so that *CBaseConduit-Monitor* will create the customer database on the handheld if it doesn't exist; it uses the type found in `rProps.m_DbType` to do the job.

We also pass our DLL's instance, `myInst`, as the third parameter. It is used to retrieve resource strings. The instance is stored as a global variable, along with three others:

```
static int ClientCount = 0;
static HINSTANCE hRscInstance = 0;
static HINSTANCE hDLLInstance = 0;
HINSTANCE myInst=0;
```

These globals are initialized when the DLL is opened.

### DLL class definition

Here's our DLL's class declaration (as created automatically by Visual C++):

```
class CSalesCondDll : public CWinApp
{
public:
    //CSalesCondDll();
    virtual BOOL InitInstance(); // Initialization
    virtual int ExitInstance();  // Termination

// Overrides
    // ClassWizard generated virtual function overrides
    //{{AFX_VIRTUAL(CSalesCondDll)
    //}}AFX_VIRTUAL

    //{{AFX_MSG(CSalesCondDll)
        // NOTE - the ClassWizard will add/remove member functions here.
        //    DO NOT EDIT what you see in these blocks of generated code !
    //}}AFX_MSG
    DECLARE_MESSAGE_MAP()
};
```

### Initializing function

*InitInstance* must initialize the table's DLL. This contains some field functions beyond those in the *basetable.cpp* file. It must also initialize the PDCmn DLL, which contains some resources for the dialog shown in *ConfigureConduit*:

```
BOOL CSalesCondDll::InitInstance()
{
    // DLL initialization
    TRACE0("SALESCOND.DLL initializing\n");
```

```
    if (!ClientCount ) {
        hDLLInstance = AfxGetInstanceHandle();

        hRscInstance = hDLLInstance;

        // add any extension DLLs into CDynLinkLibrary chain
        InitTables5DLL();
        InitPdcmn5DLL();
    }
    myInst = hRscInstance;
    ClientCount++;

    return TRUE;
}
```

### *Exit function*

We also need an *ExitInstance*:

```
int CSalesCondDll::ExitInstance()
{
    TRACE0("SALESCOND.DLL Terminating!\n");

    // Check for last client and clean up potential memory leak.
    if (--ClientCount <= 0)
    {
        PalmFreeLanguage(hRscInstance, hDLLInstance);
        hRscInstance = hDLLInstance;
    }

    // DLL clean up, if required
    return CWinApp::ExitInstance();
}
```

### *DLL resources*

There are a variety of strings that the Conduit Manager loads from resources (including all the logging strings). These strings have to be stored within our DLL. In our resource file, *SalesCond.rc*, we don't have any explicit resources. Instead, in the Resource Includes panel, we add a compile-time directive:

```
#include "..\include\Res\R_English\Basemon.rc"
```

This makes all the standard *basemon* resource strings part of our DLL.

## *Testing the Conduit*

Before testing, make sure you use *CondCfg.exe* to register the Remote Database name for the Sales conduit as "Customers-Sles". This is what tells your conduit what database to sync.

There are some good tests you can perform to ensure that your conduit is working properly:

*Sync having never run your application*
: Your database(s) won't yet exist. This simulates a user syncing after installing your software but before using it. If your conduit performs correctly, any data from the desktop should be copied to the handheld.

*Sync having run your application once*
: Do this test after first deleting your databases. This simulates a user syncing after installing your software and using it. If everything works as expected, data from the handheld should be copied to the desktop.

*Add a record on the handheld and sync*
: Make sure the new record gets added to the desktop.

*Add a record on the desktop and sync*
: Make sure the new record gets added to the handheld.

*Delete a record on the handheld and sync*
: Make sure the record gets deleted from the desktop.

*Delete a record on the desktop and sync*
: Make sure the record gets deleted from the handheld.

*Archive a record on the handheld*
: Make sure the record gets deleted from the main desktop file and gets added to the archive.

There are other tests you can make, but these provide the place to begin.

# Generic Conduit

Generic Conduit is the other approach to creating a conduit that handles two-way syncing. It is based on a new set of classes (currently unsupported) that Palm Computing has recently started distributing. Having seen all that is involved in creating a conduit based on the *basemon* and *basetabl* classes, you can understand why Palm Computing wanted to offer a simpler solution to developers. Generic Conduit is one of Palm's solutions to this problem—these classes are intended to make it easier to get a conduit up and running.

## Advantages of Using Generic Conduit

There are some powerfully persuasive advantages to basing a conduit on these new classes:

*In some cases, you don't need to write any code*
: Generic Conduit contains everything, including *ConfigureConduit*, *GetConduitName*, etc. If you compile and register it, it'll be happy to two-way sync

your Palm database to a file on the desktop. This approach requires the use of its own file format, however. If you don't like that format, you need to customize the Generic Conduit classes to some extent.

*If you do have to write code, it might not be much*
: The number of classes and the number of methods are much less daunting than those found in the *basemon* and *basetabl* classes.

*All the source code is available*
: The entire source code is provided; you don't have to rely on any DLLs (*basemon* uses *Tables.DLL* for the CBaseTable class and MFC for serialization). Further, if you so desire, you can change any or all of the source code.

*There's less work involved in handling records*
: Generic Conduit is unlike *basemon*, which has a schema and attempts to represent your record as fields in memory. Generic Conduit treats your record as just a sequence of bytes. Thus, records are copied from the handheld to the desktop and left untouched; the default file format stores them as is. Record comparison is accomplished by comparing all the bytes in each record to see if they are identical. This is a far cry from *basemon*'s approach, which represents records in memory as fields and does field-by-field comparison.

*The approach to conduit creation makes more sense*
: This Generic Conduit approach makes a great deal of sense. All that's needed for synchronization to work correctly is to compare two records to see whether they are the same or different. There's no need to know what fields exist or anything else; you just compare the bytes.

## Disadvantages of Using Generic Conduit

There are also disadvantages to this approach. The good news is that they may possibly fade over time:

*Generic Conduit is not supported by Palm*
: Palm Computing provides the Generic Conduit code as an unsupported sample. The supported way to do two-way syncing is with the *basemon* classes. It is certainly worth checking for the latest version of Generic Conduit and Palm's current support position before making a decision regarding its use (see *http://www.Palm.com/devzone* for information).

*It's new*
: The *basemon* classes are used for Palm's shipping conduits and by numerous third parties. That means they work very well, and, presumably, most of the bugs have already been found and fixed. If you're an early user of Generic Conduit, you are at risk for as yet unfound bugs of who knows what nature.

Once again, it is worth checking on the most recent version of Generic Conduit—as time passes this will become less of a problem.

*The suggested way to create conduits is duplicate/modify*

Palm Computing's suggested way to use the Generic Conduit is to duplicate the Generic Conduit source folder and then go to work making changes to their source. This approach flies in the face of good C++ inheritance programming practices, which should be to derive classes from the Generic Conduit classes and override only those routines that require modification.

Here is why this approach has two major problems:

— If and when changes are made to the Generic Conduit classes (for example, bug fixes or added features), the source code to every single Generic Conduit–based conduit will need to incorporate those changes. You, the developer, need to apply any changes that were made in the Generic Conduit code to your own modified version of the code.

  On the other hand, in our subclassing model, the conduits just need to be recompiled to take advantage of the newly changed code.

— Sample conduits are massive. The Generic Conduit comes with two samples: one for the address book and one for the date book. Unfortunately, these two samples have as much additional code as the Generic Conduit itself (actually, they have more, since they've got all the code from the Generic Conduit plus their own specific code). This intermingled code in the samples means they are very bad guides to creating a conduit. It is wretchedly difficult to figure out which code is for the conduit and which is specifically for the address book. Until you do, you won't know what needs to be done to write a new conduit.

## Solution to the Disadvantages

We can't do anything about the first two problems (only time and Palm Computing have control of these issues), but we can address the third problem. Our sample that uses the Generic Conduit doesn't duplicate the original code; instead, it makes use of derived classes and virtual functions—our code consists only of the differences from the original. By doing this, we can easily use new versions of the Generic Conduit classes, and it should be very easy for you to use our code as a sample for creating a conduit.

## Generic Conduit Classes

There are eight classes that affect your use of Generic Conduit. As might be expected, each has a different responsibility. Figure 13-2 shows you the inheritance relationship.

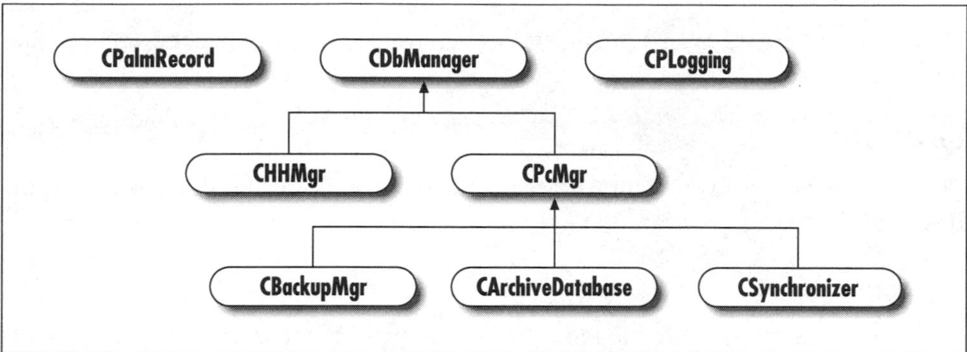


*Figure 13-2. Inheritance relationship of Generic Conduit classes*

Now let's look at what each class does.

### *CPalmRecord*

This represents a Palm record; it stores attributes, a unique ID, a category number, a record length, and a pointer to the raw record data.

### *CDbManager*

This is the class that is responsible for a database. It defines methods for iterating through the records, adding and deleting records, etc. As you can see from Figure 13-2, it is also an abstract class; there are four derived classes that implement these methods.

### *CHHMgr*

This class is derived from CDbManager and implements the CDbManager member functions by using the Sync Manager. This concrete subclass uses the interface of the abstract class. It can be used just like any other database, but its implementation is different. For example, its method to add a record is implemented using *SyncWriteRec*.

### *CPcMgr*

This class implements the CDbManager member functions for a file on the desktop. When a file is opened, it reads all the records into memory and stores them in a list. Changes to the database are reflected in memory until the database is closed; at that point, the records are rewritten to the database.

You often create your own derived class of CPcMgr and override the functions *RetrieveDB* and *StoreDB* to read and write your own file formats.

#### *CArchiveDatabase*

This class is derived from CPcMgr. It is responsible for handling the archive files on the desktop.

#### *CBackupMgr*

This class is also derived from CPcMgr. It is responsible for the backup file on the desktop.

#### *CPLogging*

This class is responsible for logging when any type of failure occurs during syncing.

#### *CSynchronizer*

This class is responsible for handling the actual synchronization. It creates the database classes and manages the entire process (it has many of the same duties as CBaseConduitMonitor). You often override one of its member functions, *CreateDBManager*, to create your own class derived from CPcMgr.

Amazing as it may seem, that is all there is worth noting about the Generic Conduit classes. Now let's turn to the code based on Generic Conduit that we create for the Sales application conduit.

# *Sales Conduit Based on Generic Conduit*

This sample was based on an early beta version of the Generic Conduit and may not compile with the version available to you. For a more current version of the sample, see *http://www.oreilly.com/catalog/palmprog/*.

## *CSalesPCMgr*

We have derived a new class from CPcMgr, because we want to support the same a tab-delimited text format we used with the alternative conduit classes. Here is our new class:

```
class CSalesPcMgr: public CPcMgr
{
public:
    CSalesPcMgr(CPLogging *pLogging, char *szDbName,
      TCHAR *pFileName = NULL, TCHAR *pDirName = NULL,
```

```
        DWORD dwGenericFlags,
        eSyncTypes syncType = eDoNothing);

protected:
    virtual long StoreDB(void);
    virtual long RetrieveDB(void);
};
```

### *CSalesPCMgr constructor*

Our constructor just initializes the base class:

```
CSalesPcMgr::CSalesPcMgr(CPLogging *pLogging, char *szDbName,
   TCHAR *pFileName, TCHAR *pDirName,
   DWORD dwGenericFlags, eSyncTypes syncType)
   :CPcMgr(pLogging, szDbName, pFileName, pDirName, dwGenericFlags,
      syncType)
{
}
```

### *StoreDB function*

Our *StoreDB* routine writes the list of records in text-delimited format:

```
long CSalesPcMgr::StoreDB(void)
{
   if ( !m_bNeedToSave) { // if no changes, don't waste time saving
       return 0;
   }

    long retval = OpenDB();
    if (retval)
        return GEN_ERR_UNABLE_TO_SAVE;

    for (DWORD dwIndex = 0; (dwIndex < m_dwMaxRecordCount) && (!retval);
       dwIndex++){
        if (!m_pRecordList[dwIndex]) // if there is no record, skip ahead
            continue;
        retval = WriteRecord(m_hFile, m_pRecordList[dwIndex]);

        if (retval != 0){
            CloseDB();
            return GEN_ERR_UNABLE_TO_SAVE;
        }
    }

    CloseDB();
    m_bNeedToSave = FALSE;
    return 0;
}
```

It calls *WriteRecord*, which writes line by line.

### WriteRecord

This writes the record:

```
long WriteRecord(HANDLE hFile, CPalmRecord *pPalmRec)
{

    DWORD           dwPut;
    unsigned long   len;
    const int       kMaxRecordSize = 1000;
    char            buf[kMaxRecordSize];
    char            rawRecord[kMaxRecordSize];
    DWORD           recordSize = kMaxRecordSize;
    long            retval;

    retval = pPalmRec->GetRawData((unsigned char *) rawRecord,
       &recordSize);
    if (retval) {
        return retval;
    }

    Customer *aCustomer = RawRecordToCustomer(rawRecord);


    // Write the record to the file as (if private):
    // <customerID>\t<name>\t<address>\t<city>\t<phone>\tP\t<recID>
    //    or, if not private:
    // <customerID>\t<name>\t<address>\t<city>\t<phone>\t\t<recID>
    sprintf(
        buf,
        "%d\t%s\t%s\t%s\t%s\t%s\t%d\r\n",
        aCustomer->customerID,
        aCustomer->name,
        aCustomer->address,
        aCustomer->city,
        aCustomer->phone,
        pPalmRec->IsPrivate() ? "P": "",
        pPalmRec->GetID()
    );
    len = strlen(buf);
    WriteFile(
        hFile,
        buf,
        len,
        &dwPut,
        NULL
    );

    delete aCustomer;

    return dwPut == len ? 0 : GEN_ERR_UNABLE_TO_SAVE;
}
```

It calls *RawRecordToCustomer*, which converts the bytes in a record to a customer:

```
Customer *RawRecordToCustomer(void *rec)
{
    Customer *c = new Customer;
    PackedCustomer *pc = (PackedCustomer *) rec;
    c->customerID = SyncHHToHostDWord(pc->customerID);
    char * p = (char *) pc->name;
    c->name = new char[strlen(p)+1];
    strcpy(c->name, p);
    p += strlen(p) + 1;
    c->address = new char[strlen(p)+1];
    strcpy(c->address, p);
    p += strlen(p) + 1;
    c->city = new char[strlen(p)+1];
    strcpy(c->city, p);
    p += strlen(p) + 1;
    c->phone = new char[strlen(p)+1];
    strcpy(c->phone, p);
    return c;
}
```

### *Retrieving a database*

We also have a function, *RetrieveDB*, that reads a text file and creates records from it. Even though `m_HFile` is already an open `HFILE` that we could read, it's easier to do it another way. We read text from a *CStdioFile* (it provides a routine to read a line at a time), so we open the file read-only with *CStdioFile* and close it once we're done:

```
long CSalesPcMgr::RetrieveDB(void)
{
    m_bNeedToSave = FALSE;
    if (!_tcslen(m_szDataFile))
        return GEN_ERR_INVALID_DB_NAME;

    CStdioFile *file = 0;
    TRY
    {
        file = new CStdioFile(m_szDataFile, CFile::modeRead);
    }
    CATCH_ALL(e)
    {
        if (file)
            file->Abort();
        delete file;

        return GEN_ERR_READING_RECORD;
    }
    END_CATCH_ALL

    TRY
```

```
    {
        CPalmRecord newRecord;
        while (ReadCustomer(*file, newRecord)) {
            AddRec(newRecord);
        }
        file->Close();
    }
    CATCH_ALL(e)
    {
        file->Abort();
        delete file;
        return GEN_ERR_READING_RECORD;
    }
    END_CATCH_ALL
    delete file;

    return 0;

}
```

### *Reading customer information*

The previous routine relies on a utility routine that we need to write. This routine simply reads in the tab-delimited text file and turns it into a Palm record:

```
bool ReadCustomer(CStdioFile &file, CPalmRecord &rec)
{
    static char gBigBuffer[4096];
    if (file.ReadString(gBigBuffer, sizeof(gBigBuffer)) == NULL)
        return false;
    char *p = gBigBuffer;
    char *customerID = FindUpToNextTab(&p);
    char *name = FindUpToNextTab(&p);
    char *address = FindUpToNextTab(&p);
    char *city = FindUpToNextTab(&p);
    char *phone = FindUpToNextTab(&p);
    char *priv = FindUpToNextTab(&p);
    char *uniqueID = FindUpToNextTab(&p);
    char *attributes = FindUpToNextTab(&p);

    if (!address)
        address = "";
    if (!city)
        city = "";
    if (!phone)
        phone = "";
    if (!priv)
        priv = "";
    if (!attributes)
        attributes = "";
    if (!uniqueID)
        uniqueID = "0";
    if (customerID && name) {
        rec.SetID(atol(customerID));
```

```
            rec.SetIndex(-1);
            rec.SetCategory(0);

            rec.SetPrivate(*priv == 'P');

            // 'N' -- new, 'M' -- modify, 'D'-- delete, 'A' -- archive
            // if it's Add, it can't be modify
            rec.ResetAttribs();
            if (strchr(attributes, 'N'))
                rec.SetNew();
            else if (strchr(attributes, 'M'))
                rec.SetUpdate();
            if (strchr(attributes, 'D'))
                rec.SetDeleted();
            if (strchr(attributes, 'A'))
                rec.SetArchived();

            static char buf[4096];
            PackedCustomer *pc = (PackedCustomer *) buf;
            pc->customerID = SyncHostToHHDWord(atol(customerID));
            char *p = (char *) pc->name;
            strcpy(p, name);
            p += strlen(p) + 1;
            strcpy(p, address);
            p += strlen(p) + 1;
            strcpy(p, city);
            p += strlen(p) + 1;
            strcpy(p, phone);
            p += strlen(p) + 1;

            rec.SetRawData(p - buf, (unsigned char *) buf);

            return true;
        } else
            return false;
    }
```

## CSalesSynchronizer

We also have a derived a class from CSynchronizer, because we want to do three things:

- Create our derived class of CPcMgr.
- Set a bit field specifying that we don't use the AppInfo block (for sort info or categories).
- Copy our orders database from the handheld and our products database to the handheld.

Unlike the previous occasion, we don't have to perform a bunch of copying tricks to handle a simple override. Everything works as expected.

### Class definition

Here's our class declaration of CSalesSynchronizer:

```
class CSalesSynchronizer: public CSynchronizer {
public:
    CSalesSynchronizer(CSyncProperties& rProps);

protected:
    virtual long Perform(void);
    virtual long CreatePCManager(void);
};
```

### Creating a CSalesPcMgr class

Here's the routine that creates a CSalesPcMgr:

```
long CSalesSynchronizer::CreatePCManager(void)
{
    DeletePCManager();

    m_dbPC = new CSalesPcMgr(m_pLog,
                         m_remoteDB->m_Name,
                         m_rSyncProperties.m_LocalName,
                         m_rSyncProperties.m_PathName,
                         m_dwDatabaseFlags
                         m_rSyncProperties.m_SyncType);
    if (!m_dbPC)
        return GEN_ERR_LOW_MEMORY;
    return m_dbPC->Open();
}
```

### The constructor

Our constructor sets the bit field, specifying that we don't support categories, or the AppInfo block or the sort info block:

```
CSalesSynchronizer::CSalesSynchronizer(CSyncProperties& rProps) :
    CSynchronizer(rProps)
{
    // m_dwDatabaseFlags is a bit-field with
    //    GENERIC_FLAG_CATEGORY_SUPPORTED
    //    GENERIC_FLAG_APPINFO_SUPPORTED
    //    GENERIC_FLAG_SORTINFO_SUPPORTED

    // we don't want any of the flags set, so we just use 0
    m_dwDatabaseFlags = 0;
}
```

### Modifying perform to add uploading and downloading products and orders

As we found in the *basemon* case, there's a fairly large routine that opens the conduit, does the appropriate kind of syncing, and closes the conduit. We need to insert our code to copy the Products database and Orders database in there. We've copied that routine and inserted our code (our added code is bold):

```
long CSalesSynchronizer::Perform(void)
{
    long retval = 0;
    long retval2 = 0;

    if (m_rSyncProperties.m_SyncType > eProfileInstall)
        return GEN_ERR_BAD_SYNC_TYPE;


    if (m_rSyncProperties.m_SyncType == eDoNothing) {
        return 0;
    }
    // Obtain System Information
    m_SystemInfo.m_ProductIdText = (BYTE*) new char [MAX_PROD_ID_TEXT];
    if (!m_SystemInfo.m_ProductIdText)
        return GEN_ERR_LOW_MEMORY;
    m_SystemInfo.m_AllocedLen = (BYTE) MAX_PROD_ID_TEXT;
    retval = SyncReadSystemInfo(m_SystemInfo);
    if (retval)
        return retval;

    retval = RegisterConduit();
    if (retval)
        return retval;



    for (int iCount=0; iCount < m_TotRemoteDBs && !retval; iCount++) {
        retval = GetRemoteDBInfo(iCount);
        if (retval) {
            retval = 0;
            break;
        }

        switch (m_rSyncProperties.m_SyncType) {
            case eFast:
                retval = PerformFastSync();
                if ((retval) && (retval == GEN_ERR_CHANGE_SYNC_MODE)){
                    if (GetSyncMode() == eHHtoPC)
                        retval = CopyHHtoPC();
                    else if (GetSyncMode() == ePCtoHH)
                        retval = CopyPCtoHH();
                }
                break;
            case eSlow:
                retval = PerformSlowSync();
                if ((retval) && (retval == GEN_ERR_CHANGE_SYNC_MODE)){
                    if (GetSyncMode() == eHHtoPC)
                        retval = CopyHHtoPC();
                    else if (GetSyncMode() == ePCtoHH)
                        retval = CopyPCtoHH();
```

```
                }
                break;
            case eHHtoPC:
            case eBackup:
                retval = CopyHHtoPC();
                break;
            case eInstall:
            case ePCtoHH:
            case eProfileInstall:
                retval = CopyPCtoHH();
                break;
            case eDoNothing:
                break;
            default:
                retval = GEN_ERR_SYNC_TYPE_NOT_SUPPORTED;
                break;
        }

        DeleteHHManager();
        DeletePCManager();
        DeleteBackupManager();
        CloseArchives();
    }

// added here for sales conduit
    if (retval == 0 && m_rSyncProperties.m_SyncType == eHHtoPC ||
        m_rSyncProperties.m_SyncType == eFast ||
        m_rSyncProperties.m_SyncType == eSlow)
        retval = CopyOrdersFromHH(m_rSyncProperties);
    if (retval == 0 && m_rSyncProperties.m_SyncType == ePCtoHH ||
        m_rSyncProperties.m_SyncType == eFast ||
        m_rSyncProperties.m_SyncType == eSlow)
        retval = CopyProductsAndCategoriesToHH(m_rSyncProperties);
// done added here for sales conduit
// Unregister the conduit
    retval2 = UnregisterConduit((BOOL)(retval != 0));

    if (!retval)
        return retval2;
    return retval;
}
```

## *Creating the Conduit*

In our *OpenConduit* DLL entry point, we create our CSalesSynchronizer and call it's *Perform* function to do the work of synchronization:

```
ExportFunc long OpenConduit(PROGRESSFN pFn, CSyncProperties& rProps)
{
    long retval = -1;
    if (pFn)
    {
        CSalesSynchronizer* pGeneric;
```

```
            pGeneric = new CSalesSynchronizer(rProps);
            if (pGeneric){
                retval = pGeneric->Perform();

                delete pGeneric;
            }

        }
        return(retval);
    }
```

At this point, we can test the code. It works just as the *basemon* version did, so we will use the same tests.

As you can see, Generic Conduit makes the task of supporting two-way mirror image syncing much easier. It is simpler to derive classes, since there are no real problems with functions that should be virtual that are not. In either case, we hope that it is clearer how to add support for two-way syncing after this description of each method.

# 14

# Debugging Conduits

*In this chapter:*
- *HotSync Flags*
- *Source-Level Debugging*
- *Avoiding Timeouts While Debugging*
- *Conduit Problems You Might Have*
- *Test with POSE*
- *Turn Off Other Conduits During Testing*
- *Use the Log, Luke*

Two of the most important tools you have in your debugging arsenal are a number of flags you can set during a sync and source-level debugging in CodeWarrior. After we discuss these, we give some advice on specific problems you might encounter.

Last but not least, we will look at how to clean things up. Mucking about in your conduit code is a good way to mess things up; we show you how to tidy up the registry when you are through.

## HotSync Flags

You can launch a sync with several different flags that give you information on what is occurring. These useful flags are:

`-v` Verbose mode

`-L1` Different verbose mode

`-L2` Different verbose mode with packet information

Besides these flags there is another flag, `-c`, that you can use to verify your connection.

### Running HotSync in Verbose Mode with -v

If you want to run HotSync in verbose mode, you set the `-v` flag by hand from the Run dialog:

```
c:\PalmDesktopDir\hotsync.exe -v
```

If you are already running HotSync, you need to exit before you can launch it by hand. Just choose Exit from the menu (see Figure 14-1).

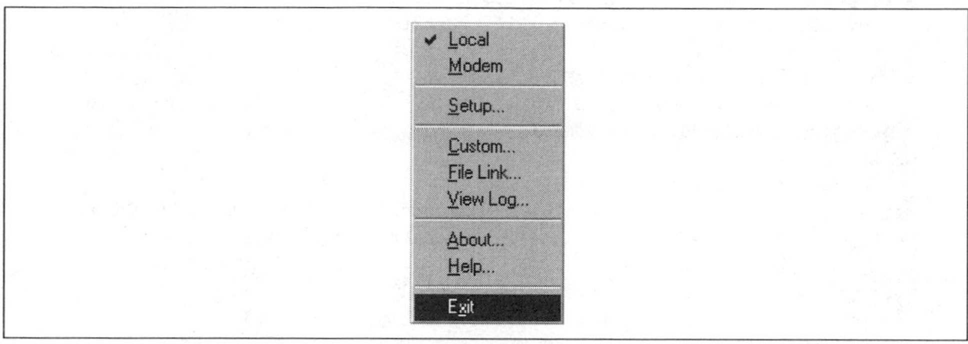


*Figure 14-1. Exiting the running version of HotSync*

Once you are in HotSync verbose mode, the log contains a great deal of additional information regarding its activities. Here's an example verbose log (abridged for space):

```
---Initializing User Manager---
---Discovering Communication State---
---Identifying Viewer user---
Found user name
---Establishing Sync Locale---
---Performing HotSync---
   Validating User.
   User match exists.
HotSync started 07/31/98 11:52:13
Setting up local HotSync environment.
   User is  Fen Rhodes
ROM Listing
   System                          0001 70737973 02/20/1998 02/20/1998 0003
   AMX                             0001 70737973 02/20/1998 02/20/1998 0003
   UIAppShell                      0001 70737973 02/20/1998 02/20/1998 0003
...
   Mail                            0002 6D61696C 02/20/1998 02/20/1998 0003
   Expense                         0001 65787073 02/20/1998 02/20/1998 0003
RAM Listing
   Unsaved Preferences             0000 70737973 04/14/1998 07/30/1998 0001
   Net Prefs                       0000 6E65746C 04/14/1998 06/29/1998 0001
...
   Sales                           0001 536C6573 07/30/1998 07/30/1998 0001
   Sles_Customers                  0000 536C6573 07/30/1998 07/30/1998 0000
   Sles_Orders                     0000 536C6573 07/30/1998 07/30/1998 0000
   Sles_Products                   0000 536C6573 07/30/1998 07/30/1998 0000
Attempting to Sync with Conduit:  datcn20.dll
   Key is Software\U.S. Robotics\Pilot Desktop\Component0
   Sync type is Fast
Local path is C:\Pilot\RhodesF\datebook\
   Remote name 0 is DatebookDB
   Loading   datcn20.dll   conduit
OK Date Book
   Conduit successful
```

```
Attempting to Sync with Conduit:  addcn20.dll
   Key is Software\U.S. Robotics\Pilot Desktop\Component1
   Sync type is Fast
Local path is C:\Pilot\RhodesF\address\
   Remote name 0 is AddressDB
   Loading  addcn20.dll  conduit
OK Address Book
   Conduit successful
Attempting to Sync with Conduit:  d:\poscond\todcnd21\debug\todcn20d.dll
   Key is Software\U.S. Robotics\Pilot Desktop\Component2
   Sync type is Fast
Attempting to Sync with Conduit:  memcn20.dll
   Key is Software\U.S. Robotics\Pilot Desktop\Component3
   Sync type is Fast
Local path is C:\Pilot\RhodesF\memopad\
   Remote name 0 is MemoDB
   Loading  memcn20.dll  conduit
OK Memo Pad
   Conduit successful
Attempting to Sync with Conduit:  bakcn20.dll
   No Registry Key
   Sync type is Backup
Local path is C:\Pilot\RhodesF\Backup\
   Remote name 0 is System MIDI Sounds
   Remote name 1 is Saved Preferences
   Remote name 2 is Graffiti ShortCuts
   Remote name 3 is NetworkDB
   Remote name 4 is LauncherDB
   Loading  bakcn20.dll  conduit
OK System
   Set PC ID and last sync time on Palm organizer
Cleaning up local HotSync environment
```

The log has two very useful pieces of information:

- A list of all the databases
- An entry whenever a conduit is about to be synced to

## A Different Verbose Mode with -L1

HotSync 3.0 and later versions have two additional verbose mode flags: `-L1` and `-L2`. Although some of the messages printed when using the `-v` flag are printed when using either of these new flags, not all are. Therefore, you may want to use `-L1` or `-L2` in addition to the `-v` flag.

When you use the `-L1` or `-L2` flags, the *HotSync.log* file is located in the top-level directory. It is located with *HotSync.exe* (as opposed to its normal location within the user's directory).

Here's an example output from using the -L1 flag:

```
A Direct serial connection is pending  08/01/98 14:40:49
Establishing Connection with the Palm organizer
Direct Serial Connection: Baud rate = 57600

Port speed is 57600 bps
Initialized Sync Manager Successfully

---Initializing User Manager---
---Discovering Communication State---
---Identifying Viewer user---
 An account is found for Palm organizer user: Fen Rhodes

The primary Hotsync PC for this user is unknown

---Establishing Sync Locale---
---Performing HotSync---
   Validating User.
   User match exists.
HotSync started 08/01/98 14:40:52
Setting up local HotSync environment.
   User is  Fen Rhodes
Attempting to Sync with Conduit:  datcn20.dll
   Key is Software\U.S. Robotics\Pilot Desktop\Component0
   Sync type is Fast
Local path is C:\Pilot\RhodesF\datebook\
   Remote name 0 is DatebookDB
   Loading   datcn20.dll   conduit
   Conduit failed
Attempting to Sync with Conduit:  addcn20.dll
   Key is Software\U.S. Robotics\Pilot Desktop\Component1
   Sync type is Fast
Local path is C:\Pilot\RhodesF\address\
   Remote name 0 is AddressDB
   Loading   addcn20.dll   conduit
   Conduit failed
Attempting to Sync with Conduit:  d:\poscond\todcnd21\debug\todcn20d.dll
   Key is Software\U.S. Robotics\Pilot Desktop\Component2
   Sync type is Fast
Local path is C:\Pilot\RhodesF\todo\
   Remote name 0 is ToDoDB
   Loading   d:\poscond\todcnd21\debug\todcn20d.dll   conduit

Trying to open database: ToDoDB
 08/01/98 14:41:08
OK To Do List
   Conduit successful
Attempting to Sync with Conduit:  memcn20.dll
   Key is Software\U.S. Robotics\Pilot Desktop\Component3
   Sync type is Fast
Local path is C:\Pilot\RhodesF\memopad\
   Remote name 0 is MemoDB
   Loading   memcn20.dll   conduit
   Conduit failed
```

```
Attempting to Sync with Conduit:  C:\SalesCond\Debug\SalesCond.DLL
   Key is Software\U.S. Robotics\Pilot Desktop\Component4
   Sync type is Do Nothing
Local path is C:\Pilot\RhodesF\Sales\
   Remote name 0 is CustomerDB
   Invalid conduit version
   Loading   C:\SalesCond\Debug\SalesCond.DLL   conduit
Sales - sync configured to Do Nothing
   Conduit successful
Attempting to Sync with Conduit:  bakcn20.dll
   No Registry Key
   Sync type is Backup
Local path is C:\Pilot\RhodesF\Backup\
   Remote name 0 is System MIDI Sounds
   Remote name 1 is Saved Preferences
   Remote name 2 is Graffiti ShortCuts
   Remote name 3 is NetworkDB
   Remote name 4 is LauncherDB
   Loading   bakcn20.dll   conduit
```

The -L1 flag includes, among other things, the baud rate at which the connection was made.

## *A Different Verbose Mode with Packets Using -L2*

The -L2 flag includes all the output from -L1 plus a trace of all the packets sent to and received from the handheld. Please note that the log becomes quite large. Here's a small excerpt of some output:

```
A Direct serial connection is pending  08/01/98 14:47:38
Establishing Connection with the Palm organizer
Direct Serial Connection: Baud rate = 57600

Port speed is 57600 bps
Sending Command ReadSysInfo . Packet size = 8
Packet Trace:
12 01 20 04 00 01 00 02                                    | .. .....

Response Received. Packet size = 34
Packet Trace:
92 02 00 00 20 0E 03 00   30 00 00 01 00 00 00 04          | .... ...0.......
00 01 00 00 21 0C 00 01   00 02 00 03 00 00 00 00          | ....!..........

Initialized Sync Manager Successfully

---Initializing User Manager---
---Discovering Communication State---
Sending Command (null) . Packet size = 14
Packet Trace:
39 01 22 0A 00 80 68 74   61 6C 68 74 63 70                | 9."...htalhtcp

Response Received. Packet size = 4
Packet Trace:
B9 00 00 05                                                | ....
```

```
Sending Command ReadFeature . Packet size = 10
Packet Trace:
38 01 20 06 6E 65 74 6C   00 00                        | 8. .netl..

Response Received. Packet size = 10
Packet Trace:
B8 01 00 00 20 04 02 00   30 00                        | .... ...0.
```

We can't think of a reason you'd need to see the packets going back and forth between HotSync and the handheld, but we've provided this option for completeness.

### *Quick-Connect Mode*

HotSync 3.0 and later versions have a `-c` flag that immediately disconnects from the Palm OS handheld after connecting and obtaining the user name. This is a handy way to verify your connection to the handheld.

### *Rebuilding the Registry*

Occasionally, you may find that your Conduit Registry is totally fouled or that you've unregistered (or changed) one or more of the default conduits.

To repopulate the Conduit Registry with the default settings for each of the default conduits, first use `CondCfg` to delete the entries for the default conduits and then use the `-r` flag of HotSync, which adds back entries for each of the default conduits:

```
hotsync.exe -r
```

You can accomplish the same thing while using the debug version of things. Simply use the `-r` flag with the debug version of HotSync:

```
hotsyncd.exe -r
```

This repopulates the registry with entries for the debug versions of each of the built-in conduits rather than entries for the release versions.

## *Source-Level Debugging*

Source-level debugging can be an invaluable aid to finding problems in your code. It does require careful setup and building, however. First, you need to build and run a debug version (which requires special libraries). Next, you need to set your breakpoints. In the following sections, we describe how to do this.

### *Building a Debug Version*

To build a debug version of your conduit, select Set Active Configuration in the Build menu. This specifies the debug rather than the release version of the conduit. To complete the build of a debug version, you also need to link with debug versions of the libraries. These libraries end in *d.lib* (for example, *hotsyncd.lib* is the debugging version of *hotsync.lib*). You can specify the debug versions of your libraries in the Link panel of the Project Settings dialog.

## Running a Debug Version

To run a debug version of your conduit, you need to do a number of things:

1. Run a debug version of HotSync (*hotsyncd.exe*).
2. Debug versions of the DLLs need to be in the HotSync directory. A release version of HotSync won't load a conduit built to run with debug. The 3.0 Conduit SDK ships with debug versions of HotSync and the DLLs. Copy them to the directory, where they can reside with the nondebug versions.
3. Run `CondCfg`, so that the entry for your conduit points to the debug directory rather than the release directory. Use *path\debug\MyConduit.DLL* rather than *path\release\MyConduit.DLL*.
4. In the Debug panel of the Project Settings dialog, specify the full pathname to *hotsyncd.exe* as the executable (see Figure 14-2).

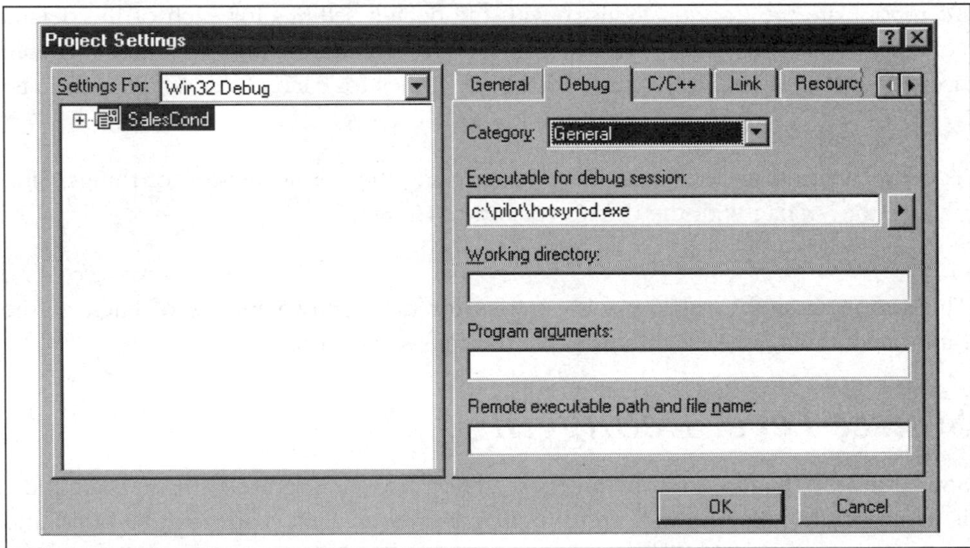


*Figure 14-2. Specifying the application to run when debugging the conduit*

## Setting Breakpoints

To set breakpoints in your code, you right-click on a line and choose Insert/Remove Breakpoint, as shown in Figure 14-3.

```
__declspec(dllexport) long OpenConduit(PROGRESSFN progress,
                                        CSyncProperties &sync)
{
    AFX_MANAGE_STATE(AfxGetStaticModuleState());
    long err = 0;

    if (sync.m_SyncType == eDoN
        LogAddEntry("Sales - syr
            false);
            return 0;
    }

    CONDHANDLE myConduitHandle;
    if ((err = SyncRegisterCondu
        return err;

    LogAddEntry("", slSyncStarte

    if (sync.m_SyncType == eHHtc
        if ((err = CopyOrdersFrc
            goto exit;
        if ((err = CopyCustomers
            goto exit;
    } else if (sync.m_SyncType =
        if ((err = CopyProductsA
            goto exit;
```

Cut
Copy
Paste
Insert File into Project
Open Document " if (... eDoNothing) {"
Go To Definition Of if (sync.m_SyncType == eDoNothing) {
Go To Reference To if (sync.m_SyncType == eDoNothing) {
Insert/Remove Breakpoint
Enable Breakpoint
ClassWizard...
Properties

*Figure 14-3. Setting a breakpoint in your code at a particular line*

Once you have gotten this far, you are almost ready to roll. You have just two more steps:

1. Exit the HotSync Manager if it's currently running.
2. Choose Go from the Start Debug submenu of the Build menu. You can also use the F5 function key as a shortcut.

# *Avoiding Timeouts While Debugging*

When you are debugging a conduit, there are two timeouts that you need to avoid. The first is an automatic-off timeout, the second a HotSync one.

## *Auto-off Timeout*

There is a timeout that causes the handheld to go to sleep after a certain time (a power-saving feature). If you're in the middle of single-stepping through your conduit and the handheld goes to sleep, you'll have one thoroughly ruined debugging session. To avoid this problem, use the ℓ..3 shortcut (see "Device Reset" on page 289 for a full discussion). It stops the Palm OS handheld from going to sleep.

Until you do a reset, the Palm OS handheld won't go to sleep again automatically. Try not to wander away from your debugging to other things. If you do, when you come back to your debugging after a good night's sleep, your batteries will quite likely have expired.

## HotSync Timeout

The other timeout you need to worry about is the timeout of the HotSync protocol. If you are stopped at a breakpoint while in the middle of a synchronization, the HotSync application is not sending information to the handheld. The handheld then thinks that the connection has been lost and ends the HotSync session.

### Opening the secret handheld option

To convince the handheld not to give up, you need to use a secret option that lies hidden within the handheld HotSync application. To get to it, you open the HotSync application on the device. Next, carefully place the handheld in a brown paper bag and wave it over your head while screaming like a chicken—okay, just kidding. What you really do is:

1. Hold down the scroll-up button on a Palm OS 3.0 device or both the scroll-up and scroll-down keys on a pre-3.0 device.

In POSE (on Windows only), you can simulate pressing the scroll-up and scroll-down keys by holding down the keyboard Page Up and Page Down keys.

2. While holding the key(s), tap in the top-right corner of the screen.

### The secret alert

You should see an alert, as shown in Figure 14-4. Now HotSync is your dutiful servant, waiting forever and never timing out. If you quit the HotSync application and reopen it, this option is reset; the HotSync application can again timeout.

*Figure 14-4. HotSync secret alert*

# Conduit Problems You Might Have

The following are two of the most common problems you may come across when debugging a conduit.

## *When an Installed Conduit Doesn't Run*

A problem that you might encounter is having a conduit that appears to be installed but doesn't get called during a sync session. First, check the presyncing setup by choosing the Custom menu of HotSync. If your conduit doesn't show up in the list, check the items in the following sections.

### *A mismatched HotSync and conduit*

If you use a release version of one with a debug version of the other, the conduit is not called. Make sure that a debug version of your conduit is linked with debug versions of the DLL and that release versions are linked with release versions.

### *The DLL isn't where it's supposed to be*

If you provide a full pathname for your conduit, make sure it's there. If you specify only the conduit name (*MyConduit.DLL*), the conduit must be in the DLL path (a common place to put it is in the same directory as *HotSync.exe*).

Select the conduit and press the Change... button to have your *ConfigureConduit* routine called. If it doesn't work—you know because your *ConfigureConduit* dialog doesn't appear—here are some possible reasons:

*Required functions not present*

Check that your *ConfigureConduit* (or, for HotSync 3.0, *CfgConduit*) routine is in your conduit and declared as `__declspec(dllexport)`.

Also, make sure that the following are present and exported:

- *GetConduitName*
- *GetConduitVersion*
- *OpenConduit*

*HotSync hasn't been restarted*

After you make changes to the registry using *CfgCond.exe*, you should restart HotSync to make sure it rereads the registry.

Once you've got your configuration dialog up, you know that HotSync has found your DLL and called your code successfully. Now if you try to Sync and your conduit doesn't run, it's almost certainly because of one of the two following reasons:

*Your conduit requires a matching creator ID*

Run HotSync in verbose mode to check the Creator ID of your application. Check that ID against the creator registered for the conduit (in *CondCfg.exe*). They must match.

*Conduit configured to do nothing*

Your conduit may be configured to do nothing (check the Custom/Change dialog from the HotSync menu). Even if your conduit is configured to do nothing, the *OpenConduit* entry point should still be called. You can set a breakpoint and see whether it is being called or alternatively check the verbose HotSync log.

## When the Handheld Crashes After Syncing

Each application with an associated conduit that ran during a sync is sent the `sysAppLaunchCmdSyncNotify` launch code. When this launch code is sent, the application does not have any global variables available to it and therefore must not try to access them. If it does, it will most certainly crash in a large flaming wreck.

To ensure this doesn't happen to you, have your *PilotMain* check the incoming launch code, and verify that it doesn't access global variables directly or indirectly.

---

We had a problem when building the conduit: it kept crashing. Here is the story. Earlier in our code we had added the ability to keep track of what ROM version the application is running on. We did this by modifying *RomVersionCompatible* to save the ROM version in a global. Now, much later on when we are trying to get our conduit up and working, we are crashing. It turns out that our *PilotMain* was calling the *RomVersionCompatible* first, before checking the launch code. The result: our application kept crashing. Don't make the same mistake.

---

# Test with POSE

A good way to catch problems in your conduit code is by using POSE. It's possible to sync with POSE running on a different machine (in which case the cable is on the machine running your conduit) or on the same machine (in which case the cable is going out one serial port and in another). For example, this is how we debugged our handheld application that was crashing after a sync. We set a breakpoint in *PilotMain* and waited for it to get called at the end of the sync process; single-stepping through the code finally showed the problem. If that wasn't enough to convince you, remember that it saves batteries and doesn't require a cradle, either.

Some laptops have only one serial port. Consider augmenting the built-in serial card with a serial PC card (we use a Socket serial card that costs about $125—see *http://www.socketcom.com)*.

If you're using the Mac OS version of POSE, make sure that the POSE window is frontmost while you are syncing. This gives the emulator more CPU time during the sync. Trust us, it needs it.

## Turn Off Other Conduits During Testing

It is also a very good idea to turn other conduits off during your test cycle. This gives you a much faster sync cycle. To do this, have the other conduits "Do Nothing" as their default sync action. That will make them very sleepy, and they won't wake up during the sync.

## Use the Log, Luke

The HotSync log is your friend. During your development, have your code log everything that's going on during the sync. It's one of the easiest ways to see what's happening and hence find out where problems are.

That's it. You should now have a fully debugged conduit to go with your fully debugged Palm application. This is the end of the book, so that means you know everything you need to know. Have fun, and good Palm programming to you.

# Appendix: Where to Go From Here

We have put all the Palm developer resources that we could think of into this location as a handy reference guide.

## Palm Programming Book Web Site

Any updates to the source code in this book are at:

*http://www.calliopeinc.com/PalmProgramming*

You will also find helpful links to other Palm programming locations.

## The Official Palm Developer Site

3Com's official Palm developer page is:

*http://www.palm.com/devzone*

It is the place you should go to check for the most recent versions of the SDK, CDK, and information on updates to the operating system. There are also a lot of other resources at this site—everything from white papers on various topics to Palm's FAQ for developers.

### Getting Your Application Creator ID

Palm's developer site is also where you go to register your application and obtain your application's unique creator ID. A creator ID is a four-ASCII-character ID that each application needs to distinguish itself from all other applications. This is an essential part of application development and you shouldn't leave it until the last minute. For registration instructions, check:

*http://www.palm.com./devzone/crid*

## Developer Technical Support

If you have developer support questions or require further technical information, the best place to find that is at Palm Computing's official developer support site. Send questions to:

*devsupp@palm.com*

Currently, there is no charge for this support, though you should check Palm's web site for current information.

Future plans include allowing developers the ability to submit web-based questions through Palm Computing's Developer Support web site.

## Other Developer Support

General developer information, marketing, business administration, and questions should be directed to another address:

*devinfo@palm.com*

## Platinum Certification

You can have your application tested to receive Platinum certification—Palm's way of guaranteeing to a consumer that an application meets its compatibility, quality, and usability standards. Applications that pass Platinum compatibility testing receive the Palm Computing Platform Platinum logo and some marketing and developer support from Palm.

This testing is administered by a third-party provider, Quality Partners, which has a web site where you can get information about testing standards and a free developer's testing kit. Access this site primarily through Palm's own developer site (*http://www.palm.com/devzone*). The testing kit contains detailed descriptions of their entire test suite.

Quality Partners currently offers two price plans for application testing: a Base Plan ($500 for a handheld application, $1,200 for a conduit) and a Premium Plan, which offers support and better turnaround ($700 for a handheld application, $1,600 for a conduit). (Note: there are additional charges for retesting and variations.) Check the Quality Partners' web site often, as this type of information frequently changes.

No matter what, you should look over the testing cycle that Quality Partners uses on an application and do what is necessary to ensure that your application meets those guidelines. Their tests include important checks like:

- Proper Graffiti and shortcut support
- Design consistency with Palm UI guidelines
- Proper handling of errors and use of alerts
- Successful handling of one million Gremlin events

## Palm Programming Mailing Lists

The following mailing lists are hosted by Palm Computing, and it's common to see Palm employees answering questions. While these lists are not officially supported, they serve as a good self-support mechanism and are constantly used by developers to answer each other's questions.

Palm Computing's developer web site has forms to subscribe to any of these lists:

- Palm Developer Forum
- Emulator Developer Forum
- Conduit Developer Forum

## Third-Party Palm Programming Resources

Currently, there are no Palm programming newsgroups distributed on Usenet. However, Darrin Massena hosts a newsgroup server with some different newsgroups:

*news://news.massena.com/pilot.programmer*
General Palm programming questions

*news://news.massena.com/pilot.programmer.gcc*
Discussion about using the Gnu PalmPilot SDK

*news://news.massena.com/pilot/programmer.codewarrior*
Discussion about using CodeWarrior

*news://news.massena.com/pilot.programmer.pila*
: Discussion about programming in Motorola 68000 assembly language

*news://news.massena.com/pilot.programmer.jump*
: Discussion about programming in Java

Note that *http://www.dejanews.com*, a newsgroup search engine, does catalog Massena's newsgroups, so from Dejanews you can do keyword searches.

In the future, these sites may be moved to a Palm site. If you attempt to read these newsgroups and find they are no longer where you expected them to be, check Palm's web site for further information.

# Third-Party Palm Programming FAQ

This site:

*http://wademan.com*

contains numerous helpful resources. One is a fairly comprehensive FAQ. There are also code examples and some links to other PalmPilot sites.

# RoadCoders, Handheld Developers

This site:

*http://www.roadcoders.com*

contains resources on both the Palm OS and Windows CE devices. Among its useful sections are:

*Palm OS SDKs*
: A nice listing of the currently available SDKs for the Palm OS and what platforms they run on.

*Tools*
: A list of tools and utilities.

*Articles*
: Some very nice articles on various aspects of Palm programming or on using various programming tools.

*Source code*
: Example code, some good, some not.

*Developer listings*

This is a listing of developers who do Palm programing. You can also add your name to the collection.

## PalmCentral

This is a large collection of software listed by categories, located at:

*http://www.palmcentral.com*

It includes a Developer category and source code.

# Journals and Magazines

There are two good magazines that offer a wide range of both user and programming articles. They are *PalmPower* and *Handheld Systems Journal.* Check our web site for information on new electronic resources, as this area is growing rapidly.

### PalmPower Online Magazine

This magazine is devoted exclusively to the Palm Computing platform. Its web site is:

*http://www.palmpower.com*

This monthly online magazine contains many interesting articles as well a monthly programmer's column, which often contains useful coding techniques and tips.

### Handheld Systems Journal

This journal has been around for a number of years. Its web site is:

*http://www.cdpubs.com/hhsj*

This journal covers the whole gamut of handhelds, including Palm OS devices. The focus is on code-level, in-depth discussions of hardware and software. This is a bimonthly printed magazine that is also available in electronic Adobe Acrobat form. Free samples and past archived issues of the journal are available at the web site. The current price of a subscription is around $50.

# Index

## *Symbols and Numbers*



## *A*

## D

## E

## *G*



## *H*

## *M*

## Q



## R

## *T*

## *About the Author*

**Neil Rhodes** and **Julie McKeehan** are experienced authors who, through their company, Calliope Enterprises, work closely with Palm Computing to develop new training materials that are based on this book. They are both programmers with many years of experience working with handheld systems. Neil and Julie authored several books on C++ and handheld systems, and now bring their skills to the Palm Computing Platform.

Neil has been a Unix programmer (his fingers still know vi commands), a Mac programmer (shipped several commercial products), a teacher (of programmers for Apple Developer University), a Newton programmer (several commercial products, including some for Apple), and an author (of Newton books, a C++ book, and a Macintosh programming book). Neil has been working with Palm Computing on developing their training strategy and training materials for programmers. He works closely with many of the developer support engineers at Palm (many of whom he also worked with previously when they did Newton developer support).

Julie has been a systems administrator, a director of software development at a successful Macintosh software company, a teacher (of programmers for Apple Developer University), and author (of Newton books, a C++ book, and an Internet book).

## *Colophon*

The bird on the cover of *Palm Programming* is a rock dove. There are 14 subspecies of rock dove, including the domestic pigeon. These birds are widely distributed throughout the world. In their native environment, rock doves live on rocky cliffs, building their nests in crevices and caves. In the urban environment that most domestic pigeons inhabit, nest are built on the ledges of buildings. Rock doves are not migratory birds; they make a permanent residence wherever they are. Domestic pigeons often have a range as small as 500 square meters. The rock doves' diet consists mainly of grains containing meal and oil. They also feed on insects and snails, and they supplement this diet with stones, sand, and clay. There is a considerably less savory aspect of their diet, as well: rock doves often satisfy their salt requirements by feeding at dung heaps or near refuse or human waste sites.

The rock dove population has exploded as many of their natural predators, such as the falcon, hawk, and owl, have decreased in number. This population increase is also helped along by humans, who feed the birds.

Nancy Kotary was the production editor for *Palm Programming*. Sheryl Avruch was the production manager; Debby English was the copy editor; Jane Ellin was the proofreader; Claire Cloutier LeBlanc and Jeffrey Liggett provided quality control. Seth Maislin wrote the index.

Edie Freedman designed the cover of this book using a 19th-century engraving from the Dover Pictorial Archive. The cover layout was produced with QuarkXPress 3.32 using the ITC Garamond font. The CD label was designed by Hanna Dyer. Whenever possible, our books use RepKover™, a durable and flexible lay-flat binding. If the page count exceeds RepKover's limit, perfect binding is used.

The inside layout was designed by Nancy Priest and implemented in FrameMaker 5.5 by Mike Sierra. The text and heading fonts are ITC Garamond Light and Garamond Book. The illustrations that appear in the book were created in Macromedia FreeHand 8.0 and screen shots were created in Adobe Photoshop 5.0 by Robert Romano. This colophon was written by Clairemarie Fisher O'Leary.

# More Titles from O'Reilly

## C and C++

### *C++: The Core Language*

*By Gregory Satir & Doug Brown*
*1st Edition October 1995*
*228 pages, ISBN 1-56592-116-X*

A first book for C programmers transitioning to C++, an object-oriented enhancement of the C programming language. Designed to get readers up to speed quickly, this book thoroughly explains the important concepts and features and gives brief overviews of the rest of the language. Covers features common to all C++ compilers, including those on UNIX, Windows NT, Windows, DOS, and Macs.

### *Practical C++ Programming*

*By Steve Oualline*
*1st Edition September 1995*
*584 pages, ISBN 1-56592-139-9*

A complete introduction to the C++ language for the beginning programmer and C programmers transitioning to C++. This book emphasizes a practical, real-world approach, including how to debug, how to make your code understandable to others, and how to understand other people's code. Covers good programming style, C++ syntax (what to use and what not to use), C++ class design, debugging and optimization, and common programming mistakes.

### *Checking C Programs with lint*

*By Ian F. Darwin*
*1st Edition October 1988*
*84 pages, ISBN 0-937175-30-7*

The *lint* program is one of the best tools for finding portability problems and certain types of coding errors in C programs. This handbook introduces you to *lint*, guides you through running it on your programs, and helps you interpret *lint*'s output.

### *Practical C Programming, 3rd Edition*

*By Steve Oualline*
*3rd Edition August 1997*
*454 pages, ISBN 1-56592-306-5*

*Practical C Programming* teaches you not only the mechanics of programming, but also how to create programs that are easy to read, maintain, and debug. This third edition introduces popular Integrated Development Environments on Windows systems, as well as UNIX programming utilities, and features a large statistics-generating program to pull together the concepts and features in the language.

### *High Performance Computing, 2nd Edition*

*By Kevin Dowd & Charles Severance*
*2nd Edition July 1998*
*466 pages, ISBN 1-56592-312-X*

This new edition of *High Performance Computing* gives a thorough overview of the latest workstation and PC architectures and the trends that will influence the next generation. It pays special attention to memory design, tuning code for the best performance, multiprocessors, and benchmarking.

## Hand-held Computers

### *PalmPilot: The Ultimate Guide*

*By David Pogue*
*1st Edition June 1998*
*520 pages, Includes CD-ROM*
*ISBN 1-56592-420-7*

This PalmPilot "bible" covers the PalmPilot, PalmPilot Professsional, and the new software and features of the 1998 PalmPilot model, the Palm III, as well as OEM models such as the IBM Workpad. Dense with undocumented information, it contains hundreds of timesaving tips and surprising tricks to help both intermediate and advanced users master this exciting new device. Includes CD-ROM containing 900 PalmPilot programs.

# How to stay in touch with O'Reilly

## 1. Visit Our Award-Winning Web Site

**http://www.oreilly.com/**

★"Top 100 Sites on the Web" —*PC Magazine*
★"Top 5% Web sites" —*Point Communications*
★"3-Star site" —*The McKinley Group*

Our web site contains a library of comprehensive product information (including book excerpts and tables of contents), downloadable software, background articles, interviews with technology leaders, links to relevant sites, book cover art, and more. File us in your Bookmarks or Hotlist!

## 2. Join Our Email Mailing Lists

### New Product Releases

To receive automatic email with brief descriptions of all new O'Reilly products as they are released, send email to:
**listproc@online.oreilly.com**
Put the following information in the first line of your message (*not* in the Subject field):
**subscribe oreilly-news**

### O'Reilly Events

If you'd also like us to send information about trade show events, special promotions, and other O'Reilly events, send email to:
**listproc@online.oreilly.com**
Put the following information in the first line of your message (*not* in the Subject field):
**subscribe oreilly-events**

## 3. Get Examples from Our Books via FTP

There are two ways to access an archive of example files from our books:

### Regular FTP

- ftp to:
  **ftp.oreilly.com**
  (login: anonymous
  password: your email address)
- Point your web browser to:
  **ftp://ftp.oreilly.com/**

### FTPMAIL

- Send an email message to:
  **ftpmail@online.oreilly.com**
  (Write "help" in the message body)

## 4. Contact Us via Email

**order@oreilly.com**
To place a book or software order online. Good for North American and international customers.

**subscriptions@oreilly.com**
To place an order for any of our newsletters or periodicals.

**books@oreilly.com**
General questions about any of our books.

**software@oreilly.com**
For general questions and product information about our software. Check out O'Reilly Software Online at **http://software.oreilly.com/** for software and technical support information. Registered O'Reilly software users send your questions to: **website-support@oreilly.com**

**cs@oreilly.com**
For answers to problems regarding your order or our products.

**booktech@oreilly.com**
For book content technical questions or corrections.

**proposals@oreilly.com**
To submit new book or software proposals to our editors and product managers.

**international@oreilly.com**
For information about our international distributors or translation queries. For a list of our distributors outside of North America check out:
**http://www.oreilly.com/www/order/country.html**

O'Reilly & Associates, Inc.
101 Morris Street, Sebastopol, CA 95472 USA
TEL 707-829-0515 or 800-998-9938
(6am to 5pm PST)
FAX 707-829-0104

# International Distributors

## UK, Europe, Middle East and Northern Africa *(except France, Germany, Switzerland, & Austria)*

**INQUIRIES**
International Thomson Publishing Europe
Berkshire House
168-173 High Holborn
London WC1V 7AA
United Kingdom
Tel: 44-1-71-497-1422
Fax: 44-1-71-497-1426

**ORDERS**
International Thomson Publishing Services, Ltd.
Cheriton House, North Way
Andover, Hampshire SP10 5BE
United Kingdom
Tel: 44-1-264-342-832 (UK)
Tel: 44-1-264-342-806 (outside UK)
Fax: 44-1-264-364-418 (UK)
Fax: 44-1-264-342-761 (outside UK)
Email: itpint@itps.co.uk

## France

GEODIF
61, Bd Saint-Germain
75240 Paris Cedex 05, France
Tel: 33-1-44-41-46-16 (French books)
Tel: 33-1-44-41-11-87 (English books)
Fax: 33-1-44-41-11-44
Email: distribution@eyrolles.com

**ORDERS**
SODIS
128, av.du Mal de Lattre de Tassigny
77403 Lagny Cédex, France
Tel: 33-1-60-07-82-00
Fax: 33-1-64-30-32-27

**INQUIRIES**
Éditions O'Reilly
18 rue Séguier
75006 Paris, France
Tel: 33-1-40-51-52-30
Fax: 33-1-40-51-52-31
Email: france@editions-oreilly.fr

## Germany, Switzerland, Austria

**INQUIRIES**
O'Reilly Verlag
Balthasarstr. 81
D-50670 Köln, Germany
Tel: 49-221-973160-0
Fax: 49-221-973160-8
Email: anfragen@oreilly.de

**ORDERS**
International Thomson Publishing
Königswinterer Straße 418
53227 Bonn, Germany
Tel: 49-228-970240
Fax: 49-228-441342
Email: order@oreilly.de

## Canada *(French language books)*

Les Éditions Flammarion ltée
375, Avenue Laurier Ouest
Montréal (Québec) H2V 2K3
Tel: 00-1-514-277-8807
Fax: 00-1-514-278-2085
Email: info@flammarion.qc.ca

## Hong Kong

City Discount Subscription Service, Ltd.
Unit D, 3rd Floor, Yan's Tower
27 Wong Chuk Hang Road
Aberdeen, Hong Kong
Tel: 852-2580-3539
Fax: 852-2580-6463
Email: citydis@ppn.com.hk

## Korea

Hanbit Media, Inc.
Sonyoung Bldg. 202
Yeksam-dong 736-36
Kangnam-ku
Seoul, Korea
Tel: 822-554-9610
Fax: 822-556-0363
Email: hant93@chollian.dacom.co.kr

## Singapore, Malaysia, Thailand

Addison-Wesley Longman Singapore Pte., Ltd.
25 First Lok Yang Road
Singapore 629734
Tel: 65-268-2666
Fax: 65-268-7023
Email: Daniel.Loh@awl.com.sg

## Philippines

Mutual Books, Inc.
429-D Shaw Boulevard
Mandaluyong City, Metro
Manila, Philippines
Tel: 632-725-7538
Fax: 632-721-3056
Email: mbikikog@mnl.sequel.net

## Taiwan

O'Reilly Taiwan
No. 3, Lane 131
Hang-Chow South Road
Section 1, Taipei, Taiwan
Tel: 886-2-23968990
Fax: 886-2-23968916
Email: benh@oreilly.com

## China

China National Publishing
Industry Trading Corporation
504 AnHuiLi, AnDingMenWai
P.O. Box 782
Beijing 100011, China P.R.
Tel: 86-10-6424-0483
Fax: 86-10-6421-4540
Email: frederic@oreilly.com

## India

Computer Bookshop (India) Pvt. Ltd.
190 Dr. D.N. Road, Fort
Bombay 400 001 India
Tel: 91-22-207-0989
Fax: 91-22-262-3551
Email: cbsbom@giasbm01.vsnl.net.in

## Japan

O'Reilly Japan, Inc.
Kiyoshige Building 2F
12-Bancho, Sanei-cho
Shinjuku-ku
Tokyo 160-0008 Japan
Tel: 81-3-3356-5227
Fax: 81-3-3356-5261
Email: japan@oreilly.com

## All Other Asian Countries

O'Reilly & Associates, Inc.
101 Morris Street
Sebastopol, CA 95472 USA
Tel: 707-829-0515
Fax: 707-829-0104
Email: order@oreilly.com

## Australia

WoodsLane Pty., Ltd.
7/5 Vuko Place
Warriewood NSW 2102
Australia
Tel: 61-2-9970-5111
Fax: 61-2-9970-5002
Email: info@woodslane.com.au

## New Zealand

Woodslane New Zealand, Ltd.
21 Cooks Street (P.O. Box 575)
Waganui, New Zealand
Tel: 64-6-347-6543
Fax: 64-6-345-4840
Email: info@woodslane.com.au

## South Africa

International Thomson South Africa
Building 18, Constantia Park
138 Sixteenth Road
(P.O. Box 2459)
Halfway House, 1685 South Africa
Tel: 27-11-805-4819
Fax: 27-11-805-3648

## Latin America

McGraw-Hill Interamericana
Editores, S.A. de C.V.
Cedro No. 512
Col. Atlampa
06450, Mexico, D.F.
Tel: 52-5-547-6777
Fax: 52-5-547-3336
Email: mcgraw-hill@infosel.net.mx

**SPECIAL OFFER for owners of *Palm Programming: The Developers' Guide!***

# Experience Satellite Forms™ software for FREE!

Your copy of *Palm Programming: The Developers' Guide* includes a CD containing a FREE Trial Edition of award-winning Satellite Forms – the premier visual rapid application development (RAD) tool for devices based on the Palm Computing® platform.

Use Satellite Forms to develop sophisticated custom handheld applications that tightly integrate with enterprise data from Oracle®, DB2, Lotus Notes®, Microsoft Access®, and other databases. Satellite Forms' comprehensive feature set, combined with Palm Computing's one-touch connectivity, lets you easily create integrated solutions with unparalleled versatility.

Satellite Forms' App Designer visual development environment includes controls, filters, macro actions, Visual Basic®-like scripting, and even custom SFX™ controls, developed by you or third parties using the Satellite Forms API.

Try the **Trial Edition of Satellite Forms on the enclosed CD**. Then take advantage of a special offer, exclusively for owners of *Palm Programming: The Developers' Guide* – purchase Satellite Forms for the price of just **$299**, a savings of $70 off the regular price of $369.

Visit the Puma Technology web site at **www.pumatech.com/devguide** to purchase Satellite Forms for the special price of just **$299.** Or, simply call **1-408-321-3836** today to take advantage of this exclusive offer for owners of *Palm Programming: The Developers' Guide!*

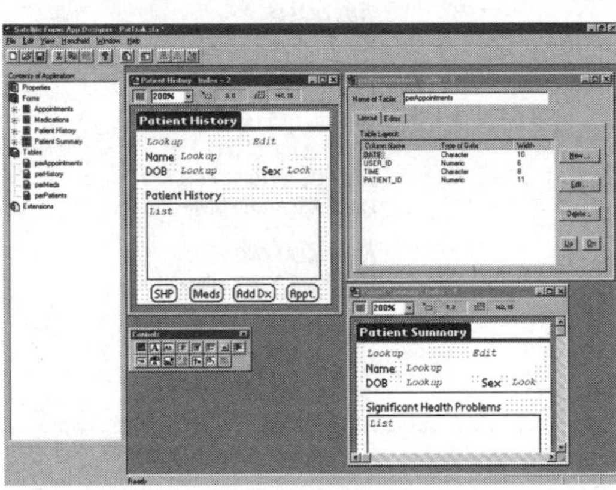

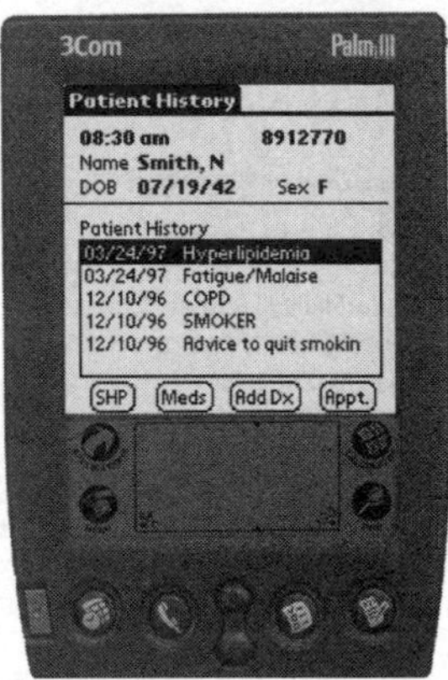


# Satellite Forms Features

Create applications on the desktop with "drag and drop" ease.

Develop multi-form applications with linked forms that share information.

Add substantial functionality without programming.

Easily integrate with corporate data using the ActiveX control or server synchronization solutions.

Add calculations, validation, conditional logic, looping, and sound, with event-driven scripts, in a Visual Basic-like syntax.

Develop solutions with a customized look and feel, including text and numeric edit fields, buttons, graphics, ink fields, timestamps, drop lists, radio buttons, and more.

Extend Satellite Forms with "C" programs, and take advantage of Satellite Forms and 3rd party SFX controls and SFX plug-ins.

Create a wide range of applications:

- Sales automation
- Health care delivery
- Inventory control
- Distribution
- Phamaceutical detailing
- Field service
- Insurance
- Inspections
- Market research
- And more

## METROWERKS CODEWARRIOR LITE DISCLAIMER AND END-USER SOFTWARE LICENSE AGREEMENT

METROWERKS DOES NOT PROVIDE ANY TECHNICAL SUPPORT FOR CODEWARRIOR LITE.

IN ORDER TO RECEIVE TECHNICAL SUPPORT YOU MUST UPGRADE TO THE COMMERCIAL VERSION OF CODEWARRIOR. PLEASE USE THE ORDER FORM IN THE DOCUMENT NAMED 'HOW TO ORDER'.

PLEASE READ THIS LICENSE CAREFULLY BEFORE USING THE SOFTWARE. BY USING THE SOFTWARE, YOU ARE AGREEING TO BE BOUND BY THE TERMS OF THIS LICENSE. IF YOU DO NOT AGREE TO THE TERMS OF THIS LICENSE, PROMPTLY RETURN THE UNUSED SOFTWARE TO THE PLACE WHERE YOU OBTAINED IT AND YOUR MONEY WILL BE REFUNDED.

**1. LICENSE.** The application and other software accompanying this License, whether on disk, in read only memory, or on any other media (the "Software") and the related documentation and fonts are licensed to you by Metrowerks and its Licensors. You own the disc on which the Software and documentation are recorded but Metrowerks and/or Metrowerks' Licensors retain title to the Software, related documentation and fonts. This License allows you to use the Software and fonts on a single computer. You may use a copy of the software on a home or a portable computer, as long as the extra copy is never loaded at the same time the software is loaded on the primary computer on which you use the Software. You may make one copy of the Software and fonts in machine-readable form for backup purposes. You must reproduce on such copy the Metrowerks copyright notice and any other proprietary legends that were on the original copy of the Software and fonts. You may also transfer all your license rights in the Software and the fonts, the backup copy of the Software and fonts, the related documentation and a copy of this license to another party, provided the other party reads and agrees to accept the terms and conditions of this License.

**2. RESTRICTIONS.** The Software contains copyrighted material, trade secrets and other proprietary material. In order to protect them, and except as permitted by applicable legislation, you may not decompile, reverse engineer, disassemble or otherwise reduce the Software to a human-perceivable form. You may not modify, rent, lease, loan, distribute or create derivative works based upon the Software in whole or in part. You may not electronically transmit the Software from one computer to another or over a network. You may not use the Software to produce software that is distributed for sale or resale or as shareware or freeware.

**3. TERMINATION.** This License is effective until terminated. You may terminate this License at any time by destroying the Software and related documentation and all copies thereof. This License will terminate immediately without notice from Metrowerks if you fail to comply with any provision of this License. Upon termination you must destroy the Software and related documentation and all related copies thereof.

**4. EXPORT LAW ASSURANCES.** You agree and certify that neither the Software nor any technical data received from Metrowerks, nor the direct product thereof, will be exported outside the United States except as authorized and as permitted by the laws and regulations of the United States. If the Software has been rightfully obtained by you outside of the United States, you agree that you will not re-export the Software nor any other technical data received from Metrowerks, nor the direct product thereof, except as permitted by the laws and regulations of the United States and the laws and regulations of the jurisdiction in which you obtained the Software.

**5. GOVERNMENT END USERS.** If you are acquiring the Software and fonts on behalf of any unit or agency of the United States Government, the following provisions apply. The Government agrees that the Software and fonts shall be classified as "commercial computer software" as that term is defined in the applicable provisions of the Federal Acquisition Regulation ("FAR") and supplements thereto, including the Department of Defense ("DoD") FAR Supplement ("DFARS"). If the Software and fonts are supplied for use by DoD, it is delivered subject to the terms of this Agreement and either (i) in accordance with DFARS 227.7202-1(a) and 227.7202-3(a), or (ii) with restricted rights in accordance with DFARS 252.227-7013(c)(1)(ii) (OCT 1988), as applicable. If the Software and fonts are supplied for use by any other Federal agency, it is restricted computer software delivered subject to the terms of this Agreement and (i) FAR 12.212(a); (ii) FAR 52.227-19; or (iii) FAR 52.227-14(ALT III), as applicable.

**6. DISCLAIMER OF WARRANTY ON METROWERKS SOFTWARE.** You expressly acknowledge and agree that use of the Software and fonts is at your sole risk. Except as is stated above, the Software, related documentation and fonts are provided "AS IS" and without warranty of any kind and Metrowerks and Metrowerks' Licensor(s) (for the purposes of provisions 6 and 7, Metrowerks and Metrowerks' Licensor(s) shall be collectively referred to as "Metrowerks") EXPRESSLY DISCLAIM ALL OTHER WARRANTIES, EXPRESS OR IMPLIED, INCLUDING, BUT NOT LIMITED TO, THE IMPLIED WARRANTIES OF MERCHANTABILITY, FITNESS FOR A PARTICULAR PURPOSE AND NONINFRINGEMENT. METROWERKS DOES NOT WARRANT THAT THE FUNCTIONS CONTAINED IN THE SOFTWARE WILL MEET YOUR REQUIREMENTS, OR THAT THE OPERATION OF THE SOFTWARE WILL BE UNINTERRUPTED OR ERROR-FREE, OR THAT DEFECTS IN THE SOFTWARE AND THE FONTS WILL BE CORRECTED. FURTHERMORE, METROWERKS DOES NOT WARRANT OR MAKE ANY REPRESENTATIONS REGARDING THE USE OR THE RESULTS OF THE USE OF THE SOFTWARE AND FONTS OR RELATED DOCUMENTATION IN TERMS OF THEIR CORRECTNESS, ACCURACY, RELIABILITY, OR OTHERWISE. NO ORAL OR WRITTEN INFORMATION OR ADVICE GIVEN BY METROWERKS OR A METROWERKS AUTHORIZED REPRESENTATIVE SHALL CREATE A WARRANTY OR IN ANY WAY INCREASE THE SCOPE OF THIS WARRANTY. SHOULD THE SOFTWARE PROVE DEFECTIVE, YOU (AND NOT METROWERKS OR A METROWERKS AUTHORIZED REPRESENTATIVE) ASSUME THE ENTIRE COST OF ALL NECESSARY SERVICING, REPAIR OR CORRECTION. SOME JURISDICTIONS DO NOT ALLOW THE EXCLUSION OF IMPLIED WARRANTIES, SO THE ABOVE EXCLUSION MAY NOT APPLY TO YOU.

**7. LIMITATION OF LIABILITY.** UNDER NO CIRCUMSTANCES INCLUDING NEGLIGENCE, SHALL METROWERKS BE LIABLE FOR ANY INCIDENTAL, SPECIAL OR CONSEQUENTIAL DAMAGES THAT RESULT FROM THE USE OR INABILITY TO USE THE SOFTWARE OR RELATED DOCUMENTATION, EVEN IF METROWERKS OR A METROWERKS AUTHORIZED REPRESENTATIVE HAS BEEN ADVISED OF THE POSSIBILITY OF SUCH DAMAGES. SOME JURISDICTIONS DO NOT ALLOW THE LIMITATION OR EXCLUSION OF LIABILITY FOR INCIDENTAL OR CONSEQUENTIAL DAMAGES SO THE ABOVE LIMITATION OR EXCLUSION MAY NOT APPLY TO YOU.

In no event shall Metrowerks' total liability to you for all damages, losses, and causes of action (whether in contract, tort (including negligence) or otherwise) exceed that portion of the amount paid by you which is fairly attributable to the Software and fonts.

**8. CONTROLLING LAW AND SEVERABILITY.** This License shall be governed by and construed in accordance with the laws of the United States and the State of California, as applied to agreements entered into and to be performed entirely within California between California residents. If for any reason a court of competent jurisdiction finds any provision of this License, or portion thereof, to be unenforceable, that provision of the License shall be enforced to the maximum extent permissible so as to effect the intent of the parties, and the remainder of this License shall continue in full force and effect.

**9. COMPLETE AGREEMENT.** This License constitutes the entire agreement between the parties with respect to the use of the Software, the related documentation and fonts, and supersedes all prior or contemporaneous understandings or agreements, written or oral, regarding such subject matter. No amendment to or modification of this License will be binding unless in writing and signed by a duly authorized representative of Metrowerks.

Should you have any questions or comments concerning this license, please do not hesitate to write to Metrowerks Corp., 9801 Metric Boulevard, Suite 100, Austin, TX, 78758, USA. attn: Warranty Information.

**DISCLAIMER**

*CODEWARRIOR LITE on enclosed CD-ROM*

METROWERKS AND METROWERKS' LICENSOR(S), AND THEIR DIRECTORS, OFFICERS, EMPLOYEES OR AGENTS (COLLECTIVELY METROWERKS) MAKE NO WARRANTIES, EXPRESS OR IMPLIED, INCLUDING WITHOUT LIMITATION THE IMPLIED WARRANTIES OF MERCHANTABILITY AND FITNESS FOR A PARTICULAR PURPOSE, REGARDING THE SOFTWARE. METROWERKS DOES NOT WARRANT, GUARANTEE OR MAKE ANY REPRESENTATIONS REGARDING THE USE OR THE RESULTS OF THE USE OF THE SOFTWARE IN TERMS OF ITS CORRECTNESS, ACCURACY, RELIABILITY, CURRENTNESS OR OTHERWISE. THE ENTIRE RISK AS TO THE RESULTS AND PERFORMANCE OF THE SOFTWARE IS ASSUMED BY YOU. THE EXCLUSION OF IMPLIED WARRANTIES IS NOT PERMITTED BY SOME JURISDICTIONS. THE ABOVE EXCLUSION MAY NOT APPLY TO YOU.

IN NO EVENT WILL METROWERKS AND METROWERKS' LICENSOR(S), AND THEIR DIRECTORS, OFFICERS, EMPLOYEES OR AGENTS (COLLECTIVELY METROWERKS) BE LIABLE TO YOU FOR ANY CONSEQUENTIAL, INCIDENTAL OR INDIRECT DAMAGES (INCLUDING DAMAGES FOR LOSS OF BUSINESS PROFITS, BUSINESS INTERRUPTION, LOSS OF BUSINESS INFORMATION, AND THE LIKE) ARISING OUT OF THE USE OR INABILITY TO USE THE SOFTWARE EVEN IF METROWERKS HAS BEEN ADVISED OF THE POSSIBILITY OF SUCH DAMAGES. BECAUSE SOME JURISDICTIONS DO NOT ALLOW THE EXCLUSION OR LIMITATION OF LIABILITY FOR CONSEQUENTIAL OR INCIDENTAL DAMAGES, THE ABOVE LIMITATIONS MAY NOT APPLY TO YOU.

FREE TECHNICAL SUPPORT FROM METROWERKS IS PROVIDED BY ACQUIRING ANY OF METROWERKS' COMMERCIAL PRODUCTS. YOU CAN UPGRADE FROM THIS LIMITED VERSION OF CODEWARRIOR TO A COMMERCIAL PRODUCT AND THEREBY BENEFIT FROM THIS TECHNICAL SUPPORT. FOR MORE INFORMATION, CONTACT METROWERKS AT 1-800-377-5416, OR VIA EMAIL AT SALES@METROWERKS.COM.

# O'REILLY WOULD LIKE TO HEAR FROM YOU

Which book did this card come from?

______________________________

Where did you buy this book?

- ❑ Bookstore
- ❑ Computer Store
- ❑ Direct from O'Reilly
- ❑ Class/seminar
- ❑ Bundled with hardware/software
- ❑ Other ______________________

What operating system do you use?

- ❑ UNIX
- ❑ Macintosh
- ❑ Windows NT
- ❑ PC(Windows/DOS)
- ❑ Other ______________________

What is your job description?

- ❑ System Administrator
- ❑ Programmer
- ❑ Network Administrator
- ❑ Educator/Teacher
- ❑ Web Developer
- ❑ Other ______________________

❑ Please send me O'Reilly's catalog, containing a complete listing of O'Reilly books and software.

Name ______________________ Company/Organization ______________________

Address ______________________

City ______________ State ______________ Zip/Postal Code ______________ Country ______________

Telephone ______________________ Internet or other email address (specify network) ______________________

Nineteenth century wood engraving of a bear from the O'Reilly & Associates Nutshell Handbook® *Using & Managing UUCP.*

PLACE STAMP HERE

NO POSTAGE NECESSARY IF MAILED IN THE UNITED STATES

**BUSINESS REPLY MAIL**

FIRST CLASS MAIL PERMIT NO. 80 SEBASTOPOL, CA

*Postage will be paid by addressee*

**O'Reilly & Associates, Inc.**
101 Morris Street
Sebastopol, CA 95472-9902